D1176039

FOOD IN THE AMERICAN GILDED AGE

Books in the American Food in History Series

FOOD

IN THE AMERICAN GILDED AGE

Edited by Helen Zoe Veit

Michigan State University Press

EAST LANSING

Copyright © 2017 by Michigan State University

♾ The paper used in this publication meets the minimum
requirements of ANSI/NISO Z39.48–1992 (R 1997) (Permanence of Paper).

Michigan State University Press
East Lansing, Michigan 48823–5245

Printed and bound in the United States of America.

26 25 24 23 22 21 20 19 18 17   1 2 3 4 5 6 7 8 9 10

Names: Veit, Helen Zoe, editor. | Turner, Katherine Leonard, writer of
introduction. | Michigan State University.
Title: Food in the American Gilded Age / edited by Helen Zoe Veit.
Description: East Lansing : Michigan State University Press, [2017] |
Series: American food in history | Includes texts originally published 1870-1903. |
Includes bibliographical references and index.
Identifiers: LCCN 2016027764 | ISBN 9781611862355 (cloth : alk. paper) |
ISBN 9781609175177 (PDF)
Subjects: LCSH: Cooking, American—History—19th century—Sources. |
Food habits—History—19th century—Sources. | Food writers—United States—
Biography. | LCGFT: Cookbooks.
Classification: LCC TX715 .F68346 2017 | DDC 641.5973/09034—dc23
LC record available at https://lccn.loc.gov/2016027764

Cover and book design by Erin Kirk New.
Cover image is *The Bookman* (poster, 1896). Art and Architecture Collection,
Miriam and Ira D. Wallach Division of Art, Prints and Photographs,
The New York Public Library, Astor, Lenox, and Tilden Foundations.

Michigan State University Press is a member of the Green Press Initiative and
is committed to developing and encouraging ecologically responsible publishing practices.
For more information about the Green Press Initiative and the use of recycled paper in
book publishing, please visit www.greenpressinitiative.org.

Visit Michigan State University Press at www.msupress.org.

CONTENTS

ACKNOWLEDGMENTS

I am delighted to have the chance to thank the many people who helped turn this project into a book. As always, thank you to Gabriel Dotto, the head of Michigan State University Press, who has been an enthusiastic supporter of the series from the beginning. Thank you also to the many other good people at the press, especially Kristine Blakeslee, Elise Jajuga, Travis Kimbel, Annette Tanner, and Anastasia Wraight. The historian Julia Irwin provided very helpful comments on a draft of this manuscript, and the book is much better as a result of her generosity. It was a pleasure to work with Katherine Leonard Tuner, who wrote a great introduction to the book during a busy time in her career.

Michigan State University's Special Collections has one of the finest historical cookbook collections in the world, and I feel extraordinarily lucky to have ready access to it. I feel even luckier because the staff of Special Collections is so welcoming and helpful. Thank you to everyone there, and especially to Peter Berg, who has been incredibly supportive and generous at all stages of producing this series. I am also extremely grateful to Leslie Behm, who digitized dozens of images from the historical cookbooks for this volume.

FOOD IN THE AMERICAN GILDED AGE

A Matter of Class:
Food in the United States, 1870–1900

KATHERINE LEONARD TURNER

In 1898, the wealthy Mrs. William Astor, known as the social "gatekeeper" for the most aristocratic level of New York society, gave a lavish ball for about four hundred in her Fifth Avenue double mansion.[1] The ball began on a January night, after the opera, and featured dancing at 11:30, followed by a cold buffet and then a hot seated supper. The menu, along with a description of the event, the ladies' gowns, and names of some of the prominent guests, was recorded in the *New York Times* the next day.

SERVICE CHAUD
Bouillon en Tasse
Cotelettes de Volailles Perigeux
Filet aux Champignons Farcis
Pommes Surprise
Terrapin
Canvasback Duck
Hominy Croquettes

SERVICE FROID
Saumon Bayadere
Filet Froid a la Russe

Galantine de Poussins
Chaud-Froid de Caliles
Pate de Fois Gras en Croute
Salade Orientale
Pate de Gibier
Tartines de Langue
Ramequins
Rilettes de Tours
Glace Fantasies
Fraises Fondants
Cerises a l'Eau-de-Vie
Petits-Fours
Marrons
Bonbons
Mandarins Glaces
Fruit
Café

(Hot dishes: cups of bouillon, chicken with butter and herbs, beef tenderloin stuffed with mushrooms, a potato dish, turtle, fried hominy cakes. Cold dishes: salmon tartare, a cold molded beef dish, jellied chicken, pâté baked in a crust, a salad of some sort, a game pâté, duck meat on toasts, cheese straws, pork on toasts, ice cream molded in fanciful shapes, strawberry fondant, cherries in liquor, chestnuts, chocolates or candies, and orange slices candied in hot syrup.)[2]

Mrs. Astor's dinner exemplified her social power: rich and expensive ingredients, presented in the most fashionable French-named dishes, in a decadent buffet eaten long after midnight amid dancing, an orchestra, and a multitude of roses and palm trees from Mrs. Astor's own conservatories. Its extravagance was emblematic of the Gilded Age.

Meanwhile, elsewhere in New York in the mid-1890s, a German-born family struggled to get by. The father worked in a restaurant, while his wife worked as a janitor to earn a reduced rent on their apartment. Two of their five daughters worked in a box factory and paid a small amount for board. The family lived in a four-room tenement apartment with two windows on the Lower East Side, about five miles away from Mrs. Astor's mansion. The children slept on mattresses in the front room because there was not enough space in the windowless bedrooms. They lived on cheap, plain food with a few treats: beef shank, mutton chops, salt pork, eggs, macaroni, condensed milk, cabbages, potatoes, peas, soup greens, canned tomatoes, cheap jelly, bakery bread, cake, and rolls. The family was rarely able to eat together, as they worked different hours, and at any rate the apartment had no dining room or table big enough to seat them all together. The oldest girls bought lunch with their coworkers, the father ate meals at the restaurant when he could, and the children bought cakes and fruit from street peddlers for their school lunches. The dietary reformers who recorded the details of their diet remarked that the food, for 13 cents per person per day, was insufficient for health, by the newly devised caloric standard of nutrition.[3]

The poverty of urban families was equally emblematic of the Gilded Age. The huge numbers of industrial workers who were creating a wealthy, modern country participated very unevenly in its riches. This was a period in which greater abundance for all (because of the industrialization of agriculture, transportation, and food processing) went hand in hand with continued inequality. The notorious elites who gave the period its moniker ate fabulous meals, unmatched in richness, luxury, and quantity. At the very same time, hordes of workers and immigrants huddled in cramped cities, eating what they could: sometimes enough, sometimes not. In the countryside, rural workers caught on the losing side of industrialization ate barren, monotonous diets. Self-consciously creating themselves between these extremes, the middle classes enshrined American food heritage and created a new public world of dining. Food was still quite regional, but it was becoming less so. The trains and steamships that moved people into cities also moved food to new markets, transported processed food, and helped disseminate new ideas about a national cuisine and a national diet. The burgeoning American empire brought exotic food and foreign influences to traditional cuisine, along with lower prices for former luxuries like sugar and coffee. Kitchens, too, were developing into a more modern form, with improved tools and utilities for some. By 1900, the United States food system was poised on the edge of modernity, as the age-old problems of hunger and seasonality receded, and new problems of processing and food safety came to the fore.

Daily Meals

In the late nineteenth century, American food was quite diverse. Everyday diets were shaped by income, work life, housing, neighborhoods, and cultural traditions, as well as regions, seasons, and new food-processing technologies.[4] Most urban Americans fell into two major categories: the working class (men and many women who worked manual-labor jobs without much stability or control over their work) and the middle class (in which mainly men worked at salaried or professional "white collar" jobs, while women stayed at home with children and maintained the home). America's many farming families, the bulk of the population until the early twentieth century, could also be divided into two groups: families who owned their own land and might be financially independent, although increasingly connected to banks and railroads, and those who did not own land and worked for others as agricultural workers, tenant farmers, or sharecroppers. In all farming families, the labor of the whole family was necessary to survive and thrive. A small elite class was numerically small but socially vital.

Farmers and working people rose early to eat breakfast, or carried it to eat on the way to work. Breakfast varied widely: coffee or tea and a roll for European immigrants, cold baked beans and bread for New England millworkers, fried pork and cornbread for southern sharecroppers. A surprising number of working-class men stopped at a neighborhood saloon for a glass of beer to brace them for the workday. Farm wives rose before dawn to prepare hot breads, mush, eggs, fried meat, and other hearty dishes before the working day began.[5]

Middle-class people generally ate a more substantial and leisurely breakfast, eaten at the table rather than on the go. Eggs were served with meat: not just breakfast meats like ham, bacon, or sausage, but also steaks, broiled chicken, and small fish might appear. Starches were multiplied: biscuits *and* pancakes, muffins *and* grits *and* toast. Traditionally, preserved fruit or jams would be on the table, but increasingly, middle-class people could afford fresh fruit throughout more of the year, transported from warmer regions.

After a long morning's work, workers ate quick and simple packed lunches: sandwiches, hard-boiled eggs, small cakes, pickles. Many workers carried their lunch in tin or aluminum lunch pails, and it was unpacked and eaten in the coal mine, outside the steel mill, or (rarely) in a company-provided lunchroom. The lunch bucket contents varied according to workers' ethnic backgrounds: Slavic miners in Pennsylvania brought sandwiches of ham and homemade bread with pastries and fruit, while locally born "mountain folk" miners brought fried or roasted rabbit or squirrel in their buckets, or simply bread and molasses. Both Cornish and Finnish miners in the upper Midwest brought pasties—pastry turnovers of meat and vegetables—carefully made by their wives or sold by other local women.[6] Workingmen in any city or industrial town often took advantage of the saloon "free lunch," whereby the purchase of a nickel beer earned them access to the free lunch counter: soup, cold cuts, bread and cheese, with vinegary vegetable salads and pickles. Urban schoolchildren bought cakes, candies, nuts, and fruit from peddlers outside their school gates. People who could return home for lunch ate a home-cooked meal that was often a preview of their evening meal.

Many middle-class men still observed the older tradition of returning home for lunch if they worked near enough. But as the twentieth century approached, more and more white-collar workers commuted from their suburban homes to jobs in urban business districts. Those men availed themselves of the city's "businessmen's restaurants": genteel saloons, chophouses, German-style eateries, and modern cafeterias that served a quick lunch for a low price. Women and young children ate at home, light luncheons of soup, egg dishes, or perhaps a creamed "entrée" of leftovers from dinner.

Working-class people often lacked the luxury of eating together with their families. Family members who worked different shifts came and went, helping themselves to food that was cooked and left out: a pot of beans or a pan of noodle kugel, bread and tea or coffee. Farm people generally kept the rural tradition of a big midday meal, so supper was simple: bread or mush and milk, or leftovers from the noon dinner. Some evening meals were cooked in a big hurry, as working women left work, stopped to buy the day's groceries, and cobbled together a quick meal; other suppers were cooked by daughters while mothers were off working.[7]

The evening meal showed the clearest distinction between middle-class people and the elites who considered themselves their social "betters." Wealthy people rose late, dined late, and supped late (when "supper" still meant a late-night meal, sometimes eaten after a ball or other evening amusement). In their homes full of servants, elaborate meals were served every evening, and frequent, formal dinner parties cemented their social standing. Middle-class people were torn between wanting to emulate the wealthy and wanting to preserve a more sober, frugal, virtuous way of life, including earlier and simpler evening meals. Yet the standard evening meal hour crept later and later over this period (a trend that also met the needs of commuting husbands who might not return until later). Sometimes children were fed and put to bed early, while their parents ate later. Elites were also likely to dine more richly: multicourse meals with many options (two soups, two entrées), expensive ingredients (out-of-season produce, wild game), and dishes that required a great deal of skilled kitchen labor, accompanied by imported wines and liquors. Middle-class people might have only two or three courses of comparatively simpler, plainer fare.[8] They were likely to have servants, but only a few, so elaborate formal meals were much more difficult to attain, never mind the expense. The authors of the 1887 *White House Cook Book* suggested the following menu for those in "ordinary" circumstances who could still afford to entertain:

> A *family dinner*, even with a few friends, can be made quite attractive and satisfactory without much display or expense; consisting first of good soup, then fish garnished with suitable additions, followed by a roast; then vegetables and some made dishes, a salad, crackers, cheese and olives, then dessert. This sensible meal, well-cooked and neatly served, is pleasing to almost any one, and is within the means of any housekeeper in ordinary circumstances.[9]

The food that Americans ate varied a great deal by region and class, but there were some items that were almost universal. Many people ate bread—spread with butter, margarine, jam, or sweetened condensed milk—with every meal, and sometimes bread was a meal in itself with milk or tea.[10] The bread might be homemade wheat yeast-risen bread or soda biscuits, or soft, white bakery loaves, or dark rye or pumpernickel from Eastern European bakeries. Farm families and many middle-class families baked their own bread each week. Beginning in the 1870s, wheat flour was processed in high-efficiency roller mills that removed the bran; people much preferred the white flour, even though it was not as healthful. In the South and parts of the West, corn (in bread and mush) was the primary grain, although Americans all over the country ate corn bread, corn cakes, or cornmeal mush sometimes. Better-off southerners ate

wheat-flour biscuits, or beaten biscuits that required the dough to be "beaten" for nearly an hour to produce a soft, almost cracker-like thin biscuit.[11] In the late nineteenth century, commercially produced baking powder was widely available to make these "quick breads." For American Indians, wheat bread was a new and not particularly welcome food. Forced onto reservations and deprived of their traditional access to food gathering and hunting, Indians had to depend on government-supplied rations, including flour and sugar. When Navajos were forced to relocate to New Mexico and could not grow their traditional beans, they transformed the flour and lard of necessity into a cultural staple, fry bread.[12]

Other starchy foods filled stomachs, instead of or alongside bread. Especially in the South along the Atlantic and the Gulf of Mexico, rice was an essential part of many meals. People of Eastern European ancestry made rich homemade egg noodles to eat alone or to enrich a soup; Jews baked their noodles into a kugel. Italians imported pasta from Italy, or bought from neighborhood pasta shops or regional pasta factories.[13] The poorest families combined their bread with more starch: bread and potatoes, bread and cornmeal mush, bread and oatmeal.[14] But for most, the daily bread was enriched and enlivened with meat, vegetables, dairy, and fats.

Red meat was a recently affordable luxury. In Europe, most people ate meat only a few times a year. When immigrants arrived in the United States, they were astonished to find that even working-class people could eat meat nearly every day. Beef steak and pork chops were the most preferred, for taste and because they

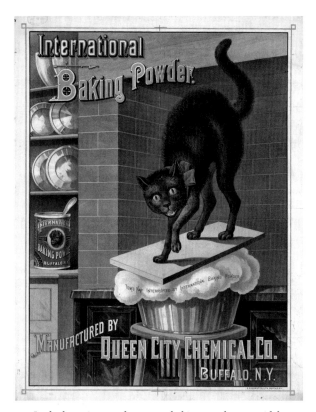

In the late nineteenth century, baking powder was widely available. It made cakes, biscuits, and other quick breads rise reliably. "Tom's nap interrupted by International baking powder." Buffalo, NY: G.H. Dunston, Lith., 1885. Library of Congress Prints and Photographs Division.

everyone ate organ meats: kidney, liver, and tongue were especially appreciated. Cold tongue, for instance, was a popular meat, pickled or jellied and served cold. Poor folks, especially black southerners, made great use of what were later called "variety meats," building thrifty, filling meals on pig's feet, chitlins, and hog maws.[15] Although fresh meat had become more widely available and cheap, preserved meat, such as bacon and salt pork, was still quite important. Southerners ate salt pork or fatback nearly every day, using the grease for cooking and flavoring.[16]

Beef and pork were the most common meats, by far. Chicken was quite expensive until intensive breeding operations were developed in the twentieth century, and chickens had more value as egg producers, so most people enjoyed chicken only rarely, as a Sunday treat. Jews particularly appreciated poultry as part of the Sabbath meal, using the meat as well as the fat (chicken or goose fat for cooking) and the innards (especially chicken livers). Fish was important for those who lived in coastal cities or along rivers, and people far from the water might get their protein from canned sardines. Canned fish like herring or kippers were popular for breakfast. Oysters and lobsters became high-status treats in this period, and were canned or rushed via refrigerated rail car even to cities far from the sea.[17] Men in rural areas, and especially Native American men, fished, hunted, or trapped to add trout, squirrel, or rabbit to the family table. All of these meats might appear at any and every meal. Apart from a few groups, notably observant Jews who ate dairy or pareve meals, meatless meals were only

could be cooked quickly and easily. Other cuts of meat (especially large, inexpensive joints like beef brisket) were simmered slowly, stretching for several meals. Leftovers from large joints might turn up in "made" dishes like hash, creamed dishes, and croquettes. Almost

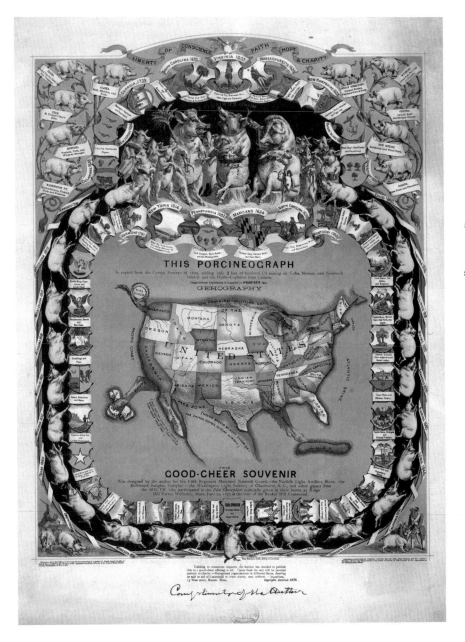

This map, depicting the importance of the hog in American history and suggesting a pork dish for every state, was commissioned as a souvenir by sewing-machine magnate William Emerson Baker for guests at a convention to promote more sanitary farming and food processing. "Porcineograph," Forbes Lithograph Manufacturing Company, ca. 1876. Library of Congress Prints and Photographs Division.

served from dire necessity. Anyone who could afford to eat meat did so.

Vegetables and fruits appeared on the table depending on season, region, heritage, and pocketbook. Cabbage, onions, and potatoes were the universal vegetables: they appeared year-round, on the tables of rich and poor, rural and urban alike, in soups and stews, or cooked by themselves. For many people, potatoes appeared at nearly every meal: boiled, fried, mashed, hashed, or creamed. Squash, fresh corn, peas, sweet potatoes, and tomatoes were also popular in their seasons. Celery was a high-status dish, grown in hothouses and presented at table in specially designed cut-glass celery vases that reflected its high price. The poorest members of the urban working class ate hardly any vegetables and no fruit, clinging instead to a dreary but filling diet of oatmeal, bread, potatoes, and cheap stew meat, with perhaps some milk or butter.

Those who had yards, or who lived in areas with a lot of vegetable farms, ate a wide variety of vegetable dishes in season, for taste and to stretch out the food budget. Farmers, of course, could raise vegetables along with their cash crop if they had the time and labor to spare. Italian immigrants, known for their passion for vegetables, established thousands of farms to supply their communities with the variety of greens, tomatoes, peppers, eggplant, broccoli, and other vegetables they demanded. Even as the twentieth century approached, Americans still foraged for produce, picking wild greens, berries, and mushrooms in the woods and fields, even in the green spaces of industrial cities. For instance,

in Pittsburgh, women and children picked dandelion greens from local parks to eat and sell. In the Pacific Northwest, American Indians confined to reservations left them without permission in order to continue gathering berries and other wild foods.[18]

Native-born Americans in all regions generally liked their vegetables well cooked, served with butter or a sauce. The Women's Centennial Committee *National Cookery Book* (1876) suggested that "fresh and young" peas and asparagus should boil an hour. Fannie Merritt Farmer's *The Boston Cooking-School Cook Book* (1896) suggested twenty to sixty minutes boiling for green peas.[19] New Americans, like the Italians, ate a wider variety of vegetables and often enjoyed them raw or lightly cooked. The tossed green salad was still considered a French dish. Fresh fruit was enjoyed in season, especially as a breakfast food or snack, but Americans generally preferred their fruit in pie form. Any fresh fruit, or canned or dried fruit, could be baked in a crust and serve as a dessert, a snack, or part of a meal.

As the nineteenth century waned, more people could afford canned vegetables and fruits, most commonly tomatoes, peas, and peaches, to add relish to bland food, especially in midwinter. People in rural places, or in urban places with large kitchens and yards, bought bushels of vegetables and fruit cheaply at the peak of the season to can or preserve. Glass mason jars, manufactured inexpensively since the 1870s, made home canning affordable and easier, and sugar was also less expensive than in the past. From cities to small towns, Eastern Europeans shredded, salted, and preserved their own cabbage into sauerkraut every year. Most people canned sweet foods (fruits and jellies) or salted or acid items like sauerkraut and pickles at home, since home-canned nonpickled vegetables were not safe from spoilage until the widespread use of the pressure cooker after World War I.[20]

In the first half of the nineteenth century, only people who owned cows or lived near dairy farms could be sure of a fresh, clean source of milk, and most people drank little fresh milk. After the 1870s, newly established milk trains brought fresh milk into cities from country dairies, and demand increased. City dwellers drank more fresh milk and fed it to their babies as an alternative to breast milk. However, fresh milk could carry bacteria and diseases like typhoid and tuberculosis, especially when it was watered down with dirty water to lower the price, a common practice. Some milk was pasteurized after the 1870s, but this mainly benefited the wealthier people who could afford to pay more for pasteurized milk.[21] Cheese and butter became cheaper, as they were manufactured on a larger scale. Refrigeration also made cheese and butter available throughout more of the year. Butter was still relatively expensive, especially during the winter when cows produced less milk. Because it was valuable, it was a prime target for adulteration; cheaply priced butter was sometimes very bad indeed. Working-class people bought butter substitutes like margarine (made from animal and vegetable fats) when they were available, or they spread condensed milk or lard on their bread instead. Even middle-class people shared tips for conserving butter, such as serving it in portioned "pats"

rather than letting diners help themselves. Americans recently arrived from Northern and Eastern Europe were most likely to drink milk, and to eat other dairy products like sour cream, yogurt, fresh cheese, and buttermilk. Irish immigrants supplemented their potatoes with butter and buttermilk. Russians ate sour cream with beets and cucumbers. Southerners who kept dairy cows were more likely to drink buttermilk than fresh liquid milk.

Although changes in agriculture, transportation, and food processing tended to unify the nation and its food, regional differences persisted. Especially after the resurgence of interest in colonial America after the 1876 Centennial, northern whites enshrined New England's traditional cuisine as the symbolic cuisine of America. Dishes like fish chowders, "Indian" cornmeal pudding or mush, pumpkin pie, baked beans, steamed brown bread, doughnuts, codfish, and "New England boiled dinner," meaning a large joint of beef, such as a brisket, simmered with potatoes and other vegetables, seemed to carry Puritan values like sobriety and frugality. The "traditional" Thanksgiving menu of a large turkey with stuffing and pies was solidified in the late nineteenth century, based on romanticized ideas about colonial New England foods. By the 1870s New Englanders ate much like other regions in the North, with perhaps more seafood, beans, and potatoes. The Mid-Atlantic region was known mainly for the oysters, game, and turtles from the waters and wetlands around New York, New Jersey, Philadelphia, and Delaware.[22]

Immigrants also shaped regional cuisine. Generations of German immigrants had influenced the cuisine in

Pennsylvania, where pretzels, scrapple, and souse were common. Germans also influenced food in the Midwest, not least by founding breweries like Pabst, Schlitz, and Blatz. Norwegians, Swedes, and Finns helped create the cuisine of the upper Midwest, which included lutefisk (pickled fish) and pasties (meat turnovers). In the Far West and California, Asian immigrants and Hispanic residents influenced local cuisines.[23] Los Angeles, for example, did not have a regional source for wheat flour until the 1870s, as the mostly Mexican-ancestry population ate homemade corn tortillas, and its vegetable and fruit peddlers were largely Chinese-born. Chinese immigrants provided themselves with abundant dried vegetables, mushrooms, rice, and tea from China to supplement local fresh vegetables and seafood.[24] Quite the opposite of immigrants, American Indians throughout the West attempted to maintain their traditional diet based on gathering, hunting, and traditional vegetables: bighorn sheep, mule deer, and cushaw squash in the Sonora Desert; deer, corn, wild rice, and milkweed in Nebraska.[25] However, Indians often had to adopt a "white" diet based on wheat flour and lard when their access to land was limited by reservation policy or land appropriation.

A number of distinct cuisines flourished in the South: the French and Creole influences in New Orleans and the Gulf Coast; pork in the Upland South; rice and seafood in the Low Country. African food culture, transmitted in the time of slavery, continued to influence southern cuisine, as black cooks served peanuts, okra, beans and rice, and fried chicken to their employers and to their own families. Poor southerners, especially tenant farmers and sharecroppers, clung to the "hog and hominy" diet of fat pork and cornmeal mush, corn bread, or grits.[26]

For wealthy and middle-class Americans, the British Empire provided a culinary inspiration. Foods like chutney, mulligatawny soup, and curried or "Hindoo" eggs (eggs in a white sauce mildly flavored with curry) offered a way for Americans to experience the power of empire secondhand.[27] As the twentieth century approached, new "foreign" foods would become an increasingly popular way for native-born white Americans to add some exotic interest to their diet, while still reinforcing imperialism and white supremacy.

The Food System Transformed

In the late nineteenth century, agriculture was industrializing. Small family farms were being gradually replaced by larger, more efficient "factory farms," using more complex machinery and chemical fertilizers that required bank loans for financing. Railroads brought food from further away, and lowered the price. Refrigeration extended fresh foods' life span. Taken together, these changes began to reduce seasonality. And while Americans had always enjoyed food imported from overseas, in the late nineteenth century, U.S. food imports increased, as American began to expect to enjoy European delicacies and the fruits of American empire.

These structural developments meant that nearly everyone was able to eat at least a bit better than in the past, with more access to previously high-status foods like meat, white flour, and sugar, and more access to fresh produce throughout the year. Middle-class people in particular benefited from the greater variety of food available. However, these changes to the food system occurred at the same time that America's "second industrial revolution" concentrated new immigrants and American rural migrants into crowded industrial cities. Despite the long-term movement toward lower food prices, frequent industrial depressions (especially in the 1870s and 1890s) and job insecurity meant that working-class city-dwellers frequently had trouble stretching their food dollars to feed the family. And lower farm prices and endemic rural poverty meant that poor farmers, such as sharecroppers and tenant farmers, often struggled to maintain an adequate diet.

In the 1870s, food was becoming available outside of its traditional time of year through transportation and new technologies in farming and food processing. Faster transportation had effectively shortened distances, so that ripe fruit could be brought from southern or western states or even from other countries, and sold before it rotted.[28] Refrigerated train cars meant that meat could be slaughtered and shipped year-round, not just in the cold months. New technologies in farming could also reduce seasonality. Canned food, which became widely available in the late nineteenth century, was much closer to fresh in taste and texture than dried or salted food, and so it seemed like an impressive reduction of seasonality.

The industrialization of agriculture made food production more like factory production, with increased use of mechanization, increased dependence on capital and credit, economies of scale, and market specialization. This kind of production eventually helped diminish seasonal variations and pressures on the prices of staples and grains. In the thirty years after 1870, homesteading farmers began to flood into the Great Plains and Far West, although much of the land was eventually found too dry for farming.[29] During the same years, the Dawes Act, intended convert Indians into property-owning farmers, allowed widespread white appropriation of Indian lands, especially the most fertile and valuable lands.[30] More land under cultivation meant a larger supply of food on the market and lower prices, especially for grains and meat. Farmers changed their tools, as well. Innovations such as mechanical planters, reapers, and binders (tools that still used horses as the motive power, rather than steam or gasoline) increased the amount of crop farmers could produce with less labor. Wheat production increased 250 percent in the last quarter of the century, and by 1898, one dollar could buy twice as much flour as in 1872.[31] These new techniques worked best in large farms, requiring significant capital and leading to increased dependence on banks. Larger farms resulted in lower commodity prices, which in turn made it even harder for small farmers to compete.[32] These changes in American farming combined to bring a greater variety of food into American markets and, at least for a while, lowered prices for food as well.

Railroad transportation and related technological changes altered the nature of food as a commodity. The railroads transformed food by increasing the radius of supply. Food could be transported quite cheaply over long distances, lowering prices and increasing the variety of food available. By the 1880s, the use of ice-refrigerated railroad cars was changing agriculture, as fruits, vegetables, meat, and other perishable goods could be shipped long distances. In some instances, the railroad system transformed entire industries.

The development of the refrigerated railroad car made it possible to develop a centralized meat-processing center in Chicago. In the 1850s and 1860s, cattle from Texas were herded to Kansas, brought into Chicago by rail, and then shipped, still "on the hoof," to slaughterhouses throughout the East. In the 1870s, Gustavus Swift, a livestock agent born in Massachusetts who moved his business to the Midwest along with the expanding railroads, built a more efficient system, shipping chilled, butchered meat rather the entire, living cow. His plan required refrigerated cars that would chill the meat without damaging it, and icehouses along the way to refresh the car refrigeration. Local butchers were pressured to sell "chilled beef" instead of beef that they had butchered themselves; those who resisted found themselves ruthlessly undercut by Swift's low prices. Once Swift was able to perfect this system, other packers followed suit. As this "Western beef" flooded the market in the last quarter of the nineteenth century, beef prices plunged,

falling as much as 30 percent between 1882 and 1893.[33] Americans could afford to eat fresh meat instead of preserved meat, replacing salt pork with fresh beef. The changes in the meat industry affected individual neighborhoods as well: local slaughterhouses disappeared, and retailers concentrated on selling the most desirable, standardized cuts, rather than having to dispose of all the parts of a locally slaughtered animal.[34]

As inexpensive butchered meat poured out of centralized industries, wild game and shellfish declined in numbers due to overhunting and overfishing. By 1900, for example, Americans living in New York, Philadelphia, and Baltimore could easily buy inexpensive beef butchered and packed in Chicago, but the ducks, oysters, and crabs that had once been plentiful in the Chesapeake were becoming scarce.[35]

The milk supply was drastically altered by the railroads. Until the 1870s, if city dwellers drank milk, it came from cows in crowded, dirty, local dairies. The cows ate discarded distillery and brewery mash, were penned in small, filthy stalls, and produced sour, dirty milk. In the 1880s and 1890s, newly established milk trains, soon with ice-refrigerated cars, brought fresh country milk quickly into cities, making it less expensive. However, railroads increased the distance and time that milk could travel between cow and consumer, and bacterial contamination plagued urban milk supplies until pasteurization became widespread in the 1910s.[36]

The railroads' ability to bring fresh produce seemed the most remarkable. Even before the Civil War, seasonal fruits and vegetables had been shipped from the warm South to colder northern cities, and by the 1870s shipping increased considerably on the expanded rail lines. Southern states like Florida, Georgia, and South Carolina, with their longer growing seasons, specialized in produce like tomatoes, salad greens, radishes, fresh onions, and cucumbers they could ship to New York and other northern cities.[37] Fresh produce was even shipped all the way from California back to eastern states. The first carload of California fresh fruit reached the East Coast in 1869, and the California agricultural economy boomed in the last quarter of the nineteenth century, as refrigerated cars could ship produce almost anywhere in the country without significant damage—especially after sturdy varieties like iceberg lettuce were specially developed for long transport.[38]

This meant that city dwellers, even in cold northern states, could enjoy out-of-season fruits and vegetables. Boston cooking teacher and home economist Maria Parloa, in an 1880 cookbook, wrote about the temptations of supplementing northeastern produce with southern items, warning of its higher cost: "The railroads and steamers connect the climes so closely that one hardly knows whether he is eating fruits or vegetables in or out of season. The provider, however, realizes that it takes a long purse to buy fresh produce at the North while the ground is yet frozen."[39]

Long before frozen food was sold at retail, American's food supply was already shaped by cold storage. Cold-storage warehouses, often attached to the railroad network, were common in large cities after the 1880s. Perishable food like eggs, meat, and fresh fruit could be chilled at or below freezing for weeks or months and then sold as fresh. In 1891, *Harper's Weekly* reported that large cold-storage warehouses in New York and Chicago were keeping eggs, meats, and other items fresh for weeks or months out of their seasons. The buying public was often suspicious of cold-storage food: the food seemed unnaturally fresh though months old, and the cold could conceal spoilage.[40] To *Harper's*, however, cold storage promised a "peaceful revolution," in which eggs would sell for the same low price year-round, spring lamb would be available any time, and "people of very small incomes will be able to enjoy a bill of fare such as the richest man was unable to procure within the memory of the reader."[41] The changes in food distribution promised a sort of democracy of goods, in which even poor people would be able to buy plenty of fresh, luxurious food.[42] Although this promise was not quite achieved, most Americans did benefit from the wider seasonal availability of food. Height and weight measurements suggest that the better nutrition from refrigerated meat and dairy was one factor that allowed Americans to grow a little taller and heavier in subsequent generations.[43] Rural people, who lived far from railroad terminals or shipping ports, benefited less from this new transportation technology, of course; they were still largely limited to produce that grew locally or could survive longer, slower hauls.

Urban people also benefited most from the United States' increasingly active role in global commerce. Importers provided Latin American coffee, European cheese and pasta, Chinese tea, Caribbean sugar and bananas, Pacific coconuts, and spices from all around the world.[44] Wealthy urban consumers in particular could flatter themselves that their nation was a cornucopia of all the world's finest delicacies: an impression supported by the U.S. government's willingness to use military force and diplomatic pressure to protect trade. But almost all Americans benefited from the low prices for coffee, sugar, and other staples—low prices protected by the United States' growing international power. By 1900, the United Fruit Company, backed by U.S. military power, had exported more than a million stems of bananas to the United States, grown in the company's extensive holdings in Caribbean nations.[45] The expanded railroad networks in the United States were part of a global system of food production, one shaped by unequal power.

Industrial Food Processing

The railroads transported new varieties of processed food, in addition to fresh food. In the late nineteenth century, there were two major sets of changes to American food processing. Traditional processes such as cheese making, brewing, bread making, and meat curing were accelerated and converted from small-batch, artisan production to continuous factory production. And newer processes such as commercial canning and breakfast cereal manufacture produced new processed foods that radically changed American eating habits.

Food had been canned since the early 1800s, but for most of the nineteenth century, canned food was an expensive way for wealthy people to enjoy out-of-season or rare delicacies. In the 1850s, a small can of oysters, salmon, lobsters, tomatoes, corn, or peas might cost 50 cents in an eastern grocery store. At that time, a skilled mason working on the Erie Canal earned about $1.50 each week.[46] Canned food was often sold in "boom" areas such as the Far West, where canned fruits and vegetables were sometimes the only ones available at any price. Newly rich miners in California lavished money on canned delicacies, paying exorbitant prices for exotic "prepared" foods like turtle soup and lobster salad in cans.[47] In the late nineteenth century, the industry expanded, and canned food's retail price dropped as manufacturers found ways to eliminate costly human labor: that of the skilled tinsmiths who made and soldered the cans, as well as that of the unskilled, low-paid women and children who prepared the food to be canned.[48]

Canned food finally became affordable for the middle classes in the 1880s, and for most people around 1900. The technological advances and elimination of high labor costs lowered the prices of common canned foods, especially tomatoes, corn, and peas, to within the reach of many: about 5–25 cents per can for vegetables, fruits, or salmon. Middle-class cooks grew accustomed to using canned fruits and vegetables when fresh ones were seasonally unavailable.[49] Even poor working-class families used a small amount of canned food. Working-class families, like the German family in New York City in the 1890s that spent only $10 per week for food, regularly spent 10 cents for a can of tomatoes.[50] There was, however, some resistance to canned food. Some recent immigrants, especially Italians, refused to use canned foods, finding them to be a totally unacceptable version of "fresh."[51]

Some new products heralded twentieth-century changes in diet. Canned ready-to-eat baked beans and soups had been sold since the 1880s. The Campbell's Soup Company developed condensed soup in 1898. In the 1890s, new processed breakfast cereals, like Kellogg's Corn Flakes and Post's Grape-Nuts, offered a completely new kind of breakfast, marketed as a healthy alternative to the traditional heavy meat breakfast. The newly consolidated National Biscuit Company, later renamed Nabisco, began packaging crackers in a tightly sealed box so they would stay crisper than crackers traditionally sold in bulk from barrels. The "Uneeda Biscuit" was introduced in 1898, a bit of clever wordplay that spawned dozens of imitators and demonstrated the huge power of marketing for the new processed, packaged foods.[52]

As food was being processed more heavily and produced far from where it was sold and consumed, unscrupulous producers had more opportunity to adulterate the products to increase profits. To the old tricks

(wooden "nutmegs," chalk in flour) were added new techniques: copper in canned peas to make them bright green, unspecified filler in canned meat products, jelly that was nothing but glucose syrup, food coloring, and artificial flavor. In 1898, the "Embalmed Beef" scandal broke when the U.S. Army accused meatpackers of providing supposedly "fresh" canned beef that was heavily dosed with chemicals to cover its rottenness, sickening the troops who ate it.[53] Before the passage of the Pure Food and Drug Act in 1906, consumers concerned about adulteration had little choice but to trust their grocer's recommendations. Consumer advocates suggested, not very practically, that people could perform tests to check for additives, although surely few people actually did. On an 1884 cover of *Puck*, a humor magazine, a man tests for water in the milk, sand in the sugar, and other suspicious substances in his butter, bread, and hash. The idea that consumers might need to understand chemistry to ensure safe food was one of the factors that led women like Ellen Richards to pursue university degrees in chemistry (at Vassar and MIT) and to establish the field of home economics, applying science to traditional household arts. One of her books, *Food Materials and Their Adulterations* (1885), helped spur passage of state pure food and drug acts before the federal act in 1906.[54]

By the end of the nineteenth century, the path food took from farm to kitchen had changed almost beyond recognition. Farms were larger, food traveled faster and farther to market, and some food was transformed along the way into a growing selection of packaged and

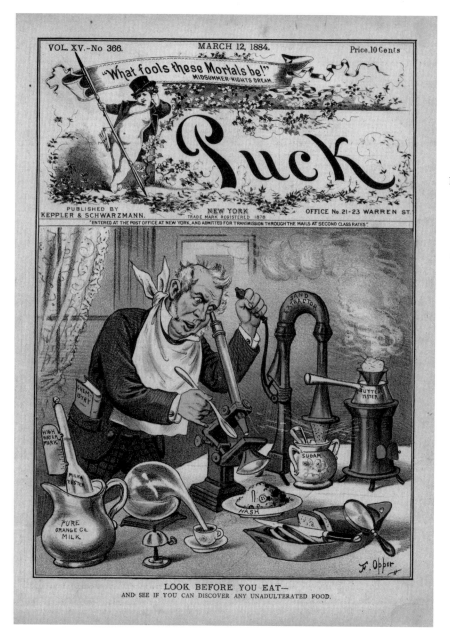

Food that was produced and processed far from the final consumer might be adulterated to increase its profitability. Consumers had to take it upon themselves to test for suspicious ingredients in their food. "Look before you eat," Frederick Burr Opper. Published by Keppler and Schwarzmann, New York, March 12, 1884. Library of Congress Prints and Photographs Division.

processed food. The kitchens where this food was processed for the last time before it was eaten had changed, too. The kitchens of working-class people were quite different from those of middle-class people, in both form and function. And rural people of all classes were mostly left out of the technological changes that made kitchen work lighter, cleaner, and easier for urban people by 1900.

Kitchens, Tools, and Utilities

For middle-class people, the kitchen was a necessary evil. The kitchen was a workplace, ideally one where servants would toil and the lady of the house would merely supervise. The many middle-class women who worked alongside their help still tried to shield the formal areas of the house from the noise, smells, and mess of the kitchen. Yet in the second half of the century, there was a move to modernize this room, in hopes of improving the working conditions both for servant and for mistress. In 1869, sisters Catharine Beecher and Harriet Beecher Stowe published *The American Woman's Home: Or, Principles of Domestic Science; Being a Guide to the Formation and Maintenance of Economical, Healthful, Beautiful, and Christian Homes*. They urged American women to take housekeeping seriously, insisted on the social and moral importance of a well-kept home, and suggested ways to make housework more efficient. They recommended kitchen innovations like continuous work surfaces, separate areas for cooking and washing up, and built-in cabinets and storage. Homes built after the 1870s might have more "modern" kitchens, built to facilitate workflow, with a well-designed coal stove, running water, built-in sinks, and perhaps cupboards or cabinets for storage. Kitchens were usually closed off by a door from the rest of the house, and guests (apart from women in the family) were never invited in.

Working-class and farm kitchens were more central to the family's life. They were busy places, with constant cooking, eating, bathing, socializing, and working. Working-class homes, whether apartments or houses, were generally small in size and full of people, with little in the way of built-in storage or single-function rooms. Practically speaking, working people could not afford to light and heat several rooms of the home at once, so families huddled around the source of heat or light. In summer, people tried to use the stove as little as possible or used small tabletop gasoline or oil stoves to save fuel and reduce heat in their living and working area.[55] Farm kitchens were large, designed for heavy productive work like canning fruit. Both working-class and farm kitchens might surprise a present-day observer. They might contain a bed, because people slept in the kitchen if that was the most comfortable room, or if there was no other space. Working-class kitchens also lacked formal dining spaces. People ate wherever it was convenient and com-

THE KITCHEN

An idealized image of a middle-class kitchen. There is running water and a built-in sink,
but the low kitchen table is the only work surface. The coal stove dominates the room.
"Prang's aids for object teaching—The kitchen." Boston: L. Prang and Co., 1874.
Library of Congress Prints and Photographs Division.

fortable: near the stove in winter, near the open door or windows in summer.

Utilities and tools made huge differences in the never-ending work of a kitchen. Modern utilities like running water made kitchen work much easier, but they were not evenly distributed. The wealthiest people had indoor running water after the Civil War. Less well-to-do people may have had a pump in the kitchen, pumping city water, well water, or water from their own cistern. Most working-class people had to haul water, either from a single sink in their apartment building, or from a pump in the back-yard or on the corner. Farm families hauled water from a spring, or from a well or pump in the yard.[56] This meant that every drop of water used for cooking, cleaning, and bathing had to be carried in and heated on the stove, and sometimes carried back out again. The large cook stoves of middle-class houses had hot-water reservoirs—large, covered metal basins attached to the stove, with a faucet for access—that could produce a constant supply of hot water as long as the stove was kept lit and the reservoir filled as it was used. But someone in those houses still had to carry water, and carry coal to heat it with.

The stove was the most important tool in the kitchen, a tool that remained essentially unchanged from the

Stove manufacturers advertised endless minor improvements, but stove technology did not actually improve much. Women's labor, rather than the stove, was the main force responsible for turning out endless loaves of perfect bread. "The new Sterling did it. Sterling ranges," ca. 1896. Library of Congress Prints and Photographs Division.

Civil War until the widespread adoption of gas stoves around 1900. The only major innovation in stoves during that time was the change in fuel, from wood to coal. Most stoves could burn wood or coal interchangeably, so cooks could switch back and forth depending on what was cheaper. Hard (anthracite) coal was more expensive, but it burned cleaner and hotter than the cheaper soft coal. Cooking on a coal stove of 1900 was more or less the same experience it had been on a wood stove of 1850. Though perhaps slightly more efficient and more convenient to use, the stove still required fuel hauling, constant fire-tending, and standing uncomfortably close to the source

of heat in order to cook. The experience of cooking began to change only with different types of fuels and stoves that could be turned on and off more easily and that did not emit so much radiant heat.

Cooking stoves required a great deal of experience to learn to operate properly, and they needed constant maintenance. If the ashes were not removed each day, the fire would not light; and if the stove was not cleaned regularly, it would smoke up the room. Any stove would rust if not "blacked" with stove polish as often as every few days. Inexpensive stoves were more or less simple boxes, whose heat was hard to control; a complicated system of dampers controlled the heat in more expensive models, requiring time and attention to learn. Wood and coal stoves did not have temperature gauges. To test the heat, cooks used traditional methods that were essentially unchanged from the days of brick hearth ovens, such as holding one's hand near the heat and counting the seconds till it was unbearable.[57] They were dangerous appliances to have in the home. Stoves could emit noxious gas if used improperly. They could topple over, hot-water reservoirs might spill and scald, or children might burn themselves on the stove's hot cast-iron surfaces.[58]

Unlike our gas and electric ranges today, wood and coal stoves could not be turned on or off quickly; they were slow to heat and slow to cool. They were better suited to a full-time housekeeper, whose other tasks kept her in the house where she could maintain the fire and cook a variety of dishes at different temperatures as the fire waxed and waned, than to a wage-worker who returned home only to eat. Middle-class women gladly employed cooks when they could afford to do so, because it meant they could be freed from the constant attendance at the stove for club meetings, volunteer or charity work, more time with children, or even wage work. Farm women rarely had cooks, and spent much of their lives in company with the huge, smoking stove. And although any kind of food could be produced on a stove, they were most practical and economical when used for slow-cooking dishes like stews, or when used for a several dishes at once to get the most use from the fuel. In this way, they were still more like the old-fashioned hearth.

Stoves using coal oil, kerosene, or gasoline were patented beginning in the 1860s, for use as portable, camping, or other temporary or supplementary stoves. These new stoves were inexpensive and relatively easy to use, but the burning fuel smelled bad and there was great risk of fire and explosion.[59] The 1897 Sears, Roebuck catalog offered one-burner oil stoves for as little as 85 cents and gasoline stoves for $2.63 and added, "There is positively no danger in using the Acme Gasoline Stove. It cannot explode"—suggesting that consumers were aware of gasoline stoves that *did* explode.[60]

Stoves had not changed much, but kitchenware had. In the late nineteenth century, kitchen cookware on the American market was made from new, lightweight, and inexpensive materials. Formerly expensive items like ceramic dishes and pressed glassware were now mass produced, and thus sold more cheaply. Pots, pans, kettles, buckets, and other vessels, previously made of heavy and relatively expensive cast iron, were made in lighter metals such as aluminum, which appeared after the 1880s. Enameled goods (the lightweight, white or blue-speckled pans called enamelware, agateware, or graniteware) were made by a process developed in Germany in the eighteenth century. They were manufactured in large quantities in the United States after the 1870s.[61] Enamel pots and pans sold in the Sears, Roebuck catalog for between 15 cents and $1.00 in 1897.[62] Through Rural Free Delivery, begun in the 1890s, farm families could buy this kitchenware from catalog retailers like Sears and Montgomery Ward, rather than at country stores or from traveling peddlers.

Americans of the Gilded Age enthusiastically adopted specialized kitchen implements and serving ware. In an era when factory work was increasingly rationalized and mechanized, inventors and manufacturers created kitchen tools for very specialized tasks. Labor-saving patented gadgets like rotary eggbeaters became more common, and farm families embraced tools that could lighten their food-processing work, such as cherry pitters and apple peelers, and food choppers to speed up sausage making.[63] From the midcentury, domestic advisors like Catharine Beecher advocated having the right utensil or dish for table service. It seemed more appropriate to use precisely the right item for each dish. Beecher, writing for a middle-class audience, suggested a full complement of at least 144 items for the service of an ordinary middle-class dinner party for twelve, counting only cutlery, plates, and bowls.[64] Other items for table service included sauce boats, soup tureens, vegetable and pudding dishes, platters for meat, and specialized dishes for desserts, fruit, and other courses. Wealthy Victorians delighted in even more specialized items, such as cake baskets, condiment caster sets, ice-water pitchers, doilies, celery vases, asparagus forks, grape scissors, and so on.[65] Working-class people, too, aspired to a profusion of goods: inexpensive dishware, pressed glass, cooking pots, and linens filled their kitchens, often bought secondhand or from cheap outlets like pushcart vendors.[66]

Markets

As the United States became more urbanized, the seemingly timeless act of buying food at market became a more complex, more challenging, and more time-consuming task.[67] Shopping required knowledge and skill: where and when to get the best-quality food for the lowest prices, how to judge the quality of food and avoid adulterated products. As farming, processing, and transportation transformed food, the way that most people bought food changed, too. In rapidly growing industrial cities and towns, a dizzying and ever-changing array of retailers sold fresh food and groceries. Late nineteenth-century city dwellers could choose between different places and ways to buy food as the types of retailing evolved. Most still bought fresh food—meats, dairy, and produce—every few days or every day. The most important decision to make was where to buy: from small, specialized retailers, such as grocers, butcher shops, dairy stores, bakeries, or greengrocers, to stands at outdoor or partly covered public markets, to peddlers on the street. Meanwhile, farm families continued to trade far less often, in traditional "country stores," until mail-order merchants like Montgomery Ward and Sears could fulfill the promise of home grocery delivery.

At public markets, the rich and poor of a city rubbed elbows. Consumers could buy from wholesalers, or directly from producers who hauled their fruits, veg-

Rich and poor rubbed elbows in the public markets, where a wide range of food was available. "New York City—rich and poor; or, the two Christmas dinners—a scene in Washington Market, sketched from real life." Illustration from Frank Leslie's illustrated newspaper 35 (January 4, 1873): 265. Library of Congress Prints and Photographs Division.

demand. The markets opened early: New York City's markets opened at 4:00 a.m., for example. Restaurant and fashionable hotel caterers and housekeepers of the wealthy came first and paid the highest prices for the freshest, best-quality food. After they had made their selections, ordinary housewives and boardinghouse keepers arrived around 6:00 or 7:00 a.m. to look for bargains. As the day went on, the food became cheaper, as the produce wilted and the fish began to stink.[69] Shopping at this type of market required considerable confidence and skill. A buyer had to know just what he or she wanted and how much could be stored, had to judge the quality of what was offered and determine how long it would keep in the storage facilities available, and had to evaluate the seller's need to unload his produce and his willingness to make a bargain. Indeed, despite the bargains available, many buyers shied away from the hectic markets and this battle of wits.

If they would not come to the market, the market would come to them. People in cities and towns could also buy food from peddlers and hucksters who sold from pushcarts, wagons, or baskets. Pushcart peddlers sold fresh fruits and vegetables, meat and fish, bread and bakery products, groceries, and all manner of prepared snacks, in addition to clothing, shoes, fabric, household goods, books, and other items. Peddlers and hucksters took the advantages of the public market and added mobility: they traveled about the city, enabling consumers to buy right outside their doors or on nearby streets. Pushcart sellers had a lot of flexibility: they could sell fruit just about to go bad, slightly damaged vegetables,

etables, meats, or dairy products into the city. Public markets offered low prices and sometimes fewer middlemen, but they could also be crowded and unsanitary.[68] The markets offered flexible pricing: customers could shop early in the day, for the best quality, or late in the day, for the lowest prices, and vendors could change their prices quickly based on inventory, supply, and or other odd-lot produce to bargain-seekers.[70] Pushcart vendors could also sell in quantities to suit their buyers. Peddlers in New York's Jewish community could find buyers for damaged eggs, or a single white or yolk from a broken egg, or a single chicken wing or an ounce of butter, among residents of tenement houses with little storage space who bought food every day.[71]

Not every neighborhood had pushcarts or access to public markets, but virtually all had a few small, local grocers. At the beginning of the nineteenth century, grocers had supplied a very small proportion of the food that Americans ate. Dried, preserved, or long-keeping foods such as flour, cornmeal, and dried fruits were sold by grocers in cities, or in general stores in the country. Grocers also offered imported or luxury items, such as coffee, tea, spices, liquors, and preserved foods, as well as staples like salt. Families who lived far from cities, or on very small means, might buy almost no groceries at all except for grains, some sugar, coffee or tea, or whatever food they could not grow or trade for locally. People who could afford to buy staple foods in bulk (and had the storage space to keep them) usually did so, buying perhaps several barrels of flour and sugar and boxes of dried apples per year. People in cities who lived more hand-to-mouth, or who lacked storage space, might buy small quantities of staple foods—for instance, two cents' worth of sugar, enough for a few days—several times a week. During the nineteenth century, grocers gradually became a more important part of daily food shopping. After the 1880s, canned foods, packaged crackers, breakfast cereal, and other processed foods filled grocers'

shelves. And as the twentieth century approached, more people bought even staple foods like flour in smaller brand-name packages, rather than in bulk.[72]

Groceries were small local businesses that offered flexible credit and other services to meet their customers' needs. They were usually full-service, meaning that they offered credit and home delivery. Both wealthy and poor households availed themselves of credit to buy food. In wealthy households, servants could be sent food shopping without being entrusted with money; in poor ones, credit kept food on the table during periodic unemployment. Retail grocery and food stores were easy businesses to enter but hard ones in which to prosper. A relatively small capital cost was required to start a store, but it was a very competitive field, and the expenses of making deliveries and extending credit put many retailers out of business.[73] Local grocery stores could be miniscule and quite casual. For instance, one street in Boston in the 1890s featured within its tenements "one corner and two basement groceries, with bread, bundled kindling-wood, milk, and salt pickles for staple articles of traffic."[74]

Lack of storage space made shopping more difficult, and more expensive, for poor urban people. Middle-class houses and farmhouses generally had greater storage space, including features like cellars, porches, attics, and cabinets and closets inside the home. Middle-class people had ice boxes, which must be supplied with ice every few days, while rural people often had some kind of cold storage in icehouses or spring houses (where food was kept cool by spring water). Working-class people, lacking those spaces, bought food daily in small quantities, even staples like butter, flour, and sugar. In 1893, housing reformer Marcus T. Reynolds explained that low-income families bought in small quantities for lack of both money and storage space. Working people "cannot buy a barrel or even a bag of flour, for if they did they would be without other provisions. They do not want a pound of butter or a leg of meat, for they have no ice to keep it on."[75] By the end of the century, even middle-class people were moving into smaller city homes that often lacked the large storage spaces of their former homes. The days when people bought flour by the barrel and potatoes by the bushel were already receding.

The living conditions in crowded cities made it impossible for many people to store up food in the old-fashioned way. But the cities did offer one important innovation: they provided ever more ways for people to buy ready-to-eat food. The restaurant culture that grew in American cities in the late nineteenth century paved the way for the huge expansion of eating out that would follow in the twentieth century.

Restaurants and Food Businesses

Restaurants blossomed in the late nineteenth century. Elites demonstrated their social standing with lavish banquets at culinary institutions like Delmonico's in New York. People who worked long hours bought snacks, lunches, and ready-to-eat food, rather than cook in their cramped kitchens. Recent immigrants ate and drank traditional foods with their countrymen, sometimes attracting curious or adventurous native-born Americans to sample the food. And middle-class people began asserting their right both to the formerly guarded elite spaces and to the homey neighborhood ethnic and working-class spots.

Throughout the first half of the nineteenth century, public dining had been rare, limited primarily to taverns and inns that served travelers or local businessmen. Street vendors sold food such as oysters, roasted corn ears, fruit, and sweets at low prices to all classes. These hucksters, such as Philadelphia's vendors of "hot corn" and "pepper pot soup" (a spicy tripe soup), remained traditional in many cities until the twentieth century.[76] Oysters, in particular, were eaten by rich and poor alike. Throughout most of the nineteenth century, they were a cheap and popular street food in eastern cities, eaten from small stands and in basement "oyster saloons" by the millions until their prices rose around 1910 due to overfishing and pollution.[77] Public dining of all kind was, of course, found only in cities. Rural people might sometimes dine out while traveling, but not on a regular basis, and they continued to eat almost entirely at home throughout the end of the century.

Over the course of the nineteenth century, restaurants began to proliferate in American cities. As cities

Rich and poor alike ate oysters on every possible occasion in the late nineteenth century. "Oyster stand in Fulton Market." Alfred R. Waud. Illustration in Harper's Weekly 14, no. 722 (October 29, 1870): 701. Library of Congress Prints and Photographs Division.

grew in size, fewer professional men were able to walk back home for lunch, so they sought meals at taverns, clubs, and chophouses. European-style fine dining began to develop in eastern cities in the century's second half. From the 1840s well into the twentieth century, Delmonico's restaurant in New York City (actually a series of restaurants in different locations around New York, operated by a Swiss family) epitomized fashionable, lavish European cuisine served in a luxurious atmosphere.

Other restaurants such as Sherry's, Rector's, and the dining rooms at the Waldorf-Astoria followed in the same vein, with French food—or at least food with French names. Wealthy Americans held sumptuous banquets in these restaurants, with many courses, elaborate table decorations of sugar work, fruit, and fresh flowers. The elegant restaurants inspired a new kind of table service at dinner parties in wealthy homes. In the old "English" or "family style," all the courses were placed on the table at once, to provide a show of abundance, with each dish in its own boat-shaped plate. The host served the plates and passed them, and guests helped themselves to side dishes. In the new "Service à la Russe," a butler carved the meat at a sideboard and filled individual plates offered to guests. Guests might also help themselves from platters brought to their seat by waiters. Printed menu cards described the dishes, emphasizing the sequence and composition of the menu and ensuring that guests knew just what they were eating. This service meant fewer dishes on the table, which made room for more elegant tables with large centerpieces and specialized utensils.[78]

Toward the end of the nineteenth century, middle-class urban Americans began to imitate social elites, eating out more often than before at more modest, but still genteel, establishments. Originally restricted to businessmen and the wealthy, the practice of fine dining gradually lost some of its masculine and extravagant connotations and became more open to unaccompanied upper-class and middle-class women, and to family dining.[79] Restaurant diners still represented a fairly small proportion of Americans, as rural people would rarely if ever have eaten at restaurants. But their numbers were steadily growing.

Urban people at all levels bought ready-to-eat food (like bakery bread or delicatessen food) and ate in a wide range of cheap local restaurants, saloons, and food stands. Increased immigration in the second half of the nineteenth century caused a major change to the restaurant scene in large cities, both in the types of res-

taurants and in the clientele who patronized them. The earliest and best-known "ethnic" restaurants were the "Biergartens," opened and patronized by German immigrants beginning in the 1860s. Biergartens offered a festive environment of live music, plentiful food, and lager beer (which took America by storm when it was first introduced in large quantities in the 1870s, despite the increasingly powerful temperance movement).[80] Other immigrants opened restaurants in ethnic neighborhoods in order to sell familiar foods to the single men who emigrated in large numbers. For the most part, these restaurants were unknown outside of the ethnic enclaves. They were small and were mostly unnoticed by those outside the community. In fact, these "restaurants" sometimes operated out of an apartment kitchen and were known only to the neighbors.

Jewish, Italian, German, Greek, and other immigrant communities were served by dozens of small restaurants, bakeries, delicatessens, butcher shops, candy stores, groceries, food importers, saloons, and food carts.[81] New York in particular was known for its Jewish and German delicatessens. Jewish "appetizing" stores sold smoked fish and dairy products, while "delicatessens" sold meats and sausages. Non-Jewish German delis offered sausages, fish salads, sauerkraut, wursts, and smoked ham.[82] Over time, the different types of delis began to mingle, as some Russian and other Eastern European Jews began to eat German-style deli meats like pastrami, as part of a homogenization of "Jewish style" food in America.[83] Much of this food could be eaten cold: salads, pickles, smoked fish, bread, cheeses, ham, sausages, desserts. Like bakeries, delis offered ready-to-eat food that was appetizing and not too expensive and that could be eaten by itself or as part of a more complex meal served at home.

Baker's bread was the staple of most nineteenth-century Americans' diets. Americans in rural areas continued to bake their own bread well into the twentieth century, partly because of a lack of any options to buy baked bread. Farming and middle-class housewives, and many working-class women as well, prided themselves on their skill in baking light, tender, consistent loaves, even when the flour available varied wildly and coal ovens were temperamental. Homemade bread was widely considered healthier, better-tasting, and more economical (unless one counted the time demanded of the cook and the overpowering heat of the stove in small apartments).

Although homemade bread remained common in many families, it was increasingly being displaced by bread from commercial bakeries. In towns and cities, many families depended on daily bread from the baker's if they didn't have the time, skill, or resources to bake at home, and often enjoyed other bakery treats as well. Especially for busy working-class women and their families, home-baked bread became a luxury, and baker's bread the norm. Most people bought bread from relatively small local bakeries with four or fewer employees, often family operations, that served neighborhoods and small towns.[84] Some neighborhood bakeries were almost microscopic. In Boston in the 1890s, a tiny bakery, "about six feet by six, opening out of Mrs. Flanagan's kitchen," served the occupants of one working-class street.[85] Larger bakeries selling mass-produced bread on a regional scale wouldn't appear until the 1920s. Through the Gilded Age, bread was consistently cheap, selling for two to five cents per loaf. Stale or day-old bread was usually available more cheaply still, and "dark" bread was cheaper than light.[86]

In saloons, men of all classes, as well as some women, found a popular meal option. Saloons began offering "free lunches" with the purchase of a drink in the last quarter of the nineteenth century. As more Americans moved to cities to work in factories and mills, more and more saloons sprang up to compete for their business. The number of saloons in the United States tripled between 1870 and 1900. In 1901, there were 6,217 saloons in Chicago, or about one for every 273 people.[87] Most of these were "tied-house" saloons, which sold beer from only one brewery in exchange for fixtures, furniture, and other start-up costs provided by that brewery.[88] In order to compete in the crowded urban market, breweries and beer distributors began providing food or funds to the saloons in order to put out a lunch spread, free with the price of a beer.[89]

Free lunches in the West and Midwest were often generous "spreads" of hot and cold dishes, supplemented with ethnic or daily specials. In his 1906 novel *The Jungle*, Upton Sinclair wrote that on Chicago's street of saloons called "Whiskey Row," "One might walk among these and take his choice: 'Hot pea soup and boiled cabbage today.' 'Sauerkraut and hot frankfurters. Walk in.' 'Bean soup and stewed lamb. Welcome.'"[90] There were fewer saloons per capita in the East, where the liquor-licensing laws were more stringent. The usual free lunch spread in New York saloons consisted either of a "hot lunch" of soup, or a cold lunch consisting of bread, cheeses, meats, and salads. A *New York Times* writer in 1904 described the summer free lunch in East Side saloons: "sliced onions and cucumbers, smothered with vinegar; sliced tomatoes, treated ditto; pickled beets, sauerkraut, potato salad, cold baked beans, leberwurst, bologna sausage, and smoked fish," as well as bread and cheese. (The writer's distaste for these free lunches, influenced by new understandings of food safety, was suggested in the title, "The Free Lunch Microbe.")[91] Most of the food offered was highly spiced, salted, or pickled: both because those foods would keep better at room temperature, and because they provoked thirst. Workingmen in these cities frequently ate their workday lunches in these places. With the free food contingent on the purchase of a beer—which usually cost only a nickel—the saloon lunch model was a powerful force pushing men to drink during the day.[92] Saloons that catered to wealthier men offered more bountiful spreads, with hot carved roasts and other rich dishes.

Women had a more complex relationship with restaurants and other sources of ready-to-eat food than men. Public dining had traditionally been a male-dominated space, and restaurants and saloons were important places for men to make personal or business connections or to seek entertainment outside the domestic circle. While restaurants did not formally bar them, women who considered themselves "respectable" did not generally eat in restaurants, unless forced to by circumstances (a boardinghouse dining room, a hotel restaurant while traveling). They might buy food from a delicatessen or a snack from a pushcart, but few women would eat in a saloon. Some saloons had "ladies' entrances" or "family entrances," often on the side, for women to enter the bar discreetly in order to eat, drink, or buy beer to take home. In general, however, most women did not go into saloons. No doubt this was partly because saloons were often prostitutes' workplaces, and partly because drunken men were likely to insult, proposition, or otherwise mistreat women.[93]

Most working-class women probably experienced restaurants as workplaces, rather than as a place to relax and enjoy a meal. The cheap restaurants that working-class men enjoyed, and which provided small competencies for immigrant families, were built on the labor of women and children. For example, a man who emigrated from Naples around the turn of the century opened a restaurant in Greenwich Village. Rather than hire workers, "he brought from Italy his parents, two brothers and a sister. This he did in the interest of himself for his relatives could be relied upon as trustworthy and industrious helpers." His daughter Josephine was kept out of school in order to wait tables and wash dishes, and she led a difficult life. "When caught on the street or daydreaming while washing dirty dishes, Josephine was frequently whipped by her father."[94]

As the turn of the twentieth century approached, middle-class women increasingly asserted their right to eat in public, at female spaces like tea shops, but also in more formal restaurants. Women expected to be able to eat lunch while shopping downtown, or to meet friends, without being mistaken for prostitutes or relegated to a back room. Restaurants which had formerly banned unaccompanied women (a policy designed to discourage prostitutes) were gradually pressed to admit women without male escorts as long as they looked sufficiently genteel.[95] As the twentieth century began, women of means were determined to enjoy the dining culture of the modern city on the same terms as men. The characteristically urban experience of going out to eat became more commonplace for all Americans, as farm people continued to migrate into towns and cities. An activity mainly practiced by the very wealthy and the poor had become more universal.

From 1870 to 1900, the United States grew from an inward-looking, largely rural nation still reeling from the effects of the Civil War, to an urbanizing, industrializing, outward-looking nation enmeshed in empire. In the midst of this transformation, social class was the most important factor that shaped individual Americans' food. People bought the best food they could afford and access. Some enjoyed a seemingly limitless abundance; some struggled to put bare meals on the table. The majority ate a little better than they had in previous generations, a greater variety of food and more luxuries like meat, with fewer seasonal limitations. They prepared the food in kitchens large and small, old-fashioned or up-to-date, with convenient new tools or with primitive techniques. In some households, women labored alone; in others, women worked alongside or supervised other women's work. They ate traditional foods but used more modern ingredients, or they enjoyed more of the rich ingredients that had always been costly and rare. Or they tried new dishes, shared recipes with newcomers, and learned new patterns of eating. They created a public food culture, which had places for urban workers, elites, and the newly cosmopolitan middle class. Throughout these changes, food remained an experience formed by class, as well as by region, race, and culture. In the twentieth century, these structural changes would accelerate, as more immigrants entered the United States, cities grew, and food traveled ever farther and was more heavily processed, but social class would remain the most important ingredient in everyone's daily bread.

Seeing the Gilded Age through Its Recipes

Let sanguine healthy-mindedness do its best with its strange power
of living in the moment and ignoring and forgetting, still the evil background is
really there to be thought of, and the skull will grin in at the banquet.
—WILLIAM JAMES, *The Varieties of Religious Experience* (1902)

The food served at the Calumet Club in Chicago on November 24, 1883, was utterly typical of Gilded Age banquets: oysters and clear soup, fish and poultry and sweetbreads, turtle and game and various vegetables. Sweets, cheeses, fruits, and coffee. The food would have been heavy, the alcohol would have flowed all night long, and those familiar with fine dining in this era would have been able to predict the general order and content of the courses without even glancing at the menu.

But the occasion inspiring this particular banquet was atypically momentous: Lieutenant General Philip Sheridan's promotion to commanding general of the U.S. Army. Like the commanding general who preceded him, William Tecumseh Sherman, Sheridan had been a Union hero in the Civil War. Also like Sherman, Sheridan was famous for his tactical ruthlessness and his willingness to target civilians' means of survival. Sheridan had continued to display this penchant for ruthlessness well after the Civil War ended. By the time of the ban-

quet, he had spent more than a decade and a half leading U.S. troops in a virtual war of extermination against American Indians in the western states and territories, not only battling Native warriors in hundreds of engagements, but also encouraging the wholesale slaughter of the buffalo herds on which Native peoples depended.[1] It was no accident that people continue to attribute the phrase "The only good Indian is a dead Indian" to Sheridan, although there is no evidence he ever said it in so many words.[2] Its genocidal sentiment perfectly captures his intent.

Mark Twain called it a "Gilded Age," not a "Golden Age," and his name stuck because so many shared the sense that the era's outward glamour hid far less savory realities.[3] Scratch the glinting surface only a little, and stark contrasts emerge, with the lavish food, glamorous clothing, and physical ease enjoyed by a few contrasting painfully with the hunger, poverty, and violence suffered by others. On the western plains, American Indians were fighting and dying in the last Indian wars. In the U.S. South, the dismal failures of Reconstruction had led to a twisted sharecropping system, systemic poverty, and exploding racial violence. Immigrants were arriving on American shores by the millions in the last decades of the nineteenth century, and many moved into congested city tenements with few sanitary accommodations and, sometimes, open sewers.

It was an era of gross income inequality, with the top 2 percent of Americans controlling nearly 30 percent of the nation's wealth.[4] The era's extremes of wealth and want played out in Americans' bodies. Hunger was regular and widespread among the rural poor as well as among those in urban slums, and poor Americans in the late nineteenth century were often shorter and drastically thinner than their better-fed counterparts. Some poor people suffered from diseases of malnutrition, with weeping sores caused by protein deficiencies or with soft, bent bones caused by a lack of vitamin D.[5] At the same time, rich Americans were indulging as never before, with multiple courses of rich, French-inspired food at every meal, and banqueting on a colossal scale. The paunches and double chins some wealthy Americans were acquiring would make the bloated fat cat physique a powerful symbol of capitalism's failures.

At the same time, the Gilded Age also saw the expansion of a robust middle class, and eating and dining were important parts of middle-class identity. Etiquette guides, particularly those that spelled out otherwise unspoken rules about table manners and entertaining, were popular in the late nineteenth century among

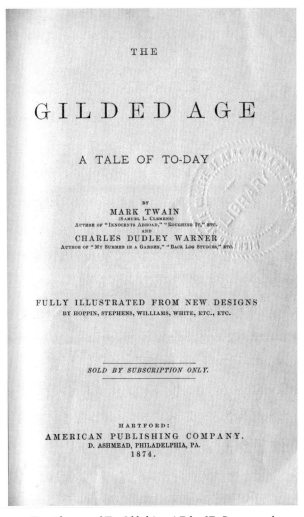

The title page of *The Gilded Age: A Tale of To-Day*, a novel published by Mark Twain and Charles Dudley Warner in 1874. From Mark Twain and Charles Dudley Warner, *The Gilded Age: A Tale of To-Day* (Hartford American Publishing Company, 1874), Special Collections, Michigan State University Libraries.

The cover of *Harper's Weekly* for the week of February 14, 1874, vividly captured the extremes of wealth and poverty in the American Gilded Age. In the engraving, the fortunes of three children are preordained by their parents' social class, symbolized by the kind of spoon they are fed with: a silver spoon, a wooden spoon, or no spoon at all. The likeliest fate for the poor, spoon-less child, according to the accompanying poem, was an early death. Cover of *Harper's Weekly: A Journal of Civilization* 18, no. 894 (February 14, 1874), Special Collections, Michigan State University Libraries.

upwardly mobile Americans who had grown up in poor or rural circumstances. So were guides that decoded the French words and phrases that were ubiquitous on elite American menus during the Gilded Age, from the ornate souvenir menus printed for the fanciest banquets to those menus handwritten for dinners in private homes. Not every American menu in the Gilded Age contained writing in French, but a stunning number of them did, with occasionally ridiculous results. Consider, for instance, the "Ris de veau, braisé, a l'Oncle Sam"—that is, "Braised Sweetbreads, Uncle Sam Style"—served at a banquet for an Ohio military order in 1887. It was in this era that the word "menu"—from the French *ménu*—decisively replaced "bill of fare" in Americans' vocabularies. French could be a big stumbling block for those hoping to appear at ease in upper-class settings; not having at least a passing familiarity with the language could instantly expose someone as a social charlatan. Indeed, the fact that only unusually privileged and well-educated individuals would have spoken French well increased the language's value as a social testing ground.[6]

In part because of its symbolic associations with money, elegance, and power, French's popularity only increased throughout the Gilded Age, and by the 1890s it was showing up even on the stained menu cards handed out at relatively humble restaurants. French cooking styles—heavy on cream and sauces and pastry—were wildly popular, although French recipe titles did not always refer to authentically French fare.[7] Why was French so widely appealing? Or, put another way, why did "croquettes de volaille" sound so much better

This engraving, titled "Remember the Poor," depicted a wealthy couple giving warm clothes and a basket of food to a poor mother and her emaciated children. From *Godey's Lady's Book* 71, no. 485 (November 1870): 486, Special Collections, Michigan State University Libraries.

Like most menus made for formal banquets, this one—printed on cloth and elaborately embroidered—was written almost entirely in French. Banquet menu for dinner given for Hon. John Reilly at Charles Duppler's Hotel, New York, November 1889, Rare Book Division, New York Public Library Menu Collection.

to Gilded Age ears than "chicken fritters"? The decades after the Civil War were a time of rapid industrialization, unprecedented levels of immigration, and tremendous and sometimes frightening technological and social changes, and Americans were suffering from a collective lack of confidence in the soundness of their own customs, culinary and otherwise. In large numbers, American turned to Europe as the source and standard of fine food and good manners.[8] "They do this in Europe, to be sure," one etiquette writer offered typically in 1894, "so that it cannot be laughed at as ridiculous."[9] American writers enthusiastically described European habits—German styles of proposing a toast, Russian styles of serving food—and advocated their adoption on the sole grounds, often, that they *were* European. European aris-

tocracy held a special appeal. Advertisements in middle-class American magazines like *Everyday Housekeeping* and *Ladies Home Journal* routinely featured queens and kings, whether or not the product had any relation to royalty, and magazines regularly printed descriptions of the everyday lives of European monarchs. This imaginative proximity to European power showed up in cookbooks, too, where authors created recipes with titles like Potage à la Reine, Imperial Soup, Duchess Potatoes, Royal Custard, and Consommé à la Royale. And was it really *consommé*, or should it be *consommeè*? Or perhaps *consomme*? All three spellings show up in the culinary materials excerpted here, because many of the Americans writing French in the Gilded Age did not actually know it very well, and their stabs at French culinary

OUR SABBATH-DAY TEA.

An engraving of an idealized middle-class family calmly enjoying Sunday tea, a quasi-meal eaten by some late-nineteenth-century Americans in imitation of English habits. From Julia McNair Wright, *Ladies' Home Cook Book: A Complete Manual of Household Duties* (L. M. Palmer, 1896), plate between pp. 242 and 243, Special Collections, Michigan State University Libraries.

Imitating an English custom, some wealthy Americans printed special calling cards to indicate when they would be at home to receive guests. From *Our Deportment, or the Manners, Conduct and Dress of the Most Refined Society*, comp. John A. Young (Springfield, MA: W. C. King and Co., 1882), 144, Special Collections, Michigan State University Libraries.

terms are riddled with misspellings, grammatical errors, and accent problems.

Besides their heavy reliance on French words and phrases, many of these recipes would have looked distinctively modern to readers at the time because the American recipe format was undergoing a revolution. While recipes from the mid-nineteenth century and before virtually always consisted only of vague prose instructions, by the 1880s recipes increasingly started with a list of all required ingredients before moving into more detailed and concrete directions. At the same time, older measuring terminology like "dessertspoonful" or "tumblerful" or "the weight of three eggs in sugar" was

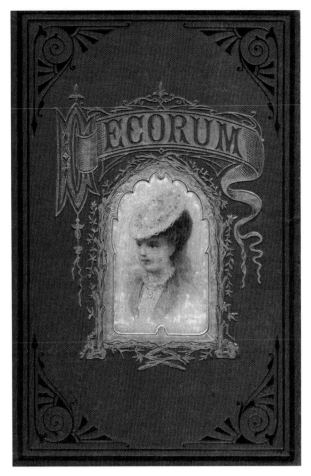

Books like John Ruth's 1880 *Decorum* were part of a rapidly growing genre of etiquette literature in the late nineteenth century. Rules about food were particularly complicated, and table manners could be a social stumbling block for the uninitiated. Cover of John Ruth, *Decorum: A Practical Treatise on Etiquette and Dress of the Best American Society* (Chicago: J. A. Ruth and Co., 1880), Special Collections, Michigan State University Libraries.

Venison occasionally appeared on elegant tables in the East in the Gilded Age, but it was a
common and necessary staple in rural places. In the winter of 1887–1888, John C. H. Grabill
photographed two miners posed in a campsite tableau with recently slaughtered deer near
Deadwood in the Dakota Territory. South Dakota would become a state the following year.
"Hunting Deer," photographic print, Library of Congress Prints and Photographs Division.

disappearing, in favor of standardized measurements. Although the transition to the modern recipe format was not yet complete, and recipe instructions were not yet reliably comprehensive, Gilded Age recipes on the whole were vastly more precise and accurate than recipes had even been before. As a result, we have an unprecedentedly accurate sense of how Gilded Age dishes would have been made and how they would have tasted.

Of course, the more accurately we can reproduce a recipe the clearer it is that historical tastes were sometimes very different. Nineteenth-century Americans relished foods that later became unpopular, such as offal. All sorts of Gilded Age recipes called for liver, tripe, tongue, brains, kidneys, feet, or sweetbreads—the sweet, tender thymus gland found only in the brain of young calves. People then also regularly ate a much greater variety of animals than Americans today, including venison, mutton, game birds, turtles, and frogs. Poor, rural Americans ate the greatest variety of all. For instance, the people conducting dietary studies among poor southern African Americans in Virginia noted that some people supplemented their diets with possum, raccoon, muskrat, and snakes.

Mundane recipe titles hide other surprises. "Pickles" in this era referred to pickled cantaloupes or mushrooms or oysters as often as it meant pickled cucumbers. In other dishes, meanwhile, cucumbers were sometimes boiled or fried. Dishes can also slip into unexpected categories. Irish Potato Pudding turns out to be a sweet dessert, while Hygienic Soup was a salty oatmeal gruel. Frozen Beef Tea was a cold, slushy beef broth meant for sipping, while Cocoa Cordial was a mix of hot chocolate and port wine. And then there are dishes that simply sound dreadful to modern palates, like Christine Herrick's Canned Pea Pancake or Fannie Farmer's Banana Salad, which called for cooks to stuff empty banana skins with cubes of banana marinated in French dressing.

Beyond the precision of modern recipes, we also know an unusual amount about Gilded Age eating because for the first time in American history people were regularly publishing menus. That is, they were recording detailed descriptions of meals, including information about which dishes were paired with which, in what order different dishes were eaten, and what time of day people were eating certain foods. Menus show up all the time in Gilded Age sources on food, in descriptions of banquets, in suggestions about how to entertain, and in cookbooks proposing recipe pairings. Menus make clear that meal planning in this era was influenced by the changeable availability of different foods in this era, as reflected in Christine Herrick's seasonal menus, for instance.

But while seasonality still mattered, by the late nineteenth century more and more foods were becoming available year round, thanks to the growing reach and speed of food transportation networks and the expansion of cold-storage facilities. Note, for instance, the Florida oranges, California pears, and other fresh fruits served at one February banquet in Detroit in 1891.[10] National distribution of industrial food products was also changing how Americans cooked and ate. Note how regularly the cookbook authors here assumed readers would have access to brand-name products like Maillard's chocolate, Cerealine, or Quaker Oats, or how

Starting in the 1870s, Quaker Oats became one of the first food companies to launch a national advertising campaign for its product. Quaker Oats Nursery Rhymes advertisement, 1895, The Alan and Shirley Brocker Sliker Collection, MSS 314, Special Collections, Michigan State University Libraries.

In this trade card produced by the Akron Milling Company, an enthusiastic customer orders a variety of grains by telephone, a recent invention. Trade card, AMC Perfect Cereals (Akron, OH: Akron Milling Co., 1885), The Alan and Shirley Brocker Sliker Collection, MSS 314, Special Collections, Michigan State University Libraries.

regularly canned goods appeared in these recipes.[11] For instance, in one of her recipes Fannie Farmer casually called for a can of "Kornlet," a commercially processed pulp made from the inner kernel of sweet green corn.[12] But the industrialization of the food supply was hardly complete in the Gilded Age. Some items we may think of as exclusively industrial products—like noodles and yeast—would have regularly been made at home in the late nineteenth century, while other products would have been less processed than we would expect: many cooks were still shelling peas and removing spinach roots themselves, for instance, and many still had to singe and pluck pinfeathers every time they wanted to cook a chicken. Sometimes, too, a recipe calling for a can of food was not referring to an industrial product at all, but to food canned at home, as in the *Kentucky Housewife* recipe for Canned Turtle Soup that was followed by instructions on how to can turtle meat by hand.

Growing material prosperity meant that some people had the luxury to think more about food's visual aesthetics than ever before. For instance, Mrs. Peter White advised soaking pickles with grape leaves to turn them green, or adding a whopping half pound of turmeric to turn them yellow. Mary Henderson commented that raw oysters served in a block of ice created "a pretty effect in the gas-light." Food and entertaining writers also obsessed over the importance of a clean, appealing table. "Too much can not be said as to the pleasant effect of a dinner," Henderson wrote, "when the table-linen is of spotless purity, and the dishes and silver are perfectly bright." Dietary reformers studying poor American eat-

Decorative arrangements of food were the height of fashion at elite tables in the Gilded Age, such as this dish of diced, sugared pineapple surrounded by slices of sponge cake. Henderson recommended this elaborate arrangement not only for its aesthetic value, but also because otherwise she found imported pineapples— which often arrived in the American Northeast the worse for wear—to be tough and tasteless. From Mrs. Mary F. Henderson, *Practical Cooking and Dinner Giving* (New York: Harper and Bros., 1877), 339, Special Collections, Michigan State University Libraries.

ing eagerly praised one family that, under their influence, began setting their table with a white tablecloth, in contrast to other "slovenly and shiftless" families whose lack of civilization, as reformers saw it, was reflected in their lack of interest "in the appearance of their homes and tables."

Another aesthetic consideration was noise, and middle-class writers believed the less of it the better.

Etiquette writers condemned loud breathing, noisy chewing, and slurping of any kind, and they reminded diners not to clatter their silverware or scrape their chairs. Herrick praised a restaurant for its "noiseless serving," while Henderson suggested that a thick mat should be placed under the tablecloth to muffle the sound of moving dishes and that servants should wear slippers to minimize the sound of their footfalls. Commentators prized quiet at the table because it indicated that eaters were self-controlled and servants were well trained.

Excerpts from a variety of culinary sources create an unusually nuanced portrait of food in the Gilded Age. One of the most popular books excerpted here is Mary Henderson's 1877 Practical Cooking and Dinner Giving. An experienced hostess and natural tastemaker, Henderson was a wealthy woman who used her book as a forum to share opinionated advice that would have been exceptionally valuable to those with least experience themselves. In fact, Henderson's book fits into the larger genre of etiquette writing from the era, a varied selection of which is excerpted here. The complexity of the era's etiquette proscriptions give a keen sense of how high the stakes of proper behavior seemed to those in the perilous process of class ascension.

But not all Americans used food to show off before strangers or to jockey for social position. The handwritten culinary manuscript from Massachusetts, written in the 1870s and 1880s and never before published, is a valuable reminder of how older forms of recipe writing and cooking were still very much alive in private

homes in the era, while Mrs. Peter White's 1885 *Kentucky Housewife* demonstrates the endurance of regional cooking even as it increasingly appeared alongside more homogenous national styles. The 1891 *What to Eat, How to Serve It*, written by Christine Herrick, who would become one of the most trusted American authorities on food and entertaining by the turn of the century, offers a valuable view into middle-class meal planning, with menus influenced not only by seasonal availability but also by newly pressing concerns about digestion and hygiene. For nineteenth-century Americans, her title would have brought to mind the famous 1863 cookbook, *What to Eat and How to Cook it*, written by the French chef Pierre Blot, and it is noteworthy that by the 1890s Herrick chose to emphasize the serving and presentation of food over the work that went on in the kitchen.

A great many Americans, however, would never have planned menus using a book or cooked using printed recipes at all, for that matter. One of the best sources we have on what poor people were eating in the late nineteenth century comes from a series of dietary studies conducted in the 1890s by reformers in the emerging field of nutrition. This volume includes excerpts from studies conducted in Alabama, New York, Chicago, Virginia, and New Mexico, and they give a glimpse of the deprivations and culinary monotony endured by many impoverished Americans. In glaring contrast, a collection of Gilded Age banquet menus from the 1880s and 1890s reveals the excess that marked fine dining for the wealthiest Americans, whose unbelievable quantities of food functioned as much as displays of power as they did as gastronomic events. Finally, this volume concludes with an excerpt from Fannie Farmer's *The Boston Cooking-School Cook Book*, originally published in 1896, a Gilded Age blockbuster that would become one of the most iconic cookbooks in American history. Its popularity resulted in part from its very modern emphasis on accurate recipes and precise measurements, and in part from Farmer's passion for delicious food that was decidedly less in thrall to French styles of cooking than her counterparts.

A Note on Spelling, Punctuation, and Unfamiliar Terms

Nineteenth-century Americans sometimes spelled words differently. In these recipes you'll occasionally see words like egg yelks, pease, and other archaic or nonstandard spellings. Occasionally authors (or maybe editors) were inconsistent, and different spellings of one word appear in the same text. Likewise, French terms appeared frequently in Gilded Age writing on food. American writers had often not studied French formally, and errors riddle the "cook's French" found in many sources.[13] In general, I haven't changed nineteenth-century spelling or grammar—whether in English or French—to conform to modern rules unless I thought the text contained a typo that the authors themselves would have corrected if they had noticed it. In those cases, I either used brackets to insert a missing word or punctuation mark, or I corrected a typo and indicated that change in a note. I have inserted "[sic]" only very occasionally, when I thought there might be confusion over whether an error was original to the text.

Cookbook authors sometimes provided several versions on one recipe and numbered the variations, as when Fannie Farmer created Egg Sauce I and Egg Sauce II, for example. In those cases when only one of the variations appeared in these excerpts, I removed the number. I also occasionally made other extremely minor changes for stylistic consistency across the different excerpts. At the end of the book is a glossary of terms that appeared multiple times in the cookbooks, which I judged likely to be unfamiliar to modern readers.

Mrs. Mary F. Henderson, *Practical Cooking and Dinner Giving*, 1877

First published in 1877 by Harper and Brothers and reprinted many times thereafter, Mary Henderson's *Practical Cooking and Dinner Giving* remains one of the most famous books on dining and etiquette in the Gilded Age. Born Mary Newton Foote in 1846 in Seneca Falls, New York, two years before the groundbreaking convention on women's rights there, the author grew up in a wealthy household and received an extensive education. In her early twenties, she married Senator John Henderson of Missouri. Although John Henderson only stayed a senator for a year after their wedding, the Hendersons became immensely rich in the years that followed, thanks to savvy investments. (On the 1900 census, John Henderson would list his occupation as "Capitalist.")[1] Besides being wealthy, Mary Henderson was worldly, handsome, and highly intelligent, and she became a star of the social scene in St. Louis, where she wrote *Practical Cooking and Dinner Giving*, and later in Washington, DC, where the Hendersons built a mansion so massive and ornate it was known as Boundary Castle.[2] They had three sons, although only one survived, a tragically ordinary occurrence in the nineteenth century.[3]

Practical Cooking and Dinner Giving offers the decided opinions of an elite woman deeply invested in her social world. Yet despite Mary Henderson's profound classism and her insistence on the importance of social rituals, the very act of writing an advice book detailing housekeeping routines that were usually hidden behind the scenes shows that she was either generous enough or entrepreneurial enough—and very possibly both—to want to share her domestic secrets with others. Henderson's secrets were hardly "practical" for everyone, of course. At a time when many Americans struggled to obtain adequate food, the prosaic title would have struck many as laughable. To begin to follow Henderson's advice on dinner giving, a reader would have needed massive holdings of china and silver and linen—enough for more than a dozen people to have new dishes and cutlery at each course of a long meal, in addition to lavish quantities of fine foods and wines themselves.

In part, Henderson's nonchalance was a way of showing off, because downplaying luxury was a way for her to emphasize that she was completely accustomed to it. She would have been aware, for instance, that her

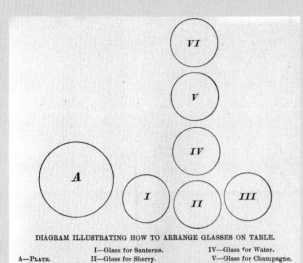

DIAGRAM ILLUSTRATING HOW TO ARRANGE GLASSES ON TABLE.

A—Plate.	I—Glass for Sauterne.
	II—Glass for Sherry.
	III—Glass for Rhine Wine.
	IV—Glass for Water.
	V—Glass for Champagne.
	VI—Glass for Burgundy.

Besides the cost of the food itself, another major obstacle to hosting a formal dinner in the Gilded Age was the number of use-specific dishes and utensils thought to be necessary. Wealthy households in this era had mammoth holdings of dishes, cutlery, and glassware. Diagram illustrating how to arrange glasses in a formal table setting from Fanny Gillette, *The White House Cook Book: A Selection of Choice Recipes Original and Selected* (Chicago: R. S. Peale and Co., 1887), 467, Special Collections, Michigan State University Libraries.

description of a simple "every-day" dinner would have sounded like a feast to most people: "For reasonable and sensible people, there is no dinner more satisfactory than one consisting first of a soup, then a fish, garnished with boiled potatoes, followed by a roast, also garnished with one vegetable; perhaps an entrée, always a salad, some cheese, and a dessert." And a formal meal, by her lights, would have been grander in every way.

Based on her sample menus, a breakfast party was an enormous meal with six or seven courses, various kinds of meats and fish, a variety of breads and pastries, and at least one or two different wines. Lunches were even more elaborate and alcohol-soaked. For example, one of Henderson's lunch menus—a twelve-course ladies' lunch—had three different alcoholic drinks (milk punch, claret, and champagne), and such disconcerting details as a course of chocolate (probably hot chocolate) with whipped cream served in between courses of beef fillet and spinach on tongue. Even while describing such abundance, Henderson found ways to make clear that nothing was terribly grand by her standards. For instance, after outlining the intricate steps involved in making preparations for a formal, multicourse dinner, she wrote offhandedly, "one can see that it requires very little trouble to serve the dinner . . . It is a simple routine." She went on to refer blandly to the possibility of stamping personalized menu cards with a family crest and to entertaining "foreign embassadors." In calling such advice "practical" and such elaborate preparations "simple," Henderson emphasized her own privilege by making it clear that, for her, having vast resources, sophisticated connections, and a staff of servants to command was absolutely ordinary.

Yet Henderson's book title was not entirely ironic: for some people, her advice would actually have been quite practical. As the professional classes expanded throughout the late nineteenth-century United States, there was a growing cohort of newly middle-class or wealthy Americans who had grown up in poor or rustic circum-

Spinach, cooked and molded into decorative towers. From Mrs. Mary F. Henderson, *Practical Cooking and Dinner Giving* (New York: Harper and Bros., 1877), 199, Special Collections, Michigan State University Libraries.

Mrs. Smith requests the pleasure of Mr. Jones's company at dinner, on Thursday, January 5th, at seven o'clock.

R. S. V. P.

12 New York Avenue, January 2d, 1875.

Mary Henderson advised readers to send formal invitations for their dinner parties, and she provided sample cards giving the correct form for such an invitation. She also explained that R.S.V.P. stood for "'Answer, if you please'" or *"Répondez s'il vous plait."* From Mrs. Mary F. Henderson, *Practical Cooking and Dinner Giving* (New York: Harper and Bros., 1877), Special Collections, Michigan State University Libraries.

stances and who needed help navigating an intimidatingly complex elite social world. In fact, elite rules could be all the more forbidding precisely because decorum was supposed to seem natural. For people in newly comfortable financial circumstances, Henderson's concrete advice on topics like sending an invitation or setting the table or planning a menu for a gentlemen's supper would have been valuable.

Practical Cooking and Dinner Giving would have been particularly useful as a French language cheat-sheet. Henderson, fluent in French herself, recognized that the language's dominance of American menus could be a major obstacle for others, and she advised her read-

ers to use tact in choosing whether to write a menu in English or French, since for some guests an all-French menu "might as well be written in Choctaw." Moreover, she tacitly acknowledged that readers of her book might well be among those who did not already know French. She provided translations of common terms in passing, explaining, for instance, that a *boutonnière* was "a little bunch of three or four flowers," and that R.S.V.P. stood for *"Répondez s'il vous plait,"* or "Answer, if you please." Perhaps most practical of all, she appended a glossary, not included here, translating more than two hundred common French culinary words and phrases.

Setting the Table and Serving the Dinner

[A] round table five feet in diameter is the best calculated to show off a dinner. If of this size, it may be decorated to great advantage, and conveniently used for six or eight persons, without enlargement.

Put a thick baize under the table-cloth. This is quite indispensable. It prevents noise, and the finest and handsomest table-linen looks comparatively thin and sleazy on a bare table.

Do not put starch in the napkins, as it renders them stiff and disagreeable, and only a very little in the table-cloth. They should be thick enough, and, at the same time, of fine enough texture, to have firmness without starch. Too much can not be said as to the pleasant effect of a dinner, when the table-linen is of spotless purity, and the dishes and silver are perfectly bright.

Although many ornaments may be used in decorating the table, yet nothing is so pretty and so indicative of a refined taste as flowers. If you have no épergne for them, use a *compotier* or raised dish, with a plate upon the top, to hold cut flowers; or place flower-pots with blossoming plants on the table. A net-work of wire, painted green, or of wood or crochet work, may be used to conceal the roughness of the flower-pot. A still prettier arrangement is to set the pot in a *jardinière* vase.

At a dinner party, place a little bouquet by the side of the plate of each lady, in a small glass or silver bouquet-holder. At the gentlemen's plates put a little bunch of three or four flowers, called a *boutonnière*, in the folds of the napkin. As soon as the gentlemen are seated at table, they may attach them to the left lapel of the coat.

Place the dessert in two or four fancy dessert-dishes around the centre-piece, which, by-the-way, should not be high enough to obstruct the view of persons sitting at opposite sides of the table. The dessert will consist of fruits, fresh or candied, preserved ginger, or preserves of any kind, fancy cakes, candies, nuts, raisins, etc.

Put as many knives, forks, and spoons by the side of the plate of each person as will be necessary to use in all the different courses. Place the knives and spoons on the right side, and the forks on the left side, of the plates. This saves the trouble of replacing a knife and fork or spoon as each course is brought on. Many prefer the latter arrangement, as they object to the appearance of so many knives, etc., by the sides of a plate. This is, of course, a matter of taste. I concede the preferable appearance of the latter plan, but confess a great liking for any arrangement which saves extra work and confusion.

Place the napkin, neatly folded, on the plate, with a piece of bread an inch thick, and three inches long, or a small cold bread roll, in the folds or on the top of the napkin.

Put a glass for water, and as many wine-glasses as are necessary at each plate. Fill the water-glass just before the dinner is announced, unless caraffes are used. These are kept on the table all the time, well filled with water, one caraffe being sufficient for two or three persons.

All the wine intended to be served decanted should be placed on the table, conveniently arranged at different points.

At opposite sides of the table place salt and pepper stands, together with the different fancy spoons, crossed by their side, which may be necessary at private dinners, for serving dishes.

Select as many plates as will be necessary for all the different courses. Those intended for cold dishes, such as salad, dessert, etc., place on the sideboard, or at any convenient place. Have those plates intended for dessert already prepared, with a finger-bowl on each plate. The finger-glasses should be half filled with water, with a slice of lemon in each, or a geranium leaf and one flower, or a little *boutonnière*: a sprig of lemon-verbena is pretty, and leaves a pleasant odor on the fingers after pressing it in the bowl. In Paris, the water is generally warm, and scented with peppermint.

Some place folded fruit-napkins under each finger-bowl; others have little fancy net-work mats, made of thread or crochet cotton, which are intended to protect handsome painted dessert-plates from scratches which the finger-bowls might possibly make.

The warm dishes—not *hot* dishes—keep in a tin closet or on the top shelf of the range until the moment of serving. A plate of bread should also be on the sideboard.

Place the soup-tureen (with soup that has been brought to the boiling-point just before serving) and the soup-plates before the seat of the hostess.

Dinner being now ready, it should be announced by the butler or dining-room maid. Never ring a bell for a meal. Bells do very well for country inns and steamboats, but in private houses the *ménage* should be conducted with as little noise as possible.

With these preliminaries, one can see that it requires very little trouble to serve the dinner. There should be no confusion or anxiety about it. It is a simple routine. Each dish is served as a separate course. The butler first places the pile of plates necessary for the course before the host or hostess. He next sets the dish to be served before the host or hostess, just beyond the pile of plates. The soup, salad, and dessert should be placed invariably before the hostess, and every other dish before the host. As each plate is ready, the host puts it upon the small salver held by the butler, who then with his own hand places this and the other plates in a similar manner on the table before each of the guests. If a second dish is served in the course, the butler, putting in it a spoon, presents it on the left side of each person, allowing him to help himself. As soon as any one has finished with his plate, the butler should remove it immediately, without waiting for others to finish. This would take too much time. When all the plates are removed, the butler should bring on the next course. It is not necessary to use the crumb-scraper to clean the cloth until just before the dessert is served. He should proceed in the same manner to distribute and take off the plates until the dessert is served, when he can leave the room.

This is little enough every-day ceremony for families of the most moderate pretensions, and it is also enough for the finest dinner party, with the simple addition of more waiters, and distribution of the work among them.

It is well that this simple ceremony should be daily observed, for many reasons. The dishes themselves taste better; moreover, the cook takes more pride, and is more particular to have his articles well cooked, and to present a better appearance, when each dish is in the way subjected to a special regard: and is it not always preferable to have a few well-cooked dishes to many indifferently and carelessly prepared? At the same time, each dish is in its perfection, hot from the fire, and ready to be eaten at once; then, again, one has the benefit of the full flavor of the dish, without mingling it with that of a multiplicity of others. There is really very little extra work in being absolutely methodical in every-day living. With this habit, there ceases to be any anxiety in entertaining. There is nothing more distressing at a dinner company than to see a hostess ill at ease, or to detect an interchange of nervous glances between her and the servants. A host and hostess seem insensibly to control the feelings of all the guests, it matters not how many there may be. In well-appointed houses, a word is not spoken at the dinner between the hostess and attendants. What necessity, when the servants are in the daily practice of their duties?

If one has nothing for dinner but soup, hash, and lettuce, put them on the table in style: serve them in three courses, and one will imagine it a much better dinner than if carelessly served.

Let it be remembered that the above is the rule prescribed for every-day living. With large dinner parties, the plan might be changed, in one respect, i.e., in having the dishes, in courses, put on the table for exhibition, and then taken off, to be carved quickly and delicately at a side-table by an experienced butler. This gives the host time to entertain his guests at his ease, instead of being absorbed in the fatiguing occupation of carving for twelve or fourteen people . . .

At small dinners, I would not have the butler to be carver. It is a graceful and useful accomplishment for a gentleman to know how to carve well. At small dinners, where the dishes can not be large, the attendant labor must be light; and, in this case, does it not seem more hospitable and home-like for the gentleman to carve himself? Does it not disarm restraint, and mark the only difference there is between home and hotel dinners? . . .

There are several hints about serving the table, which I will now specify separately, in order to give them the prominence they deserve.

1st. The waiters should be expeditious without seeming to be in a hurry. A dragging dinner is most tiresome. In France, the dishes and plates seem to be changed almost by magic. An American senator told me that at a dinner at the Tuileries, at which he was present, twenty-five courses were served in an hour and a half. The whole entertainment, with the after-dinner coffee, etc., lasted three hours. Upon this occasion, a broken dish was never presented to the view of a guest. One waiter would present a dish, beautifully garnished or decorated; and if the guest signified assent, a plate with some of the same kind of food was served him immediately from the broken dish at the side-table.

Much complaint has been made by persons accustomed to dinners abroad of the tediousness of those given in Washington and New York, lasting, as they often do, from three to five hours. It is an absolute affliction to be obliged to sit for so long a time at table.

2d. Never overload a plate nor oversupply a table. It is a vulgar hospitality. At a small dinner, no one should hesitate to ask for more, if he desires it; it would only be considered a flattering tribute to the dish.

At large companies, where there is necessarily a greater variety of dishes, the most voracious appetite must be satisfied with a little of each. Then, do not supply more than is absolutely needed; it is a foolish and unfashionable waste. "Hospitality is not to be measured by the square inch and calculated by cubic feet of beef or mutton."

At a fashionable dinner party, if there are twelve or fourteen guests, there should be twelve or fourteen birds, etc., served on the table—one for each person. If uninvited persons should call, the servant could mention at the door that madam has company at dinner. A sensible person would immediately understand that the general machinery would be upset by making an appearance. At small or private dinners, it would be, of course, quite a different thing.

The French understand better than the people of any other nation how to supply a table. "Their small family dinners are simply gems of perfection. There is plenty for every person, yet every morsel is eaten. The flowers or plants are fresh and odoriferous; the linen is a marvel of whiteness; the dishes are few, but perfect of their kind."

When you invite a person to a family dinner, do not attempt too much. It is really more elegant to have the dinner appear as if it were an every-day affair than to impress the guest, by an ostentatious variety, that it is quite an especial event to ask a friend to dinner. Many Americans are deterred from entertaining, because they think they can not have company without a vulgar abundance, which is, of course, as expensive and troublesome as it is coarse and unrefined.

For reasonable and sensible people, there is no dinner more satisfactory than one consisting first of a soup, then a fish, garnished with boiled potatoes, followed by a roast, also garnished with one vegetable; perhaps an *entrée*, always a salad, some cheese, and a dessert. This, well cooked and neatly and quietly served, is a stylish and good enough dinner for any one, and is within the power of a gentleman or lady of moderate means to give. "It is the exquisite quality of a dinner or a wine that pleases us, not the multiplicity of dishes or vintages."

3d. Never attempt a new dish with company—one that you are not entirely sure of having cooked in the very best manner.

4th. Care must be taken about selecting a company for a dinner party, for upon this depends the success of the entertainment. Always put the question to yourself, when making up a dinner party, Why do I ask him or her? And unless the answer be satisfactory, leave him or her out. Invite them on some other occasion. If they are not sensible, social, unaffected, and clever people, they will not only not contribute to the agreeability of the dinner, but will positively be a serious impediment to conversational inspiration and the general feeling of ease. Consequently, one may consider it a compliment to be invited to a dinner party.

5th. Have the distribution of seats at table so managed, using some tact in the arrangement, that there need be no confusion, when the guests enter the dining-room, about their being seated. If the guest of honor be a lady, place her at the right of the host; if a gentleman, at the right of the hostess.

If the dinner company be so large that the hostess can not easily place her guests without confusion, have a little card on each plate bearing the name of the person who is to occupy the place. Plain cards are well enough; but the French design (they are designed in this country also) beautiful cards for the purpose, illustrated with varieties of devices: some are rollicking cherubs with capricious antics, who present different tempting viands; autumn leaves and delicate flowers in chromo form pretty surroundings for the names on others; yet the designs are so various on these and the bill-of-fare cards that each hostess may seek to find new ones, while frequent dinner-goers may have interesting collections of these mementoes, which may serve to recall the occasions in after-years.

6th. If the dinner is intended to be particularly fine, have bills of fare, one for each person, written on little sheets of paper smoothly cut in half, or on French bill-of-fare cards, which come for the purpose. If expense is no object, and you entertain enough to justify it, have cards for your own use especially engraved. Have your crest, or perhaps a monogram, at the top of the card, and forms for different courses following, so headed that you have only to fill out the space with the special dishes for the occasion.

Bills of fare are generally written in French. It is a pity that our own rich language is inadequate to the duties of a fashionable bill of fare, especially when, perhaps, all the guests do not understand the Gallic tongue, and the bill of fare (*menu*) for their accommodation might as well be written in Choctaw. I would say that some tact might be displayed in choosing which language to employ.

menu

Dîner du 15 Février.

Potages.

Poissons.

Hors-d'oeuvres.

Relevés.

Entrées.

Rôtis.

Entremêts.

Glaces.

Dessert.

If you are entertaining a ceremonious company, with tastes for the frivolities of the world, or, perhaps, foreign embassadors, use unhesitatingly the French bills of fare; but practical uncles and substantial persons of learning and wit, who, perhaps, do not appreciate the merits of languages which they do not understand, might consider you demented to place one of these effusions before them. I would advise the English bills of fare on these occasions.

7th. The attendants at table should make no noise. They should wear slippers or light boots . . . No word should be spoken among them during dinner, nor should they even seem to notice the conversation of the company at table.

8th. The waiter should wear a dress-coat, white vest, black trousers, and white necktie; the waiting-maid, a neat black alpaca or a clean calico dress, with a white apron.

9th. Although I would advise these rules to be generally followed, yet it is as pleasant a change to see an individuality of a characteristic taste displayed in the setting of the table and the choice of dishes as in the appointments of our houses or in matters of toilet. At different seasons the table might be changed to wear a more appropriate garb. It may be solid, rich, and showy, or simple, light, and fresh.

10th. Aim to have a variety or change in dishes. It is as necessary to the stomach and to the enjoyment of the table as is change of scene for the mind. Even large and expensive state dinners become very monotonous when one finds everywhere the same choice of dishes. Mr. Walker, in his "Original," says: "To order dinner is a matter of invention and combination. It involves novelty, simplicity, and taste; whereas, in the generality of dinners, there is no character but that of routine, according to the season."

11th. Although many fashionable dinners are of from three or four hours' duration, I think every minute over two hours is a "stately durance vile." After that time, one can have no appetite; conversation must be forced. It is preferable to have the dinner a short one than a minute too long. If one rises from a fine dinner wearied and satiated, the memory of the whole occasion must be tinged with this last impression.

12th. There is a variety of opinions as to who should be first served at table. Many of the *haut monde* insist that the hostess should be first attended to. Once, when visiting a family with an elegant establishment, who, with cultivated tastes and years of traveling experience, prided themselves on their *savoir faire*, one of the members said, "Yes, if Queen Victoria were our guest, our sister, who presides at table, should always be served first." The custom originated in ancient times, when the hospitable fashion of poisoning was in vogue. Then the guests preferred to see the hostess partake of each dish before venturing themselves. Poisoning is not now the order of the day, beyond what is accomplished by rich pastry and plum puddings. If there be but one attendant, the lady guest sitting at the right of the host or the oldest lady should be first served. There are certain natural instincts of propriety which fashion or custom can not regulate. As soon as the second person is helped, there should be no further waiting before eating.

13th. Have chairs of equal height at table. Perhaps every one may know by experience the trial to his good humor in finding himself perched above or sunk below the general level.

14th. The selection of china for the table offers an elegant field in which to display one's taste. The most economical choice for durability is this: put your extra money in a handsome dessert set, all (except the plates) of which are displayed on the table all the time during dinner; then select the remainder of the service in plain white, or white and gilt, china. When any dish is broken, it can be easily matched and replaced.

A set of china decorated in color to match the color of the dining-room is exceedingly tasteful. This choice is not an economical one, as it is necessary to replace broken pieces by having new ones manufactured—an expense quite equal to the extra trouble required to imitate a dish made in another country.

By far the most elegant arrangement consists in having different sets of plates, each set of a different pattern, for every course. Here is an unlimited field for exquisite taste. Let the meat and vegetable dishes be of plated silver. Let the épergne or centre-piece (holding flowers or fruit) be of silver, or perhaps it might be preferred of majolica, of bisque, or of glass. The majolica ware is very fashionable now, and dessert, oyster, and salad sets of it are exceedingly pretty. A set of majolica plates, imitating pink shells, with a large pink-shell platter, is very pretty, and appropriate for almost any course. Oyster-plates in French ware imitate five oyster-shells, with a miniature cup in the centre for holding the lemon. There are other patterns of oyster-plates in majolica of the most gorgeous colors, where each rim is concaved in six shells to hold as many oysters. The harlequin dessert sets are interesting, where every plate is not only different in design and color, but is a specimen of different kinds of ware as well. In these sets the Dresden, French, and painted plates of any ware that suits the fancy are combined.

A set of plates for a course at dinner is unique in the Chinese or Japanese patterns. Dessert sets of Bohemian glass or of cut-glass are a novelty; however, the painted sets seem more appropriate for the dessert (fruit, etc.), white glass sets are tasteful for jellies, cold puddings, etc., or what are called the cold *entremêts* served just before the dessert proper.

But it seems difficult, in entering the Colamores' and other large places of the kind in New York, to know what to select, there are such myriads of exquisite plates, table ornaments, and fairy-lands of glass.

I consider the table ornaments in silver much less attractive than those in fancy ware. There are lovely maidens in bisque, reclining, while they hold painted oval dishes for a jelly, a Bavarian cream, or for flowers or fruit; cherub boys in majolica, tugging away with wheel-barrows, which should be loaded with flowers; antique water-jugs; cheese-plates in Venetian glass; clusters of lilies from mirror bases to hold flowers of *bonbons*; tri-pods of dolphins, with great pink mouths, to hold salt and pepper.

If a lady, with tastes to cultivate in her family, can afford elegancies in dress, let her retrench in that, and bid farewell to all her ugly and insipid white china; let wedding presents consist more of these ornaments (which may serve to decorate any room), and less of silver salt-cellars, pepper-stands, and pickle-forks.

Senator Sumner was a lover of the ceramic art. His table presented a delightful study to the connoisseur, with its different courses of plates, all different and *recherché* in design. Nothing aroused this inimitable host at a dinner party from his literary labors more effectu-ally than a special announcement to him by Marley of the arrival from Europe of a new set of quaint and ele-gant specimens of China ware. He would repair to New York on the next train.

15th. I will close these suggestions by copying from an English book a practical drill exercise for serving at table. The dishes are served from the side-table.

"Let us suppose a table laid for eight persons, dressed in its best; as attendants, only two persons—a butler and a footman, or one of these, with a page or neat wait-ing-maid; and let us suppose some one stationed outside the door in the butler's pantry to do nothing but fetch up, or hand, or carry off dishes, one by one:

While guests are being seated, person from outside
   brings up soup;
Footman receives soup at door;
Butler serves it out;
Footman hands it;
Both change plates.
Footman takes out soup, and receives fish at door;
   while butler hands wine;
Butler serves out fish;
Footman hands it (plate in one hand, and sauce
   in the other);
Both change plates.
Footman brings in *entrée*, while butler hands wine;
Butler hands *entrée*;
Footman hands vegetables;
Both change plates,
Etc., etc. . . ."

The Dinner Party

It is very essential, in giving a dinner party, to know precisely how many guests one is to entertain. It is a serious inconvenience to have any doubt on this subject. Consequently, it is well to send an invitation, which may be in the following form:

Mrs. Smith requests the pleasure of Mr. Jones's company at dinner, on Thursday, January 5th, at seven o'clock.

R. S. V. P.

12 New York Avenue, January 2d, 1876.

The capital letters constitute the initials of four French words, meaning, "Answer, if you please" (Répondez s'il vous plait). The person thus invited must not fail to reply at once, sending a messenger to the door with the note. It is considered impolite to send it by post.

If the person invited has any doubt about being able to attend the dinner at the time stated, he should decline the invitation at once. He should be positive one way or the other, not delaying the question for consideration more than a day at the utmost. If Mr. Jones should then decline, he might reply as follows:

Mr. Jones regrets that he is unable to accept Mrs. Smith's polite invitation for Thursday evening.

8 Thirty-seventh Street, January 3d.

Or,

Mr. Jones regrets that a previous engagement prevents his acceptance of Mrs. Smith's polite invitation for Thursday evening.

Thirty-seventh Street, January 3d.

A prompt and decided answer of this character enables Mrs. Smith to supply the place with some other person, thereby preventing that most disagreeable thing, a vacant chair at table.

If the invitation be accepted, Mr. Jones might say in his note:

Mr. Jones accepts, with pleasure, Mrs. Smith's invitation for Thursday evening.

Thirty-seventh Street, January 2d.

The more simple the invitation or reply, the better. Do not attempt any high-flown or original modes. Originality is most charming on most occasions; this is not one of them.

In New York, many, I notice, seem to think it elegant to use the French construction of sentences in formal notes: for instance, they are particular to say, "the invitation of Mrs. Smith," instead of "Mrs. Smith's invitation;" and "2d January," instead of "January 2d." In writing in the French language, the French construction of sentences would seem eminently proper. One might be pardoned for laughing at an English construction, if ignorance were not the cause. So, when one writes in English, let the sentences be concise, and according to the rules of the language.

On the appointed day, the guest should endeavor to arrive at the house not exceeding ten minutes before the time fixed for dinner; and while he avoids a too early arrival, he should be equally careful about being tardy. It is enough to disturb the serenity and good temper of the most amiable hostess during the whole evening for a guest to delay her dinner, impairing it, of course, to a great extent. She should not be expected to wait over fifteen minutes for any one. Perhaps it would be as well for her to order dinner ten minutes after the appointed hour in her invitation, to meet the possible contingency of delay on the part of some guest.

When the guests are assembled in the drawing-room, if the company be large, the host or hostess can quietly intimate to the gentleman what ladies they will respectively accompany to the dining-room. After a few moments of conversation and introductions, the dinner is to be announced, when the host should offer his arm to the lady guest of honor, the hostess taking the arm of the gentleman guest of honor; and now, the host leading the way, all should follow; the hostess, with her escort, being the last to leave the drawing-room. They should find their places at table with as little confusion as possible, not sitting down until the hostess is seated. After dinner is over, the hostess giving the signal by moving back her chair, all should leave the dining-room. The host may then invite the gentleman to the smoking-room or library. The ladies should repair to the drawing-room. A short time thereafter (perhaps in half an hour), the butler should bring to the drawing-room the tea-service on a salver, with a cake-basket filled with fancy biscuits, or rather crackers or little cakes.

Placing them on the table, he may then announce to the host that tea is served. The gentlemen join the ladies; and, after a chat of a few minutes over the tea, all of the guests may take their departure. If the attendant is a waiting-maid, and the tea-service rather heavy, she might bring two or three cups filled with tea, and a small sugar-bowl and cream-pitcher, also the cake-basket, on a small salver; and when the cups are passed, return for more.

I do not like the English fashion, which requires the ladies to retire from the table, leaving the gentlemen to drink more wine, and smoke. Enough wine is drunk during dinner. English customs are admirable, generally, and one naturally inclines to adopt them; but in this instance I do not hesitate to condemn and reject a custom in which I see no good, but, on the contrary, a temptation to positive evil. The French reject it; let Americans do the same.

Cooking as an Accomplishment

The reason why cooking in America is, as a rule, so inferior is not because American women are less able and apt than the women of France, and not because the American men do not discuss and appreciate the merits of good cooking and the pleasure of entertaining friends at their own table; it is merely because American women seem possessed with the idea that it is not the fashion to know how to cook; that, as an accomplishment, the art of cooking is not as ornamental as that of needle-work or piano-playing. I do not undervalue these last accomplishments. A young lady of esprit should understand them; but she should understand, also, the accomplishment of cooking. A young lady can scarcely have too many accomplishments, for they serve to adorn her home, and are attractive and charming, generally. But of them all—painting, music, fancy work, or foreign language—is there one more fascinating and useful, or one which argues more intelligence in its acquisition than the accomplishment of cooking?

What would more delight Adolphus than to discover that his pretty *fiancée*, Julia, was an accomplished cook; that with her dainty fingers she could gracefully dash off a creamy omelet, and by miraculous manoeuvres could produce to his astonished view a dozen different kaleidoscopic omelets, *aux fines herbes*, *aux huîtres*, *aux petits pois*, *aux tomates*, etc.; and not only that, but scientific croquettes, mysterious soups, delicious salads, marvelous sauces, and the hundred and one savory results of a little artistic skill? Delighted Adolphus—if a sensible man, and such a woman should have no other than a sensible man—would consider this as the *chef-d'oeuvre* of all her accomplishments, as he regarded her the charming assurance of so many future comforts.

From innate coquetry alone the French women appreciate the powers of their dainty table. Cooking is an art they cultivate. Any of the *haut monde* are proud to originate a new dish, many famous ones doing them credit in bearing their names.

One thing is quite evident in America—that the want of this ornamental and useful information is most deplorable. The inefficiency, in this respect, of Western and Southern women, brought up under the system of slavery, is somewhat greater than that of the women of the Northern and Eastern States; however, as a nation, there is little to praise in this regard in any locality. Professor Blot endeavored to come to the rescue. Every *man* applauded his enterprise; yet I can myself testify to the indifference of the women—his classes for the study of cookery numbering by units where they should have numbered by hundreds. He soon discontinued his instructive endeavors, and at last died a poor man.

There is little difficulty abroad in obtaining good cooks at reasonable prices, who have pursued regular courses of instruction in their trade: not so in America. Hospitality demands the entertaining of friends at the social board; yet it is almost impossible to do so in this country in an acceptable manner, unless the hostess herself not only has a proper idea of the serving of a table, but of the art of cooking the dishes themselves as well. In some of the larger cities, satisfactory dinners and trained waiters may be provided at an enormous cost at the famous restaurants, where the meal may appear home-like and elegant. But unfortunate is the woman, generally, who wants to do "the correct thing," and, wishing to entertain at dinner, relies upon the sense, good taste, and management of the proprietor of a restaurant. She may confidently rely upon one thing—an extortionate bill; and, generally, as well, upon a vulgar display, which poorly imitates the manner of refined private establishments.

However, "living for the world" seems very contemptible in comparison with the importance of that wholesome, satisfactory, every-day living which so vitally concerns the health and pleasure of the family circle.

But why waste time in asserting these self-evident facts? They are acknowledged and proclaimed every day by suffering humanity; yet the difficulty is not remedied. Is there a remedy, then? Yes. This is a free country, yet Dame Fashion is the Queen. Make it the fashion, then, that the art and science of cookery shall be classed among the necessary accomplishments of every well-educated lady. This is a manifest duty on the part of ladies of influence and position, even if the object be only for the benefit of the country at large. Let these ladies be accomplished artists in cookery. The rest will soon follow. There will be plenty of imitators . . .

Breakfast

After a fast of twelve or thirteen hours, the system requires something substantial as preparation for the labors of the day; consequently, I consider the American breakfasts more desirable for an active people than those of France or England.

In France, the first breakfast consists merely of a cup of coffee and a roll. A second breakfast, at eleven o'clock, is more substantial, dishes being served which may be eaten with a fork (*déjeuner à la fourchette*), as a chop with a potato *soufflé*. No wonder there are *cafés* in Paris where American breakfasts are advertised, for it takes one of our nationality a very short time to become dissatisfied with this meagre first meal.

In England, breakfast is a very informal meal. After some fatiguing occasion, if one should desire the luxury of an extra nap, he is not mercilessly expected at the table simply because it is the breakfast-hour; for there the breakfast-hour is any time one chances to be ready for it. Gentlemen and ladies read their papers and letters in the breakfast-room—a practice which, of course, is more agreeable for guests than convenient for servants. However, if one can afford it, why not? This habit requires a little different setting of the table. It is deco-rated with flowers or plants, and upon it are placed several kinds of breads, fruits, melons, potted meats, and freshest of boiled eggs. But the substantial dishes must be served from the sideboard, where they are kept in silver chafing-dishes over spirit-lamps. As members of the family or guests enter, the servant helps them each once, then leaves the room. If they have further wants, they help themselves or ring a bell.

The American breakfast is all placed upon the table, unless oatmeal porridge should be served as a first course. Changes of plates are also necessary when cakes requiring sirup or when melons or fruits are served.

Let us now set the American breakfast-table.

The coffee-urn and silver service necessary are placed in a straight line before the hostess. The one or two kinds of substantials are set before the host; vegetables or *entrées* are placed on the sides. Do not have them askew. It is quite as easy for an attendant to place a dish in a straight line as in an oblique angle with every other dish on the table.

I advocate the general use of oatmeal porridge for breakfast. Nothing is more wholesome, and nothing more relished after a little use. If not natural, the taste should be acquired. It is invaluable for children, and of no less benefit for persons of mature years. Nearly all the little Scotch and Irish children are brought up on it. When Queen Victoria first visited Scotland, she noticed the particularly ruddy and healthy appearance of the children, and, after inquiry about their diet and habits, became at once a great advocate for the use of porridge. She used it for her own children, and it was at once introduced very generally into England. Another of its advantages is that serving it as a first course enables the cook to prepare many dishes, such as steaks, omelets, etc., just as the family sit down to breakfast; and when the porridge is eaten, she is ready with the other dishes "smoking hot."

It would be well if more attention were given to breakfasts than is usually bestowed. The table might have a fresher look with flowers or a flowering plant in the centre. The breakfast napery is very pretty now, with colored borders to suit the color of the room, the table-cloth and napkins matching.

The beefsteaks should be varied, for instance, one morning with a tomato sauce, another à la maître d'*hôtel*, or with a brown sauce, or garnished with water-cresses, green pease, fried potatoes, potato-balls, etc., instead of being always the same beefsteak, too frequently over-cooked or undercooked, and often floating in butter.

Melons, oranges, compotes, any and all kinds of fruits, should be served at breakfast. In the season, sliced tomatoes, with a French or *Mayonnaise* dressing, is a most refreshing breakfast dish. A great resource is in the variety of omelets, and with a little practice, nothing is so easily made. One morning it may be a plain omelet; another, with macaroni and cheese; another, with fine herbs; another, with little strips of ham or with oysters . . . The different arrangements of meat-balls are croquettes, with tomato, cream, apple, or brown sauces, are delicious when they are freshly and carefully made.

As there are hundreds of delicious breakfast dishes, which only require a little attention and interest to understand, how unfortunate it must be for a man to have a wife who has nothing for breakfast but an alternation of juiceless beefsteak, greasy and ragged mutton-chops, and swimming hash, with unwholesome hot breads to make up deficiencies!

Breakfast parties are very fashionable, being less expensive than dinners, and just as satisfactory to guests. They are served generally about ten o'clock, although any time from ten to twelve o'clock may be chosen for the purpose. It seems to me that ten o'clock, or even nine o'clock (it depends upon the persons invited), is the preferable hour. Guests might prefer to retain their strength by a repast at home if the breakfast-hour were at twelve o'clock, and then the fine breakfast would be less appreciated. At breakfast parties, with the exception of the silver service being on the table all the time for tea and coffee, the dishes are served in courses precisely as for dinner . . .

Three bills of fare are given for breakfast parties, which will show the order of different courses:

Winter Breakfast.

1st Course.—Broiled sardines on toast, garnished with slices of lemon. Tea, coffee, or chocolate.

2d Course.—Larded sweet-breads, garnished with French pease. Cold French rolls or petits pains. Sauterne.

3d Course.—Small fillets or the tender cuts from porter-house-steaks, served on little square slices of toast, with mushrooms.

4th Course.—Fried oysters; breakfast puffs.

5th Course.—Fillets of grouse (each fillet cut in two), on little thin slices of fried mush, garnished with potatoes à la Parisienne.

6th Course.—Sliced oranges, with sugar.

7th Course.—Waffles, with maple sirup.

Early Spring Breakfast.

1st Course.—An Havana orange for each person, dressed on a fork.

2d Course.—Boiled shad, maître d'hôtel sauce; Saratoga potatoes. Tea or coffee.

3d Course.—Lamb-chops, tomato sauce. Château Yquem.

4th Course.—Omelet, with green pease, or garnished with parsley and thin diamonds of ham, or with shrimps, etc., etc.

5th Course.—Fillets of beef, garnished with water-cresses and little round radishes; muffins.

6th Course.—Rice pancakes, with maple sirup.

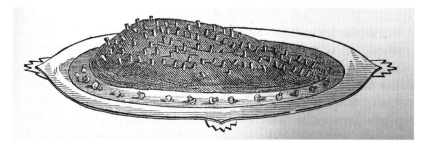

A fillet of beef, garnished with vegetables. From Mrs. Mary F. Henderson, *Practical Cooking and Dinner Giving* (New York: Harper and Bros., 1877), 135, Special Collections, Michigan State University Libraries.

Summer Breakfast.

1st Course.—Melons.

2d Course.—Little fried perch, smelts, or trout, with a sauce Tartare, the dish garnished with shrimps and olives. Coffee, tea, or chocolate.

3d Course.—Young chickens, sautéd, with cream-gravy, surrounded with potatoes à la neige. Claret.

4th Course.—Poached eggs on anchovy-toast.

5th Course.—Little fillets of porter-house-steaks, with tomatoes à la Mayonnaise.

6th Course.—Peaches, quartered, sweetened, and half-frozen.

Lunch

This is more especially a ladies' meal. If one gives a lunch party, ladies alone are generally invited. It is an informal meal on ordinary occasions, when every thing is placed upon the table at once. A servant remains in the room only long enough to serve the first round of dishes, then leaves, supposing that confidential conversation may be desired. Familiar friends often "happen in" to lunch, and are always to be expected.

Some fashionable ladies have the reputation of having very fine lunches—chops, chickens, oysters, salads, chocolate, and many other good things being provided; and others, just as fashionable, have nothing but a cup of tea or chocolate, some thin slices of bread and butter, and cold meat; or, if of Teutonic taste, nothing but cheese, crackers, and ale, thus reserving the appetite for dinner . . .

The principal dishes served are *patés*, croquettes, shell-fish, game, salads—in fact, all kinds of *entrées*, and cold desserts, or I may say dishes are preferred which do not require carving. *Bouillon* is generally served as a first course in *bouillon* cups, which are quite like large coffee-cups, or coffee or tea cups may be used, although any dinner soup served in soup-plates is *en regle*. A cup of chocolate, with whipped cream on the top, is often served as another course.

I will give five bills of fare, reserved from five very nice little lunch parties:

Fried smelts, a kind of small fish, skewered in a variety of ways. From Fannie Farmer, *The Original 1896 Boston Cooking-School Cook Book* (Mineola, NY: Dover Publications, 1997), 311, Special Collections, Michigan State University Libraries.

Mrs. Collier's Lunch (February 2d).

Bouillon; sherry.

Roast oysters on half-shell; Sauterne.

Little vols-au-vent of oysters.

Thin scollops, or cuts of fillet of beef, braised; French pease; Champagne.

Chicken croquettes, garnished with fried parsley; potato croquettes.

Cups of chocolate, with whipped cream.

Salad—lettuce dressed with tarragon.

Biscuits glacés; fruit-ices.

Fruit.

Bonbons.

Mrs. Sprague's Lunch (March 10th).

Raw oysters on half-shell.

Bouillon; sherry.

Little vols-au-vent of sweet-breads.

Lamb-chops; tomato sauce; Champagne.

Chicken croquettes; French pease.

Snipe; potatoes à la Parisienne.

Salad of lettuce.

Neuchâtel cheese; milk wafers, toasted.

Chocolate Bavarian cream, molded in little cups, with a spoonful of peach marmalade on each plate.

Vanilla ice-cream; fancy cakes.

Fruit.

Mrs. Miller's Lunch (January 6th).

Bouillon.

Deviled crabs; olives; claret punch.

Sweet-breads à la Milanaise.

Fillets of grouse, currant jelly; Saratoga potatoes.

Roman punch.

Fried oysters, garnished with chow-chow.

Chicken salad, or, rather, Mayonnaise of chicken.

Ramikins.

Wine jelly, and whipped cream.

Napolitaine ice-cream.

Fruit.

Bonbons.

Mrs. Well's Lunch.

Bouillon; sherry.

Fried frog's legs; French pease.

Smelts, sauce Tartare; potatoes à la Parisienne.

Chicken in scallop-shells; Champagne.

Sweet-bread croquettes; tomato sauce.

Fried cream.

Salad; Romaine.

Welsh rare-bit.

Peaches and cream, frozen; fancy cakes.

Fruits.

Mrs. Filley's Lunch.

Mock-turtle soup; English milk-punch.

Lobster-chops; claret.

Mushrooms in crust.

Lamb-chops, en papillote.

Chetney of slices of baked fillet of beef.

Chocolate, with whipped cream.

Spinach on tongue slices, sauce Tartare.

Roast quail, bread sauce.

Cheese; lettuce, garnished with slices of radishes and
nasturtium blossoms, French dressing.

Mince-meat patties; Champagne.

Ices and fancy cakes.

Fruit.

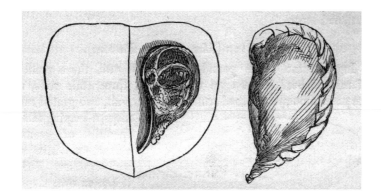

To cook lamb chops *en papillote*, a cook would broil each chop and then place it on buttered paper, cover it with sauce and other accompaniments, and then seal the paper up tightly before baking. From Mrs. Mary F. Henderson, *Practical Cooking and Dinner Giving* (New York: Harper and Bros., 1877), 149, Special Collections, Michigan State University Libraries.

Gentlemen's Suppers

As ladies have exclusive lunches, gentlemen have exclusive suppers. Nearly the same dishes are served for suppers as for lunches, although gentlemen generally prefer more game and wine. Sometimes they like fish suppers, with two or three or more varieties of fish, when nightmare might be written at the end of the bill of fare.

If one has not a reliable cook, it is very convenient to give these entertainments, as the hostess has a chance to station herself in the *cuisine*, and personally superintend the supper.

One bill of fare is given for a fish supper:

1st Course.—Raw oysters served in a block of ice. [The ice has a pretty effect in the gas-light.]

2d Course.—Shad, maître d'hôtel sauce, garnished with smelts.

3d Course.—Sweet-breads and tomato sauce.

4th Course.—Boiled sardines, on toast.

5th Course.—Deviled chicken, Cunard sauce.

6th Course.—Fillets of duck, with salad of lettuce.

7th Course.—Mayonnaise of salmon, garnished with shrimps.

8th Course.—Welsh rare-bit.

9th Course.—Charlotte Russe.

10th Course.—Ice-cream and cake.

Evening Parties

If people can afford to give large evening parties, it is less trouble and more satisfactory to place the supper in the hands of the confectioner.

For card parties or small companies of thirty or forty persons, to meet some particular stranger, or for literary reunions, the trouble need not be great. People would entertain more if the trouble were less.

If one has a regular reception-evening, ices, cake, and chocolate are quite enough; or for chocolate might be substituted sherry or a bowl of punch.

For especial occasions for a company of thirty or forty, a table prettily set with some flowers, fruit, chicken salad, croquettes or sweet-breads and pease, one or two or more kinds of ice-cream and cakes, is quite sufficient. Either coffee and tea, Champagne, a bowl of punch or of eggnog, would be sufficient in the way of beverage.

Selected Advice on Table Manners, 1872–1903

Etiquette guides were popular in the late nineteenth century, and nowhere more so than in America. Enough Americans bought etiquette advice books to sustain a lively genre, which in turn supported a widespread belief that manners mattered.[1] And indeed, they did. Behind every query on etiquette and every article about its advice lurked concern about class. Even when etiquette writers described the intricacies of formal dinners, they rarely wrote with the uppermost echelons of American society in mind. Instead, their descriptions of the most rarefied and aristocratic entertainments were generally aimed not at those most secure in their social positions but at those in the precarious process of social ascension. Etiquette writers, in other words, wrote for individuals in the middle and lower-middle classes.[2] Advice on manners functioned as a powerful social tool that was most useful to people who were least certain about the rules.[3]

Urbanization fueled the need for advice. As immigrants and former farmers poured into American cities throughout the second half of the nineteenth century, they had to navigate dynamic social worlds in which they could no longer rely on established reputations or family connections. Instead, urban Americans had to prove and re-prove themselves in a world populated mainly by strangers. Manners became shorthand for experience, education, and class. Many of what had been acceptable public behaviors in the early nineteenth century, like blowing the nose or scratching, came to be seen as shamefully private actions by the late nineteenth century. Embarrassment—the uncomfortable awareness of doing in public what should have been done in private—became a routine part of American urban life in the nineteenth century.[4] Etiquette writers gave specific instructions about which actions were acceptable and which were embarrassingly incorrect.

Table manners were especially tricky, in part because of basic embarrassment about the animalistic nature of eating. Although eating was "necessary to satisfy hunger," the etiquette writer Julia Dewey almost lamented, "it is a requirement of our lower nature, and we should try to invest our manner of eating with enough refinement and delicacy to distinguish us, in this respect, from the brute."[5] To guard against coarseness, etiquette writers emphasized the need to eliminate all traces of the animal. "Take small mouthfuls," Margaret Livings-

GENTLEMAN MEETING A LADY.

Etiquette guides offering advice on everything from table manners to behavior on the street abounded in the late nineteenth-century United States. *Our Deportment, or the Manners, Conduct and Dress of the Most Refined Society*, comp. John A. Young (Springfield, MA: W. C. King and Co., 1882), 144, Special Collections, Michigan State University Libraries.

ton advised, and "masticate slowly with the lips closed. There is a strong and unappetizing suggestion of animalism in the society at breakfast or dinner of the man or woman who smacks, grinds his or her food noisily between the teeth, regards with eager glance the contents of the plate, drains off a glass of water, sips coffee and soup with a loud hissing sound, and clears his or her plate before any one is through."[6]

The danger of appearing animal-like was keen when eating messy foods—foods that were sticky or juicy, foods that were large or unwieldy, foods that dripped. Diners used utensils to dissect their meat, sawing flesh from bone with their knives and conveying edible pieces to the mouth on forks. Fruits—with their peels, seeds, and pits, and with their anthropomorphic forms and textures—presented a special challenge. Improvements in shipping and railways throughout the nineteenth century offered middle-class Americans—even those living in the inclement North—an unprecedented range of fresh fruits and vegetables throughout the year. By the end of the nineteenth century, tropical fruits, especially bananas, had become popular fare at formal dinners. Utensils helped mediate the awkwardness of fruit, although refined nineteenth-century fruit eating can sound absurd today, like advice to peel and eat oranges with a knife and spoon, and to peel and eat bananas with a knife and fork.[7]

Late nineteenth-century etiquette made an art form out of ignorance about and removal from the production of food. Good table manners meant demonstrating a tangible distance from the hard labor involved in all stages of getting food to the table: removal from the sweat and manure of the farmyard, from dusty miles of transportation, from the steam and splattering grease of the kitchen. In fact, middle-class Americans in all sorts of realms came to define themselves by this very distance from manual labor; one major class distinction that emerged during the nineteenth century was that middle-class women and children did not work for wages. Table etiquette replicated this distance in miniature in nearly every command, from orders about the way to spoon soup away from the body to the physical distance necessary between plates and laps to the necessity of seeming to be unconcerned about spills or accidents. Middle- and upper-class Americans at table worked hard to maintain attitudes of leisure and nonchalance.

In an era when many Americans enthusiastically associated progress with efficiency, table manners of the era were conspicuously antiefficient. While it would be more efficient to load up a fork while still chewing the previous mouthful, for instance, etiquette writers insisted that one should never put food on the fork until one had quietly swallowed.[8] Likewise, writers warned it was rude to blow on or to stir soup or hot drinks. Instead, they advised, simply wait while the liquids slowly cooled.[9] Even the famous injunction against eating with the knife was antiefficient since it required American eaters to switch the fork and knife from right to left hand every time the eater wished to cut off a bite of food. Eating slowly and quietly not only de-emphasized the labor of eating, but it also visibly demonstrated physical self-restraint.

As some newly rich Americans worked to appear at home in unfamiliar social circumstances by copying wealthy habits, sometimes exceeding old wealth in ostentation and display, a lively discussion played out about the relationship between upper-class consumption and identity. What was authentically fine and high? What was vulgar, ostentatious, and false? How could you tell the difference? By the turn of the century, uncertainty on these points—and tensions surrounding them—would contribute to the decline of the most extravagant Gilded Age habits.

Florence Hartley, *The Ladies Book of Etiquette, and Manual of Politeness* (Boston: Lee & Shepard, 1872)

Avoid making any noise in eating, even if each meal is eaten in solitary state. It is a disgusting habit, and one not easily cured if once contracted, to make any noise with the lips while eating.

Never put large pieces of food into your mouth. Eat slowly, and cut your food into small pieces before putting it into your mouth.

If you are asked at table what part of the meat you prefer, name your favorite piece, but do not give such information unless asked to do so. To point out any especial part of a dish, and ask for it, is ill-bred. To answer, when asked to select a part, that "it is a matter of indifference," or "I can eat any part," is annoying to the carver, as he cares less than yourself certainly, and would prefer to give you the piece you really like best.

Do not pour coffee or tea from your cup into your saucer, and do not blow either these or soup. Wait until they cool.

Never put poultry or fish bones, or the stones of fruit, upon the table-cloth, but place them on the edge of your plate.

Never pile up the food on your plate. It looks as if you feared it would all be gone before you could be helped again, and it will certainly make your attempts to cut the food awkward, if your plate is crowded.

Cecil B. Hartley, *The Gentlemen's Book of Etiquette and Manual of Politeness* (Boston: J. S. Locke & Co., 1874)

It may seem a very simple thing to eat your meals, yet there is no occasion upon which the gentleman, and the low-bred, vulgar man are more strongly contrasted, than when at the table.

There are a thousand little points to be observed in your conduct at table which, while they are not absolutely necessary, are yet distinctive marks of a well-bred man.

If, when at home, you practice habitually the courtesies of the table, they will sit upon you easily when abroad; but if you neglect them at home, you will use them awkwardly when in company, and you will find yourself recognized as a man who has "company manners" only when abroad.

I have seen men who eat soup, or chewed their food, in so noisy a manner as to be heard from one end of the table to the other; fill their mouths so full of food, as to threaten suffocation or choking; use their own knife for the butter, and salt; put their fingers in the sugar bowl, and commit other faults quite as monstrous, yet seem perfectly unconscious that they were doing anything to attract attention.

Far from eating with avidity of whatever delicacies which may be upon the table, and which are often served in small quantities, partake of them but sparingly, and decline them when offered the second time.

Observe a strict sobriety; never drink of more than one kind of wine, and partake of that sparingly.

If in the leaves of your salad, or in a plate of fruit you find a worm or insect, pass your plate to the waiter, without any comment, and he will bring you another.

Be careful to avoid the extremes of gluttony or over daintiness at table. To eat enormously is disgusting, but if you eat too sparingly, your host may think that you despise your fare.

Put your napkin upon your lap, covering your knees. It is out of date, and now looked upon as a vulgar habit to put your napkin up over your breast.

Never blow your soup if it is too hot, but wait until it cools. Never raise your plate to your lips, but eat with your spoon.

If a dish is distasteful to you, decline it, but make no remarks about it. It is sickening and disgusting to explain at a table how one article makes you sick, or why some other dish has become distasteful to you. I have seen a well-dressed tempting dish go from a table untouched, because one of the company told a most disgusting anecdote about finding vermin served in a similar dish.

Never put fruit or bon-bons in your pocket to carry them from the table.

Always wipe your mouth before drinking, as nothing is more ill-bred than to grease your glass with your lips.

If you are invited to drink with a friend, and do not drink wine, bow, raise your glass of water and drink with him.

Do not put your glass upside down on the table to signify that you do not wish to drink any more; it is sufficient to refuse firmly. Do not be persuaded to touch another drop of wine after your own prudence warns you that you have taken enough.

It is excessively rude to leave the house as soon as dinner is over. Respect to your hostess obliges you to stay in the drawing-room at least an hour.

Perfect Etiquette; or *How to Behave in Society: A Complete Manual for Ladies and Gentlemen* (New York: Albert Cogswell, 1877)

Never find fault with your food.

Do not lean back in your chair when finished.

Do not spread your elbows, for it is looked upon as very vulgar.

Do not be ashamed to eat all on your plate, if you can.

When a plate is handed to you, keep it and commence eating.

Eat slowly.

Whenever anything disagreeable is found in your solids or fluids, remove it without making any remark that will cause the appetite of others to fail.

Harrietta Oxnard Ward, *Sensible Etiquette of the Best Society* (Philadelphia: Porter & Coates, 1878)

The more truly religious a man is, the more polite he will spontaneously become, and that, too, in every rank of life, for true religion teaches him to forget himself, to love his neighbor, and to be kindly even to his enemy; and the appearance of so being and doing is what good society demands as good manners. High moral character, a polished education, a perfect command of temper, delicate feeling, good habits, and a good bearing, are the indispensable requisites for good society. These constitute good breeding, and produce good manners.

John Ruth, *Decorum: A Practical Treatise on Etiquette and Dress of the Best American Society* (New York: Union Publishing House, 1879)

Nothing indicates the good breeding of a gentleman so much as his manners at table. There are a thousand little points to be observed, which, although not absolutely necessary, distinctly stamp the refined and well-bred man. A man may pass muster by dressing well, and may sustain himself tolerably in conversation; but if he be not perfectly "au fait" dinner will betray him.

It is not good taste to praise extravagantly every dish that is set before you; but if there are some things that are really very nice, it is well to speak in their praise. But, above all things, avoid seeming indifferent to the dinner that is provided for you, as that might be construed into a dissatisfaction with it.

Avoid picking your teeth, if possible, at the table, for however agreeable such a practice might be to yourself, it may be offensive to others. The habit which some have of holding one hand over the mouth, does not avoid the vulgarity of teeth-picking at table.

It is considered vulgar to dip a piece of bread into the preserves or gravy upon your plate and then bite it. If you desire to eat them together, it is much better to break the bread in small pieces, and convey these to your mouth with your fork.

Soup should be eaten with the side of the spoon, not from the point, and there should be no noise of sipping while eating it. It should not be called for a second time.

Fish follows soup, and must be eaten with a fork, unless fish-knives are provided. Put the sauce, when it is handed you, on the side of your plate.

Never take up a piece of asparagus or the bones of fowl or bird with your fingers to suck them, possibly making the remark that "fingers were made before forks." These things should always be cut with a knife and eaten with a fork. If fingers *were* made before forks, so were wooden trenchers before the modern dinner service. Yet it would rather startle these advocates of priority to be invited to a dinner-party where the dining-table was set with a wooden trencher in the centre, into which all the guests were expected to dip with their fingers.

A guest should never find fault with the dinner or with any part of it.

When you are helped, begin to eat without waiting for others to be served.

A knife should never, on any account, be put into the mouth. Many even well-bred people in other particulars think this an unnecessary regulation; but when we consider that it is a rule of etiquette, and that its violation causes surprise and disgust to many people, it is wisest to observe it.

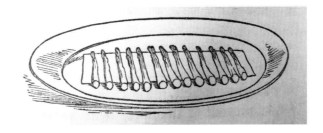

Asparagus served on a platter, from Mrs. Mary F. Henderson, *Practical Cooking and Dinner Giving* (New York: Harper and Bros., 1877), 198, Special Collections, Michigan State University Libraries.

Eat slowly.

Never bite fruit. An apple, pear or peach should be peeled with a silver knife, and all fruit should be broken or cut.

Mrs. S. O. Johnston, "Hints upon Etiquette and Good Manners," *Ladies Home Journal* 3, no. 6 (April 1886)

Good manners at the table are of the greatest importance, for one can, at a glance, discern whether a person has been trained to eat well, i. e. to hold the knife and fork properly, to eat without the slightest sound of the lips, to drink quietly, and not as a horse or cow drinks; to use the napkin rightly; to make no noise with any of the implements of the table, and last, but not least, to eat slowly, and masticate the food thoroughly. All these points should be most carefully taught to children and then they will always feel at their ease at the grandest tables in the land. There is no position where the innate refinement of a person is more fully exhibited, than at the table; and nowhere, that those who have not been trained in table etiquette feel more keenly their deficiencies. The knife should never be used to carry food to the mouth, but only to cut it up into small mouthfuls, then place it upon the plate at one side, and take the fork in the right hand, and eat all the food with it.

Be careful to keep the mouth shut closely while masticating the food. It is the opening of the lips which causes the smacking which is so disgusting, and reminds one of the eating of animals in the pig sty.

Soup is always served for the first course, and it should be eaten with dessert spoons, and taken from the tips of

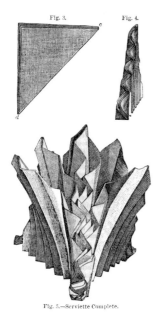

Popular publications like *Godey's Lady's Book* often included tips on etiquette and entertaining, including instructions like these on elaborate napkin folding. From "Dinner Serviettes," *Godey's Lady's Book* (Philadelphia) 88, no. 525 (March 1874), Special Collections, Michigan State University Libraries.

them, without any sound of the lips, and not sucked into the mouth audibly from the side of the spoon. Never ask to be helped to soup a second time. The hostess may ask you to take a second plate, but you will politely decline.

Finger bowls are not a general institution, and yet they seem to be quite as needful as the napkin, for the fingers are also liable to become a little soiled in eating. They can be had quite cheaply, and should be half filled with water and placed upon the side table, or butler's tray, with the dessert, bread and cheese, etc. They are passed to each person when the dessert is placed upon the table. A leaf or two of sweet verbena, an orange flower, or a small slice of lemon, is usually put into each bowl, to rub upon the fingers. The slice of lemon is most commonly used. The finger tips are slightly dipped into the bowl, the lemon juice is squeezed upon them, and then they are dried softly upon the napkin. At dinner parties and luncheons, they are indispensable.

In many families there is no waitress, then everything should be placed upon the table before the family are called, and the dessert can be put on a little table at your right. Always make your eldest daughter set the table, and do it neatly. Lay the cloth straight, and put the salt cellar and the butter plate, with the tumbler or cup, at the right hand of each person. Have crocheted macramé twine mats to keep the table cloth from being soiled, and at the head and foot of the table place a napkin cornerwise to the centre, or straight as one prefers. This will prove a great saving of table cloths, and the napkins can be retrieved often. Then tell her to look carefully over the table to see that not one thing is omitted. Look at your place, and see that there are enough cups and saucers placed neatly at the left hand, for breakfast or tea, and that the sugar bowl is well filed, and the cream and milk pitcher are prepared for use. Have a stand of metal at the right hand, to hold the coffee or tea pots, and the water pot, and a spoon cup should be placed beside the sugar bowl, with the tea-spoons and sugar spoon in it. Also see that the carving knife, fork and steel are laid beyond the plates at your husband's seat. And have these plates well heated, and all the food as hot as possible. It is a decided annoyance to have this child, or that one, asked to leave the table to procure needed appliances, that ought to have been upon it.

"Good Form" in England. By an American Resident in the United Kingdom
(New York: D. Appleton and Company, 1888)

Wherever else a person may slip, through ignorance or inadvertence, into "bad form," he may hope for forgiveness, or, at least, allowance-making; but not so at a dinner party. It fairly bristles with rules, which, while they represent "good form," stifle, through their iron restraint, every feeling of natural enjoyment.

Mrs. Florence Marion Hall, *The Correct Thing in Good Society*
(Boston: Estes and Lauriat, 1888)

IT IS THE CORRECT THING

To remember that "hurry was made for slaves."
To eat celery and olives with the fingers.
To use a fork for conveying back to one's plate as quietly as possible, fish bones, scraps of gristle, etc.
To use a spoon for soup, puddings, tea, coffee and chocolate, preserves, berries (especially where milk or cream is served with them), custards, or for any dishes too soft to be managed conveniently with a fork.
To use a silver knife for fruit where one is required.
To prepare and eat fruit with special nicety and care.
To remove fruit stones and seeds from the mouth with the thumb and fingers, or with a fork.
To remove the skins and stones of grapes from the mouth with the thumb and fingers.
To use a fork as well as a knife with any juicy fruit, such as a juicy pear or a pineapple.

To peel and slice bananas with a knife and fork, and then eat them with a fork.

To peel an orange with a knife or spoon, divide it into pegs, and eat it with the aid of the fingers, or to cut it up nicely with a knife and fork, and eat it with the latter.

To use a finger-bowl after eating fruit,—dipping the tips of the fingers in it, and passing them nicely over the mouth, then wiping both fingers and mouth on the napkin.

To hold the fork in the right hand, when eating with it, with the tines curving down in the middle so as to form a bowl, that is to say, in the reverse position from that in which the fork is held for carving.

Oranges are now often cut in two with a sharp knife, and the pulp eaten with an orange-spoon, or with an ordinary teaspoon.

To put on only one plate where the fish or meat is served with salad and no other accompaniment.

To raise the fork to the mouth laterally with the right hand, so that the fork will be nearly parallel with the mouth.

To lay the knife and fork side by side on the plate, with the handles together, when sending it back for a second helping. This is the modern custom.

To eat a boiled egg out of the shell with an egg-spoon.

For grown people to break bread in pieces before buttering it or eating it.

To break open hot rolls, muffins, and gems.

To ask the servant quietly for what you wish, after waiting for a suitable length of time.

IT IS NOT THE CORRECT THING

To eat rapidly.

To raise and spread out the elbows when cutting up one's food, or to cut it all up at once, as if for a child.

To display too much vigor in grasping one's knife and fork.

To cut potato, or touch it with a knife.

To use a spoon where one can conveniently use a fork.

To cut salad into little pieces on one's plate, so that it looks like mince-meat. This should be done in the kitchen if at all.

To leave a spoon standing in a teacup instead of laying it in the saucer.

To take asparagus in one's fingers when it is covered with sauce.

To drink tea out of the saucer, or to pour it into the saucer to cool.

When pouring out tea, to fill the cup so full that it runs over.

To put sugar, cream, or lemon in the tea without first ascertaining whether any of these are desired, and in what quantity.

To leave the spoon in the cup while drinking.

To use a steel knife with fruit of any sort.

To eat fruit in a mussy or unpleasant manner, getting one's fingers or mouth covered with juice.

To spit the stones, seeds or skins of fruit into one's plate.

To eat pineapples with the fingers.

To eat bananas with the fingers, except at a very informal meal.

To peel a pear or peach, and take up the juicy pieces in one's fingers, instead of using a fork.

To suck an orange, or to eat it in public at all, if one cannot do so in a delicate way.

To dip the whole hand in the finger-bowl.

To open the mouth unduly wide in eating.

To double up a large slice of meat or cake, or to "bolt" the same.

To pack food on the back of the fork, thus necessitating the use of the fork wrong side up.

To put the skins of potato, orange-peel, etc., on the table-cloth.

To place the plate from which one has finished eating at one side instead of waiting for the waitress to remove it.

To tip the plate in order to secure the last drops of soup.

To tuck the feet up on the rounds of one's chair, or to place them on the stand of the table.

Lady M. Colin and M. French-Sheldon, *Everybody's Book of Correct Conduct* (New York and London: Harper & Brothers Publishers, 1893)

If you are asked what you will take, choose what is already on the table, unless it is positively disagreeable to you. Do what you can to avoid giving trouble; it will make you liked by your hostess and by the servants.

It is the correct thing . . . [t]o remember that you are invited to enjoy a good dinner certainly, but not to gormandize or drink too much.

It is the correct thing . . . [t]o be invariably civil to all dependents and servants. Even if you have reason to correct them, you can do so best by preserving your own dignity.

G. H. Sandison, *How to Behave and How to Amuse: A Handy Manual of Etiquette and Parlor Games in Two Parts* (New York: The Christian Herald, 1895)

Should you unfortunately overturn or break anything, make no apology, but let your regret appear in your face.

When you eat fruit that has a pit or a skin that is not to be swallowed, the pit and the skin must be removed from the mouth with the fingers of the left hand, or with a spoon or fork in the right.

The farmer's boy, the intelligent mechanic and the humblest clerk or artisan, in these days of widely-diffused knowledge, may familiarize themselves with the customs and observances of polite society to an extent that will go far toward placing them on a level with those who would otherwise be regarded as their superiors.

The Complete Bachelor: Manners for Men
(New York: D. Appleton and Company, 1896)

The American is unfortunately too often in a hurry. He bolts his food. He is a victim of the "quick-lunch" system. Again, a bachelor eating a solitary meal at a club or a restaurant is apt from sheer loneliness to try and dispose of it as rapidly as possible. Drill yourself into eating leisurely. Persons of refinement take only small morsels at a time. One can not be too dainty at table.

I pass over the man who leaves traces of each meal on his shirt or his clothes. Such a being, I have no doubt, would convey food to his mouth with his knife, would blow on his soup, tea, or coffee with the idea of cooling it, or would pour the two latter cheering fluids into a saucer and drink them therefrom.

Coffee and milk are never served during dinner, nor again is iced milk. These are barbarisms.

Julia M. Dewey, Lessons on Manners: Arranged for Grammar Schools, High Schools, and Academies (New York: Hinds & Noble, 1899)

We should take our seat at the table when the lady of the house takes hers and rise only when she gives the signal. If necessary to leave the table before the meal is over, permission should be asked of her.

In rising, the chair should not be pushed back noisily, but quietly, just far enough to enable us to rise easily. Every movement at the table should be made with as little noise as possible. All moving of feet, leaning upon the table, clattering of knives, forks and dishes show ignorance of good manners.

Americans, as a rule, eat too rapidly, which induces ill health and causes them to be set down by their English brethren as coarse and ill-mannered.

[When drinking, it] is against good form to throw the head back and invert the glass or to draw the breath in noisily.

The knife is used in cutting up the food but not in conveying it to the mouth; the fork is used for this purpose.

In using the spoon care should be taken not to put it too far into the mouth.

Although it is necessary to satisfy hunger, it is a requirement of our lower nature, and we should try to invest our manner of eating with enough refinement and delicacy to distinguish us, in this respect, from the brute.

In order to eat with propriety and grace we must begin to observe table manners when young and constantly practise [sic] them in the home; otherwise when we attempt them in other places we shall seem rustic and awkward.

Cheerful conversation is good for digestion as well as for enjoyment; therefore we should avoid any depressing topic. The table is not the place to tell bad news, nor to discuss sickness, accident, or death, or whatever is painful or disagreeable to hear . . . Relaxation from care and a reasonable amount of "cheerful jollity" are hygienic and entirely consistent with good table manners.

If an accident occur, such as breaking a dish, spilling a glass of water, or dropping food upon the cloth, we should not add to the confusion and annoyance of the one through whom the mishap comes by noticing it, unless we can help to repair the mischief in a way not to attract attention to the unlucky person.

"Mrs. Rorer's Answers to Questions," *Ladies Home Journal 16*, no. 1 (December 1898)

Do not feel it necessary to put anything more upon the tea-table for guests than you would for your own family. Make a rule about serving each meal; have enough plain, well-cooked food, and if the Queen of England should happen in do not make an apology nor add one thing to what is already on the table. Hospitality, after all, is good sauce for the appetite, and if your guest feels that she has upset the routine she will not enjoy the best meal you could put before her.

"Mrs. Rorer's Answers," *Ladies Home Journal 16*, no. 5 (April 1899)

Little neck clams and oysters should be served first. The soup follows, and with it bread is served. After this the fish course. At a large dinner boiled fish with a sauce, potatoes and cucumbers, or potatoes alone. Following the fish at an elaborate dinner comes a small entrée, such as chicken patty, mushroom patty, chicken cutlet, or any small made dish, with which serve bread. Then comes the main meat dish of the dinner, which may be a larded fillet, a truffled capon or a roasted turkey or a joint of any kind. With this serve one or two vegetables, but not potatoes, and a fruit sherbet. Then the game course, with which is served either a lettuce salad with French dressing or baked macaroni; if the latter, have a salad course alone to follow the game, and with it serve toasted wafers and cheese. If the salad is served with the game, follow with a dessert and then close with coffee. For an elaborate dinner, such as this outline would make, the pudding should be rather elegant, but simple—either a frozen pudding, ice cream, whipped cream or omelet soufflé. If salad is served with the game, the coffee at the close of the dinner may be served either at the table or in the dining room.

Mrs. Burton Kingsland, *The Book of Good Manners: "Etiquette for All Occasions"* (New York: Doubleday, Page and Company, 1902)

The line of social demarcation begins at the table. We eat only with our equals.

The English are the least open to reproach, perhaps, and their higher classes give to the world laws for the proper behavior at table which we recognize as binding.

It is growing to be "unfashionable" to serve many wines, and in better taste for ladies to confine themselves to a single glass or refuse them altogether.

No one uses a knife in eating fish, unless silver ones, made for the purpose, are provided. A bit of bread, broken but never cut, is usually sufficient as an auxiliary to the fork.

It is never proper to hold the fork with the tines turned upward in the left hand. It is exclusively the privilege of the right.

Fruit must never be bitten, but cut in small pieces and eaten either in the hand or with a fork.

No form of selfishness is so repulsive as that exhibited at table. Preferences for special dishes should not be made prominent.

No hostess apologizes, no guest observes anything amiss. If an accident occur, all ignore it.

There is one supreme rule of table etiquette. It is that to the lapses of others we shall be a little blind, and concentrate all our attention upon our own improvement.

All unpleasant subjects should be banished from conversation at table.

The more quietly a table is served, the more it appears to be well served.

Margaret Livingston, "Table Etiquette," in *Correct Social Usage: A Course of Instruction in Good Form Style and Deportment by Eighteen Distinguished Authors, vol. 1* (New York: The New York Society of Self-Culture, 1903)

Let the china fall, let the champagne be poured smoking hot, and let the soup arrive at a temperature of forty-five degrees, but do not scold a servant, complain, nor frequently explain and apologize at meals.

Only at an informal meal is it in good taste to comment upon the food and offer the housekeeper compliments upon its savory quality.

Take small mouthfuls; masticate slowly with the lips closed. There is a strong and unappetizing suggestion of animalism in the society at breakfast or dinner of the man or woman who smacks, grinds his or her food noisily between the teeth, regards with eager glance the contents of the plate, drains off a glass of water, sips coffee and soup with a loud hissing sound, and clears his or her plate before any one is through. Rattling the knife, fork, or spoon against the plate is a common mistake, as is also the attempt to speak while the mouth is full.

A banana should be wholly peeled and broken with the fingers, or cut with the fruit knife into mouthfuls as needed, and these mouthfuls are to be transferred to the lips by the fingers, not on the knife blade.

Cynthia Westover Alden, "Etiquette for Smaller Towns and Villages," in *Correct Social Usage: A Course of Instruction in Good Form Style and Deportment by Eighteen Distinguished Authors, vol. 1.* (New York: The New York Society of Self-Culture, 1903)

There is no necessity of being nervous about going to the table. Wait for the hostess. When she is ready to sit down, take your own chair. If there are dishes before you that you do not know exactly what to do with, note what the others do, or steer clear of the entirely. When one follows the rule of eating with the fork and not the knife, and making as little noise as possible with the mouth while eating, there is going to be no awkwardness to speak of that will prove embarrassing.

Massachusetts Recipe Manuscript, 1870s and 1880s

Never before published, this handwritten cookery manuscript reveals little about its origins or author. On the notebook's front cover, someone—presumably the writer of the manuscript—wrote neatly, "Receipt Book, 1870," and on the first inside page, she wrote her initials and the year: "L. J. B. 1870." Who was the writer? One hint is that several times in the notebook, someone—writing in a different handwriting than the one in which most of the recipes were written—referred to "Aunt Laura." Did the "L" in L. J. B. stand for Laura? It seems likely, and it also seems probable that she lived in Massachusetts. The state name never appears in the manuscript, but Massachusetts place-names are everywhere, including Boston, Worcester, Marlboro, Greenfield, Easthampton, and Conway. One recipe probably came from Hillsboro, a town in Massachusetts that was thriving in the second half of the nineteenth century but that would become a ghost town in the early twentieth century. There is also a recipe called Charlestown Pudding, possibly named for the once-independent city that was annexed to Boston in the 1870s.

The one fact that seems absolutely certain about the writer of this manuscript is that she had a whopping sweet tooth. There are a handful of savory recipes, like those for Ripe Cucumber Pickles, Chicken Salad, and Tomato Chop—sweetened tomatoes stewed with peppers, vinegar, horseradish, and spices. There are also a few homemade medical remedies. For the most part, however, this was a notebook lovingly devoted to desserts—jumbles and puddings and candies and doughnuts and, most of all, cakes. And many of the recipes are delicious. There are recipes for Cookies with caraway seeds, Gold and Silver Cakes (classic nineteenth-century recipes where the presence or absence of egg yolks determined the cake's color), Chocolate Carousels, and Delmonico's Pudding. The last was almost certainly named in reference to the famously grand Delmonico's Restaurant in New York, which had been helping to define American fine dining since it opened in the 1830s and which had become, by the Gilded Age, a household name synonymous with elegant high cuisine.[1] This version of Delmonico's Pudding was a delicate, milky dessert topped with a layer of meringue.

Nineteenth-century recipes were often vague and inconsistent, and recipe writers routinely made all sorts of assumptions that can frustrate a modern cook trying to puzzle them out. Those deficiencies are magnified in this handwritten recipe collection because the writer seems to have been writing primarily for herself, and in most cases she already knew what she was doing. She noted ingredient quantities with some precision, but she often left out directions altogether. And why not? Obviously an experienced cook, the author clearly felt she needed few reminders about how to combine fats and sugars, when to add eggs or fold in the dry ingredients, how hot she should make her fire or when she should test for doneness. This was not a cookbook intended for public consumption; it was a series of personal notes.

Curiously, some of the recipes appear out of chronological order. The "1870" that appears on both the front cover and the first page suggests strongly that the author started the manuscript that year. Yet, later in the notebook, several recipes appear with dates from the 1860s. While it is possible the author started the notebook earlier and only later wrote on the cover and filled in the early pages, it seems most likely that she later copied older recipes from her files as this manuscript became her primary clearinghouse for personal recipes.

Hat[']s Cup Cake

[Added in more recent handwriting: "Laura's sister"]

1 cup butter

2 cups sugar

4 eggs

1 cup sweet milk

3 cups flour

2 tea spoon soda

Ophelia's Cup Cake

[Added in more recent handwriting: "Aunt Laura's oldest sister"]

1 cup butter

2 cups sugar

4 eggs

1 cup sour milk or cream

1 tea spoon soda

First beat sugar and butter, then add eggs without beating, then milk with soda—and flour from 3 to 4 cups. Spice to taste.

Hattie Howe's Cup Cake

1 cup butter

1 cup sugar

4 eggs—well beaten

1 cup sour milk

1 tea spoon soda

5 cups flour

Spice of flavor to taste or add currants.

Jenny Lind Cake

Beat together 1 egg and 1 cup sugar—stir in ¼ cup
butter—Add one cup milk

1 tea spoon soda

2 tea spoons cream tartar

A little salt

2 cups flour

Flavor to taste—1 loaf.

Cob Cake

1 cup sugar

½ cup butter

1 cup flour

3 eggs

1 tea spoon soda

Put all together and stir quickly—Bake in a round pan.
1 loaf.

Easthampton

Oct. 1, 1869

Cookies

1 cup butter

2 cups sugar

1 cup sweet milk

½ tea spoon soda

nutmeg or caraway seed[s]

Flour to make stiff.

Cold Water Cake

2 cups sugar

½ cup butter

2 eggs

1 cup cold water

3 cups flour

1 tea spoon soda

2 tea spoons cream tartar

1 tea spoon extract vanilla

    Conway, Sept, 1866

    Mrs. Royce

Gold and Silver Cake

1 cup brown sugar

½ cup butter

Yolks of 5 eggs, well beaten

¼ tea spoon soda, dissolved in half a cup of milk

¾ tea spoon cream tartar

Mixed in two cups of flour.

Silver—the same, using the whites and white sugar
    with flavoring.

Sponge Cake

1 cup sugar

3 eggs

½ cup milk

1 tea spoon cream tartar

½ tea spoon soda

1½ cups flour

First beat eggs, then sugar, then flour, then milk with
soda stirred in—cream tartar with flour.

    From Eliza

American recipes throughout the nineteenth century increasingly
called for soda, sometimes called saleratus, a chemical agent that
leavened baked goods. By the Gilded Age, baking soda was widely
sold under national brand names such as Arm and Hammer.
Trade card, *Arm and Hammer Brand Church and Co.'s Soda*, The
Alan and Shirley Brocker Sliker Collection, MSS 314, Special
Collections, Michigan State University Libraries.

Currant Cake

2 cups white sugar

1 cup butter

1 cup currants

4 eggs

Tea spoon soda

Spice to taste

      Marlboro, July 1863

Ginger Cakes

1 cup sugar

1 cup molasses

1 cup butter

1 table spoon ginger

1 table spoon vinegar

1 table spoon soda

1 egg

Mix hard and roll out quarter of an inch thick[.]

      Hillsboro Bridge

      Sept. 1869

Jumbles

2 eggs

1 cup sugar

½ cup butter

3 cups flour

½ teaspoon soda, dissolved in 1 table spoonful milk

Flavor to taste[.] Roll in strips in sugar and cinnamon.

      From Mrs. Dr. Packard

      Sept. 1871

Doughnuts

1 egg

5 table spoons sugar

A large half cup milk

1 teaspoon [cream?] to ½ tea [spoon] of soda

A little salt

Flour to make stiff

      Mrs. Smith, Dec. 1874

Mock Mince Pies

1 cup chopped raisins

2 cups cider or nearly a cup of boiled cider and the
    remainder water

1 cup sugar

½ cup molasses

4 crackers made fine

Spice like mince.

      Mrs. Stevens—July 1862

Faith Cake

½ cup butter
1 cup sugar
2 eggs
½ cup milk
1 tea spoon cream to ½ [teaspoon] soda
2 small cups flour.
Flavor to taste.

Pop Overs

1 cup milk
1 cup flour
1 egg
a little salt

Bake in cups, putting about two large spoon fulls [sic] batter in a cup. Bake from 20 to 25 minutes in a quick oven.

"Charlestown" Pudding

3 eggs, two table spoons flour, and a little salt, beaten thoroughly together. Pour this into a quart of boiling milk and boil ten minutes, stirring all the time. When boiled, flavor and pour into a dish, and pour over it while hot a cup of white sugar. Serve cold.

Delmonico's Pudding

Take the yolks of three eggs to one quart of milk, 1 table spoonful corn starch, small cup of white sugar. Flavor to taste. Stir the eggs, sugar and corn starch thoroughly together and stir into the milk boiling ten minutes. [Put] in a dish and lay the whites of the eggs, well beaten, on the top. Bake a light brown. Serve cold.

Corn Starch Pie

1 cup boiling water, 1 table spoonful corn starch, dissolved in cold water, a piece of butter, 1 cup sugar, 1 egg, 1 lemon. Grate the rind and squeeze the juice. Stir the sugar, lemon and egg together. Bake with top crust.

Mrs. Osterhout[?]
June 1873

Seed or Thin Cakes

1 cup sugar
1 cup butter
1 egg
3 table spoonfuls milk
1 tea spoon cream tarter
½ tea spoon soda

Seed or not. Flour to mix hard. Bake quickly.

Mrs. Graves
Mar. 8, 1873

Bread, Brown

3 cups rye flour

3 cups indian meal

1 cup molasses

1 quart water or milk

1 heaping tea spoon soda

50 raisins

Mix thin as griddles. Bake two hours, cover with tin plate when partly baked.

    Mrs. Derby

    Worcester, 1875

Yeast

3 quarts of water

1 handful of hops

3 large potatoes grated

1 cup sugar

1 great spoon full of salt

1 great spoon full of flour

1 good sized cup of yeast will raise it.

Hard Sugar Gingerbread

1 cup butter

2 cups sugar

½ cup milk or water

3 eggs

1 table spoonfull ginger

1 tea spoon salt

1 small tea spoon soda

5 cups flour

Mix butter and flour, then add eggs well beaten, then sugar.

    Miss Rea, Boston, Feb. 1876

Oatmeal Cakes

1 cup oatmeal soaked over night. In the morning add 1 cup sour milk and 1 tea spoonful soda. Thicken with wheat flour.

    From Amy, Manchester, May 1876

To Pickle Oysters

Add a little water to the oysters and liquor, and wash the oysters, taking off all the bits of shells—strain and boil the liquor, then add the oysters while it is boiling, and let them boil one minute—take them out and to the liquor add a few pepper corns, cloves, and a blade or two of mace—Add the same quantity of vinegar as oyster juice and let the whole boil 15 minutes.

    Mrs. Allen

Tomato Chop

1 peck tomatoes, well chopped—add ½ tea spoon salt—stir together and put in a jar to remain over night. Next morn pour over them 1 pint cold water, and strain into a cullander, then put them over the fire to cook—after having added ½ tea cup full chopped bell peppers, and vinegar enough to cover them—boil until cooked, and then pour into a jar to cool. When cold, add ½ cup of horse-radish (or omit), ¾ cup of sugar, tea spoonful of cinnamon, one of cloves, and one of mustard.

Spiced Currants

5 pounds of currants, and 3 pounds of brown sugar—whole spices—boil until quite thick.

Chicken Salad

Boil a chicken tender—cut in small strips. Boil 4 eggs 3 minutes. Mash and mix with 2 tea spoons butter—12 tea spoons vinegar, 1 tea spoon mustard, 1 tea spoon salt. A little pepper, celery.

Mrs. Boomer

Chocolate for Cake

½ cup grated chocolate
½ cup milk
½ cup sugar
Yolk of 1 egg
A little salt
Add a little corn starch if not thick enough.

Jennie Gala[?], Feb. 1880

Ripe Cucumber Pickles

Pare and take out the seeds. Slice to suit your fancy. Put in good cider vinegar and salt, to remain 24 hours. Strain and make a syrup of one tea cup of sugar to one quart of vinegar—with cinnamon cloves and all spice—when the syrup is hot put in the cucumbers, and boil 20 minutes, or until clear and soft. Whole spices, or ground in a bag.

Mrs. Chittenden, Oct. 1880

Cholera Mixture

Take a tea spoonful of laudanum, peppermint, camphor, rhubarb, and tincture of cayenne, and mix. Dose—from 15 to 30 drops, repeat according to the urgency of the case.

Miss Stebbins

For Bowel Complaints

Half the yolk of an egg. 1 tea spoon castor oil, 1 tea
  spoon sugar.
Beat thoroughly and fill up slowly with cold water.
  Dose two tea spoons after each of operation[?].
    Mrs. Dr. Marsh

Chocolate Carousels

1 cup molasses
2 cups brown sugar
½ cup milk
½ pound chocolate cut up in small peices [sic]. A small
  piece of butter. Boil 20 minutes, stirring all the time.
    Boston—Lucy Foote

Taffy

1 cup light brown sugar
1 tea spoon butter

Water enough to make it as thick as cream. Mix the
sugar and water together. When it begins to boil, put
in the butter. Boil without stirring. Try it in water and
when it hardens it is done. Flavor if you like[.]
  Greenfield. March, 1870

Candy

1 cups molasses
1 cup sugar
1 table spoonful vinegar
A piece of butter the size of an egg—or smaller. Boil 20
  or 25 minutes[.]
    From Mrs. Foster

Mrs. Peter A. White, *The Kentucky Housewife: A Collection of Recipes for Cooking*, 1885

Almost certainly, Mrs. Peter A. White called her 1885 cookbook *The Kentucky Housewife*, published by Belford, Clarke & Co., as an attempt to capitalize upon a much more famous cookbook by the same name—Mrs. Lettice Bryan's 1839 *The Kentucky Housewife*, one of the best-known antebellum southern cookbooks and by far the most famous cookbook from Kentucky.[1] Using a proven title would have been a way to attract second glances from book buyers who might have ignored an unfamiliar name, and it would also have been a way for White to nod respectfully to her celebrated predecessor. Of course, using "Kentucky Housewife" also established White's cookbook as an explicitly regional one. She included recipes for biscuits, gumbo, grits, sweet potato pie, hog feet, jambalaya, Kentucky cured hams, hominy fritters, and many more self-consciously southern dishes. She also presumed an intimacy with food that hinted that she was writing for rural cooks more than urban ones; for instance, her recipe for green peas tells readers to gather them from the garden just before cooking them. Twenty years after the end of the Civil War, as the popularity of southern cookbooks was growing in both the North and the South, White went out of her way to style her work as a homely, regional, southern book.

Yet despite its clear regionalism, in other ways *The Kentucky Housewife* was very much a book of the Gilded Age. Cheek by jowl with resolutely southern foods were French-influenced dishes like Boudins à la Richelieu, Champignons with Sweetbreads, Potatoes à la Lyonnaise, and Crème Diplomate—a creamy gelatin dessert made with sherry, gelatin, and candied cherries. She also included recipes for some of the most fashionable dishes of the era, like canvasback ducks, lobsters, oysters, truffles, and turtle, as well as classic Gilded Age accompaniments like Chestnut Soup, Aspic Jelly, and Hollandaise Sauce. In part, White's decision to include foods that would have been perfectly at home on Delmonico's menu simply reflected national food trends. But the diversity of the book's recipes also points to the eclectic ways many southerners were eating by the 1880s, at least those financially stable and educated enough to be able to buy and read a cookbook. For instance, she also included classic nineteenth-century recipes that were popular all over the country, such as Washington Pie (a mild dessert honoring George Washington), croquettes (savory, deep-fried balls that were golden and crispy on the outside and filled with warm, creamy meat mixtures on the inside), and jumbles (a kind of cookie). In Kentucky and elsewhere in the South, diets strayed far outside of regional stereotypes.

More subtly, White's modern recipe format also made *The Kentucky Housewife* distinctively modern. Unlike recipes from earlier decades, which tended to plunge readers immediately into a descriptive paragraph that called for ingredients as it went, by the late nineteenth century writers increasingly listed ingredients first and gave cooking instructions afterward. This format was just starting to show up regularly in cookbooks by the 1880s, and White was one of the first cookbook writers to use it consistently. Partly, she explained, she wrote precisely so that "any cook who can read can take this book and be her own teacher." Yet despite her fairly consistent inclusion of an ingredient list with each recipe, the lists themselves were often incomplete. For instance, her ingredient list for Simple Chicken Soup omits the chicken, while the ingredient list for Cauliflower Served with Fried Chicken fails to mention either chicken or cauliflower. Her ingredient list for Corn Grits leaves out the milk; her ingredient list for Crème Diplomate leaves out the sherry. Yet most of White's omissions feel less like oversights than like a genre in the midst of transition. Even as she said she aimed for precision, she retained parts of the casual attitude toward recipe writing that defined the mid-nineteenth-century cookbooks she would have grown up reading. Ultimately, she must have reasoned, an intelligent reader could figure out such obvious points herself.

Preface

Having always regarded a cookery book as a book for the kitchen, I have, in order to carry out my idea, not only been explicit in giving proportions, but have endeavored to express myself so simply that any cook who can read can take this book and be her own teacher.

Mrs. P. A. W.

Breads, Etc.

Light Biscuits

One pint of sweet milk,
One quarter of a pound of butter,
One teacupful of yeast,
Three well-mashed potatoes,
A saltspoonful of salt.

Warm the milk and butter, put in flour enough for a soft sponge, then put in the yeast and salt. Let it rise, work in the potatoes, and add more flour, until a nice dough is made, but don't have it quite as thick as bread dough. Let this rise again, and one hour before kneaded [*sic*], roll, cut, put into pans, and bake in a quick oven. These are for tea; but if wanted for breakfast, make them up the night before, and work the first thing in the morning. Use a small teacup in measuring the yeast.

Hominy Meal Muffins

One quart of hominy meal,
One cooking-spoonful of butter,
One teaspoonful of salt,
Three eggs.

Scald the meal well and stir in milk enough to make a stiff batter; add the yelks of the eggs well beaten; salt; lastly, the whites beaten to a froth. Warm and grease the molds, and bake in a well-heated oven thirty minutes.

Waffles

One pint of flour,
One pint of sour cream, or buttermilk,
One dessertspoonful of lard and butter mixed,
Half a teaspoonful of soda,
A little salt,
One egg.

Stir the soda in the milk until it foams, then add the flour and lard and butter melted, beating well all the time. Beat the egg separately, adding the yellow first, then the white. The salt should be put in the flour dry. Bake in well-greased and well-heated irons.

Good Egg Bread

One quart of corn meal,
One tablespoonful of lard and butter,
One teacupful of milk,
One teaspoonful of salt,
Three eggs.

Pour a little boiling water over the meal to scald it; add the salt; stir in briskly the well-beaten yelks of the eggs, then the milk and lard and butter melted; lastly, the well-beaten whites of the eggs. Bake in a slow oven nearly an hour.

Baking Powder Biscuits

One quart of flour,
Three teaspoonfuls of baking powder,
One large cooking-spoonful of butter,
One teaspoonful of salt,
One pint of milk.

Sift the flour, then put in the baking powder, salt and butter; mix thoroughly with the hands, and pour in the milk. Roll only once, half an inch thick; cut with a biscuit cutter, and bake twenty minutes in a quick oven. Begin to make these biscuits just half an hour before they are to be eaten, allowing ten minutes to mix them. The dough should only be stiff enough to roll, so add more milk if needed.

Pounded Biscuit

One quart of flour,
One cooking-spoonful of lard and butter, mixed,
One teaspoonful of salt.

Sift the flour into a bowl, sprinkle the salt, then rub in the lard and butter. Now add milk, or milk and water enough for a stiff dough. Pound, or work, for fifteen or twenty minutes. If the dough blisters, and snaps when you pull it, it is worked enough. Roll, cut, and stick with a fork. Have a good oven; bake and brown nicely.

Cream Biscuits

One pound of flour,
One pint of sweet cream,
Half a teaspoonful of salt.

Sprinkle the salt over the flour, mix in the cream with the hands thoroughly, and pound or work until the dough blisters. Shape or cut, then prick as for pounded biscuits, and bake in a well-heated oven.

Baking Powder Flannel Cakes

One quart of well-sifted flour,
Three well-beaten eggs,
One cooking-spoonful of butter and lard,
Three heaping teaspoonfuls of baking powder,
Milk enough for a thick batter,
Salt to the taste.

Mix the flour, salt and milk, and beat hard, then add the well-beaten yelks, and lard and butter melted. Beat the whites of the eggs very stiff, and stir in slowly. Lastly, sift in the baking powder.

Spanish Buns

One pound of granulated sugar,
Three-quarters of a pound of flour,
One coffeecupful of cream,
One coffeecupful of dried currants,
Six ounces of butter,
Two teaspoonfuls of baking powder,
Four eggs.

Cream the butter and flour. Beat the yellows of the eggs very light with the sugar, and add to the flour. Wash, pick and dry the currants; flour well, and mix through. Beat the whites of the eggs to a stiff froth, and stir in slowly. Lastly sift in the baking powder. Bake in a well-heated oven.

To Cook Corn Grits

One coffeecupful of grits,
Three coffeecupfuls of boiling water,
One teaspoonful of salt.

Put the grits in the water with the salt, and boil steadily an hour and a half, stirring frequently while boiling. Just before it is done add a small cupful of milk.

Oatmeal Grits

One coffeecupful of fine oatmeal,
One quart of boiling water,
One teaspoonful of salt.

Put the salt in the boiling water, sprinkle the meal lightly in with one hand while stirring it with the other. When thoroughly mixed, let it boil steadily for one hour without stirring it more than necessary to keep it from sticking, for the steam swells the grains and makes them light.

Ham Omelette

One teacupful of chopped ham,
One dessertspoonful of butter,
Black pepper to the taste,
Six eggs.

Cold boiled ham must be used for chopping. Put in black pepper to the taste, and add the well-beaten yelks and a tablespoonful of butter melted. Lastly, beat the whites of the eggs very light, and stir slowly in. Have ready a hot pan with some butter in it, pour in the mixture, and when done, fold over and serve in a well-heated dish.

Eggs with Cheese

Two ounces of grated Parmesan cheese,
Two chopped spring onions,
Two tablespoonfuls of sherry wine,
One ounce of butter,
Six eggs.

Put the grated cheese into a sauce-pan with the chopped onion and sherry wine, stir all over the fire until the cheese is thoroughly melted. Beat the eggs, put them into the sauce-pan with the cheese and stir over a slow fire until done. Have some nicely cut pieces of hot fried toast, and pour the mixture over them. A teaspoonful of chopped parsley would be a pleasant addition stirred in the cheese before it is melted.

Welsh Rare Bit

Half a pound of new cheese,
The yelk of one raw egg,
Salt and cayenne pepper to the taste.

Melt the cheese slowly, and add by degrees dry mustard to the taste, then the salt and cayenne pepper; thin with beer. Have some nicely-cut pieces of buttered toast and spread the cheese on them.

Tongue Toast

One boiled tongue,
A teacupful of cream,
Yelk of one egg,
A half-teaspoonful of mixed mustard.

After the tongue has been well boiled and is perfectly cold, either grate or mince very fine. Mix with it the cream, the well-beaten yelk of the egg and the mustard. Simmer two or three minutes. Cut off the crust of some slices of bread, toast nicely, and butter well. Heat a flat dish, lay the slices of toast on it, spread the mixed tongue on them, and send to the table hot in a covered dish. This makes a nice breakfast or supper dish. For tongue, substitute cold boiled ham.

Meats for Breakfast

One Way to Cook a Steak

A nice, tender beefsteak,
Butter, black pepper and salt.

Wipe the steak dry, and pepper it well with black pepper. Put it on a gridiron before a bright fire. Broil one side until half done, and do the other side the same way. Have ready a pan over hot water, with a large piece of butter, black pepper and salt. Press the steak well on each side, return to the fire, and broil a few minutes longer. Have a dish heated, put the steak on it, and pour over the butter in which the steak was pressed. Never salt a steak until half cooked.

To Devil Ham

A few thin slices of cold boiled ham,
Mixed mustard, bread-crumbs, and black pepper.

Pepper the slices of ham, spread the mustard on them, and sprinkle with grated bread crumbs. Roll each piece and tie a thread loosely around. Put them in the oven, with some butter in the pan, for about ten minutes, basting the pieces with the butter as they are cooking. The thinner the slices are cut, the better.

Beef Stew for Breakfast

One quart of beef cut in dice,
One dessertspoonful of chopped onion,
One pint of cold boiled potatoes cut in dice,
One cooking-spoonful of butter,
Salt and black pepper to the taste,
One dessertspoonful of flour.

Put the beef and onion into a skillet, with water enough to cover, and simmer for twenty minutes, and add the potatoes and cook five minutes longer. Put the flour and batter together, stir in, and when it thickens, season. Have ready, in a heated dish, some nicely-cut pieces of buttered toast, and pour the stew over them. A little summer savory can be added if desired. Cold roast beef must be used.

Dry Beef Hash

One pint of chopped beef,
One pint of mashed potato,
Half a teacupful of cream,
A teaspoonful of chopped onion,
A teaspoonful of chopped parsley,
Salt and cayenne pepper to the taste.

Have the beef, that has either been boiled or roasted, free from all fat; mix with the potato, cream, onion and parsley, add the salt and cayenne pepper to the taste. Stir in a skillet or bake in an oven for twenty minutes. If baked, put in a dish, sprinkle some bread crumbs on top, and put here and there some small pieces of butter. A tablespoonful of butter can be added when mixing.

Lamb Chops

They should be neatly trimmed; the bone scraped, peppered and rolled in butter; then broiled with great care. When done, put more butter on them, also some salt and black pepper. Wrap little ruffles of white paper around the ends of the sticks; place the chops nicely around the dish, and have a center of tomatoes, peas, champignons or mashed potatoes. Chops are also nice dipped in bread crumbs, after broiling, and browned in lard, and served as above [Dry Beef Hash].

Mutton or Lamb Stew

One pound of lamb or mutton,
One medium sized onion,
One cooking-spoonful of butter,
One teaspoonful of flour,
Salt, and cayenne pepper to the taste,
Half a pint of milk,
Six potatoes.

Take cooked mutton and cut into dice. Boil the potatoes, and cut them also into dice. Have the milk boiling in the skillet, then put all in, and stew for ten minutes. Cream the butter and flour and stir in the mutton until it thickens. Have in the dish some hot buttered toast, and pour the stew over them. The onion should also be boiled before putting in the stew, and chopped fine.

To Make Veal Hash

One quart of chopped veal,
One teaspoonful of chopped onion,
Two tablespoonfuls of tomato catsup,
One cooking-spoonful of butter,
Salt and black pepper to the taste,
One teaspoonful of flour,

Cut in dice a quart of the cold fillet of veal, cook the onion before chopping, put it with the veal, a pint of hot water, salt and pepper into a skillet. While it is simmering, wet the flour and butter together and stir in until it thickens, then add the catsup. Have pieces of buttered toast about four inches square in a heated dish and pour the hash over them. The stuffing can be added instead of the flour if preferred.

Cold Mutton Hash

One pint of chopped mutton,
One pint of chopped potatoes,
One medium sized onion chopped fine,
Half a teaspoonful of powdered summer savory,
A cooking-spoonful of butter,
Salt and black pepper to the taste.

Put the potatoes and onion in a skillet with enough water to cover. Stew for half an hour, and add the butter, summer savory, mutton, salt and pepper. Stir for ten minutes, and serve on pieces of buttered toast. Should the hash be thin, mix with the butter a teaspoonful of flour. Cold beef hash can be made in the same way.

Turkey Hash

One quart of chopped turkey,
One pint of potatoes cut in dice,
One cookingspoonful of chopped celery,
Half a coffeecupful of cream,
A dessertspoonful of flour,
Salt and black pepper to the taste.

Put the potatoes and celery in a skillet, with water enough to cover, and stew for half an hour. Then put in the turkey, cream, salt and pepper, and let all come to a boil. Mix the flour with a little of the liquid of the hash and stir in until it thickens. If cream is not to be had substitute milk and a tablespoonful of butter, and if celery is not convenient, put in a teaspoonful of chopped onion and summer savory, to the taste.

Sausage Meat

Eleven pounds of tenderloins,
Seven pounds of leaf fat,
Four heaping tablespoonfuls of powdered sage,
Three teaspoonfuls of salt,
Four tablespoonfuls of ground black pepper,
One teaspoonful of cayenne pepper.

Chop or grind the meat as fine as possible. Put in the salt and pepper; lastly, the sage. Mix well with the hands, and fry in little cakes.

To Cook Sausages

Make into small cakes half an inch thick, dredge with a little flour and fry in a skillet with a small piece of lard until a dark brown.

To Prepare Hogs' Brains

When they are taken from the heads they must be picked, skinned and washed, changing the water while washing until it is clear. Put them into a bucket of cold water with some salt, soak for fifteen minutes, and they will be ready for use. Stew or fry. They can be kept for ten days by soaking them in salt and water, and changing the water every third day.

To Fry Hogs' Brains

One quart of brains,
One large cooking-spoonful of butter,
Salt, black pepper and powdered sage to taste,
Four eggs.

Beat the eggs together and mix with the brains. Heat the skillet, put in the butter, and when melted add the brains. Stir rapidly all the time, as you do when scrambling eggs. When half done add the salt, black pepper and powdered sage; continue to stir, and when they cease to stick to the skillet they are done. This makes a delicious dish for breakfast. Be sure to wash all the blood from the brains and pick out all the pieces of bone, and the strings.

To Prepare Tripe

Cold water,
Tripe,
Vinegar,
Salt.

Scrape and wash the tripe thoroughly. Put it in cold water and salt, and soak for ten days. Don't put much salt in, and just keep it covered with water, and change it every other day. Boil it for nine hours steady, and it will be ready to fry, stew or boil. If it is to be kept any length of time, it should be put in brine or vinegar.

To Stew Tripe

One teacupful of cream,
One tablespoonful of butter,
One teaspoonful of flour,
Three hard-boiled eggs,
Salt and pepper to the taste.

Cut the quantity of tripe you intend stewing into small pieces, about two inches square. Put it into a sauce pan, with equal quantities of milk and water, enough to cover well. Boil half an hour, then stir in the cream. Put the flour and butter together and add to it; after it has boiled five minutes longer, chop the hard-boiled eggs and stir them in. A little vinegar and mixed mustard is an improvement. This is a nice breakfast dish.

To Boil Hogs' Feet

Two dozen pigs' feet,
A good deal of water,
A large cooking-spoonful of salt.

Put the feet into a large pot, and cover with lukewarm water, adding the salt. Simmer slowly until thoroughly done, which will take four or five hours. The bones must be loose, but they must not be allowed to remain in the water until they are ready to fall out. When done, put in a large, wide-mouthed jar and cover with the water they were boiled in; then put in the following spices: one coffeecupful of whole allspice, half a teacupful of whole cloves, one coffeecupful of whole black pepper grains.

Lastly, add a third as much vinegar as you have water. Watch them closely, so as not to let the water and vinegar be absorbed entirely, but when you see it disappearing add more according to directions.

To Stew Hogs' Feet

Some cold boiled hogs' feet,
Cream according to the quantity of feet,
Salt and pepper to the taste,
A little sweet marjory.

Take the quantity of feet you wish to serve, put them into a sauce pan with a little hot water. Cover, and steam until perfectly soft, and put in the cream. Let it boil up once, rub the butter and flour together, add to the feet, boil up once more, season, and put in a little sweet marjory to the taste.

Bouillon, or Clear Soup

Four pounds of lean beef,

Four quarts of clear water,

One teaspoonful of celery seed,

Four large onions,

Six large carrots,

One bunch of parsley,

Six blades of mace,

Sixteen whole cloves,

The whites of four eggs,

Salt and pepper to the taste.

Cut the beef into pieces the size of a walnut, taking care not to leave a particle of fat on them. Pour on the four quarts of water, and let it boil up three times, skimming well each time; for if any of the grease is allowed to go back into the soup, it will be impossible to get it clear. Scrape the carrots, stick four whole cloves firmly into each onion, and put them in the soup. Then add the celery seed, parsley, mace, pepper and salt. Let this boil until the vegetables are tender, then strain through a bag, return to the soup pot, and stir in the well-beaten whites of the eggs. Boil until the eggs gather to one side, skim off, and color a delicate amber by burning a dessertspoonful of brown sugar, and stirring it into the soup until sufficiently colored. Wash the bag in warm water, pour the soup through again, and serve.

Okra Soup

One chicken, or a small knuckle of veal,

Two quarts of clear water,

Six large tomatoes,

Four large onions,

One quart of okra,

One bunch of parsley,

Salt and cayenne pepper to the taste,

One teaspoonful of summer savory,

Half a teaspoonful of powdered allspice.

Put on the chicken, or veal, in the water and let it boil up twice, skimming carefully until all of the grease is taken off; add the tomatoes, parsley, onions, summer savory, allspice, cayenne pepper and salt. Put this on at breakfast time: at 12 o'clock, put in a separate saucepan the quart of okra, cut up in thin slices. Boil for an hour, or until perfectly tender. Half an hour before dinner strain the soup and add the okra. This is for a 2 o'clock dinner; if for a late dinner put on the meat and vegetables at 1 o'clock and the okra at 5 o'clock.

Black Soup

One veal shank,
One gallon of water,
Two large carrots,
One large onion,
Three medium-size potatoes,
One bunch of parsley,
One bunch of summer savory,
Half a pint of browned flour,
One pint of Madeira wine,
Salt and black pepper to the taste.

Cut up the shank and put it on with the vegetables, salt and pepper, to boil slowly for four hours, skimming constantly while boiling; strain, put into a clean pot with the parsley, summer savory and browned flour. Boil for one hour; take out the parsley and summer savory, and, just before serving, heat the wine and put it in. Put in the soup as many yelks of hard-boiled eggs, thin slices of lemon and force-meat balls as you have guests to serve, allowing one yelk, one force-meat ball and a slice of lemon for each plate.

Canned Turtle Soup

Two quarts of beef soup,
Two tablespoonfuls of brown flour,
One tablespoonful of butter,
One dessertspoonful of chopped parsley,[2]
Two carrots cut in dice,
Three tablespoonfuls of ham cut in dice,
One tablespoonful of chopped onion,
Yelks of six hard-boiled eggs,
Salt, cayenne pepper and wine to the taste,
One can of turtle.

Stir the ham, butter, onion, parsley and carrots together in a soup pot over the fire for five minutes. Add the beef soup, brown flour, turtle, salt and cayenne pepper. Boil fifteen minutes and add the hard-boiled eggs, chopped very fine, with the wine. Have some thin slices of lemon, and serve two with each plate. Have the tureen heated with hot water before pouring in the soup.

Calf's-Head Soup

One pelted calf's head,
A knuckle of veal,
A pint of turtle beans,
Three gallons of water.

Soak the head in water over night, putting in a cooking-spoonful of salt in the water. Take out the brains and put them in another pan of salted water, changing the water until the blood is all drawn out. The next morning, put in the calf's head and veal, or a set of calf's feet, into the three gallons of water, and boil six or seven hours, until the head is perfectly tender; then take it out of the water; remove the bone, cut the meat into small pieces, and put them back into the soup. Season with black-pepper, salt, sweet marjoram and summer savory, to the taste. Put the Mexican beans also to soak over night, and boil until thoroughly done. Then pass through a sieve, and add the soup. Make egg balls with the yelks of two hard-boiled eggs; one raw egg, and flour enough to mix them with. Roll out the size of a hazel-nut. Take two pounds of cooked fillet of veal; chop very fine, season with salt, pepper, sweet majoram [sic], and one small onion chopped fine. Add half a cupful of bread crumbs, and one egg. Mix all together with a wooden spoon, and make into small balls with a little flour. Fry in boiling lard, a cinnamon brown. Put this in the ice-chest with the soup, and fry the balls as you wish each day. When serving, put some slices of lemon in the tureen, and pour the soup over them, adding the force meat-balls, egg-balls, and wine to the taste; also, the yelks of two hard-boiled eggs mashed fine. If you do not use the black beans, brown a little flour or sugar to color the soup with. Put the brains in a cloth, boil till tender. Mash the yelks of two hard-boiled eggs, and mix with the brains, adding black pepper and salt. Boil the calf's tongue until tender, and put the brains in spoonfuls around the tongue, alternating with a slice of lemon. This will make a nice side dish.

Force-Meat Balls for Calf's Head Soup

Half a pound of well-cooked veal,
One calf's brains,
Salt, cayenne pepper and nutmeg to taste,
Two eggs.

Chop the brains and veal as for mince meat; mix with the eggs, salt, cayenne pepper and nutmeg. Flour a board, drop a small piece here and there, roll into balls in the flour, using as little flour as possible. Throw them into boiling lard, and fry a dark brown. Drain, and when cool put into the soup. A spoonful or two of fine bread crumbs can be used in mixing the balls if desired.

Gumbo Soup

Two large chickens,
Two quarts of okra,
Three large onions,
One teaspoonful of allspice,
One bunch of parsley,
Three quarts of water,
One teaspoonful of summer savory.

Skin and quarter the chickens, cut up the onions, and put all into a saucepan with three slices of pickled pork and two tablespoonfuls of butter. Fry until the chickens are a light brown, and put all into a soup-pot, adding the allspice, parsley, summer savory; salt and cayenne pepper to the taste. Let this boil slowly from ten o'clock, skimming frequently. At twelve o'clock put on the okra, whole, in a separate pot, with water enough to cover well; boil for an hour and a quarter. Half an hour before dinner, take the chicken out of the soup; pick out the bones, and cut the meat in small pieces. Put back into the pot, and add the okra. Let it come to a boil and serve. This soup can be made in the winter out of canned okra and tomatoes. To the above quantity of soup two cans must be used. This quantity is for a large family. Half the quantity can be made if preferred.

Simple Chicken Soup

One coffeecupful of cream,
One teacupful of well-boiled rice,
One blade of mace,
A saltspoonful of celery seed,
One dessertspoonful of corn starch.

When boiling a pair of chickens for dinner, put in the water a blade of mace and a saltspoonful of celery seed. After the chickens are done, take out two quarts of the water; skim well, and add the cream, or rich milk; then the rice and the dessertspoonful of corn starch; season to the taste. It will require about three quarts of water for a pair of chickens.

Crab Gumbo Soup

One knuckle of veal,
Three good-sized onions,
A quarter of a peck of okra,
Six large crabs,
Two gallons of boiling water,
Two tablespoonfuls of butter,
Salt and pepper to the taste.

Cut up the onions, slice the okra, and fry them in butter with pepper and salt. When browned, put all into a pot with the boiling water, and when half cooked, divide the crabs, fry them in butter and stir them in. Let this simmer for five hours; then it will be done. If wanted in the winter use the canned okra, one quart, and three pints of oysters in the place of the crabs. Serve quickly.

Oyster Gumbo

One large chicken,
One can of oysters,
Half a pound of boiled ham,
Two quarts of boiling water,
One bunch of summer savory,
One bunch of parsley,
One tablespoonful of filee powder,
Salt, black and cayenne pepper to the taste.

Divide the chicken, skin and flour each piece well; cut the ham in dice, and, with a cooking-spoonful of butter, fry until brown. Then pour on it two quarts of boiling water, the bunches of summer savory and parsley tied together, salt and cayenne pepper. Let this boil slowly for four hours. Take out the summer savory and parsley, pull the chicken to pieces, return it to the pot, and about fifteen minutes before serving, heat the oysters and their liquor, and add to the soup. While they are simmering very slowly, take out a tea cupful of the soup and mix with the filee powder. When perfectly smooth put it in the soup; let it boil up once and it will be done. Pour into a heated tureen and serve with some nicely-boiled rice in another dish.

Chicken Soup for the Sick

One large chicken,
Three pints of cold water,
Three tablespoonfuls of rice,
One bunch of parsley,
Salt and pepper to the taste.

Cut the chicken into four parts, and wash in cold water; put the pieces into a sauce-pan with the three pints of water, a little salt, the rice and parsley. Let it boil gently for an hour and a half, skimming constantly. Take out the meat and parsley, and pour the soup into a bowl.

Purée of Chicken

One large chicken,
One small knuckle of veal,
Three quarts of water,
A quarter of a pound of rice,
One bunch of parsley,
One blade of mace,
Half a teaspoonful of celery seed,
A coffeecupful of boiling cream,
Salt and pepper to the taste.

Put the chicken and veal on with three quarts of water, together with the rice, parsley, mace and the celery seed, tied in a muslin bag. Boil gently until the chicken is thoroughly done, taking care to skim well all the time it is boiling. Take out the veal, bone, cut, and pound the chicken in a mortar; moisten it with a little of the stock, and pass it through the colander. Strain the stock, pressing the rice through the sieve. Return the chicken to the stock, season, and just before serving, pour in the cream. Heat thoroughly, but don't boil.

Chestnut Soup

Two quarts of Spanish chestnuts,
Two quarts of chicken stock,
One pint of rich cream,
Salt, nutmeg and cayenne pepper to taste.

Shell the chestnuts, put them in a pan and cover with cold water. Let them scald until the inner skin can be taken off. Put them on a sieve, to allow the hot water to drain off, and while draining, pour on some cold water, so as the skins can be removed with the hand. When they are well skinned, put them into a sauce pan with the chicken stock, and let them simmer until perfectly tender. Then mash through the sieve into the same stock. Season with nutmeg, salt and cayenne pepper to the taste. Put it into a saucepan with hot water underneath, stirring all the time until it begins to simmer; then pour in the pint of cream, and after stirring five minutes longer, serve.

Lobster Soup

Two pounds of fresh lobster, or one can of preserved, weighing two pounds,
One quart of milk,
One quart of boiling water,
Two tablespoonfuls of corn starch,
One teaspoonful and a half of salt,
Two tablespoonfuls of butter,
Mace and cayenne pepper to the taste.

Canned lobster was increasingly available around the country during the late nineteenth century, making it possible for cooks far from the coasts to serve it at home. "Trade cards depicting food including: fish, lobster, poultry, lemons, eggs and drinks," ca. 1876–1890, The Miriam and Ira D. Wallach Division of Art, Prints and Photographs: Print Collection, The New York Public Library Digital Collections.

Put the milk in a saucepan, with hot water underneath. When it comes to a boil, stir in the corn starch, previously dissolved in a little cold water. In the meantime, cut the lobster in very small pieces; put it in the pint of water with the seasoning and butter, and boil until the lobster is done. Strain, and pour into the thickened milk. Pound the coral very fine, and add to the soup, which will give it a pretty pink color.

Fish

To Broil Oysters

Four dozen large oysters,
A quarter pound of butter,
Salt, and black pepper.

Drain, and wipe the oysters. Place them carefully on the wire broiler; have the butter, salt, and pepper, in a sauce pan with hot water underneath. Broil the oysters before the fire, turning the broiler to have them nicely browned; and as you broil them, put them in the butter, until all are broiled, and serve quickly in a heated dish. This quantity can be reduced, or increased, according to the number to be served.

To Griddle Oysters

Select the largest and finest oysters, drain the liquor from them. Have the griddle hot, and butter it well. Lay the oysters on it in single layers, and when browned on one side, turn on the other, to brown too. While they are cooking, a small piece of butter maybe added; this, combined with the juice given out by the oyster, forms a brown skin. When done to a nice brown, remove both oysters and skin with a tin cake turner; put them on a hot dish, pour over them some plain melted butter, seasoned with a little black and cayenne pepper.

A Fricasse of Lobster

Two large lobsters,
One pint of cream,
The juice of one lemon,
Salt and cayenne pepper to the taste.

Parboil the lobsters, allowing ten minutes to the pound. Take out all of the meat, and the coral; cut the meat into small pieces, and with the coral, put into a sauce-pan, and pour on the cream. Cover, and let it stew gently for the same time it took to cook the lobster; then add the lemon juice and curry powder to the taste. Simmer for five minutes and serve very hot.

Lobster Balls

One large hen lobster,
One pint of bread crumbs,
Curry powder, salt and cayenne to the taste,
Two eggs.

Parboil the lobster, allowing ten minutes to the pound. Take out the meat and coral, and pound well in a mortar; mix with it the bread crumbs, curry, salt and cayenne pepper, and the two eggs. Shape into balls the size of a small potato; roll in bread crumbs; fry a nice brown in hot lard, and serve on a napkin.

To Devil Crabs

One dozen crabs,
Inside of a baker's loaf of bread,
Yelks of four hard-boiled eggs,
Parsley and Worcestershire to the taste,
Salt and cayenne pepper to the taste,
A quarter of a pound of butter.

Boil the crabs twenty minutes, then dissect. Chop the parsley very fine, mash the eggs smooth, and mix all with the meat, sauce, salt and cayenne pepper. Wash the shells, fill and dip each one in egg, roll in pounded crackers, and fry a nice brown.

To Select Crabs

Select the thickest and heaviest crabs, which are generally considered the best, though the medium-sized are the most delicate. When perfectly fresh, the shell should be a bright red, and the joints of the legs stiff. Boil them as you would lobsters, only boil them longer.

To Fry Soft-Shell Crabs

Six soft-shell crabs,
One teacupful of milk,
One teaspoonful of flour,
One egg,
Salt and pepper.

The crabs must be perfectly fresh. Wipe them dry; sprinkle over them a little salt and pepper. Beat the egg and milk together; roll the crabs, first in the flour, then in the egg and milk, and fry in boiling lard until well browned. Another way is, simply to sprinkle them with salt and pepper and roll them in cracker powder, then drop them in boiling lard, and fry as you would croquettes.

To Fry Frogs

As much cracker crumbs as will be needed,
Two eggs, salt and pepper to taste,
One teacupful of milk.

First boil them in salt and water for about three minutes; take them out and wipe well; beat the eggs, and stir in the milk, adding salt and pepper to the taste; dip each frog, first in the egg, then in the cracker crumbs; when they have all been dipped, put them carefully into a wire frying basket, and put it into a skillet of boiling lard; let them fry a nice brown, and serve at once.

For Cooking and Dressing Terrapins

Place the terrapin in boiling water for five minutes; then take it out, throw that water away, and put on fresh water to boil. Remove the outside skin, which is on the legs and flesh between the upper and lower shells. This can be easily done at this stage by rubbing with a towel. Put the terrapin back into the boiling water, and cook until it is done, which will take from three-quarters of an hour to an hour and a quarter, according to the size and toughness of the terrapin. When the joints of the leg break under a slight pressure it has boiled enough.

To Open.—Place it on its back with the head from you. The gall bladder is then in the left-hand liver. This must be removed very carefully. The other liver, and all that part which is not too close to the gall should be cut up and put in. The only other part which cannot be used is the sand-bag. If the pipes are used, they should be chopped almost to a hash, and will serve as thickening. Be sure to leave out the nails and bones of the head. The eggs should have the slight film which surrounds them pulled off, and then put them in cold water for a short time.

To Dress the Terrapin

The yelks of three hard boiled eggs,
A quarter of a pound of butter,
Half a teacupful of sherry or Madeira wine,
One teacupful of sweet cream.

Mash the eggs, and add the butter; but if they do not mix nicely, a little heat can be applied. Put a sauce-pan on the fire, and put in some terrapin, then a little cream dressing, and so on, until it is thoroughly heated, and the dressing is all dissolved. Then stir in the small eggs, wine, cayenne pepper, black pepper and salt to the taste. This will be enough for one large terrapin, or three small ones.

Terrapin Dressing

One good sized terrapin,
One teaspoonful of made mustard,
Half a tumblerful of sweet cream,
A large wineglassful of sherry wine,
The yelks of two hard boiled eggs,
The eighth of a pound of butter.

Put the terrapin on in a saucepan with hot water underneath, and let it steam. Heat the cream and butter and stir in the terrapin with the mustard, and hard-boiled eggs rubbed very fine. Let this boil for about five minutes, put salt and cayenne pepper to the taste, and just before serving, heat the wine and pour in. Serve very hot, with the dish garnished with thin slices of lemon. Take out the seeds.

Egg Balls for Terrapins

Yelks of two hard-boiled eggs,
The white of one raw egg,
A saltspoonful of butter,
Salt and cayenne pepper to the taste.

Mash the yelks smoothly with the butter, then add the white of the egg. Salt and cayenne pepper to the taste. After mixing thoroughly, take bits of the mixture and roll the size of terrapin's eggs; then roll in flour and fry carefully in butter, but don't let them change color in frying. If wanted for turtle soup, shape the eggs as large as a medium-sized marble.

To Can Terrapins

Terrapins can be canned as tomatoes or peaches. Parboil them, and seal very hot. As they are so delicate, it would be better to put them up in glass jars. A little salt, cayenne and black pepper should be put in while boiling.

To Feed Oysters in the Shell

Wash them clean, lay the bottom downwards and pour over them salt and water; allowing six ounces of salt, one quart of corn or oatmeal to each gallon of water. Mix well and sprinkle over the oysters. Do this every other day, and keep them in a cellar.

To Roast Ribs of Beef

A roast of two or three ribs,
Some flour for dredging,
Salt and black pepper.

Put the beef into a pan, season with pepper and salt, and pour in the pan a pint of hot water to baste with. Keep the oven well heated, and closed until it begins to roast, then baste well every fifteen minutes; add more hot water as it begins to simmer away, so as the gravy will not burn. Allow about fifteen minutes to the pound, and half an hour before it is done, dredge well with flour, and baste often, so as to brown nicely. Take the meat up, dredge in more flour, and add seasoning and boiling water, but don't let the gravy be too thin. Let it boil up once, and strain into a gravy boat.

To Corn Beef

Four gallons of water,
Five pounds of salt,
Two ounces of saltpetre,
One pound and a half of brown sugar.

Mix the above, and boil fifteen minutes, being careful to take off the scum as it rises. Let it stand until cold, then having packed the meat you wish to corn in a vessel, pour the pickle on it, taking care to have the meat well covered with it. Before putting the pickle on the beef, it will be better to rub it well with salt and saltpetre, and let it stand three days. Let the beef remain a week in the pickle. This pickle will also be excellent for tongues.

Lamb

The best pieces of lamb for roasting, are the forequarter and hindquarter. If preferred rare, allow fifteen minutes to the pound. If preferred well done, allow twenty minutes to the pound, and serve either with a mint sauce or brown gravy and jelly.

Tongue à la Mode

One fresh beef tongue,
Half a teaspoonful of whole black pepper,
One teaspoonful of ground cloves,
One teaspoonful of ground cinnamon,
One teaspoonful of celery seed,
One teaspoonful of ground allspice,
One dozen bay leaves,
Two medium sized onions,
One pint of vinegar, one lemon,
Water enough to cover.

Get a stone crock, one foot in diameter and six inches high. Put a fresh beef tongue in it, with the above ingredients, and boil until tender. Cook one can of champignons three quarters of an hour, take out a pint of the broth, thicken with soft gingerbread, and pour over the tongue. The onions and lemon must be sliced, and be sure to take the seeds from the lemon. Add salt to the taste, when boiling. Add also, half a tumbler of sherry wine.

A Delicious Way to Use up Cold Roast Beef

One cupful of turnips, cut in dice,
One cupful of carrots, cut in dice,
One chopped onion,
Some slices of cold roast beef,
One cooking-spoonful of butter,
One tablespoonful of flour,
Two tablespoonfuls of currant jelly,
Half a teacupful of wine.

Put the vegetables into a skillet with a quart of water, some salt and some pepper. Let them boil for one hour, then put in the beef and currant jelly. While the meat is heating, rub the butter and flour together, and stir in until it thickens. Then heat the wine and add. Use a medium sized coffee cup for measuring.

Boiled Marrow Bones

Some marrow bones,
Some nicely cut squares of toast.

Saw the bones according to fancy, make a little paste of flour and water, and cover the ends with it, so as the marrow will not come out in boiling. Put them into a kettle and cover them with boiling water. Cook for two hours, and if served without taking the marrow out, take the paste off; wrap each end with white fringed paper, and arrange nicely on the dish. In this case, the bones ought to be four inches long. If served with the toast, have the squares nicely cut, buttered while hot, and spread the marrow on the squares.

A Kentucky Recipe for Curing Hams

Some red and black pepper,
Some saltpetre and brown sugar.

Make a strong red pepper tea of the pods, moisten the salt with it, and add some brown sugar, allowing about a quarter of a pound to each ham; mix all well together, and rub the hams thoroughly with it. Put a teaspoonful of saltpetre on the fleshy side of each ham; let them stand in the salt three weeks, then smoke with green hickory or red oak until a good color. Canvas them by mixing red and black peppers together; about three-fourths black pepper. Wrap in paper, put them in cotton bags, and hang in a cool, dry place.

To Boil a Ham

One ham,
One pint of vinegar,
Enough water to cover well.

If the ham is one year old, soak it over night. If two years old, soak a day and a night. If three years old soak two days and two nights. Wash well and put it on in cold water, having the water at least four inches above the ham. If small, let it simmer six or seven hours. If large, it will require at least nine hours simmering, and never let it boil hard. After it has been on the fire three hours, pour off the water, and add fresh boiling water with the pint of vinegar. Skin while the ham is warm.

To Bake a Ham

Half a teaspoonful of mixed mustard,
The yelks of two eggs,
Some grated bread crumbs.

After the ham has been well boiled and skinned, before allowing it to get cold, mix the mustard with the yelks of the eggs, and spread nicely over the ham, then sprinkle the bread crumbs over, put it in the oven and bake half an hour. It is a great improvement to pour over the ham half a tumblerful of sherry or port wine, just about ten minutes before taking it out of the oven.

To Roast a Pig

Have a very young pig,
Two medium-sized onions,
A coffeecupful of bread crumbs,
Two teaspoonfuls of summer savory,
Two tablespoonfuls of butter,
One saltspoonful of salt,
One egg, black pepper to the taste.

Clean the pig well and chop the onions very fine. Put the butter and bread crumbs together; add the egg, chopped onion, and powdered summer savory, salt and black pepper. Stuff the pig with this and sew it up with coarse thread. Truss the fore legs forward, and hind legs backward. Rub the pig with butter, sprinkle with black pepper and salt, and dredge with flour. Just before putting it in the pan, take a sharp knife and cut the skin of the body in squares, but don't cut any deeper than the skin. Put hot water in the pan, and have a moderate oven. Baste very often, and cook for three hours and a half. Make a gravy of the drippings, by adding a little summer savory and dredging with a little flour.

Veal Loaf

Three pounds of lean veal,
Two pounds of fresh pork,
Two teaspoonfuls of black pepper,
A small saltspoonful of cayenne pepper,
Two teaspoonfuls of salt,
One tablespoonful of summer savory,
Ten pulverized crackers,
Six eggs.

Chop the veal and pork as fine as possible; mix the salt and pepper together and put into the meat; then the crackers, eggs; lastly the summer savory—rubbed very fine. Mix well with the hands; mold into a loaf, and put it in a pan with a teacupful of water. Add occasionally a few small pieces of butter on the top, which will assist in basting, cooking and browning nicely. Bake carefully in a good oven for two hours, but don't let it be too hot.

Calf's Head à la Terrapin

One calf's head,
One pint of the water the head has boiled in,
One teaspoonful of allspice,
One tablespoonful of white flour,
One teaspoonful of browned flour,
Two large cooking-spoonfuls of butter,
Half a tumblerful of Madeira wine,
Salt, cayenne pepper, and mace to the taste.

Boil the calf's head until perfectly done. Chop up the meat with the brains, taking out the bones and gristle. Put into a saucepan, with the pint of water it has boiled in. Let it simmer. Mix perfectly smooth the butter and flour, adding two tablespoonfuls of the liquor. Stir into the calf's head. Add the allspice, mace, salt and cayenne. Let it simmer until it thickens, and just before taking it off the fire, pour in the wine. Garnish the dish with thin slices of lemon. This is just as delicious baked.

Take out the brains and parboil. Put the head in a pot with cold water enough to cover it, and the onions whole, with a little salt. Boil until tender enough to take out all the bones. Then season with cayenne pepper, salt, cloves, and nutmeg to the taste. Dredge with flour, and fry a light brown. Season the brains also with salt, nutmeg, cayenne pepper, to the taste. Add the butter, yelk of the egg, and two rolled crackers. Mix well with the hands, shape into little cakes, and fry a light brown.

To Fry Sweetbreads

Three sets of sweetbreads,
One large coffeecupful of sweet milk,
One teaspoonful of flour,
One dessertspoonful of butter,
Salt and black pepper to the taste,
One well-beaten egg.

Three sets means six sweetbreads. Wash them clean; put them into a kettle of boiling water, with a teaspoonful of salt. Boil slowly for twenty minutes, then throw them into cold water. After five minutes, take them out and set them away to get cold. Have ready the batter made of the above ingredients; split the sweetbreads, dip each piece into the batter, and fry a nice brown in hot lard.

Fried sweetbreads, from Mrs. Mary F. Henderson, *Practical Cooking and Dinner Giving* (New York: Harper and Bros., 1877), 152, Special Collections, Michigan State University Libraries.

To Cook Champignons with Sweetbreads

Two cans of champignons,

Two sets of sweetbreads,

Three teaspoonfuls of white flour,

One teaspoonful of brown flour,

One pint of clear soup,

One large cooking-spoonful of butter,

Two wineglassfuls of wine,

Mace, salt and cayenne pepper to the taste.

Cook the sweetbreads thoroughly, and break into small pieces, taking care to get off all the skin and gristle. Cut up the champignons and put them, with their liquor, into a saucepan with the clear soup. Boil three-quarters of an hour, then add the salt, pepper and mace, also the sweetbreads. Mix the butter with the flour, put into the sweetbreads and stir until it thickens. Just before taking the saucepan off the fire add the wine. Serve very hot.

Croquettes

Half a pound of the breast of chicken or turkey,

Half a pound of sweetbreads,

Half a pound of bread crumbs,

Half a pound of butter,

Three teaspoonfuls of chopped parsley,

One teaspoonful of grated onion,

Four eggs,

Nutmeg, salt and cayenne pepper to the taste.

Put the bread crumbs into a saucepan and pour over them hot water enough to mash perfectly smooth. Add the yelks of two eggs, stir over the fire until a moderately stiff panada is made, and set aside to cool. Chop the meat and sweetbreads as fine as possible, add the panada, butter, parsley, salt and cayenne pepper. When thoroughly mixed, add the other two eggs, both whites and yelks, and shape as pears. Break into a pan two more eggs, and have ready some stale bread crumbs. Roll each croquette in the egg, then in the crumbs, and let them stand for a while to dry. Drop in boiling lard, and fry a cinnamon brown. Be sure to cook the sweetbreads before chopping, and if they are not to be had, substitute for them four tablespoonfuls of rich cream. The more creamy the croquettes are, the more delicious they will be.

Quenelles

One pound of ground chicken or turkey breast,

Six ounces of panada,

A quarter of a pound of chopped beef suet,

A quarter of a pound of butter,

A tablespoonful of scraped pork,

Two tablespoonfuls of cream sauce,

One teaspoonful of chopped onion,

Nutmeg and grated lemon rind to the taste,

Salt and pepper to the taste.

Mix the panada and meat well together with the hand; add the butter, salt, pork, and cream sauce, and work for two or three minutes, then put in the onion, nutmeg, pepper, salt, and grated lemon rind. Let the seasoning be so delicate, that the taste of no one ingredient can be detected above the other. Shape about three inches long, two inches wide and two inches thick; roll in flour, and cook as croquettes. Serve with a white champignon sauce poured over them.

Boudins à la Richelieu

Some raw turkey breast,
One half as much butter,
Three eggs,
Salt, nutmeg and pepper to taste.

Take as much turkey breast as you wish, say a heavy pound; grate and pound in a mortar until it can be passed through a fine sieve; add half as much butter as there is turkey breast, and one-third as much paste, made as follows: Take the inside of a loaf of bread, soak it in milk, and dry on the range, but don't let it get in the least hard, then add the butter until it becomes a stiff paste, lastly the eggs, nutmeg, salt, and pepper to the taste. Fry a small piece in boiling water, to see that it is not too stiff or too soft. If too stiff add more yelks. The above should be a light-yellow in color.

To Make the Sauce for the Boudins

One fourth of a box of truffles,
One large wineglassful of sherry wine,
One aschalot.

Chop and cook the aschalot; put into a pan with the sherry wine, then add the chopped truffles. Let all cook again until nearly dry, then stir in a tablespoonful of brown sauce. Simmer for ten minutes, and put into a

dish to cool. The boudin should be the shape and size of a wafer cake, and rolled in heavy white paper, wet with sweet oil inside and outside. Then boil in clear soup for twenty-five minutes, and serve with the sauce.

Aspec Jelly

Three pints of clear soup,
One box of Cox's gelatine,
Half a pint of wine,
One tablespoonful of vinegar,
Whites and shells of three eggs,
Six whole cloves,
Salt to the taste,
One lemon.

Put the soup in a saucepan with the wine, gelatine, vinegar, cloves, rind and juice of a lemon, salt and egg shells. Lastly, stir in the well-beaten whites of the eggs. Boil twenty minutes, let it settle for five minutes and strain through a jelly bag.

How to Mold Aspec Jelly

Put the mold on ice, pour in until about one-third full; let the jelly get stiff, then cut some thin slices of cooked sweetbreads, champignons and truffles, which place tastefully on the jelly, with some cooked peas here and there. Pour on some more jelly, let it get stiff, put some more champignons, etc., and so on, until the mold is full. This is a delightful dish to be served as a course at a dinner, lunch, or supper.

Brains in Shells

One quart of brains,
One tumblerful of sweet cream,
One cooking-spoonful of butter,
Salt and black pepper to the taste,
One teaspoonful of flour.

Soak the brains until the blood has disappeared entirely from them; pick the gristle and bone from them, and parboil until white and tender; then add the cream, butter, flour, pepper and salt, and stew until done; break up the brains with a spoon until fine, put them in shells with grated bread crumbs and small pieces of butter on top, and put them into the oven to brown. This recipe applies to hogs' brains. Calves' brains can be cooked the same way, and a little of the extract of celery put in just before filling the shells is a great improvement.

To Roast a Chicken

One tender, fat chicken,
Two-thirds of a pint of bread crumbs,
Half a teaspoonful of summer savory,
One dessertspoonful of butter,
Salt and black pepper to the taste.

Wash the chicken and wipe dry. Rub the butter with the bread crumbs and the powdered summer savory, then the salt and pepper. Stuff the inside of this and skewer well. Put two thin slices of pickled pork across the breast bone, and a pint of hot water in the pan. Have a good oven; baste frequently for an hour and a half. Put the giblets on to cook at the same time you put the chicken to roast; chop very fine, dredge some flour in the pan, and when the gravy thickens stir, [sic] in the giblets, adding salt and pepper. Serve the gravy in a boat.

Fricasee of Chicken

One tender chicken,
One teacupful of butter,
One tablespoonful of flour,
One bunch of parsley,
A saltspoonful of celery seed.

Wash the chicken and cut it up as for frying; put into a stewpan, with hot water enough to cover it, the celery seed and salt; let it boil gently, taking off the scum as it rises, until it is tender, which will take about one hour; then rub the butter and flour together, put into the stewpan with the well chopped parsley; let it stew fifteen minutes; add the yelks of two raw eggs; stir as you would for custard, and boil five minutes longer. Serve on a dish with boiled rice arranged nicely around it. When putting the celery into the stewpan, put it in a thin piece of muslin.

Jambalaya of Chicken and Rice

One good sized chicken,
Two large tomatoes,
One thin slice of pickled pork,

A French-inspired cooking style popular among American home cooks throughout the nineteenth century, fricassees were stewed meat, usually served with a white sauce. From Mrs. Mary F. Henderson, *Practical Cooking and Dinner Giving* (New York: Harper and Bros., 1877), 173, Special Collections, Michigan State University Libraries.

One teacupful of rice,
Salt and cayenne pepper to the taste,
One large onion.

Prepare the chicken as for gumbo; peel and cut up the tomatoes and onions, and fry all together; while frying, slowly, have the rice boiling, and boil until it swells; add it to the chicken, etc., and fry until a light brown.

Curry

Two tablespoonfuls of curry,
One teaspoonful of ground ginger,
One teaspoonful of salt,
Three tablespoonfuls of flour,
Yelks of two hard-boiled eggs,
One quart of clear water.

Prepare the meat as for a stew; mash the yelks well; add to them the curry, ginger and salt; mix well with the water; then put in the flour; stew the meat in this mixture until done; serve with rice. Put the meat in the center of the dish, pour the sauce over it, and put the rice around it. By the sauce is meant what the meat was stewed in.

Chicken Pie

One tender chicken,
Two pints of sweet milk,
Half a pound of butter,
Two tablespoonfuls of flour,
Salt and black pepper to the taste,
One quart of water.

Divide the chicken as for frying, and put it on with the quart of water, which should be freshly boiled. When it is done, take it out of the pot; then simmer the water until reduced to a pint; then add the salt, pepper, milk, butter and flour. Boil ten minutes, and line a dish with pie crust; fill it with the chicken; cover with a top crust, and bake slowly one hour. A little celery can be boiled with the chicken or a bunch of parsley. Just keep the chicken covered with water, while it is cooking.

To Roast Ducks

One medium sized onion,
One teaspoonful of powdered summer savory,
One teacupful of bread crumbs,
One tablespoonful of butter,
Salt and pepper to the taste.

The above ingredients are for stuffing one duck. Select a young duck, and fill it with the stuffing; sprinkle a little salt and black pepper on top, and dredge with flour. Lay two thin pieces of pickled pork across the breast bone, and put it into a pan with a little hot water. Baste frequently, and cook for an hour. Serve with brown gravy, made of the giblets and currant jelly.

To Roast Wild Ducks

Some currant jelly,
A few thin slices of lemon,
One thin slice of pickled pork,
Salt, pepper and flour.

Do not stuff, but put a teaspoonful of black pepper inside of the duck; sprinkle flour and salt on the outside, and lay the slice of pork across the breast bone. Put it in the pan with a pint of hot water; have a hot fire, and baste frequently for twenty or twenty-five minutes, according to the size. Make a brown gravy; stir in currant jelly to the taste, and serve in a boat. Garnish the dish with thin slices of lemon and small sprigs of parsley.

To Cook Canvas Back Ducks

One canvas back duck,
Some currant jelly,
Salt and black pepper.

Wipe out the inside of the duck, and if at all strong, wash out with a little saleratus water; sprinkle the inside with black pepper, also sprinkle a little on the outside, with some salt and flour; lay a thin slice of pickled pork across the breast bone; have a very hot fire, baste every five minutes, and let the duck cook just eighteen minutes; when putting the duck in the pan, a pint of hot water could be put in to baste with.3 Make a brown gravy of clear soup, currant jelly, and wine to the taste. Serve quickly, as a canvas-back should never be overdone, or allowed to stand; some like it just red hot through. The gravy can be omitted if objected to.

To Broil Prairie Chicken

One fat young prairie chicken,
Four tablespoonfuls of butter,
Salt and black pepper to the taste.

Pepper the chicken, and rub with a little butter; have a hot fire; broil a little on one side, then on the other; have some more butter in a pan, with pepper and salt; press the chicken well in it, then broil until done. Put on a hot dish, and pour over it the melted butter in which it was pressed; garnish with sprigs of parsley, and serve immediately.

A Nice Dish of Quails and Truffles

Eight fat young quails,
One wineglassful of wine,
Half a pound of truffles,
One pint of clear soup,
Salt and pepper to the taste.

Cut out the breasts of eight quails; divide them and broil very delicately; cook the truffles for three-quarters of an hour in the pint of clear soup; thicken with a teaspoonful of browned flour and a tablespoonful of butter; then add the wine; arrange the quails' breasts nicely on a dish; sprinkle the truffles over them; then pour over the sauce.

To Roast Reed Birds

Some nice, fat reed birds,
Black pepper, butter and salt.

Rub them with butter, and sprinkle with black pepper. Have a good fire; put them in a pan with a little butter, and baste well for fifteen minutes. These little birds are so delicate that you can eat bones and all. They can be fried also in the following manner: Split them down the back; place each bird on pieces of buttered toast to catch the juices; sprinkle them with pepper, and have butter in the pan; baste well, and allow about twelve minutes, as they will cook quicker when split open.

To Roast Snipe and Woodcock

Some snipe or woodcock,
Some thin slices of pickled pork,
Butter, black pepper and salt.

First pluck them and take the skin off the heads and necks. Put the heads under the wings, pepper each one well, lay one thin slice of pickled pork across the breast bone of each bird and skewer it. Have a bright fire; put each bird over a slice of buttered toast, to catch the trail. Put a little butter in the pan to start the basting, and baste each bird well every five minutes, cook twenty minutes; sprinkle a little salt over each bird, and serve quickly on the pieces of toast they were cooked on; garnish with sprigs of parsley, and slices of lemon.

To Broil Venison Steaks

Some nicely cut venison steaks,
A few thin slices of lemon,
Some currant jelly, and sherry wine.

Have a good fire, pepper the steaks well, broil partly on one side, then on the other. Take them off, rub with butter, return to the gridiron, broil a few minutes longer, and put them on a hot dish. Melt some currant jelly, and while hot, add wine to the taste. Put a few small pieces of butter on each steak, then pour the wine and jelly over, which must be very hot. If wine and jelly are objected to, then broil as you would a beef steak. Arrange some thin slices of lemon and sprigs of parsley around the dish.

Mint Sauce

Two tablespoonfuls of fresh mint,
One teaspoonful of brown sugar,
Half a teacupful of vinegar,
Half a teacupful of water.

Put the vinegar, sugar and water in a gravy-boat. Chop the mint very fine and stir in. Let this stand for half an hour before using it. This quantity can be increased according to the number of guests to be served.

Brown Sauce for Meats

One pint of clear soup,
One teaspoonful of browned flour,
One dessertspoonful of butter,
Salt and cayenne pepper to the taste.

Put the soup into a saucepan with hot water underneath, with the salt and cayenne pepper. While it is boiling, rub the flour and butter together, and stir in the sauce until it thickens, then serve. A small wineglassful of sherry or Madeira wine can be added just before serving if preferred.

Sauce for Quenelles

Two cans of champignons,
One pint of cream,
A heaping tablespoonful of butter,
One tablespoonful of flour,
Nutmeg, salt and cayenne pepper to the taste.

Cut the champignons up in small pieces, and put them into a saucepan with their own liquor, to cook gently for half an hour. Stir in the cream, and while boiling, mix the butter and flour well together, and add to the champignons by degrees. Boil for five minutes, then season with the nutmeg, salt and cayenne pepper. Use two tablespoonfuls of this sauce for the quenelles, leaving out the champignons.

Truffle Sauce

One pound can of truffles,
One pint of clear soup,
One tablespoonful of butter,
One teaspoonful of white flour,
One teaspoonful of browned flour,
Two tablespoonfuls of sherry wine,
Salt and cayenne pepper to the taste.

Chop the truffles, and put them with their liquor into a saucepan with the clear soup. Boil steadily for half an hour. Rub the flour and butter together, stir in the truffles, and simmer until thick, then add the wine, salt and cayenne pepper. This sauce is delicious in an omelette, only don't put as much of the sauce as of the truffles. This is also delicious for meats and entrees.

Sauce à la Hollandaise for Fish

One pint of boiled milk,
Two tablespoonfuls of butter,
One tablespoonful of flour,
One tablespoonful of Madeira wine,
One tablespoonful of capers,
Salt and cayenne pepper, to the taste,
One egg.

Put the milk into a saucepan, and when it comes to a boil, stir in the well-beaten eggs, salt and cayenne pepper, also extract of celery, to the taste. Cream the butter and flour until perfectly smooth, and stir into the milk until it thickens. Have the capers in the sauce boat, and pour the sauce over them, and serve very hot.

Champignon Sauce

Two cans of champignons,
One quart of clear soup,
One dessertspoonful of flour,
One cooking-spoonful of butter,
Two tablespoonfuls of wine,
Salt and cayenne pepper to the taste.

Cut the champignons into small pieces, and cook in their own liquor for half an hour. Let the clear soup come to a boil, and add to the champignons, with the salt and

cayenne pepper. Rub the flour and butter, and stir in the champignons until quite thick, say the thickness of rich cream. Heat the wine and pour in just before serving.

Tartare Sauce for Fish

The yelks of two hard-boiled eggs,
The yelks of two raw eggs,
Eight tablespoonfuls of olive oil,
Three dessertspoonfuls of vinegar,
One teaspoonful of chopped onion,
One tablespoonful of capers,
Salt and cayenne pepper, to the taste.

Mash the hard-boiled eggs; add the raw eggs to them, and beat until perfectly smooth and light. Then beat in well, the oil and vinegar, in alternation. Add the onion and capers; lastly the salt and cayenne pepper. Serve cold in a sauce-boat.

Salad Dressing

The yelks of sixteen eggs,
Twenty tablespoonfuls of oil,
Fifteen tablespoonfuls of vinegar,
Nine tablespoonfuls of water,
Salt and cayenne pepper to the taste.

Beat the eggs, add the oil, vinegar and water in alternation, beating well all the time, then the salt and cayenne pepper; put this into a saucepan with boiling water underneath, and stir constantly and rapidly until the consistency of very thick custard; put it away to get perfectly cold. This will be sufficient for one large turkey. Always cut up as much celery as you have turkey, which must never be chopped, but cut in dice. The advantage of this dressing is, the proportions are so perfect that enough for six turkeys can be made in less than three-quarters of an hour. The water is put in to keep the vinegar from tasting too strong, or it would destroy the taste of the oil and make the salad too acid. I always use this dressing when making a large quantity of salad.

Sweetbread Salad

The yelks of two hard-boiled eggs,
The yelks of two raw eggs,
One teaspoonful of dry mustard,
Two cruets of the best oil,
One tablespoonful of vinegar,
Salt and cayenne pepper to the taste.

Mash the yelks of the eggs smoothly together, then sprinkle in the mustard, and beat in by degrees the oil and vinegar. Season to the taste, and beat hard for a few minutes. If it is too stiff, add the juice of one lemon. Have the sweetbreads well cooked and picked to pieces, taking off all of the skin. Put the dressing on in alternate layers with the sweetbreads, and garnish the dish with small heads of crisped lettuce.

Shrimp Salad

Two cans of shrimps,
Yelks of two hard boiled eggs,
Yelks of two raw eggs,
Twelve tablespoonfuls of oil,
Salt, cayenne pepper to taste.

Mix the eggs perfectly smooth, then beat in the oil slowly, alternating every third tablespoonful with half a teaspoonful of vinegar and three drops of lemon juice. When very light add the salt and cayenne pepper to the taste. Don't put this over the shrimps until they are to be served. In the winter, cut up as much celery as you have shrimps, and mix in. In the summer, put the shrimps in the center of the dish, pour the dressing over them, and put delicate pieces of lettuce around. Always put the dressing on the ice for a while before serving. If this quantity should not be enough, more oil, vinegar and lemon juice can be beaten in.

A Salad of Cabbage and Celery

One pint of cabbage,
One pint of celery,
One teacupful of vinegar,
A tablespoonful of butter,
A teaspoonful of mixed mustard,
A tablespoonful of rich cream,
Salt and cayenne pepper to taste,
Yelks of two eggs.

Beat the eggs, stir in the vinegar, mustard, melted butter, salt and cayenne pepper. Put all into a saucepan with boiling water underneath, and stir steadily until it thickens. When cold, add the cream. Cut the cabbage and celery in small pieces; mix well, and pour the dressing over.

Dressing for Cold Slaw

Yelks of two hard-boiled eggs,
Yelks of two raw eggs,
Five tablespoonfuls of oil,
Three dessertspoonfuls of vinegar,
Salt and cayenne pepper to the taste.

Shave the cabbage with a sharp knife until you have a quart. Put it in a dish and set it on the ice for an hour. Mash the hard-boiled eggs smoothly, then mix the raw ones with them. Beat the oil and vinegar in the eggs, alternately, and carefully, to prevent curdling. Lastly, add the salt and cayenne pepper. Have the dressing in a small bowl, and pour it over the cabbage as you serve it. The above quantity will be sufficient for six persons.

Mashed Potatoes

One quart of mashed potatoes,
Half a teacupful of cream,
One tablespoonful of butter,
Salt to the taste.

Boil them properly, then throw them into a colander and mash them well through it. After they are thoroughly mashed, put them into a saucepan with hot water underneath, and add the butter, cream and salt. Beat well for five or ten minutes and serve. If cream is not to be had, use milk and increase the quantity of butter. If preferred to be baked, put into a baking dish, and brown in the oven for about ten minutes.

A decorative serving dish intended for potatoes or rice. From Mrs. Mary F. Henderson, *Practical Cooking and Dinner Giving* (New York: Harper and Bros., 1877), 59, Special Collections, Michigan State University Libraries.

Saratoga Potatoes

Three large potatoes,
Half a pint of fresh lard,
A little salt.

Peel the potatoes, and cut them with a potato cutter into slices as thin as a wafer. Put them into a pan of ice-water for half an hour. Have the collander in a pan in the oven with the door open. Put a few slices at the time in the boiling lard, and when a delicate yellow, take them out, and put them in the collander to dry, sprinkling a little salt over them as you put them in. When all are fried, put them in a heated dish and serve. A frying basket made of fine wire is exceedingly nice for frying the potatoes in, as you can take them out of the lard without any trouble, by merely lifting the basket and pouring them into the collander to drain. The pan underneath the collander is intended to catch the grease.

Potatoes à la Lyonnaise

One pound of cold boiled potatoes,
Two teaspoonfuls of minced onion,
Two teaspoonfuls of chopped parsley,
One large cooking-spoonful of butter,
Salt and black pepper to the taste.

Slice the potatoes. Put the butter into a skillet; when hot, throw in the potatoes and onions, and fry until a light brown; then put in the chopped parsley, and when thoroughly mixed put into a heated napkin, which must be in a heated dish. Don't put the cover on the dish, simply close the napkin over the potatoes.

Shoe-Fly Potatoes

There is a machine that comes expressly for cutting shoe-fly potatoes. The potatoes are cut in strips like macaroni. Have the boiling lard in the skillet, put the potatoes in a frying basket, then put the basket into the hot lard, fry a nice brown and they will be done. Then sprinkle salt through them. Serve in a heated dish with the top off.

To Fry Tomatoes

Six large ripe tomatoes,
Half a tumblerful of cream,
Some brown sugar,
Salt and black pepper.

Slice the tomatoes half an inch thick, but don't peel them. Put a few slices at a time into a hot skillet with a cookingspoonful of butter. Fry a good brown; take them out carefully, place them in a dish which you must have over hot water; and over each layer, sprinkle about a dessertspoonful of sugar, a little salt and black pepper. When all are fried, pour the cream into the skillet and dredge in flour enough to make it as thick as a drawn butter; stir until smooth, and pour over the tomatoes. If cream is not convenient, they will be just as good without it.

To Fry Cabbage

Two quarts of cut up cabbage,
Two thick slices of pickled pork,
Salt and cayenne pepper to the taste.

Put the chopped cabbage with the pork into a skillet, and cover with hot water. Keep it steadily frying for two hours, add the salt and cayenne pepper, and fry half an hour longer. Should the water boil down, add a little more, but not during the last half hour. Have a heated dish ready, put the pork in the center, and the cabbage around it. The cabbage must be freshly cut.

How to Cook Beets

Some sugar beets,
Butter, salt and pepper.

Wash the beets, but don't trim the roots too close, or they will bleed, and lose their sweetness. If they are young, cook three hours; if old, cook four hours. When done, slice them, put into a hot dish; add butter, pepper and salt. If any should be left, pour vinegar over them, and they will be nice the next day.

Asparagus

Scrape the outside of the stalks, and cut off about an inch of the end. Tie them evenly in bundles, keeping the heads one way. Put them in well salted boiling water, and cook for a half an hour, or three quarters, according to the size of the stalks. Drain; have some nicely cut pieces of buttered toast at the bottom of a heated dish; lay the stalks in regularly, and pour over them some melted butter, or asparagus sauce.

Asparagus Sauce

One pint of water the asparagus has cooked in,
One cookingspoonful of butter,
One dessertspoonful of flour,
Salt and black pepper to taste,
Yelk of one egg.

Take the pint of water the asparagus was cooked in, put into a saucepan with hot water underneath; when it comes to a boil, add the egg, salt and pepper. Rub the butter and flour well together, and stir in until the sauce is the consistency of boiled custard. When putting in the egg first, stir in it a tablespoonful of the boiling asparagus water, then put in the saucepan. This precaution is to keep it from curdling.

Cauliflower Served with Fried Chicken

One quart of sweet cream,
One dessertspoonful of butter,
One dessertspoonful of flour,
Salt to the taste.

Put the cream into a saucepan with hot water underneath; cream the butter and flour, and when the cream boils, stir in until it thickens, then add the salt. Put in a teaspoonful of chopped parsley just before taking it off the fire. Place the heads of cauliflower in the center of the dish, and pour some of the dressing over them. Arrange the pieces of fried chicken around them, pour the rest of the dressing over, and serve very hot.

Green Peas

Gather them just before being cooked; shell and put them on in boiling water, just enough to keep them well covered, and when fresh, they will only take twenty minutes boiling. If young and tender, wash some of the pods and put them with the peas, always keeping the water a little above them. Do not let them boil too hard, or they will be mushy. If the water is allowed to boil down, they will be tough. If old, they will require longer cooking than twenty minutes. Put in the water, when putting the peas to cook, about a teaspoonful of salt. Some persons like a little sugar; in that case a dessertspoonful of granulated sugar can be put into a quart of peas.

To Cook Marrowfat Peas

Three pints of hulled peas,
Hot water enough to cover them,
A teaspoonful of salt,

These peas are later, somewhat richer in flavor, but not quite so delicate as the earlier ones. Put the peas into a saucepan, with the salt and hot water, and keep them covered while they are cooking. If very young, let them boil for twenty minutes. Throw off that water, and cover them with fresh hot water, giving them ten minutes

more boiling. Now mix a teaspoonful of flour with a dessertspoonful of butter, and stir in until the water thickens, then serve. Don't allow them to boil too hard, or they will be mushy.

To Boil Green Corn

Trim off the husks and silk; put the corn into a pot of boiling water, with a dessertspoonful of salt, and cook twenty minutes.

Another way: Leave on the silk and husks; put into a pot of boiling water, and a dessertspoonful of salt, and boil twenty-five minutes; and take off the husks and silk as quickly as possible and serve.

Corn Pudding

Twelve ears of corn,
Half a pint of sweet milk,
Half a pound of butter,
A teaspoonful of flour,
Salt and black pepper to the taste,
Two eggs.

Grate the corn; then scrape the cob so as to get out the milk; then add the sweet milk to it, salt, pepper, melted butter and flour, lastly, stir in slowly the well-beaten eggs. Bake in a slow oven one hour.

Egg-Plant Pudding

Two egg-plants,
Yelks of six hard-boiled eggs,
A quarter of a pound of butter,
A teaspoonful of chopped onion,
A teaspoonful of sweet marjoram,
Three teaspoonfuls of chopped parsley,
Salt and cayenne pepper to the taste,
One raw egg.

Split the egg-plants and soak them in cold salt and water for two hours. Parboil them, peel and press out all the water. Chop very fine, mash the yelks of the hard-boiled eggs very smooth, and mix with the above. Add the onion, parsley and sweet marjoram, rubbed and sifted. Beat the raw egg and mix well, adding lastly, the butter melted, salt and cayenne pepper. Put into a baking-dish with some grated cracker on top, and bake slowly for half an hour.

Lima or Butter Beans

Shell them and lay them in cold water for an hour (or a little longer, but not less) before cooking, as this makes them more delicate. When ready for cooking, put them into a saucepan with boiling water enough to cover them, and a little salt. Let them boil steadily for an hour, and if young, they will be done and tender; if old, they will take half an hour longer. When done, pour off nearly all the water, rub a teaspoonful of butter with a teaspoonful of flour; let it simmer for ten minutes, add salt and black pepper to the taste and serve.

To Boil Rice

One teacupful of rice,
Four teacupfuls of water,
One teaspoonful of salt.

Pick and wash the rice, rubbing it hard with the hands, and changing the water until it ceases to be milky. Put it in the saucepan with the salt, and pour over it the four teacupfuls of clear water. Let it boil steadily for fifteen minutes. Strain through a colander, return to the saucepan, and, with the top off, let it stand on the back of the range for half an hour to dry.

To Stew Onions with Cream

Six Spanish onions,
Three teaspoonfuls of butter,
One dessertspoonful of flour,
Half a pint of cream,
Salt and black pepper to the taste.

Boil the onions steadily, but not too rapidly, for two hours and a half, changing the water three times. Drain, put them into a saucepan with the cream, and let them simmer very gently. Rub the flour and butter, stir in the onions, until the cream is quite thick; add salt and black pepper, and serve immediately. Put the onions in the dish first, and pour the sauce over them.

Parsnip Fritters

Six good sized parsnips,
One teaspoonful of flour,
One tablespoonful of butter,
One egg.

Boil the parsnips for an hour and a half; skin and mash very fine, add the flour, the well beaten egg, and salt to the taste; shape into small round cakes, sprinkling a pinch of sugar over each cake. Put some lard and butter into a hot skillet, put in the cakes, and when nicely fried on each side, serve.

To Bake Pumpkins

Three pints of stewed pumpkin,
One teacupful of cream,
One tablespoonful of cornstarch,
Salt to the taste.

Drain the pumpkin through a sieve, and add to it the cream, cornstarch and salt. Put into a baking dish and bake slowly for three-quarters of an hour. In place of the cream and cornstarch a coffeecupful of mashed sweet potatoes, mixed well with the pumpkin, and baked half an hour, is very nice.

Hominy Fritters

Two teacupfuls of boiled hominy,
One teacupful of sweet milk,
Four tablespoonfuls of flour,
Half a teaspoonful of baking powder,
Salt to the taste,
One egg.

The hominy must be well boiled and cold; mash well with a spoon; stir in the flour and milk alternately, with the well beaten yelk of the egg, then put in salt to the taste; sprinkle the baking powder lightly through, lastly the white of the egg beaten to a froth; fry in boiling lard, as you would fritters.

To Boil Hominy

One quart of hominy,
Two quarts of water,
One teaspoonful of salt.

Wash well in two or three waters, rubbing the grains well with the hands, so as to whiten them. Soak over night, and boil in the same water, from four to six hours, according to the size of the grains. Put the salt in the water in the morning, and add boiling water continually, so as to keep it an inch above the hominy while boiling. After boiling the time required, press a grain with the fingers, and if it is soft it is done. Drain through a colander, and keep where it will not get musty. This quantity will do for two or three times. When heating it over, put it in a saucepan with a little milk, and after it has simmered about twenty minutes, rub a little butter and flour together, which must be according to the quantity of milk, and stir in until it thickens.

To Fry Apples

Two pints of apples,
One teacupful of brown sugar,
Half a teacupful of butter.

Peel and seed the apples, and slice as you would for preserves. Have the skillet hot; put in a dessertspoonful of lard, and when melted add one-half of the butter. Now put in one-half of the apples; in a few minutes turn, and when nearly done, put in one-half of the sugar. When they look clear and like a peach preserve, take off, and put in a dish over hot water. Do the rest the same way. Turn them carefully, but do not stir them.

Tapioca and Apples

Take a pint of tapioca, pour some hot water over it, and continue to add more hot water to it until it swells; peel and core some juicy apples, fill each hole with granulated sugar, and sprinkle sugar freely over the apples. When the tapioca is perfectly soft, put in extract of lemon and sugar to the taste, with a little salt. Pour it over the apples and bake slowly for two hours. The tapioca should be put to soak before breakfast. Serve with cream.

Pastry

One pound of the best flour,
Three-quarters of a pound of butter,
A wine glass of ice water,
The whites of two eggs.

Take three-quarters of a pound of the flour and put in a bowl; put the other quarter of a pound in a plate. Beat the whites of the eggs very light, and mix in the flour, with the wine glass of ice water, so as to make a stiff dough; beat well with a rolling pin for ten minutes; roll, adding the butter in four rollings, and the quarter of a pound of flour. Put the pastry on the ice for two hours. This quantity will make three large pies.

Washington Pie

One cup of granulated sugar,
Half a cup of butter,
Half a cup of milk,
One egg,
Two cups of flour,
One teaspoonful of cream of tartar,
Half a teaspoonful of soda.

Cream the sugar and butter, add the flour, milk, and well beaten egg, cream of tartar and soda; flavor delicately with vanilla. Put in two round tins, about an inch deep, and bake in a moderately quick oven.

Cream for Washington Pie

One tablespoonful of flour or cornstarch,
One-third of a cup of granulated sugar,
One cup of milk,
One egg.

Put the milk on to boil, add the sugar, egg and corn starch; stir until it thickens, and flavor with vanilla. Cut the cake in two, and when the cream is cold, not stiff, spread it on one-half of the cake; put back the other half, making two layers for each cake. A little grated cocoanut can be sprinkled over the cream before putting the cake on it. This must be served cold.

Lemon Pies

Two teacupfuls of granulated sugar,
One tablespoonful of butter,
One teacupful of cream,
One tablespoonful of cornstarch,
Juice and grated rind of three lemons,
Six eggs.

Beat the eggs separately, then together; add the sugar, butter, cream, juice and grated rind of the lemons; lastly, the cornstarch. Stir over the fire until it thickens, and when perfectly cold, pour into pie plates lined with pastry.

Orange Pie

Three-quarters of a cupful of sugar,
Two tablespoonfuls and a half of butter,
Juice and grated rind of one orange,
One dessertspoonful of corn starch,
Three eggs.

Beat the sugar and butter, then the well-beaten yelks of the eggs, the juice and grated rind of the orange, nutmeg and cornstarch. Lastly, the whites of the eggs beaten to a stiff froth. Put into a saucepan with hot water underneath, and stir until thick and perfectly smooth. Line the plates with pastry, and when cool pour into the plates and bake quickly.

Bread Fritters

One quart of sweet milk,
Two teacupfuls of bread crumbs,
One teaspoonful of soda,
Two teaspoonfuls of cream of tartar,
Nutmeg and salt to the taste,
Two tablespoonfuls of granulated sugar,
Two eggs.

Boil the milk, and soak the bread crumbs in it for ten minutes, in a covered bowl. Beat until smooth; add the well-beaten yelks of the eggs, then the salt, nutmeg, soda, and cream of tartar dissolved in a little hot water. Lastly the whites of the eggs, beaten to a stiff froth. Serve with butter and sugar, or maple molasses.

A mold for blanc-mange, a popular nineteenth-century custard. From Mrs. Mary F. Henderson, *Practical Cooking and Dinner Giving* (New York: Harper and Bros., 1877), 59, Special Collections, Michigan State University Libraries.

Blanc Mange

Three pints of new milk,
One ounce of gelatine,
Sugar and vanilla to taste.

Put one quart of milk in the saucepan with the gelatine, and boil until it is thoroughly dissolved; add the other pint with the sugar, and let it boil once more, strain and set it aside to cool. When it begins to congeal, flavor with vanilla to the taste, and then mold. Any other extract that may be preferred can be used.

Irish Potato Pudding

One pint of mashed potato,
One tablespoonful of butter,
One pint of cream,
Granulated sugar to the taste,
Juice and rind of one lemon,
Four eggs.

Rub the potato through a sieve before measuring; stir in the cream and well beaten yellows of the eggs, with the melted butter, sugar, rind and juice of the lemon. Mix thoroughly, and add the well beaten whites. Bake half an hour in a pudding dish. Serve with a hot or cold sauce. This can also be baked in pastry.

Sweet Potato Pie

Two pounds of boiled, mashed sweet potatoes,
One pound of sugar, one pound of butter,
Two tablespoonfuls of wine, two of brandy,
One tablespoonful of rose water,
One pint of rich, sweet cream.

Cream the butter and sugar together. Boil and mash the sweet potatoes; beat them by degrees into the sugar and butter; add five well beaten eggs; then the wine, brandy and rose water mixed; lastly the cream. Line your pie plates with some nice well-made pastry; fill them with the potato, and bake until a nice brown.

Brown Betty

Two cupfuls of chopped apples,
One cupful of bread crumbs,
Half a cupful of brown sugar,
One teaspoonful of ground cinnamon,
Two tablespoonfuls of butter.

Have a deep dish; first put in a layer of chopped apples, tart ones; then some of the brown sugar, cinnamon and bread crumbs, and small pieces of butter; then another layer of apples, and so on until the dish is full, having the last layer, of bread crumbs, and small pieces of butter. Steam three-quarters of an hour, by putting the dish in a pan of hot water and a cover over it; then uncover and bake until well browned. Eat either with sugar and cream, or a hot sauce. Use a coffeecup for measuring.

Baked Indian Pudding

Two coffeecupfuls of Indian meal,
One coffeecupful of molasses,
A large cooking-spoonful of butter,
Milk enough for a batter.

Scald one cupful of the meal with a little hot water, then add the other cupful not scalded, the molasses and butter. Lastly, thin with the milk, and bake three hours in a slow oven.

Suet Pudding

One teacupful of chopped suet,
One teacupful of molasses,
One teacupful of sweet milk,
Three teacupfuls and a half of flour,
One teaspoonful of soda,
Two teaspoonfuls of cream of tartar,
Half a teaspoonful of ground cloves,
One teacupful of raisins and currants mixed.

Chop the suet as fine as possible, and mix well with the milk and molasses, then sift in the flour and cloves. Dredge the currants and raisins with flour, and add. Lastly, the cream of tartar and soda, mixed with a little milk. Steam three hours, and serve with a hot sauce. Butter can be used instead of suet; in that case, put in two-thirds of a teacupful.

Yankee Cake Pudding

One pint of flour,
One coffeecupful of sweet milk,
Two teacupfuls of granulated sugar,
One teaspoonful of cream of tartar,
Half a teaspoonful of soda,
One large cooking-spoonful of butter,
One egg.

Beat the butter and sugar together until very light; then add the flour and milk in alternation, with the extract of lemon or vanilla to the taste. Lastly, mix the cream of tartar and soda in a tablespoonful of milk, and stir in the mixture; bake in a slow oven. Serve with a hot or cold sauce.

Cocoanut Pudding

One teacupful of desiccated cocoanut,
One quart of sweet milk,
Two tablespoonfuls of cornstarch,
One tablespoonful of butter,
Sugar and nutmeg to the taste,
Three eggs.

Boil one pint of the milk, and soak the cocoanut in it for half an hour. Put it into a saucepan, and as soon as it boils, add the remainder of the milk, yelks of the eggs, sugar, nutmeg; lastly, the cornstarch. Stir until it thickens, then put into a pudding dish, and bake quickly for fifteen minutes. Beat the whites of the eggs until stiff, add a tablespoonful of granulated sugar, cover the top of the pudding with it, and brown nicely.

Pumpkin Pudding

Half a pound of stewed pumpkin,
A quarter of a pound of butter,
A quarter of a pound of sugar,
Half a pint of sweet milk,
One wineglassful of wine,
Nutmeg or cinnamon to the taste,
Three eggs.

Mix the milk and pumpkin, add the sugar, well-beaten eggs and melted butter. Put into a saucepan with hot water underneath, and stir until it thickens. When cool add the wine, and put into plates lined with pastry. Bake in a quick oven.

Chocolate Pudding

Twelve tablespoonfuls of grated bread crumbs,
Six tablespoonfuls of grated vanilla chocolate,
One cookingspoonful of butter,
One quart of sweet milk,
Yelks of six eggs.

Boil the milk and sweeten to the taste with granulated sugar, then add the butter to it while boiling; cool, and add the well beaten yelks of the eggs, and grated chocolate. Bake for half an hour. Beat the whites of the eggs to a stiff froth, adding, while beating, two tablespoonfuls of pulverized sugar, then spread evenly over the pudding and brown nicely. Eat with cream.

Pudding Sauce

One cupful of boiling water,
Half a cupful of butter,
Half a cupful of granulated sugar,
Two wineglassfuls of Madeira wine,
One teaspoonful of cornstarch,
Nutmeg to the taste.

Cream the butter and sugar; stir in the hot water, then the nutmeg; lastly the corn starch. Put into a saucepan with hot water underneath, and stir until it thickens. Just before taking off the fire, add the wine. This will make sauce enough for a medium-size pudding, say for a family of six. Should the pudding be a large one, then the proportions must be doubled. Use a coffeecup for measuring.

Hard Sauce for Pudding

Two cupfuls of powdered sugar,
Half a cupful of butter,
Juice and grated rind of one lemon,
A teaspoonful of grated nutmeg.

Cream the butter, and beat in the sugar, lemon juice, grated rind and nutmeg, for about ten minutes. A wine-glass of sherry wine might be added. Pile lightly on a pretty dish and set it away to cool.

Charlotte Russe

Half a pint of sweet milk,
A quarter of a pound of granulated sugar,
Two pints and a half of rich cream,
One teacupful of boiling water,
Half a box of Cox's gelatine,
Half of a vanilla bean,
Yelks of two eggs.

Put the milk on to boil, beat the eggs and stir in; add the sugar and vanilla bean, split and cut in small pieces, and boil five minutes. Pour the boiling water over the

gelatine, and let it boil up once; sweeten the cream to the taste, beat the cream to a stiff froth, and when the custard is cool, not cold, mix all together. Line the molds with sponge cake, and pour the mixture in. Keep in a cool place. Before molding take out the pieces of vanilla bean.

Ice Cream

Half a box of Cox's gelatine,
A quarter of a pound of granulated sugar,
Four pints of rich cream,
One pint of boiling water,
Half of a vanilla bean.

Split the vanilla bean, cut into small pieces, and put into a saucepan with the gelatine, sugar, and boiling water. Let this boil until the gelatine is dissolved. Strain, and let it get cool, but not cold. Take out the pieces of bean, scrape the inside into the gelatine, and stir in the cream. If not sweet enough, add sugar to the taste. Put into a freezer, and stir constantly until well frozen.

Macaroon Ice Cream

One gallon of rich cream,
One dozen macaroons,
Three large oranges,
One teaspoonful of extract of vanilla.

Sweeten the cream to the taste, put it into the freezer, and when partially frozen, roll the macaroons very fine and stir in; grate the rind of one of the oranges and add, with the juice of the three; then the vanilla. Freeze hard; pack the freezer well with ice broken in small pieces, and a quantity of salt, which will keep the cream until wanted to serve.

Frozen Sherbet

Three pints of clear water,
One pound and a half of sugar,
The whites of two eggs,
The juice of four lemons.

Take six lumps of sugar, and rub them on the rinds of the lemons until the sugar is perfectly yellow. This is done to get the flavor of the rind. Put them in the water with the rest of the sugar. While it is dissolving squeeze, strain the juice, and stir it in the water. Put all into a freezer, and when half frozen, add the well-beaten whites of the eggs, and finish freezing. Pack well with salt, and ice to keep from melting.

Jelly

Two boxes of Cox's gelatine,
Three pints of clear water,
One pint and a half of granulated sugar,
One teacupful of brandy or whisky,
One quart of sherry wine,
Juice of six lemons and rinds of three,
Two tablespoonfuls of stick cinnamon,

Six whole cloves,
Eighteen raisins,
Whites of three eggs.

Put the water on to boil, add the gelatine, sugar, juice of lemons, and thinly cut rinds; also the cloves, cinnamon and well beaten whites of the eggs and raisins. Boil until the whites gather to one side, then pour in the wine and brandy. Strain through a bag and mold. Be careful not to stir the jelly when taking it up to pour through the bag.

Orange Jelly

Twelve large oranges,
One pound of granulated sugar,
Two ounces of isinglass,
A teacupful of hot water,
The whites of two eggs.

Cut the oranges in pieces and squeeze out all the juice. If this should not make a pint, squeeze more until you get a pint cup full. Put in the sugar, and when it is dissolved put it on the fire. Dissolve the isinglass in the hot water and stir into the juice; then add the well beaten whites of the eggs. Boil steadily for twenty minutes; strain slowly through a bag and mold. To be eaten with cream.

Crème Diplomate

One pint of whipped cream,
Half an ounce of gelatine,
One teacupful of candied cherries,
Vanilla and sugar to the taste.

Dissolve the gelatine in a little water, and stir in the whipped cream. Sweeten and flavor to the taste, and beat well. Then add sherry wine to the taste, and the candied cherries. Put into a mold, and leave it in a cool place until it gets stiff.

Chocolate Custard

A quarter of a pound of vanilla chocolate,
Half a pound of granulated sugar,
Two quarts of sweet milk,
Yelks of twelve eggs,
Whites of five eggs.

Grate the chocolate and put it into the milk. When near a boil stir in the well-beaten yelks of the twelve eggs, the well-beaten whites of five, and sugar. Boil for about five minutes, stirring well to keep from curdling. Serve cold.

Cookies

One teacupful of butter,
Three teacupfuls of granulated sugar,
One teaspoonful of soda,
One grated nutmeg,
Four eggs.

Beat the eggs very light, then beat with the sugar; add the nutmeg and soda, mixed with a teaspoonful of sour cream. Then work in flour until stiff enough to roll. Roll very thin; cut and bake in a quick oven. This will make a large number if rolled thin, as directed, and are delicious.

Doughnuts

Two pounds of flour,
One pound of sugar,
One pint of milk,
One tablespoonful of rosewater,
One teaspoonful of soda,
One nutmeg,
Four eggs.

Cut the butter into the flour, and mix well with the hands. Add the sugar, rosewater, milk and soda. Lastly, the well-beaten eggs. Fry a nice brown in boiling lard. Sugar each doughnut well while hot.

Crullers

Two pounds of flour,
Half a pound of butter,
Three quarters of a pound of sugar,
A teaspoonful of powdered cinnamon,
Nutmeg to the taste,
Six eggs.

Cream the butter and flour, add the sugar and well-beaten yelks with the cinnamon and nutmeg. Beat the whites very light and stir in slowly. Roll out, cut into strips, twist into shape and fry in boiling lard a light brown.

Horse Manders

One pound of flour,
One pound of granulated sugar,
Half a pound of butter,
Cinnamon and mace to the taste,
Five eggs.

Wash the butter well in a little cold water, or rose-water. Beat it to a cream, add the sugar, then the eggs, leaving out the whites of two. Throw all into the flour, and mix lightly. Take out small pieces, roll in sugar as for jumbles, and bake in a moderate oven.

Cinnamon Jumbles

One pound and a half of flour,
One pound of butter,
One pound of sugar,
Two tablespoonfuls of ground cinnamon,
Three eggs.

Rub the flour and butter together, add the sugar and eggs beaten well together, lastly the cinnamon. Roll, cut, and bake in a quick oven. Should the above quantity of flour not be sufficient to make the dough stiff enough to roll well, add more.

Ginger Cake

Three cupfuls and a half of flour,
Two cupfuls of brown sugar,
One cupful of molasses,
One cupful of butter,
Three teaspoonfuls of ground ginger,
One pint of milk,
The yellows of three eggs,
One teaspoonful of baking powder.

Beat the sugar and eggs together, add the other ingredients and the milk; lastly, the baking powder. Bake quickly.

White Cake

Two cupfuls of flour,
One cupful and a half of sugar,
Half a cupful of sweet milk,
Half a cupful of butter,
Half a teaspoonful of soda,
Half a teaspoonful of cream of tartar,
Flavor with vanilla or lemon to the taste,
The whites of five eggs.

Cream the butter and sugar, add the well-beaten eggs; dissolve the soda and cream of tartar in a little milk, and stir in, while adding the flour; then the milk, and lastly the flavoring. Bake immediately, in a moderately warm oven. Use a coffee cup in measuring.

Spice Cake

One pound of flour,
One pound of brown sugar,
One tablespoonful of ground cinnamon,
One tablespoonful of ground cloves,
One tablespoonful of ground allspice,
One wineglassful of brandy or sherry,
One teacupful of sour cream,
One teaspoonful of soda,
Half a pound of butter,
One grated nutmeg,
Six eggs.

Cream the butter and flour, add the yelks of the eggs, well beaten; sugar, spices and brandy. Mix the soda with the cream, and stir in. Lastly beat the whites of the eggs to a froth and mix in very slowly. Bake slowly for an hour and a quarter. This is delicious served hot as a pudding with a hot sauce.

A Cheap Sponge Cake

Two cupfuls of flour,
One cupful of pulverized sugar,
A tablespoonful of butter,
One cupful of sweet milk,
One teaspoonful of cream of tartar,
Half a teaspoonful of soda,
Flavoring to the taste,
One egg.

Cream the butter and flour, add the sugar and milk alternately, then the well-beaten yelk of the egg. Sift in the soda and the cream of tartar and flavor to the taste. Lastly, beat the white of the egg very light, and stir in gradually. Bake in square tins twenty minutes. Measure with a coffee cup.

Chocolate Fruit Cake

A quarter of a pound of Maillard's chocolate,
One pound of flour,
One pound of sugar,
Half a pound of butter,
One teacupful of sour milk,

One teaspoonful of soda,

Half a pound of seeded raisins,

Half a pound of dried currants,

Two teaspoonfuls of cream of tartar,

Half a teaspoonful of vanilla,

Six eggs.

Beat the eggs separately, then together, and then with the sugar. Sift the flour and cream of tartar twice together, cream with the butter, and mix well with the eggs. Beat the soda in the milk. Pour enough boiling water on the chocolate to dissolve it, and add to the above. Seed the raisins, wash, pick and dry the currants, dredge well with flour and stir lightly into the cake. Grease a cake-mold well, pour in, and bake slowly until thoroughly done.

Preserves, Syrups, Cordials and Candies

Cherry Preserves

Twelve pounds of stoned cherries,

Twelve pounds of granulated sugar.

Stone the cherries, and save the juice that escapes while stoning them. Pour this on the sugar, and when dissolved, put it on the fire. After it has boiled about fifteen minutes, put in the fruit, and boil steadily one hour. Seal in glass jars.

Citron or Watermellon Preserve

One pound of pared watermellon rind,

One pound of granulated sugar,

The thinly cut rind of one lemon,

Half a teaspoonful of ground ginger.

The rind of the mellon must be carefully pared and cut in pieces before weighing. Cut in any shape you choose. Soak the pieces a day and night in a little weak alum and salt water. Rinse and boil in clear water until you can pierce them with a fork. Make a syrup of the sugar, adding enough vinegar to keep from turning to sugar, and boil the lemon rind in it (cut thin) and ginger until clear. Pour over the fruit while hot. These proportions can be increased as required.

Red Raspberry Jam

Eight pints of red raspberries,

Two pints of currant juice.

Mash the raspberries well, and mix with the currant juice. Weigh, and add an equal quantity of granulated sugar. Boil slowly until quite thick, then seal in glass jars. Old currant jelly can be used, if the juice cannot be had. In that case only put in sugar in proportion to the berries.

To Brandy Greengages

Take the quantity of greengages you wish to brandy; wipe them dry and throw them into boiling water, and boil only until they are tender, but don't let them burst open. Spread them on dishes to cool, and when cold put them into jars, and fill the jars with equal portions of syrup, and white brandy. The syrup should be made rich and strong, as the gages are very acid. The proportions for a rich syrup are, to every pint of granulated sugar, put in half a pint of water. Boil slowly, and skim carefully until it is thick and clear. The gages must be sealed tightly.

Tomato Figs

One peck of tomatoes,
Six pounds of brown sugar.

Scald the tomatoes, remove the skin in the usual way, and weigh them. Put them in a kettle with the sugar, and boil them until the sugar penetrates, and they are clarified. Take them out, spread them on dishes, flatten, and dry them in the sun. Sprinkle small quantities of syrup occasionally over them until dried. Then pack them in boxes in layers, sprinkling each layer with powdered white sugar. They will keep well from year to year, and retain surprisingly their flavor, which is nearly as good as the best quality of figs. The pear shaped or single tomato answers the purpose best.

Peach Marmalade

Ten pounds of soft yellow peaches,
Six pounds of brown sugar.

Get the full ripe, open stone, yellow peach. Peel, take out the stone and weigh. Then chop very fine, and mix the sugar thoroughly with them. Put into a preserving kettle, let them simmer steadily but not too rapidly, for two hours, stirring constantly, to keep them from burning. Put into glass jars, and when cooled, cover with paper saturated with brandy, and seal with flour paste.

Orange Marmalade

As many oranges as are to be preserved,
Granulated sugar according to the quantity of fruit.

Remove the rind and seeds from the oranges. Cut the rind of one half in very fine strips, and parboil in water until enough of the bitter has been removed, and sufficient taste remains to flavor the pulp nicely. Cut up the pulp as fine as possible and mix with the rind. Add to every pound of the fruit, one pound of granulated sugar. Put into a preserving kettle and stir slowly all the time it is boiling. When it is a clear golden color it is done. This is delicious with ice cream, plain cream, or on pastry puffs.

Apple Butter

Take as much new sweet cider as you wish to use, fresh from the press. Boil it down to one half the original quantity. Have ready some fine juicy apples, pared, cored and quartered. Put as many in the kettle as can be kept moist by the cider. Stew until the consistency of soft marmalade and a dark brown color, stirring frequently. It is quite an improvement to have one fourth as many quinces as apples. If well boiled, it will keep a year.

Egg Nogg

Yelks of two dozen eggs,
Three quarts of rich cream,
One tumblerful of brandy and whisky, mixed,
One tumblerful of sherry wine,
Sugar and nutmeg to the taste.

Beat the eggs and sugar together, and stir in the brandy and whisky to cook the eggs. Then add the sherry wine and nutmeg. Beat the cream very light, and stir gradually in the eggs.

Peach Cordial

Three dozen yellow peaches,
One gallon of peach brandy,
One pound and three quarters of loaf sugar.

Peel and cut the peaches in half; crack the stones, and take out enough of the kernels to make a half a tumblerful, and put all into a stone jar.[4] Pour about a teacupful of water over the sugar, and let it boil until a rich syrup, skimming carefully while it is boiling. Mix it with the brandy and pour over the fruit. Let this stand for six weeks, then strain and bottle.

Blackberry Cordial

Two quarts of blackberry juice,
One pound of granulated sugar,
Half an ounce of grated nutmeg,
Half an ounce of ground cinnamon,
A quarter of an ounce of ground allspice,
One pint of the best brandy.

Prepare the blackberries as you would currants, by putting them into a stone jar, and keeping it in boiling water until the quantity of juice required is extracted from them. Put in the sugar, tie the spices in a muslin bag, and boil all for one hour. Strain through a flannel bag; add the brandy, and cork tightly.

Whisky Punch for Bottling

One gallon of whisky,
One quart of Jamaica rum,
Three pints of clear water,
Ten lemons.

Squeeze the lemons, strain and stir the juice in the water; add the rum and whisky, and sweeten to the taste. Let it simmer slowly for twenty minutes, cover until cold, then bottle. Drink either cold or hot, and add water if too strong. Use Bourbon whisky.

Currant Wine

One gallon of currant juice,
Two pounds of granulated sugar,
One quart of clear water,
One pint of Jamaica rum.

Put the juice, sugar and water, into a preserving kettle; let it boil for five minutes, taking care to skim it well while boiling. Take it off and pour into a stone jar to stand for a week. If necessary, skim again, then add the rum.

Blackberry Wine

Fifteen gallons of blackberries,
Five gallons of water.

Mash the berries, but do not bruise the seed; allow them to stand twenty-four hours, strain and add three pounds of the best white sugar to each gallon of juice. When the sugar is thoroughly dissolved, put all into a cask with the water. Put a piece of muslin over the hole, and allow it to stand until fermentation ceases, after which cork tightly or bottle.

Taffy

Two cupfuls of brown sugar,
One-half a pound of butter,
One teaspoonful of extract of vanilla.

Put the above ingredients into a saucepan, melt together and stir over a bright fire for twelve minutes; add the vanilla and cook three minutes longer. Grease a marble slab, pour on it the mixture, and when cool enough, cut in small squares, and before it is perfectly cold, grease a knife and loosen it from the marble to keep it from sticking.

Caramels

One fourth of a cupful of chocolate,
One cupful and a half of brown sugar,
A quarter of a pound of butter,
One cupful of sweet milk.

Mix the sugar and butter well together, then add the sweet milk and chocolate. Stir until thoroughly dissolved, then boil half an hour, and just before it is ready to be taken off the fire, flavor to the taste with the extract of vanilla. Pour into pans, and when nearly cool take a sharp knife and cut it in squares. Measure with a coffee cup.

Chocolate Caramels

One quarter of a pound of chocolate,
One pound and a half of brown sugar,
One teacupful of cream,
Extract of vanilla to the taste.

Grate the chocolate; scald the cream and pour it over the chocolate, stirring until smooth. Then add the vanilla, put into a saucepan and cook until it thickens. Grease a pan, pour in the mixture, and when cool cut in squares with a greased knife. Use Baker's chocolate.

Philadelphia Walnut Candy

One quart of New Orleans molasses,
One pint of walnut meats,
One tablespoonful of butter,
One tablespoonful of soda.

Boil the molasses until a nice candy is made from it, and when done, stir in the soda, butter and walnut meats. Beat hard until it gets light; then pour into buttered pans.

Pickles and Catsups

To Prepare Vinegar for Cucumber Pickles

Two gallons of the best cider vinegar,
Half a pint of black mustard seed,
Half a pint of white mustard seed,
One teacupful of horseradish,
Eight medium sized onions,
Two pounds of brown sugar,
Two ounces of celery seed,
Three ounces of black pepper grains,
Three ounces of whole allspice,
Two ounces of stick cinnamon.

Pound the allspice, cinnamon and pepper grains together until well broken up. Scrape and cut the horseradish into thin pieces; peel and quarter the onions, and with the spices, put into the vinegar to boil until it tastes well of the spices. Put the pickles into stone jars, with the spices sprinkled through, and a teaspoonful of alum in each jar. Pour the vinegar on while hot, and cover closely. This will be sufficient for four hundred small cucumbers.

To Make Yellow Pickle

One pound of sliced ginger,
One pound of scraped horseradish,
One pound of white mustard seed,
A quarter of a pound of celery seed,
One ounce of ground mace,
One ounce of grated nutmeg,
One ounce of white pepper grains,
Three gallons of strong cider vinegar,
Half a pound of turmeric.

Put all of the articles intended for the yellow pickle into a stone jar, pour on them boiling salt and water, and let them stand forty-eight hours. Then press out the water and lay them on a table covered with a soft cloth in the full sunshine. When dried, put them into stone jars with cold vinegar and a little turmeric in it; let them stand about twelve days, draw off the water, and put them into clean jars and cover with vinegar prepared in the following manner: Put the above spices, horseradish, turmeric, etc., with the three gallons of vinegar into a brass kettle, boil until the vinegar tastes strongly of the ingredients, let it get cold, then pour over the pickles.

Rough and Ready Pickle

Six dozen cucumbers,
Half a peck of green tomatoes,
One dozen green bull nose peppers,
One dozen white onions,
Half a teacupful of ground black pepper,
Half a teacupful of ground cloves and allspice, mixed,
Half a pound of white mustard seed,
Two ounces of celery seed.

Peel and slice the cucumbers, onions, tomatoes and peppers. Salt them separately and let them stand over night. The next morning press them dry and chop very fine. Then add the spices, ground pepper, celery seed, and to every gallon of mixture put a pound of brown sugar. Cover with good vinegar, stir well and boil five minutes. Put in jars and cover tightly.

Sweet Cantelope Pickle

One gallon of good cider vinegar,
Five pounds of white sugar,
Half an ounce of ground mace,
Two ounces of ground cloves,
Two ounces of ground cinnamon,
Two ounces of ground allspice,
The peelings of three oranges.

Take cantelopes that are just beginning to ripen; remove the rinds, and throw away the seeds. Cut the rinds into narrow slices and put them into stone jars. Fill a kettle with two thirds vinegar and one third water, and add a piece of alum the size of a partridge egg. Boil it five minutes, and, while hot, pour it over the melon. Let this stand thirteen or fourteen hours, take out the melon, and throw away the vinegar. While the melon is draining, put the spices and vinegar on to boil for ten minutes, and, while hot, pour over the melon. Every morning boil this vinegar over for three mornings, and the last time put the melon in the kettle and boil until tender. Put into jars, and seal while hot. These proportions can be increased according to the quantity of melon to be pickled.

To Pickle Mushrooms

Nine quarts of mushrooms,
One tablespoonful of ground mace,
One dessertspoonful of ground cloves,
One dessertspoonful of ground allspice,
One teaspoonful of cayenne pepper,
One tablespoonful of black pepper,
One teaspoonful of salt.

Wash and peel the mushrooms, then put them in the jars in which they are to be kept. As you put them in, say in layers, sprinkle spices over each layer; cover them with boiling vinegar, tie them up tightly, and in two weeks they will be ready for use.

Green Tomato Pickle

One peck of green tomatoes,
Three tablespoonfuls of dry mustard,

One ounce of yellow mustard seed,

An ounce and a half of whole black pepper,

One ounce of whole cloves,

One ounce of whole allspice,

One dozen white onions,

Half a pound of brown sugar.

Slice the tomatoes thin, sprinkle them with salt, and let them stand over night. The next morning drain them through a colander, peel and slice the onions, and put into the kettle in the following order: First, a layer of tomatoes and onions, then seed and spices, and so on until all are in the kettle. Mix the mustard with a quart of vinegar and the sugar, and pour over the tomatoes. Add more vinegar until they are covered. Place the kettle over the fire, and boil twenty minutes. Put in stone jars, and cover tightly with paper.

Chow-Chow

Two large heads of cauliflower,

One quart of sliced cucumbers,

Half a pint of mixed English mustard,

One tablespoonful of cayenne pepper,

One tablespoonful of black pepper,

Three ounces of turmeric.

Cut the cauliflower and cucumbers into small, nicely shaped pieces, and put them into brine for twenty-four hours. Drain through a colander for an hour or two; then put them in a kettle. Cover with vinegar, in which two teaspoonfuls of celery seed has [sic] been previously boiled for twenty minutes and strained. Let the vegetables simmer with the spices in the vinegar until perfectly tender, stirring well all the time. Put into wide-mouthed jars and tie up closely. It would be well to put a piece of alum, the size of a hickory nut, into each jar to keep the pickle from getting soft.

Tomato Catsup

Two bushels of ripe tomatoes,

Half a peck of onions,

One teacupful of salt,

One teacupful of whole allspice,

Half a teacupful of ground cloves,

One teacupful of black pepper grains,

One tablespoonful of ground mace,

Two tumblerfuls of Madeira wine,

One dessertspoonful of celery seed,

Cayenne pepper to the taste,

Three grated nutmegs.

Wash the tomatoes well, and cut in slices a half an inch thick. Peel the onions, and slice thin. Put them in a preserving kettle, with the salt, on the fire, and let them boil slowly for three hours, taking care to stir frequently. Mash through a sieve with a wooden ladle, and pour into a stone jar to stand over night. The next morning, return to the preserving kettle, with the spices and wine, and simmer until thick, then mash again through a sieve with the wooden ladle, and bottle and seal well.

Cucumber Catsup

One peck of full-grown cucumbers,
Two large onions,
Half a pint of salt,
Six blades of mace,
A gill of Madeira wine,
A gill of sweet oil,
A teaspoonful of cayenne pepper,
A teaspoonful of ground black pepper.

Peel the cucumbers and cut them in thin slices. Cover them with the half pint of salt, to draw out the water, and let them stand six hours. Cut the onions also in thin slices, and put them in stone jars, in alternate layers with the cucumbers, pepper, and blades of mace, broken very fine. Stir the oil and wine in the vinegar, and pour over the cucumbers cold.

Chili Sauce

One dozen large ripe tomatoes,
Six tablespoonfuls of brown sugar,
Four teacupfuls of vinegar,
Two teaspoonfuls of ground cinnamon,
Two teaspoonfuls of ground ginger,
One teaspoonful of ground cloves,
One tablespoonful of mixed mustard,
One red pepper pod,
Four large white onions,
Salt to the taste.

Peel and slice the tomatoes; chop the onions very fine; put in the other ingredients, and boil slowly for two hours. Rub through a sifter, and seal in bottles or glass jars. Keep in a cool place in the summer, but not too cold a place in the winter. This is delicious on cold meats or fried oysters.

French Mustard

A quarter of a pound of Coleman's English mustard,
Half a pint of water,
Half a pint of vinegar,
A tablespoonful of flour,
A teaspoonful of pulverized sugar,
A saltspoonful of salt.

Put the mustard in a saucepan, and pour over it the vinegar and water; add the salt and a pinch of calamus root the size of a pea. Put it on the fire, and when it is boiling add the flour. Let it boil twenty minutes, stirring all the time. Just before taking it off stir in the sugar. When cool, put it in small wide-mouth bottles and cork tightly.

To Pickle Oysters

One quart of vinegar,
One gallon of oysters,
One pint of sherry wine,
Two quarts of oyster liquor,
Half an ounce of ground cloves,
Half an ounce of ground allspice,
Half an ounce of ground mace,

Six small red pepper pods,
One dessertspoonful of salt,
Two lemons.

Put the oysters into a porcelain kettle with their liquor and let them simmer slowly until the edges curl. When done take them out of their liquor, drop them in cold water and let them remain in it ten minutes, then drain. Take two quarts of the liquor, the vinegar, spices, salt and pepper pods; let this boil for about three minutes, then pour into a bowl to get cold. Cut the lemons into thin slices, taking care to throw away all of the seeds. Put them with the wine into the mixture, then put the oysters into wide-mouth bottles and pour it over. Cork tightly.

Oyster Catsup

Four pints of fresh oysters,
One heaping teaspoonful of ground mace,
Half a teaspoonful of cayenne pepper,
Four ounces of salt,
Three pints of white wine,
Half a tumblerful of brandy.

Wash the oysters in their own liquor, then put them into a marble mortar, with the mace, salt and cayenne pepper, and pound all well together. Now put the mixture into a saucepan with the wine, and let it boil ten minutes; rub through a sieve, boil five minutes longer, skim well, and when cold, add the brandy; bottle, cork and seal tightly. This gives a fine flavor to meat sauces, and will keep for some time.

To Prepare Horseradish

Wash the horseradish clean and let it lie in cold water for about an hour, then scrape into very fine shreds with a sharp knife. Put into a wide-mouth bottle, cover with vinegar, and cork tightly.

Menus for Breakfasts, Lunches & Dinners

spring breakfast

Fruit

Broiled Shad—Tartare Sauce,
Saratoga Potatoes.
Broiled Lamb Chops and Peas,
Hot Rolls.

Coffee and English Breakfast Tea.

Sweetbreads and Champignons.
Broiled Snipe on Toast.

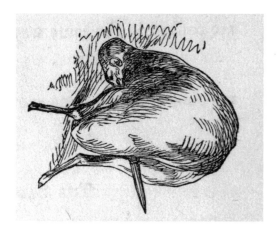

Snipe and woodcock are small wading birds that were both popular as game in the nineteenth century. In this illustration, the legs of the bird were skewered with its own slender beak, before it would have been quickly broiled or fried and served on toast. From Mrs. Mary F. Henderson, *Practical Cooking and Dinner Giving* (New York: Harper and Bros., 1877), 187, Special Collections, Michigan State University Libraries.

Americans who could afford to do so regularly ate a variety of meats and seafood for breakfast, among other foods. Breakfast menu cover for Oakland Beach Hotel, Warwick, Rhode Island, 1880, Rare Book Division, New York Public Library Digital Collections.

summer breakfast

Cantelopes.
Broiled Chicken,
Hot Rolls,
Corn Fritters.

Lamb Chops—Hot Biscuits,
Boiled Tomatoes.

Coffee and English Breakfast Tea.

Ham Omelette.
Peaches and Cream.

fall breakfast

Broiled White Fish,
Plain Omelette.
Broiled Doves, or Pheasants on Toast,
Hot Rolls.

Coffee and English Breakfast Tea.

Waffles,
Golden Syrup.

winter breakfast

Fruit.

Beefsteak with Champignons,
Hot Pounded Biscuits,
Omelette with Herbs.
Quail on Toast.

Coffee and English Breakfast Tea.

Terrapins,
Hot Rolls.

spring lunch

Clear Soup.
Fish, Sauce a la Hollandaise,
Scalloped Potatoes.
Baked Sweetbreads,
Green Peas.

Frozen Punch.

Quenelles with Truffles.
Tomato Salad—Mayonnaise Dressing.
Ice Cream and Strawberries—Cakes.
Coffee.

summer lunch

Clear Soup—Parmesan Cheese.
Broiled Salmon Steaks—Tartare Sauce.
Chicken a la Curry.

Frozen Punch.

Sweetbreads in Shells.
Tomato Salad.
Raspberry Ice Cream—Cakes.
Chocolate.

fall lunch

Lobster Soup.
Broiled White Fish—Tartare Sauce.
Broiled Chickens,
Fresh Fall Mushrooms.

Frozen Punch.

Calf's Head a la Terrapin.
Reed Birds.
Tomato Salad.
Neapolitan Brick—Cakes.
Candied Fruits.
Chocolate.

winter lunch

Oysters on the Half Shell.
White Soup.
Quails with Truffles,
Stewed Potatoes.

Frozen Punch.

Croquettes and Green Peas.
Salad.

Neapolitan Brick—Cakes.
Coffee.

spring dinner

Okra Soup.
Baked Shad—Tartare Sauce,
Mashed Potatoes.
Roast Lamb—Mint Sauce,
Green Peas.

Roman Punch.

Fillet of Veal—Brown Sauce,
Macaroni.
Salad.
Pudding—Cold Sauce.
Lemon Sherbet.
Fruit.
Coffee.

summer dinner

Lobster Soup.
Boiled Sheep's Head—Egg Sauce.
Roast Lamb—Mint Sauce,
Green Peas.

Roman Punch.

Fried Chicken—Cream Sauce,
Egg-Plant Pudding.
Croquettes—Tomato Sauce.

Salad.

Pudding—Cold Sauce.
Raspberry Ice Cream—Cakes.
Fruit.
Coffee.

fall dinner

Oyster Gumbo.
Boiled Fish—Sauce a la Hollandaise,
Baked Mashed Potatoes.
Reed Birds,
Macaroni.

Roman Punch.

Croquettes—Champignon Sauce.
Celery Salad.
Pudding.
Vanilla Ice Cream—Cakes.
Fruit.
Coffee.

winter dinner

Oysters on the Half-shell.
Clear Soup.
Boiled Fish—Shrimp Sauce,
Baked Mashed Potatoes.
Fillet of Beef with Champignons.

Roman Punch.

Boudins a la Richelieu Truffle Sauce.
Pate de Fois Gras in Aspec Jelly.
Salad.
Pudding—Hot Sauce.
Macaroon Ice Cream—Cakes.
Jelly.
Coffee.

winter supper

A supper of twelve persons to be served at one table, and in courses.
Oysters in the Shell.
Venison—Wine Sauce.
Sweet Breads and Peas.
Pheasant Breasts—Truffle Sauce.

Salad.

Ice Cream.
Fruit.
Coffee.

Christine Terhune Herrick,
What to Eat, How to Serve It, 1891

Christine Terhune Herrick would become one of the most prolific and respected American authorities on cooking, dining, and housekeeping of the turn of the twentieth century.[1] The daughter of Mary Terhune, better known by the penname Marion Harland under which she wrote dozens of novels and cookbooks, Herrick grew up in a household where female authorship was normal. Her 1891 *What to Eat, How to Serve It*, published by Harper & Brothers, a slim guide to cooking and menu planning, was one of Herrick's earlier books, but it already demonstrated the easy confidence on matters of food and entertaining that would make her a trusted guide for so many American cooks. Herrick said she aimed this book at "people of moderate means," and her menus were indeed more modest than the expensive, multicourse, alcohol-soaked meals outlined in comparable Gilded Age books like Mary Henderson's *Practical Cooking and Dinner Giving*. Yet this humility was only relative; Herrick's menus still presumed a very comfortable standard of living, and anyone hoping to make her three- and four-course meals would have needed a solid income.

Herrick arranged her menus seasonally. Her menu of roast turkey, pureed turnips, fried parsnips and onions, mashed potatoes, and orange roly-poly was unmistakably a winter dinner, with its hardy root vegetables and citrus dessert, while her dinner menu consisting of asparagus soup, chicken, peas, summer squash, and raspberry pudding was undeniably meant for the summer. In part, as she noted, she planned her menus seasonally in order to make them more economical, since fresh, locally grown foods would have been cheapest. What was more, for many nineteenth-century Americans seasonality was unavoidable: before a robust national cold chain and widespread home refrigeration, fresh ingredients were often impossible to find out of season.

Beyond food's price and availability, however, Herrick also arranged her menus around the seasons for another reason: she thought it was most healthful, and maybe even lifesaving, to eat with the weather in mind. In this era, people attributed a whole range of ills to digestive disturbances, from contagious diseases to nightmares to children's sudden deaths, and the young science of nutrition only fueled Americans' growing preoccupation with digestion's role in health. For Herrick as for many other Americans in the Gilded Age, food's digestibility was a pressing concern, and she believed it was imperative to make spring and summer meals lighter and less meaty than their cold-weather equivalents. For instance, while her spring breakfast menus contained relatively little meat, her winter breakfasts were heavy, meaty meals because she thought large quantities of meat were "almost necessary in winter" as a source of energy and warmth. While she still regularly included meat on her warm-weather breakfast menus, it tended to be fish and chicken rather than darker meats. On the most "sultry" mornings, Herrick advised, people's digestions would work best if they ate mainly fruit.

Herrick also believed that digestion was affected by the environments in which people ate. Attention to cleanliness, heat, and light was crucial. Herrick advised housekeepers to vigilantly brush crumbs off the table between meals. In summer, she told them to shoo all flies out of the dining room and to keep the shades drawn between meals to keep it cooler. Good digestion could happen much better in a clean and "deliciously cool and fresh" room than in one that was "stuffy, fly-infested," and overly bright.

As was commonplace before widespread reliable refrigeration, Herrick urged readers to eat leftovers from dinner the next day as part of their breakfasts and lunches. If you look closely, many of her breakfast dishes made use of foods that would have been cooked the night before: chicken mince made with meat from

Nineteenth-century Americans believed that indigestion could cause a host of ills, including nightmares. This advertising card, titled "Indigestion and Nightmare," was promoting Gantz's Sea Foam, a commercial yeast that supposedly aided digestion. Trade card for Gantz's Sea Foam Yeast, ca. 1880, The Alan and Shirley Brocker Sliker Collection, MSS 314, Special Collections, Michigan State University Libraries.

a roast chicken, potato hash made by chopping up cold boiled potatoes. While the practice of quickly using up perishable food had been in place for as long as humans had been eating, the term "left-over" was brand new. Appearing in print for the first time only that very year, "left-over" gave people a new way to talk about an ancient concept, and Herrick brought attention to the term's novelty by using quotation marks in her recipe for a Fish "Left-Over," which was flaked, leftover fish mixed with chopped hardboiled eggs and reheated in white sauce.[2]

Family Breakfasts for Spring

While the principal features of the home breakfast remain essentially the same throughout the year, variety is gained by adapting the different articles of food to the season of the year in which they are served. A lighter, less carbon-producing diet is not only more agreeable, but more healthful, in warm weather than one containing much animal food, while the latter is preferable and almost necessary in winter. To this consideration is added the eminent propriety of making one's bills of fare seasonable, and thus achieving fitness and economy.

With the desire to aid the housewife in her labors, a few selected *menus* for each meal and each season will be given, none of them too costly to be beyond the reach of people of moderate means, and appended to each bill of fare will be recipes for the preparation of certain dishes therein mentioned which may possibly be unfamiliar to the readers of these chapters.

Oranges.
Cracked Wheat.
Parsley Omelet.   Corn Muffins.
Buttered Potatoes.
Tea.   Coffee.

Parsley Omelet.—Five eggs, two tablespoonfuls milk, one tablespoonful butter, one tablespoonful finely minced parsley; pepper and salt to taste. Beat the whites and yolks of the eggs separately and very light; add the milk to the yolks and stir in the whites, not mixing them in thoroughly, however; season to taste. Pour into the omelet pan in which the butter has been heated, and set over the fire in a moderately hot spot. Keep the omelet from adhering to the pan by slipping a knife between them from time to time. Just before the omelet is "set," sprinkle it thickly with the chopped parsley. When done, fold one half over the other, slip to a hot dish, and serve at once, as it falls quickly.

Corn Muffins.—One and a half cups flour, one and a half cups yellow corn-meal, three tablespoonfuls sugar, two tablespoonfuls butter, two eggs, one and a half cupfuls milk, two teaspoonfuls baking-powder, half teaspoonful salt. Sift the salt and baking-powder with the flour; beat the eggs light; add the milk, the butter (melted), and the sugar. Stir in the flour and meal; beat hard, and bake in muffin-tins.

Buttered Potatoes.—Slice cold boiled potatoes, heat them in a steamer, thence transfer them to a hot dish. Put on them a large tablespoonful of butter into which have been worked a teaspoonful of chopped parsley and a saltspoonful of lemon juice. Set the dish, covered, over hot water for two minutes, and serve.

Wheat-Germ Meal.
Curried Eggs.   Rice Muffins.
Strawberries and Cream.
Tea.   Cocoa.

Curried Eggs.—One cup good gravy, six hard-boiled eggs, one teaspoonful curry-powder. Heat the gravy; stir into it the curry-powder wet up in a little cold gravy or water, and lay the eggs, each sliced in three, in the scalding gravy. Set the saucepan at the side of the stove where it will not boil, and let it stand ten minutes before sending to table.

Family Breakfast for Summer

As the season advances and the warm weather becomes settled, the preference should be given to fish and egg dishes rather than to those containing meat. For a sultry morning a breakfast of which fruit makes an important part is welcome generally to both palate and digestion.

The many kinds of delicious fresh fish that may easily be procured should hold a prominent place in summer bills of fare; while eggs, usually plentiful and cheap at this season, may be prepared in various tempting fashions.

Strawberries.
Moulded Cerealine.
Broiled Shad.   New Potatoes.
Rye Gems.
Tea.   Cocoa.

Strawberries.—When served as a first course at breakfast, it is better to have them unhulled, and to eat them with the fingers, dipping each berry into powdered sugar.

Moulded Cerealine.—Prepare the cerealine as usual the day before, and fill small cups with it. Turn it out the next morning, and eat cold, with cream.

Rice Muffins.—One cup boiled rice, two eggs, two cups flour, one tablespoonful melted butter, pinch salt, three cups milk. Stir together the milk, eggs, butter, and salt; beat in the rice and flour; bake quickly.

Rye Gems.—Three cups rye-flour, three cups milk, three eggs, one tablespoonful sugar, one tablespoonful butter. Beat hard and bake quickly.

Boiled Hominy.
Chicken Mince.   Raw Tomatoes.
Green Corn Fritters.
Blackberries and Cream.
Tea.   Cocoa.

Chicken Mince.—From the bones of a cold roast, boiled, or fricasseed chicken cut all the meat, and mince it fine with a sharp knife, chopping with it two hard-boiled eggs. Stir this into a cup of gravy . . . Season to taste, fill a pudding-dish or scallop-shells with the mixture, and serve very hot.

Green-Corn Fritters.—Two cupfuls green corn cut from the cob, two eggs, two tablespoonfuls milk, one tablespoonful melted butter, flour enough for thin batter. Whip the eggs light, beat into these the corn and the other ingredients, adding the flour last of all. Bake on a griddle.

Family Breakfasts for Autumn

During the early part of the autumn, and indeed until late in the winter, the supply of fruit is only less abundant than in the summer. Melons and peaches go first, but their place is taken by grapes, pears, apples, bananas, and, later, mandarins, tangerines, and oranges. Meat now begins to be a more necessary article in the bill of fare. By the exercise of a little ingenuity, left-overs from the dinner of the previous day may be rendered even more appetizing than they were in their first estate.

Peaches and Pears.

Oatmeal.

Veal Cutlets à la Maître d'*Hôtel.*

Potatoes hashed with Cream.

Quick Sally-Lunn.

Cocoa.   Coffee.

Veal Cutlets à la Maître d'Hôtel.—Cut veal cutlets into neat pieces, and pound each with a mallet. Broil over a clear fire, transfer to a hot dish, and lay on each cutlet a small piece of *maître d'hôtel* butter. Set in a hot corner, covered, for five minutes before sending to table.

Maître d'Hôtel Butter—Into one cupful of good butter work a tablespoonful of lemon juice and two tablespoonfuls of finely chopped parsley, with a little salt and white pepper. Pack into a small jar, cover, and keep in a cool place. It is useful to put on chops, steaks, or cutlets, or to mix with potatoes.

Potatoes hashed with Cream.—Chop cold boiled potatoes fine, and stir them into a cup of hot milk in which has been melted two tablespoonfuls of butter. Pepper and salt to taste. Let the potatoes become heated through before you serve them. If you have cream, use this and half as much butter.

Quick Sally-Lunn.—Three eggs, half cup butter, one cup milk, three cups flour, two teaspoonfuls baking-powder, half teaspoonful salt. Stir the butter, melted, into the beaten yolks; add the milk, the flour (into which the baking-powder has been sifted), and the whites last. Bake in one loaf, in a steady oven.

Apples.

Wheat Granules.

Soused Mackerel.   Potato Balls.

Quick Waffles.

Cocoa.   Coffee.

Soused Mackerel.—These may be purchased canned at nearly any good grocery, and make an excellent breakfast dish.

Potato Balls.—To two cupfuls cold mashed potato add an egg, a teaspoonful of butter, and salt and pepper to taste. Form with floured hands into small round or long balls, and fry in deep fat.

Quick Waffles.—Three cups flour, one tablespoonful butter, two eggs, two cups milk, two teaspoonfuls baking-powder, a little salt. Beat the eggs light, add the milk, butter, and salt. Stir in the flour with the baking-powder last. Grease your waffle-irons well with a piece of fat pork.

Family Breakfasts for Winter

A word may be said here about the cooking of porridges. There are as many theories about this apparently simple affair as there are denominational differences in theological circles. One housekeeper soaks the oatmeal overnight; another puts it on when the fire is made; another fifteen minutes before breakfast. Mrs. A. soaks hers in cold water, Mrs. B. uses boiling, while Mrs. C. inclines to having the water just hot. One stirs the porridge frequently; another says it is ruined if touched with a spoon.

On general principles, one may say that oatmeal is never the worse for a soaking, although some varieties need it less than others; that unless carefully and evenly cooked it is apt to become lumpy without stirring or beating; and that the degree of stiffness to which it should be brought must depend upon the taste of those who are to eat it.

Oranges.

Graham Mush.

Sausage Rolls.   Rye Muffins.

Baked Potatoes.

Tea.   Coffee.

Sausage Rolls.—Make a good pastry by chopping into two cups of flour four tablespoonfuls of butter, making this to a paste with half a cup of ice-water, and rolling out three times. Have the ingredients and utensils very cold, and handle the paste as little and as lightly as possible. Cut the pastry with a sharp knife into strips about three inches square. On one of these lay cooked and minced sausage-meat, and cover it with another square of the same size. Pinch the edges together, and bake in a moderate oven. Proceed thus until all the materials are used.

Rye Muffins.—One cup white flour, two cups rye flour, two eggs, two teaspoonfuls baking-powder, one tablespoonful butter, one tablespoonful sugar, saltspoonful salt, milk enough for stiff batter. Beat well, and bake in muffin-tins.

Wheat Germ-Meal Porridge.

Broiled Ham.   Canned Pea Pancakes.

Buttered Toast.

Baked Apples.

Cocoa.   Coffee.

Canned Pea Pancakes.—One can of green pease, one egg, one cup milk, two teaspoonfuls melted butter, half cupful flour, half teaspoonful baking-powder, salt to taste. Open the can several hours before it is to be used, and drain off the liquor. Rinse the pease in cold water. Mash them with the back of a spoon, and mix with them the butter and salt. Make a batter of the egg, the milk, and the flour, with the baking-powder. Add the pease, beat well, and bake on a griddle.

Family Lunches for Spring

These menus for simple home lunches . . . are not designed to serve as exact guides, but merely as suggestions to the housekeeper. They may easily be improved upon or altered. To some they will doubtless appear much too simple, while others may condemn them as being too elaborate.

Certain selected recipes will accompany them.

Baked Cheese Omelet.   Toasted Crackers.
Strawberry Jam.
Cocoa.

Baked Cheese Omelet.—Two eggs, two cups milk, one small cup grated cheese, one small cup fine bread-crumbs, salt and Cayenne pepper to taste, one table-spoonful melted butter. Soak the crumbs in the milk, in which you have dissolved a tiny pinch of soda; beat the eggs light, and add to the bread and milk; stir in the butter, the seasoning, and, last of all, the cheese. Bake in a well-greased pudding-dish, and eat at once, before it falls.

Toasted Crackers.—Split and toast Boston crackers. Butter them well on the inside, lay the two halves together, and serve them in a hot covered dish. They are not nearly so good when they are cold.

Ham Fritters.   Baked Bananas.
Bread-and-Butter.
Ginger Snaps.
Tea.

Ham Fritters.—Two cups minced cold ham, one egg, half-pint good stock, saltspoonful dry mustard, tea-spoonful Worcestershire sauce, tiny bit of scalded onion (chopped), half-teaspoonful minced parsley, one table-spoonful butter, one teaspoonful flour. Heat the stock to boiling, and thicken it with the butter and flour rubbed together; stir into it the ham, seasoned with the mustard, onion, Worcestershire sauce, and parsley; add the beaten egg. Pour the mixture on a flat plate to cool. When cold and firm, make into flattened balls about the size of a small plum; drop each into a batter made of a cup of flour, two teaspoonfuls of melted butter, a small cup of warm water, the beaten white of an egg, and a little salt. Lay each fritter out of the batter into boiling fat. They will puff up at once, and should be of a delicate brown.

Baked Bananas.—Select large ripe bananas, and bake them in the oven as you would potatoes. When the skin begins to split at the seams they are done. Take them out, and serve one to each person, as a vegetable. They should be peeled, and eaten with butter and a little salt.

Bread-and-Butter.—Butter bread a day old on the loaf, and cut into thin slices. Double, the buttered side inward.

Ginger Snaps.—Two eggs, two cups sugar, one cup butter, two teaspoonfuls ginger, one teaspoonful cinnamon, flour to make a stiff dough. Roll into a thin sheet, cut into rounds, and sprinkle with granulated sugar before baking. Watch closely or they will burn.

Family Lunches for Summer

In hot weather a comfortable room is essential to the enjoyment of a meal. The salle à manger must be cleared of food, the soiled dishes removed, all crumbs brushed up, and the flies beaten out the moment breakfast is over, if the apartment is to be pleasant at noon. If blinds and doors are kept closed, the room may be deliciously cool and fresh by lunch-time.

With such surroundings, good digestion is much more prone to wait on appetite than in a stuffy, fly-infested room, where neither heat nor light is excluded. Among the pleasantest recollections of at least one woman are those connected with the lunches she has eaten in midsummer in a certain city dining-room, where the subdued light, the daintily arranged table, the carefully prepared and seasonable food, and the noiseless serving inclined one to feel that there were many worse fates than being obliged to spend the summer in town.

Anchovy Toast.   Chicken Salad.
Bread-and-Butter.
Berries and Cream.
Iced Tea.

Anchovy Toast.—Spread crustless slices of toast first with butter, then with anchovy paste. Set in the oven five minutes, and send to table.

Chicken Salad.—Cut into small neat pieces half the contents of a can of boned chicken or part of a cold boiled or roast chicken. Mix this with half as much cel-ery, if you can get it; if not, arrange it in the midst of crisp lettuce leaves. Stir into it a French dressing of two tablespoonfuls of oil, as much vinegar, and a little pepper and salt, and pour over it a mayonnaise dressing.

Mayonnaise Dressing.—Into a bowl set in an outer vessel of cold or iced water place the yolk of an egg. Be careful that no vestige of the white gets in. Begin whipping in salad oil drop by drop with a Dover egg-beater, beating for nearly a minute after each addition. After

Rotary egg-beaters were one of the many kinds of tools that were becoming standard in middle-class kitchens around the country by the late nineteenth century, including double boilers, wire whisks, potato ricers, a variety of knives, and uniform measuring cups and spoons. From Fannie Farmer, *The Original 1896 Boston Cooking-School Cook Book* (Mineola, NY: Dover Publications, 1997), 30, Special Collections, Michigan State University Libraries.

ten minutes, add two or three drops at a time, and when the dressing once begins to thicken, the quantity can be increased even more. If too thick, add a little vinegar to thin it. A pint of oil can be used to every egg. When done, season with salt and white pepper. Just before serving, stir into it the whipped white of an egg. The bowl, egg-beater, and materials must all be very cold, and the dressing when made must be kept on ice until used.

Pickled Lambs' Tongues.   Egg Salad.
Boiled Corn-Bread.
Loppered Milk.

Egg Salad.—Slice hard-boiled eggs, arrange them upon crisp lettuce leaves, and pour over all a mayonnaise dressing.

Boiled Corn-Bread.—Two cups sour milk, one cup warm water, one tablespoonful lard, one tablespoonful molasses, one teaspoonful soda, one cup flour, two cups corn-meal. Mix the ingredients, beating well; pour into a Boston brown-bread mould with a tight top; set in a pot of water; boil two hours, and turn out.

Family Lunches for Autumn

Bouillon.
Cold Chicken Pie.   Potato Salad.
Cold Bread.
Gingerbread.   Cocoa.

Cold Chicken Pie.—Stew a grown chicken until tender, putting it on in cold water, and cooking very slowly; arrange the pieces in a deep pudding dish, laying in with them two hard-boiled eggs cut into slices; pour over all a cupful of the gravy, which should be well seasoned; cover the pie with a pastry crust, and bake in a moderate oven. Add to two cups of the remaining gravy a quarter-box of gelatine soaked in a little cold water, a small glassful of sherry, and a tablespoonful of vinegar; when the pie is done, pour this gravy into it through an opening which should have been left in the top. Make this pie the day before it is to be eaten. It is an excellent dish for Sunday lunch or tea.

Potato Salad.—Slice cold boiled potatoes; with three cups of these mix one sliced beet, one onion braised, and three or four stalks of celery; pour over them four tablespoonfuls of salad oil and three of vinegar, with pepper and salt to taste. Let all stand in a cold place at least an hour before serving.

Gingerbread.—Two cups milk, half-cup sugar, half-cup molasses, one teaspoonful ground ginger, one teaspoonful cinnamon, one tablespoonful butter, two teaspoonfuls baking-powder; flour enough to make a good batter. Beat hard, and bake in a steady oven.

A Fish "Left-Over."   Stewed Potatoes.
Rice Cakes.
Roast Spanish Chestnuts.

A Fish "Left-Over."—The remains of any cold boiled, broiled, fried, or baked fish; three hard-boiled eggs, if you have only a half-cupful of fish (two eggs if there is more fish); one cup white sauce. Flake the fish, chop the eggs, heat both in the white sauce, season to taste, and serve either on toast or without it.

Rice Cakes.—One egg, one cup flour, one and a half cups cold boiled rice, saltspoonful salt, three cups milk. If this amount of milk thins the batter too much, add more flour.

Roast Spanish Chestnuts.—Cut a bit off of each, and roast them in the oven. Peel, and eat with butter and salt.

Family Lunches for Winter

Curried Oysters.   Rice Croquettes.
Cold Slaw.
Crackers and Cheese.

Curried Oysters.—Heat to boiling the liquor from one quart of oysters; lay the oysters in it, and let them simmer just long enough to plump them. Take them out with a skimmer, put them where they will keep hot, and thicken the liquor by adding to it a tablespoonful of butter rubbed smooth with two of browned flour. Into this stir a teaspoonful of curry-powder wet up in a little cold water. Salt and pepper to taste, squeeze in the juice of a lemon, return the oysters to the sauce, and serve.

Rice Croquettes.—Two cups cold boiled rice, one well-beaten egg, one teaspoonful butter, one teaspoonful sugar, salt to taste. Work the butter, egg, salt, and sugar into the rice, make into croquettes with the floured hands, and fry in deep fat.

Cold Slaw.—Shred half a fine white cabbage, and pour over it a dressing made as follows: Four tablespoonfuls vinegar, half-cup milk, one tablespoonful butter, one tablespoonful sugar, one egg, pepper and salt. Beat the egg; stir the melted butter, the milk, salt, pepper, and sugar into this. Put the vinegar boiling hot into it, a little at a time. Pour the sauce over the cabbage, and let it become ice-cold before serving.

Jellied Chicken.   Hominy Croquettes.
Toasted Muffins.
Orange Cake.

Jellied Chicken.—Cut up a chicken as for fricassee, and stew until the meat slips from the bones. Take out the chicken, and cut it into neat pieces when it has become cold. Let the gravy simmer half an hour with an onion sliced, a small bunch of parsley, a couple of stalks of celery, and a bay-leaf. Strain it, and return it to the fire with the white and freshly broken shell of an egg. Let it boil up, and strain it again, this time through a cloth. While still hot pour three cups of this liquor upon a half-box of gelatine which has soaked an hour in one cupful of cold water. Stir until the gelatine is dissolved, and add a glass of pale sherry and a couple of tablespoonfuls of vinegar. Pour part of this jelly into a wet mould, and when it begins to form lay in slices of hard-boiled egg and pieces of the chicken. More jelly follows, and more chicken, until all are used up. Turn out when the jelly is perfectly firm.

Hominy Croquettes.—Make as directed for rice croquettes, using hominy instead of rice.

Toasted Muffins.—Split and toast English muffins, and butter them on the inside.

Orange Cake.—Two cups sugar, half cup butter, four eggs, three cups flour, one cup cold water, one large or two small oranges, two teaspoonfuls baking-powder. Work the butter and sugar together; add the yolks of the eggs, the juice and grated peel of the orange, the water, the whites, and the flour with the baking-powder. Bake in small cakes. If you like, reserve one of the whites of the eggs, and make an orange icing by beating with this a cup of powdered sugar and a little orange juice.

Family Dinners for Spring

Boiled Mutton, Sauce Soubise.
Mashed Turnips.   Baked Hominy.
Apple Charlotte.

Boiled Mutton, Sauce Soubise.—In purchasing your mutton, select a fine large leg, and have it cut in two, in such a way that the knuckle and the lower part of the leg will make a good piece for boiling, leaving the upper part for roasting.

Sauce Soubise.—Four onions chopped, one tablespoonful flour, one tablespoonful butter, one cup of the liquor in which the mutton was boiled; pepper and salt to taste. Stew the onions until very tender; drain them, and rub them through a colander; put the butter and flour together in a little saucepan, cook them until they bubble; add the mutton liquor, which must have been

cooled and skimmed; stir all together until thick and smooth; add the pepper, salt, and the strained onions; pass with the boiled mutton. If properly made, this is a very appetizing sauce.

Baked Hominy.—To two cupfuls of cold boiled hominy add a tablespoonful of melted butter, a tablespoonful of white sugar, one egg beaten, a cupful of milk, and a little salt; beat all together until light, and bake in a buttered pudding dish. Serve as a vegetable.

Apple Charlotte.—Two eggs, two cups milk, half-cup sugar, two cups rather stiff apple-sauce. Make a boiled custard of the yolks of the eggs, the milk, and the sugar; whip the whites of the eggs very light, and beat them into the apple sauce, which should have been well sweetened while hot. Heap the sauce and whites in a dish, and pour the custard over it. Set in the ice-box, or

LEG OF MUTTON.

Mutton—the meat of a mature sheep—was common on nineteenth-century American tables, at least in those families that could regularly afford to buy meat. Mutton would become drastically less popular in the twentieth century. Leg of Mutton. From Fanny Gillette, *The White House Cook Book: A Selection of Choice Recipes Original and Selected* (Chicago: R. S. Peale and Co., 1887), 467, Special Collections, Michigan State University Libraries.

some other cold place for half an hour before sending to the table.

Cream Corn Soup.

Stewed Pigeons.

Baked Potatoes.   Fried Bananas.

Apricot Fritters.

Cream Corn Soup.—One can corn, three cups boiling water, two cups milk, one tablespoonful butter, two tablespoonfuls flour, one egg, pepper and salt to taste. Drain the liquor from the corn, and chop the lat-ter fine; cook it in the boiling water for an hour; rub it through the colander, and return it to the fire. Have the milk hot in a farina kettle. Thicken it with the flour and butter; season, and pour a little at a time upon the beaten egg. Stir this in with the hot corn *purée*, and serve at once.

Stewed Pigeons.—Cut pigeons in half, place a layer of salt pork cut in thin strips in the bottom of a saucepan, and lay the pigeons on this; sprinkle with a little chopped onion; pour over them enough hot water to cover them, put a closely fitting top on the pot, and cook them slowly for two hours. Take out the birds and the pork, and keep them hot while you thicken the gravy left in the pot with a little browned flour wet up in cold water; boil up once, pour over the pigeons, and serve.

Fried Bananas.—Select firm bananas, peel them, and slice them lengthwise; dip them in egg, roll them in very fine cracker-crumbs, and fry them in deep fat to a light brown. Serve on a napkin laid in a deep dish.

Apricot Fritters.—Stew evaporated apricots until tender, adding, when half done, sugar in the proportion of two tablespoonfuls to every cupful of juice. When the apricots are tender, take them out, leaving the syrup to reduce by boiling until it is quite thick. Dip each piece of apricot into a frying batter made of a cup of flour, a tablespoonful of melted butter, a small cup of warm water, and the white of an egg beaten light; drop these fritters into boiling deep fat. When done, lay on a piece of brown paper in a colander for a few minutes, transfer to a hot dish, and pour the hot syrup over and around them.

Family Dinners for Summer

Asparagus Soup.
Boiled Chicken. Green Pease.
Summer Squash.
Raspberry Pudding.

Asparagus Soup.—Boil a bunch of asparagus until it is very tender. When done, cut off the green tips, and put them aside, and rub the stalks in a colander, getting all of them through that you can. Heat four cups of milk in a double boiler, add the strained asparagus to this, and thicken with a tablespoonful of butter rubbed in one of flour. Season to taste with salt and pepper, add the asparagus tops (which should have been kept hot), and serve.

Raspberry Pudding.—Two cups raspberries (red or black), three cups flour, three eggs, two cups milk, one tablespoonful butter, two teaspoonfuls baking-powder, saltspoonful salt. Beat the eggs very light, and mix with the butter, melted, and the milk. Stir into this the flour sifted with the salt and baking-powder, taking care that the batter does not lump. Dredge the berries with flour, add them to the pudding, and boil this in a plain pudding mould, set in a pot of boiling water, for three hours. Take care that the water does not come over the top of the mould. Serve with hard sauce.

Cheese Soup.
Beef à la Mode.
Fried Cucumbers.   Cauliflower.   Green Corn.
Fresh Fruit.

Roast beef. From Mrs. Mary F. Henderson, *Practical Cooking and Dinner Giving* (New York: Harper and Bros., 1877), 130, Special Collections, Michigan State University Libraries.

Cheese Soup.—One egg; a half-cupful grated cheese; one onion; two cups milk; two cups veal, chicken, or other white stock; one tablespoonful flour; one tablespoonful butter; pepper and salt to taste. Heat the milk and stock with the onion. Remove the latter, and thicken the liquid with the butter and flour rubbed smooth together. Stir in the cheese, pour a little of the soup on the egg beaten light, add this to the soup in the pot, season, and serve immediately. It is a good plan to put a tiny pinch of soda into the milk before adding the cheese.

Beef à la Mode.—Select a good piece of beef from the round, and "plug" it thickly with beef suet or with strips of fat salt pork. Make other incisions into which to crowd a force-meat made of finely chopped salt pork mixed with twice the bulk of bread-crumbs, and seasoned with herbs, allspice, onion, and vinegar. Fasten the meat securely in shape with a stout band of cotton cloth, lay it in a pot, pour over it three cups of boiling water, cover closely, and cook slowly for three hours, or until tender. Turn the meat once. Thicken the gravy left in the pot with browned flour, and pass with the meat.

This piece of meat will be as good cold as it is hot, and makes a welcome *pièce de résistance* upon which to rely for lunch or tea.

Fried Cucumbers.—Peel the cucumbers; slice them lengthwise, making about four slices of a cucumber of ordinary size. Lay them in salt and water for an hour, take out, drain, and dry. Dip first in beaten egg, then in cracker-crumbs, and fry as you would egg-plant.

Family Dinners for Autumn

Tomato Soup Maigre.
Baked White-Fish.
Mashed Potatoes.   Fried Oyster-Plant.
Rice-and-Pear Pudding.

Tomato Soup Maigre.—Fry a sliced onion brown in butter or good dripping in the bottom of the soup-pot; pour in the chopped contents of a can of tomatoes and two cups of boiling water; stew until tender, rub through a colander, return to the fire; add a half-cupful of boiled rice; thicken with a tablespoonful of butter rubbed smooth with one of flour; boil up, and serve.

Baked White-Fish.—Select a good-sized fish, and stuff it with a dressing of bread-crumbs well seasoned and moistened with a little melted butter. Sew the fish up carefully; pour a cupful of boiling water over it after it is laid in the dripping-pan, and bake (covered) for an hour, basting several times with butter. Remove the threads before sending to table.

Rice-and-Pear Pudding.—Three cups boiled rice, two eggs, one cup sugar, one cup milk, stewed or canned pears. Stir the beaten eggs, the sugar, and the milk into the rice; put a layer of this in the bottom of a pudding mould, and cover this with a stratum of pears; follow this with more rice, then more pears, and continue thus until all the materials are used; set the mould in boiling water, and boil for an hour. Eat the pudding with a hot custard sauce.

Salmon Soup.
Mutton Chops.
Baked Onions.   Stuffed Egg-Plant.
Cream Rice Pudding.

Salmon Soup.—One can salmon, one cup bread-crumbs, one quart water, two cups milk, one teaspoonful butter, pepper and salt to taste. Pick to pieces the contents of a can of salmon, removing the bones, bits of skin, etc.; put over the fire with the water and seasoning, and cook half an hour; stir in the butter, the milk, and the crumbs, and serve. Pass sliced lemon with this.

Stuffed Egg-Plant.—Boil an egg-plant thirty minutes, cut it in half, and scrape out the inside; mash this up with two tablespoonfuls of butter, and pepper and salt to taste; fill the two halves of the shell, sprinkle with crumbs, and brown in the oven.

Cream Rice Pudding.—Three cups milk, three tablespoonfuls rice, one cupful sugar, one teaspoonful vanilla. Wash the rice, put it with the milk, sugar, and flavoring into a pan, and bake in a slow oven for three or four hours. Every time a crust forms on top, stir it in, until just before taking it from the oven. Eat cold.

Family Dinners for Winter

Turnip Purée.
Roast Turkey.
Fried Parsnips.   Browned Onions.
Mashed Potatoes.
Orange Roly-Poly.

Roast turkey. From Mrs. Mary F. Henderson, *Practical Cooking and Dinner Giving* (New York: Harper and Bros., 1877), 167, Special Collections, Michigan State University Libraries.

Turnip Purée.—Eight turnips, one onion, one stalk celery, four cups water, two cups milk, one tablespoonful butter, one tablespoonful flour, pepper and salt to taste. Peel and cut up the turnips, and put them over the fire with the onion in the four cups of water; let them cook until tender, and then rub them through the colander, and put them back on the fire. Cook the butter and flour together in a saucepan; add the milk, stir into the turnip, season to taste, and serve.

Browned Onions.—Peel rather small onions, and boil them until tender; drain off the water, and pour over the onions a cupful of soup or gravy; let the onions simmer in this for ten minutes; then take them out, and keep them hot while you thicken the gravy with browned flour. Pour over the onions just before sending to the table.

Orange Roly-Poly.—Two cups flour, one and a half cups milk, one tablespoonful butter, one tablespoonful lard, two teaspoonfuls baking-powder, one saltspoonful salt, four fair-sized sweet oranges, half-cup sugar. Sift the baking-powder and the salt with the flour; rub the butter and lard into it; add the milk, and roll out the dough into a sheet about half as wide as it is long; spread this with the oranges peeled, sliced, and seeded; sprinkle these with sugar; roll up the dough with the fruit inside, pinching the ends together, that the juice may not run out; tie the pudding up in a cloth, allowing it room to swell; drop it into a pot of boiling water, and boil it steadily for an hour and a half; remove from the cloth, and lay on a hot dish. Eat with hard sauce flavored with lemon.

Roast Duck.

Canned Green Pease.   Boiled Potatoes.

Lettuce.

Crackers and Cheese.

Lemon Tarts.

Canned Green Pease.—Turn the pease from the can into a colander; pour over them several quarts of cold water, so as to rinse the pease thoroughly from the liquor in which they were canned; after this, pour as much boiling water over them, and set the colander over a pot of boiling water, covering the pease; let them steam there until heated through, dish, and put on them a couple of teaspoonfuls of butter, and pepper and salt to taste.

Lemon Tarts.—Line small patty-pans with a good puff paste, and fill them with the following mixture: Half-cup butter, one cup granulated sugar, three eggs, juice and grated rind of a lemon, two tablespoonfuls brandy, nutmeg to taste. Beat the yolks into the creamed butter and sugar; add the lemon, spice, brandy, and whites; bake in a steady oven, and eat when cold.

Dietary Studies from Alabama, New York, Chicago, Virginia, and New Mexico, 1895–1897

Dietary studies were brand new in the Gilded Age. Modern nutrition science was in its infancy, and knowledge about Americans' diets had long been limited to vague impressions and regional stereotypes.[1] Studying diet formally by choosing a group of people and carefully measuring what they ate and what it cost was a novel idea at a time when people were just starting to argue that it was important to investigate eating scientifically. The dietary studies reproduced here, from eastern Virginia, Alabama, Chicago, New York, and New Mexico, are flawed as scientific studies, with their inconsistent methods and their partial reliance on self-reported consumption. But they are precious as historical sources, not only because they represent one of the first formal attempts to document and analyze eating habits scientifically, but also because they give one of the most detailed glimpses we have into how poor Americans were eating in the Gilded Age.

These dietary studies do not talk about vitamins, which would not be discovered until around 1910, or about calories, which were just being applied to food energy for the first time while these studies were being conducted. In fact, the professor who would later make calories famous, Wilbur O. Atwater, was deeply involved

in several of these dietary studies, and his fixation on what he called the "pecuniary economy of food," that is, making eating choices along strictly economic lines, deeply influenced the studies' methodology. In their dietary studies in New York City, Atwater and Charles Woods spelled out the big idea when describing one poor family: "The great trouble here, as in so many of the poor families of the congested district, lies in unwise expenditure fully as much as in a limited income." This was a conceit beloved of middle-class reformers: that if only the poor would be stricter with themselves, if only they would deny themselves more and economize more stringently, the worst effects of poverty would not exist. According to this thinking, most hunger and deprivation were self-induced, brought about by profligacy and waste and ignorance. In the New York City studies, you can almost hear reformers clucking with disapproval as they reported families buying milk rolls and soda crackers and jumbles when they could have saved money by sticking exclusively to cheap wheat bread. Never mind if buttery milk rolls were soft and tasty, or if salty, crunchy soda crackers added variety to meals, or if jumbles were a much-anticipated treat. The value of taste and variety and treats was not measurable, and they counted

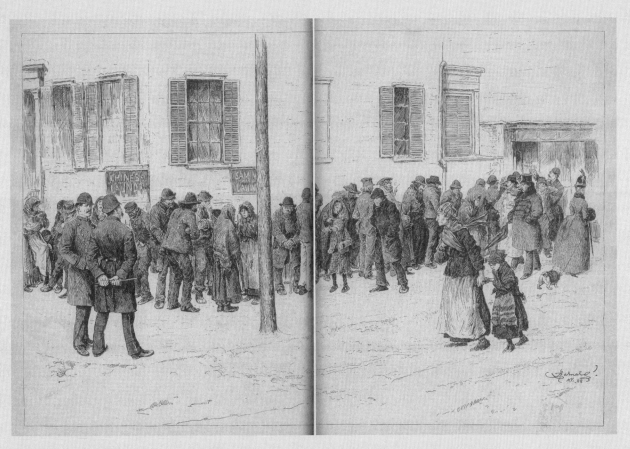

Desperately poor people waited in line for a free meal in Washington Square in New York City in 1888. This "restaurant," which gave away hot coffee, soup, and bread to the needy, was short-lived because the philanthropist running it soon became overwhelmed by the volume of need. In the foreground of the image, a poor mother leads her scantily clad daughter, hunching over with cold, while just behind them a well-dressed woman walks her dog, snug in its little jacket, a vivid reminder from the artist about how extremes of wealth and poverty coexisted in nineteenth-century New York. "Waiting in Line for a Meal," by Frederick Barnard, from *Harper's Weekly* 32, no. 1625 (February 11, 1888): 96–97, Special Collections, Michigan State University Libraries.

for nothing in the dietary tables. Reformers set about informing the poor of what they saw as superior ways to cook and eat and buy food with a messianic zeal.[2]

Dietary reformers particularly condemned immigrants' lack of culinary assimilation. Nowhere was this more pointed than with Italian immigrants, who were famously averse to changing their diets. Describing Italian immigrants in Chicago, Atwater and Arthur Bryant claimed that the "narrow range" of their food "really embarrasses their growth in every direction." In other words, as they saw it, Italians' strange diets not only impeded their physical growth but limited their economic and cultural advancement as well. They particularly denounced Italians' insistence on buying expensive, imported ingredients rather than "the more easily and cheaply secured foods in the American cities." But when reformers urged immigrants to eat the bread and boiled meat favored by "native Americans," by which they meant white people born in the United States, who can blame Italians for clinging to fruity olive oils, flavorful aged cheeses, garlic, and wine? What Atwater and Bryant saw as Italians' childish "horror" of "American food" and a mulish refusal to "adapt their tastes" looks in hindsight like the best kind of culinary sense.

By contrast, the authors gave a glowing report of one Bohemian family (that is, a family from the central European region of Bohemia that was then part of the Austro-Hungarian Empire) who "give a good example of what can be done with a small income by thrift and industry." While reformers condemned some housekeepers as "slovenly and shiftless," the Bohemian mother was "very neat," and she saved money by doing all her own baking and noodle making. Yet, strikingly, this family's diet was still not especially cheap: they spent as much or more on food as many of the other families profiled in these studies. The main difference, in fact, seems to be that their income was not actually that small to start with. In addition to his work as a tailor, the father owned a two-story tenement house and had a significant rental income as a landlord.

For those people at the bottom—those who had little education, or who were sick or disabled, or who had been born into slavery, or who spoke little English, or who were in debt—it was cruelly hard to break out of poverty, no matter how cheaply they ate. Disadvantages plagued people in these studies. Note how many were described as "sickly" or "lame" or "feeble" or "puny." Life in city tenements was brutally hard. And even worse was life as a black sharecropper in the Jim Crow South at a time of hardening legal segregation, systematic economic oppression, and exploding racial violence. The white reformers conducting these dietary studies were not primarily concerned with reporting on racism or poverty, but the brutality of life under Jim Crow comes through in the details. Some African American families had no light at night except for an open fire; some families did not even have an outhouse. Some families were impossibly in debt, like the family in Alabama who had become so indebted in the rigged sharecropping system that they had lost their farm, and all of their earthly possessions were "under mortgage" until they could pay their debts.

Sharecroppers, like these men and the woman outside a small cabin in rural Georgia in the late nineteenth century, often lived in desperate poverty. Photograph taken near Savannah, Georgia, 1867–1890, Launey and Goebel Photographers, Lot 14105, no. 10, Library of Congress Prints and Photographs Division.

Perhaps more than anything, poverty meant hunger. Poor black southerners supplemented meager diets with anything they could catch: possum, raccoon, muskrat, frogs, turtles, and even snakes. But vegetable patches and occasional game were not enough to keep everyone well fed. A woman in one eastern Virginia family weighed a skeletal ninety-two pounds; in another family, a ten-month-old baby weighed only fourteen pounds, and it died during the study. Even the seemingly neutral act of conducting the dietary studies themselves provoked animosity from white southerners. And it is important to note that the people profiled in these dietary studies would have had unusual advantages because these studies were conducted in affiliation with the two premier southern African American educational institutes of the late nineteenth century—the Tuskegee Institute in Alabama and the Hampton Institute in Virginia. And thus, unlike the vast majority of poor black southerners, some of the people interviewed here had received formal education and would sometimes have being able to draw upon these institutions' resources. For most black southerners under Jim Crow, life was even worse.

Dietary Studies in Alabama, 1895 and 1896

Food of the negro.—The staple foods of the negroes of this region are fat salt pork, corn meal, and molasses.[3] Of late, since wheat flour has become so cheap, it has been considerably used. The molasses is made from sorghum, or "millet," as it is called in this region, and sugar cane, both of which are grown in considerable quantities. The molasses from sorghum is generally preferred to that from cane. The molasses is made on the farms by a very primitive process. This consists in passing the cane between rollers to squeeze out the juice, and boiling the latter in open pans, which are set on furnaces roughly built of stone and clay. There are persons who go about from farm to farm with the rollers and make the molasses. Individual farmers who have no conveniences for making sirup carry their cane to other farms where it is worked. Only a part of the molasses used by the farmer is made on the farms, the rest is bought at the stores with other commodities.

Part of the corn meal is made from the corn grown on the farms, the rest is bought from dealers, and is uniformly unbolted.

The pork consists mostly of the fat sides, butchered and salted in the meat-packinghouses of Chicago and elsewhere, and brought in large quantities to the Southern market. Some pork is produced on the farms, but comparatively few swine were seen on those visited, nor was any kind of meat but fat pork, not even ham or shoulder, seen in any of the farmhouses. In the home of a well-to-do carpenter, which is located near the Institute, fresh beef and mutton were used during the two weeks of a dietary study. Probably this case was exceptional; indeed, the only kind of meat which seemed to be in at all common use among the country people was fat pork. Whenever they spoke of meat they always meant fat pork. Some of them knew it by no other name, nor did they seem to know much of any other meat except that of opossum and rabbits, which they occasionally hunted, and of chickens which they raised to a limited extent.

Even among the white population in the village of Tuskegee the use of fresh meat was not at all large. The table of the hotel was well supplied with fried ham and pork, but there was comparatively little beef. Fresh beef was to be had at the market on two or three days in the week. This limited use of fresh meats could not be attributed to any lack of generous diet, for the tables of white people were bountifully spread. It seemed due to the agricultural conditions which obtain in the region, and to the difficulty of keeping fresh meat in the warm climate. The climate is not favorable to the growth of ordinary grasses which are so abundant in the beef-producing regions; comparatively few cattle are raised, and the meat is less fat, and less tender and juicy than that from the grazing regions farther north. In Knoxville, Tenn., for instance, where dietary studies have been lately made, in a region where grass and corn are abundant, the native beef was much more plentiful and appetizing, and the specimens analyzed in connection with dietary studies were considerably fatter, than those from Tuskegee and elsewhere in Alabama, and were in this respect more like those of meats in the Northern markets. Veal and mutton are even less common than beef. No sheep were seen in the country about Tuskegee and there are very few in the region.

The scarcity of fresh meat and the difficulty of preserving it doubtless goes far toward explaining the dietary tastes and habits of the people in general in this region, if not elsewhere in the South. The managers of the colored schools find their students decidedly averse to a diet materially different from that of salt pork, corn meal, and molasses, to which they have been accustomed at home.

The colored families near the village of Tuskegee, and some in the country, kept cows and had milk and butter. For making butter they used small, dash churns of glazed earthenware called "splashers," which are usually about 15 inches high by 8 in diameter. The fresh milk was put directly into the churn and successive milkings were added until it contained from 1½ to 2 gallons, and the whole churned without any attempt at removing the cream. The churning was done about once in two days, and from the above amount of milk a small saucerful of a soft, white, and watery butter would be obtained. The people made no attempt at working it, nor did they add salt, but ate it fresh. The buttermilk was drunk with decided relish.

No cows or milk were seen at any one of several cabins visited on a large plantation at some distance from the village where the life was said to be like that of the aver-

age plantation negro. The food consisted almost exclusively of fat pork, corn meal, and molasses.

Cooking. The cooking is of the most simple and primitive character. It is nearly always done over the open fire. Only two of the families visited had stoves. One was that of the carpenter referred to above. He had been under the influence of the Tuskegee Institute. The following extract from a letter of Mr. Hoffman, of the Institute, who shared in the dietary investigations, is of special interest in this connection:

The daily fare is prepared in very simple ways. Corn meal is mixed with water and baked on the flat surface of a hoe or griddle. The salt pork is sliced thin and fried until very brown and much of the grease tried out. Molasses from cane or sorghum is added to the fat, making what is known as "sap" which is eaten with the corn bread. Hot water sweetened with molasses is used as a beverage. This is the bill of fare of most of the cabins on the plantations of the "black belt," three times a day during the year. It is, however, varied at times; thus collards and turnips are boiled with the bacon, the latter being used with the vegetables to supply fat "to make it rich." The corn-meal bread is sometimes made into so-called "cracklin bread," and is prepared as follows: A piece of fat bacon is fried until it is brittle; it is then crushed and mixed with corn meal, water, soda, and salt and baked in an oven over the fireplace. Occasionally the negroes may have an opossum. To prepare this for eating it is first put in hot water to help in removing a part of the hair, then covered with hot ashes until the rest of the hair is removed; thereupon it is put in a large pot, surrounded with sweet potatoes, seasoned with red pepper, and baked. One characteristic of the cooking is that all meats are fried or otherwise cooked until they are crisp. Observation among these people reveals the fact that very many of them suffer from indigestion in some form.

The food and cooking observed in the cabins visited were entirely in accordance with Mr. Hoffman's description, except that flour was used in every case. In how far this was due to the low price which has prevailed of late, and whether the use had extended generally through the black belt of course is not known. It is probable, however, that with the decline in the price of flour the negroes have been learning to use it, and liking its taste and being inclined to imitate the white man in diet as in other things, its use has become more or less common and will be likely to increase.

Dietary of a Negro Carpenter's Family in Alabama (No. 98)

This family lived in the outskirts of the Village of Tuskegee, near the Institute. The father had been under the influence of the latter institution and had learned the carpenter's trade and was in the employ of the Institute. With his savings and labor he had built a very comfortable one-story frame house with four rooms[.] The house was plainly but neatly and very comfortably furnished. A garden supplied the family with vegetables, and two cows and a number of hens and turkeys furnished milk, eggs, and fowl for the table. They had fresh meat frequently, as well as fruits and vegetables. The condition of this family had been steadily improving since the husband came under the influence of the

Institute. Instances of such thrift and comfort among the negroes of the region are extremely rare, and were found only in connection with the Institute. They illustrate not what the negro is, but what he may become.

ANIMAL FOOD

Beef, round, 455 grams, $0.10

Mutton, leg, 2,040 grams, $0.54

Pork:

    Unsmoked side bacon, 3,275 grams, $0.51

    Lard, 2,380 grams, $0.39

Chicken, 905 grams, $0.10

Eggs, 595 grams, $0.10

Butter, 990 grams, $0.44

Milk, 57,140 grams, $5.04

VEGETABLE FOOD

Cereals, sugar, etc.

    Wheat flour, 21,205 grams, $1.40

    Corn meal, 9,300 grams, $0.26

    Rolled oats, 115 grams, $0.01

    Sugar, 3,020 grams, $0.40

    Molasses, 4,410 grams, $0.44

Fruits:

    Evaporated apples, 310 grams, $0.08

    Strawberries, 665 grams, $0.10

Dietary of a Negro Farmer's Family in Alabama (No. 100)

This family was composed of husband and wife and five children. The cabin was built of logs and had two rooms.

One, used as living and sleeping room, contained two beds and a few small pieces of furniture. The kitchen was provided with a pine table, one or two chairs, a small portable cupboard, the usual pot and frying pan, and a few dishes for the table. There was no churn, as the family had no cow. In the cupboard were a piece of salt pork and a jug of molasses, and near by a sack of corn meal. The provisions were purchased each week, and toward the close there was very little left in the house. Fried pork and corn pone, cooked in the fireplace, composed the daily diet.

A mule, an ox, and a pig made up the live stock.

The farm was planted chiefly to cotton. A small patch was devoted to sugar cane. There was no garden, and the cotton was cultivated close up to the cabin door.

This farmer had been in the habit of mortgaging his crops each year, but under the influence of the Institute and the farmers' conferences he was trying to better his condition and was working this year without a mortgage.

ANIMAL FOOD
Unsmoked side bacon, 1,590 grams, $0.25
Lard, 1445 grams, $0.24

VEGETABLE FOOD
Cereals, sugar, etc.:
  Wheat flour, 9,470 grams, $0.63
  Corn meal, 20,920 grams, $0.58
  Rice, 710 grams, $0.08
Collards (cabbage), 255 grams, $0.01

Dietary of a Negro Farmer's Family in Alabama (No. 101)

This family consisted of six persons—the husband, wife, and four children. A mortgage had caused them to be sold out the year previous, and they were now clearing up a new place on a piece of land which was more than a mile back from the traveled road, and of which only a part had previously been cultivated. The cabin, however, was better than the majority. It contained four rooms, and a small log hut in the yard served as a kitchen. The soil was sandy and very poor. The land was partly covered with pine trees, full of stumps and second growth. Cotton, cane, sweet potatoes, and cowpeas had been planted. The woman worked all day in the field.

The live stock consisted of a mule, two cows, and some hens. Milk and eggs were used, and occasionally the family indulged in the luxury of sugar and coffee. The provisions were purchased by the week. The cooking was done with a stove, and the diet was somewhat better than that in several other cabins where studies were made.

All the possessions of the family were under mortgage, but their three oldest sons were working for the mortgagee to assist in payment. This accounts for their having such a good cabin after the previous year's reverses.

ANIMAL FOOD
Pork:
  Bacon, 2,990 grams, $0.52
  Lard, 905 grams, $0.15

Eggs, 3,895 grams, $0.67

Butter, 640 grams, $0.13

Milk, 595 grams, $0.26

Buttermilk, 12,460, $0.34

VEGETABLE FOOD

Cereals, sugar, etc.:

    Wheat flour, 8,390 grams, $0.56

    Corn meal, 8,280 grams, $0.23

    Sugar, 905 grams, $0.10

Dietary of a Negro Sawmill Laborer's Family in Alabama (No. 102)

This family, living on a small farm, consisted of husband and wife, an adopted daughter of 12, and two younger children. The husband worked in a sawmill and received 50 cents a day, paid in merchandise. The wife worked in the field. The husband was a step-son of the family mentioned in study No. 101. The two farms joined, and the people assisted one another in their farm work.

The cabin was made of logs and had one room, which served as living and sleeping room, and an addition in the rear, not more than 6 feet wide, which was used as a kitchen. The living room contained two beds, a few other small pieces of furniture, and a fireplace.

The kitchen had a cupboard, a pine table, and a fireplace. The house had two doors, but was without windows. The cabin was comparatively new, and better than many of its class. The furnishings, however, were as poor as those of the ordinary one-room cabins.

The food consisted of salt pork, corn meal, and molasses, with butter, buttermilk, "clabber," and a few eggs. For live stock the people had an ox, a cow, and a few hens. They had no garden, the farm crops were like those of No. 101, cotton, with a little cane, cowpeas, and sweet potatoes.

ANIMAL FOOD

Bacon, 1,630 grams, $0.29

Eggs, 425 grams, $0.07

Butter, 240 grams, $0.11

Buttermilk, 1,815 grams, $0.92

Milk, 10,435 grams, $0.05

VEGETABLE FOOD

Cereals, sugar, etc.

    Wheat flour, 3,645 grams, $0.24

    Corn meal, 5,100 grams, $0.14

    Sugar, 540 grams, $0.06

    Molasses, 3,670 grams, $0.36

Dietary Studies in New York City, 1895 and 1896

The people in whose families the studies were made represented a large number of occupations.[4] In some instances they were slovenly and shiftless and took little interest in the appearance of their homes and tables. Other families, though ignorant, were willing and anxious to learn how they might improve their habits of living . . .

Dietary Study of a Mechanic's Family (No. 30)

The family consisted of the father (Irish), the mother (English), and three daughters, aged 11 years, 8 years, and 8 months. The man was a repairer of soda-water apparatus, and until hard times came on earned good wages. The woman was sickly, and most of the work, including all of the marketing, was done by the 11-year old daughter, who was usually imposed upon by the marketmen. The family was very poor, and had received a great deal of help from the Association for the Improvement of the Condition of the Poor. The building in which they lived was in bad repair. The whole family was shiftless and careless.

The total cost of the food purchased is very high. This family paid $10.22 in ten days, or at the rate of about $31 per month for food, exclusive of beverages and condiments. Their rent was $12 per month. When the man had work, he earned about $50 per month. Deducting the cost of food and rent from this, only $7 per month remain for fuel, lights, clothing, and the numerous other requirements of a family.

With good management in its purchase and preparation, food sufficient to meet the needs of a man at moderate work for a day can be obtained at a cost ranging from 15 to 20 cents. The food of the family of a well-to-do professional man, whose dietary was recently studied, cost 18 cents per man per day, or but little more than half the cost in this family. By the proper expenditure of their money the New York family would have been able to buy their food for $15 to $20 instead of $30 per month . . .

The great trouble here, as in so many of the poor families of the congested district, lies in unwise expenditure fully as much as in a limited income.

Round steak, 10.5 oz., 15.2 cents per pound
Corned brisket, 24.5 oz., 6.5 cents per pound
Veal, breast, 39 oz., 4.1 cents per pound
Mutton
    Chuck, 23 oz., 7 cents per pound
    Loin, 9 oz., 17.8 cents per pound
    Shoulder, 14.5 oz., 11 cents per pound
Ham, 8 oz., 20 cents per pound
Chicken, 9 oz., 17.8 cents per pound
Cod (fresh), 19.5 oz., 8.2 cents per pound
Flounder, 26 oz., 6.2 cents per pound
Haddock, 19 oz., 8.4 cents per pound
Shad, 12 oz., 13.3 cents per pound
Shad-herring, 40 oz., 4 cents per pound
Eggs, 15 oz., 10.7 cents per pound
Milk, 58 oz., 2.8 cents per pound

Condensed milk, 10 oz., 16 cents per pound

Self-raising flour, 31 oz., 5.2 cents per pound

Bread, 63.5 oz., 2.5 cents per pound

Buns, 29 oz., 5.5 cents per pound

Rolls, 40 oz., 4 cents per pound

Canned asparagus, 11 oz., 14.5 cents per pound

Cabbage, [no amount given], 1.7 cents per pound

Celery, 14 oz., 11.4 cents per pound

Potatoes, [no amount given], 2 cents per pound

Bananas, [no amount given], 7.4 cents per pound

Oranges, [no amount given], 4.9 cents per pound

Peanuts, [no amount given], 18 cents per pound

Other food materials which were used by this family, but not included in the above list, were beef suet, mutton neck, pigs' feet, clam chowder, Swiss cheese, butter, crackers, starch, sugar, soup greens (carrots, leeks, onions, and parsley), radishes, rhubarb, and turnips. The great variety and unwise selection of the food purchased by the 11-year-old girl who did most of the work and all of the marketing is clearly shown by the above list. That she was imposed upon by the marketmen is brought out by the table. The excessive cost of the food of this family is due to both of these causes. The cost of their living is extravagant for a well-to-do family, and for people in their condition ("very poor") it is ruinous.

The comparatively expensive nature of most food fishes is also clearly indicated in the table. The shad-herring were very abundant and sold at a low price, so that they alone of all the fish purchased were economical. Next to veal they were the cheapest source of ani-mal food this young housekeeper found. The self-raising flour was much more expensive than wheat flour, with the necessary baking powder, would have been, and it was of such quality and cost that 10 cents did not purchase nearly as much nutriment as would be furnished by rolls, even at 4 cents a pound.

The childish taste of the girl led her to purchase peanuts. In doing so she acted wisely, though unconscious of it. The food value of the peanut is not generally appreciated. While it may be somewhat difficult of digestion, there is no reason to believe that it is not as completely digested as any similar food. It will be observed that the peanuts, even at the price paid a street vender, furnish more protein for 10 cents than any other kind of food except the breast of veal, which was bought at the unusually low price of 4 cents a pound.

Suggestions for changes and improvements.—The amount of food purchased might have been reduced 25 or 30 per cent and a considerable saving of money effected thereby. A more judicious selection of food and greater attention to the details of marketing and the preparation of the food might have still further reduced the cost. Such carefulness in purchase and preparation would also reduce the kitchen and table wastes so that practically no food would be wasted. The more intelligent selection of food, from both the nutritive and pecuniary standpoints, would preclude the purchase at the prices paid of such foods as chicken, cod, flounder, and shad, condensed milk, canned asparagus, prepared flours, radishes, celery, cherry jelly, etc., and would lead to the increased purchase of the more economical foods, including peas, beans, wheat flour, rice, and the cheap but nutritious cuts of beef, veal, and mutton. In this way a large proportion of the money spent for food could have been saved, with advantage to health and without interfering with the palatability of the food eaten. At present this end seems almost unattainable.

Dietary Study of a Jeweler's Family (No. 32).

The family consisted of the father and mother (both German); four sons, 18, 16, 10, and 8 years old; and one daughter 12 years old. The family was much neater and more thrifty than is usually the case on the crowded East Side. The husband earned $10 a week and the two eldest boys paid $10 a week to their parents. Although the husband's wages were small, the family succeeded in buying a piano and two of the children were taking music lessons.

The total cost of the food (exclusive of beverages and condiments) for the family for ten days was $9.47, or about $29 per month. The rent was $14 per month. The total income was $90. As the family, after paying for food and rent, would have nearly $50 a month unexpended, it is easy to understand how they could buy a piano and pay for music lessons for the children.

ANIMAL FOOD
Beef

Chuck, 15.5 oz., 10.3 cents per pound

Cross ribs, 11.5 oz., 13.9 cents per pound

Round, 15 oz., 10.7 cents per pound

Sirloin, 8.5 oz., 18.8 cents per pound
Bologna sausage, 12 oz., 13.3 cents per pound
Cervelat sausage, 8 oz., 20 cents per pound
Veal:

Loin and kidney, 10 oz., 16 cents per pound

Shoulder, 16 oz., 10 cents per pound
Lamb, leg, 12 oz., 13.3 cents per pound
Pork chops, 14 oz., 11.4 cents per pound
Ham, 7.5 oz., 21.3 cents per pound
Fresh cod, 16.5 oz., 9.7 cents per pound
Eggs, 16 oz., 10 cents per pound
Swiss cheese, 5.5 oz., 29.1 cents per pound
Milk, 64 oz., 2.5 cents per pound
Condensed milk, 21 oz., 7.6 cents per pound

VEGETABLE FOOD
Wheat flour, 68 oz., 2.4 cents per pound
Rice, 25 oz., 6.4 cents per pound
Bread:

Rye, 51 oz., 3.1 cents per pound

Wheat, 60 oz., 2.7 cents per pound
Milk rolls, 35 oz., 4.6 cents per pound
Sugar buns, 27 oz., 5.9 cents per pound
Doughnuts, 24 oz., 6.7 cents per pound
Red cabbage, 31 oz., 5.2 cents per pound
Canned peas, 22 oz., 7.3 cents per pound
Potatoes, [no amount given], 1.4 cents per pound
Sauerkraut, 62 oz., 2.6 cents per pound

Other food materials which were used by this family, but which were not considered of sufficient importance to include in the above table, were beef shoulder, suet, butter, oatmeal, crackers, sugar, cabbage sprouts, soup greens, lettuce, pickles, lemons, and dried peaches.

Wheat flour, in this as in all other cases where it is used, is the cheapest food purchased. It may, however, be questioned whether there is anything saved in using home-made bread when wheat bread can be purchased, as in this instance, for 2.7 cents per pound. The "milk rolls" contained shortening and had seven-eighths of the fuel value of wheat bread, but only a little more than half the amount of protein. The wheat flour, and rye and wheat breads were the cheap sources of protein in this dietary. Sauerkraut has much the same composition as the cabbage from which it is made, but as it is sold at a lower price, 10 cents will pay for 50 per cent more nutrients in sauerkraut than in cabbage. The vegetables here, as elsewhere, were expensive sources of protein. It must, however, be kept in mind that such food materials seem essential to proper nutrition and that they have a value not expressed by their chemical composition.

The food eaten furnished, perhaps, as much protein as is needed per day by a man without much muscular work. The fuel value of the food eaten, however, was considerably less than the amount needed. The lacking fuel value could be supplied at small cost by foods containing starch and sugar or by the fat of meats. Nitrogenous foods, i.e., those which supply protein, are much more expensive than those which furnish the fuel ingredients. There was very little food wasted. The small waste of fats and carbohydrates is probably due in part to the fact that the diet contained so little of these constituents. The nutritive ratio (1:5.4) is very small. The addition of

fats and carbohydrates, as suggested above, would make it larger.

Suggestions for changes and improvements.—If the members of the family were at all active in their habits, their diet would be improved by the addition of starch, sugar, or fatty foods. This would involve the more liberal use of sugar, butter, the fatter meats (as pork or mutton), or such foods as tapioca and corn starch. Such changes would only slightly increase the cost of the food and would be of undoubted advantage . . . Dr. Delaney states that this woman was very shrewd in marketing, and knew where she could get the most for the least money. While there was no extravagance in any of the foods purchased, the above opinion would seem to be founded more upon her general thriftiness than upon her selection of food and the prices which she paid. Beef sirloin at 20 cents a pound, bologna sausage and pork chops at 16 cents, and ham at 22 cents are hardly the food materials which furnish the most nutriment for the least money. Judgment in the selection of food, not so much by bulk as by the nutrients it contains, would lead here, as in other cases, to better and at the same time cheaper food.

Dietary Study of a Watchman's Family (No. 34).

The family consisted of a father (German); mother (Irish); three sons, 20, 10, and 8 years old; and four daughters, aged 14, 6, 4, and 2 years. The father was a small man and very fat. He used to own a saloon, and was rather lazy. The mother was also small. The children were all rather puny and small. The household management was not very good, and they had little knowledge of the relation of food to health and strength. Except at breakfast the family sat down together to their meals, and the table looked rather neat. They all dressed well. The father earned $8 a week. The oldest son worked in a printing office, and paid $6 a week to his parents. They paid $12 per month for rent.

ANIMAL FOOD

Pork chops, 12 oz., 13.3 cents per pound

Eggs, 22 oz., 7.3 cents per pound

Milk, 77 oz., 2.1 cents per pound

Condensed milk, 15 oz., 10.7 cents per pound

VEGETABLE FOOD

Rice, 27 oz., 5.9 cents per pound

Bread, wheat, 65.5 oz., 2.4 cents per pound

Soda crackers, 18 oz., 8.9 cents per pound

Jumbles, 18 oz., 8.9 cents per pound

Canned corn, 16 oz., 10 cents per pound

Peas:

    Dried, 32 oz., 5 cents per pound

    Green, 20 oz., 8 cents per pound

Potatoes, [no amount given], 2.2 cents per pound

Canned tomatoes, 24 oz., 6.7 cents per pound

Other food materials which were used by this family, but (with the exception of butter) in smaller amounts, were beef-soup meat, veal rib, butter, sugar, soup greens, onions, and turnips.

The soda crackers and jumbles cost two or three times as much as the wheat bread, and are practically of the same composition, except that they contain a little more fat. The dried peas were an exceedingly cheap source of protein. The difference in the cost of nutrients in green peas and dried peas is strikingly pointed out in the table, the former being about eight times that of the latter. At the prices paid the dried peas were, with the possible exception of wheat bread, the most economical food used. The green peas were, however, the most expensive, so far as the cost of nutrients is concerned, of any of the foods except the canned tomatoes. The money paid for breast of veal was the best expenditure made for animal food. This meat was probably used as a stew, and in this way was all eaten. At the prices paid condensed milk is not so economical nor so good a food as fresh milk. The corned beef cost too much; equally good could have been purchased for 8 or 10 cents a pound.

The family were underfed. The nutritive ratio (1:6) was very nearly that suggested in the dietary standards, but too little food was eaten . . . The family were trying to live economically, but in doing so failed to get enough nutriment. Instead of eating a sufficient amount of inexpensive but nutritious food, they made a poor selection and were underfed. Their income would not warrant a greater expenditure for food per man per day than was actually made (14 cents). If the daily diet had been made to contain 50 grams more protein and 1,000 more calories, it would have cost 20 or 21 cents per man per day, provided the same food materials were selected as before. It is possible to buy the needed protein and energy without exceeding the 14 cents per day actually expended, although such a diet would have no great variety.

Suggestions for changes and improvements.—The family used altogether too much butter for economy. This is the most expensive form in which animal fat is purchased. One-ninth of the total cost of the food was expended for butter. The same money spent for "breast of lamb" would have furnished as much fat as the butter and at the same time have added 1,000 grams of protein to the food. This alone would increase the protein per man per day 20 grams. The beef used in this dietary was also too expensive. More bread, less butter, more of cheaper but equally nutritious cuts of meats, and a liberal use of peas and beans would make it possible for this family to be much better nourished than was the case, and without additional cost.

Dietary Study of Family of a Carver in a Restaurant (No. 37).

The family consisted of a man, his wife, and five daughters, aged 21, 20, 13, 7, and 5 years. The mother and husband were both born in Germany. The woman had been in this country about twenty-five years and the man about twenty years. The woman's first husband, the father of the children, was also a German. The stepfather was a carver in a restaurant and had only one meal (dinner at night) at home. He earned $9 a week. The two eldest daughters worked in a box factory, and they each earned $7 to $8 per week. They paid only $3 each for board. The remaining $4 or $5 was spent in dress.

The husband used tobacco and drank beer occasionally, rarely drinking to excess. He weighed about 150 pounds, the mother about 140, and the two eldest girls about 120 pounds each. The mother was hard-working and thrifty.

The tenement in which the family lived consisted of four rooms; one was lighted from two windows in the street. The kitchen and one bedroom opened on the air shaft. The other bedroom was a "dark" room. The bedrooms were so small that there was only room for the bed. Two of the children slept on mattresses on the floor of the front room. There were set tubs and a sink in the kitchen. There was no bath tub which the family could use. The kitchen served as a dining room. The table was not set and the family did not sit down together to eat their meals. There were no regular meals, the table serving more as a lunch counter where each one went and helped himself. No meal was prepared at noon. The oldest daughter contributed to a "common spread" with her shopmates, and the children were given 5 cents each per day with which they bought cakes and fruit at the open stands on the street.

ANIMAL FOOD

Beef, shank, 44.5 oz., 3.6 cents per pound
Veal, shoulder, 18 oz., 8.9 cents per pound
Mutton chops, 17 oz., 9.4 cents per pound
Pork chops, 13.5 oz., 11.8 cents per pound
Ham, 12.5 oz., 12.8 cents per pound
Salt pork, 16 oz., 10 cents per pound
Eggs, 13 oz., 12.3 cents per pound
Condensed milk, 23 oz., 7 cents per pound

VEGETABLE FOOD

Bread

    Rye, 43.5 oz., 3.7 cents per pound

    Wheat, 57.5 oz., 2.8 cents per pound

Cake, 21 oz., 7.6 cents per pound

Rolls, 29.5 oz., 5.4 cents per pound

Beans, 29.5 oz., 5.4 cents per pound

Cabbage [no amount given], 3.8 cents per pound

Potatoes, [no amount given], 1.6 cents per pound

Jelly, 30 oz., 5.3 cents per pound

Besides the above food materials, there were also used, to a greater or less extent, beef suet, veal shoulder, lard, butter, flour, macaroni, lettuce, soup greens, onions, green peas, canned tomatoes, dried apples, and dried prunes . . .

Suggestions for changes and improvements.—Increasing the amount of food the needed [*sic*] 40 or 50 per cent would, of course, increase the cost correspondingly, provided the same food materials were selected; but this would not be the wisest plan. To furnish the required amount of nourishment it would probably be necessary to increase the cost of the food to about 15 cents per man per day. For this amount it is possible to furnish in a palatable form the nutrients needed for the proper nourishment for a man for one day, provided proper food materials are selected. For instance, it would be more economical to use fresh milk instead of condensed milk, and the cheaper cuts of meat are much more economical foods than the eggs which were used.

The great trouble here, as in most of the cases studied, is in the lack of management. Dr. Delaney interested herself in this family, and some months after the dietary study was made writes to the effect that matters grew worse before any change could be made. The mother had an attack of gastritis, and one daughter remained at home to nurse her. The rent came due and some of the furniture had to be pawned to raise the money; and then the eldest daughter left home, disgusted with the bare-looking room. On the mother's recovery the physician (Dr. Delaney) insisted on the family having a meal at noon, and the girls were urged to come home for it. A place as housekeeper of the tenement house was found for the mother, and by paying $3 a month in addition four light rooms were procured. The family have improved in their way of living. The table is now set with a white cloth and the family sit down together. The mother has improved in health and strength. When it is necessary for the girls to carry a lunch the mother prepares it for them, and it costs less than a third of what it would otherwise.

Dietary Studies in Chicago in 1895 and 1896

The purpose of the dietary studies here reported was to obtain information regarding the conditions of living and the pecuniary economy of the food of the poor of different nationalities residing in the worst congested districts of Chicago.[5] The studies were, with few exceptions, made in the vicinity of Hull House.

As is well known to all who are familiar with the philanthropic movements in the United States, Hull House is a social settlement similar in purpose to the "university," "college," and other social "settlements" which have been established in a number of our cities, as well as in England. It is situated in one of the most densely populated districts of the "West Side." This region is largely inhabited by immigrants, almost every nation of Europe being represented. Some of the residents have a very high degree of intelligence, but many are very ignorant. In purchasing food, taste and cost are usually the only points considered, as there is little appreciation of the fact that foods vary greatly in nutritive value.

The managers and residents of Hull House are very familiar with the region. They are in close touch with the people, enjoy their confidence, and exert an influence over them which is remarkable for its extent and for its great and diversified usefulness. The thorough acquaintance of Miss Addams and others of Hull House with the district, and their close sympathy with the people, were most important factors in carrying on this investigation.

These circumstances made it possible to choose representative families, to gain access to the homes selected, and to conduct the inquiry with an understanding of the problems involved which otherwise would have been out of the question.

The plan involved the selection of groups of families, each group representing a nationality, and each family being more or less typical of the people of that nationality in that part of Chicago . . . The investigations included dietary studies among families of Italians, French Canadians, Russian Jews, both orthodox and unorthodox or liberal, and Bohemians.

Studies among Italian Families

It is unusually difficult to obtain access to the homes of the Italians and gain permission to conduct dietary studies. Many families, after having consented to allow such studies to be made, refused to carry the dietary further than the first meal or day. Out of a large number of studies undertaken, only four were carried to a satisfactory close. These were conducted under the direct supervision of those carrying on the investigation.

Some peculiarities were observed in the food habits of the Italians. In correspondence concerning these studies the following statements are made:

The Italian oil, wine, arid cheese, which even the poorest family uses, are all imported, and of course expensive. These articles are comparatively cheap in Italy, and the people grow accustomed to their use. They consume a great deal of macaroni, which is now fortunately made in this country. They use very little milk, and have comparatively little idea of the use and value of indigenous vegetables and other foods.

We have almost never succeeded in getting an Italian to go to one of the county hospitals or other institutions, largely because he dreads the change of food, and insists that he would starve. On the rare occasion in which an Italian has gone to a hospital, the great complaint upon his return is of the strange food, and he spreads a horror of it among his neighbors. This dread of American food prevents, more or less, the Italians from obtaining employment under any but Italian padrones, who not infrequently impose upon their helplessness. The narrow range, so to speak, in their food really embarrasses their growth in every direction, and no pains have ever been taken to adapt their tastes to the more easily and cheaply secured foods in the American cities.

DIETARY STUDY (NO. 55)

This family consisted of the father and mother, a married daughter and her husband, and child 2 years old. The father was unemployed, and the son-in-law, usually employed in a candy shop, was out of work at the time. The mother was sick, and during the study consumed 25 cents' worth of brandy each day. They paid $8 per month rent for four rooms, three of which were light. In addition to the food 20 cents' worth of tea was consumed.

ANIMAL FOOD

Beef: Round, ½ lb., 5 cts.

Pork: Lard, 1 lb. 8½ ozs., 15 cts.

Fish: Cod (fresh), 1 lb., 8 cts.

Eggs, 2½ lbs., 35 cts.

Cheese, ½ lb., 15 cts.

Milk, 7 lbs., 21 cts.

VEGETABLE FOOD

Cereals:

    Wheat bread, 24 lbs. 2 ozs., 80 cts.

    Macaroni, 2½ lbs., 25 cts.

Sugar, 3 lbs. 9½ ozs., 15 cts.

Potatoes, 11 lbs. 11 ozs., 17 cts.

Lentils, 14½ ozs., 5 cts.

Vegetables:

    Asparagus, 1¾ lbs., 5 cts.

    String beans, 14 lbs., 25 cts.

    Cabbage, 1 lb. 5 ozs., 5 cts.

    Lettuce, 3 lbs. 3 ozs., 14 cts.

    Spinach, 1 lb. 10 ozs., 5 cts.

Studies among French-Canadian Families

Comparatively little trouble was experienced in carrying out satisfactory investigations among the French Canadians . . . The work was done under the constant supervision of those in charge of the investigations, and the results probably give a reasonably accurate idea of the food purchased by these families.

DIETARY STUDY (NO. 59)

The family consisted of the mother, about 60 years of age; a son, 35 years old; a married daughter, 26 years old, and her two children, 5 and 2 years of age. In addition to these, there were three male boarders. The son was weak-minded and did no work. The other men were employed at hard work. The family paid $15 a month for three light rooms on the third floor. During the study 50 cents' worth of coffee was consumed.

ANIMAL FOOD

Beef:

    Round, 9¼ lbs., $1.03

    Shoulder, 5 lbs. 1 oz., 53 cts.

    Soup bone, 4 lbs. 10 ozs., 30 cts.

    Corned, 5¼ lbs., 49 cts.

Veal:

    Chops, 1 lb. 9 ozs., 25 cts.

    Rib, 10 lbs., $1.13

    Shoulder, 2 lbs. 2 ozs., 15 cts.

Pork:

    Chops, 12 lbs. 3 ozs., $1.53

    Sparerib, 7 lbs. 4½ ozs., 43 cts.

    Pigs' feet, 2 lbs. 5 ozs., 21 cts.

    Bacon, 2¼ lbs., 29 cts.

    Ham, 1 lb. 13 ozs., 30 cts.

    Salt pork, 7 lbs. 3 ozs., 80 cts.

    Sausage, 4 lbs. 13 ozs., 48 cts.

Fish:

    Carp, 3 lbs. 3½ ozs., 44 cts.

    Sardines, ½ lb., 8 cts.

    Lobster (canned), 1 lb., 18 cts.

Eggs, 18 lbs. 1 oz., $1.72

Butter, 13 lbs. 3 ozs., $2.59

Milk, 41 lbs., $1.23 (44)

VEGETABLE FOOD

Cereals:

    Wheat flour, 2 lbs. 1 oz., 5 cts.

    Wheat bread, 38 lbs., $1.16

    Rice, 2 lbs., 14 cts.

    Cake, 3 lbs. 7½ ozs., 20 cts.

    Soda crackers, 2 lbs. 6 ozs., 17 cts.

    Sugar cookies, 2 lbs. ½ oz., 30 cts.

    Apple pie, 6½ lbs., 40 cts.

Sugar, 8 lbs. 10 ozs., 43 cts.

Potatoes, 67 lbs. 11½ ozs., $1.08

Vegetables:

    Asparagus. 3 lbs., 18 cts.

    String beans, 1½ lbs., 10 cts.

    Cabbage, 8 lbs., 33 cts.

    Corn (canned), 1 lb. 6 ozs., 10 cts.

    Cucumbers, 3 1bs., 20 cts.

    Lettuce, 3 lbs., 12 cts.

    Onions, 6 lbs., 30 cts.

    Radishes, 1 lb., 5 cts.

    Tomatoes (canned), 5¼ lbs., 18 cts.

Fruits: Strawberries, 3 lbs. 1 oz., 30 cts.

Studies among Families of Orthodox Russian Jews

The Russian Jews are very careful to purchase only such meat as is permitted by their ecclesiastical laws. The same care is exercised in its preparation. No especial care was observed in the purchase and preparation of vegetables, fruits, and other materials falling outside this religious prescription . . . Jewish butchers slaughter in a particular manner. The composition of the meat does not, however, appear to vary materially from similar cuts of meat as ordinarily slaughtered . . .

DIETARY STUDY (NO. 62)

The family consisted of the husband, about 25, and the wife, about 20 years of age, and one boarder (woman). The man was a pretzel peddler. They paid $8 a month for the rent of four rooms on the first floor. Two of these rooms were light and two dark.

ANIMAL FOOD

Beef:

Clod and cross ribs, 8½ lbs., 85 cts.

Chuck, 7½ lbs., 75 cts.

Plate, 1½ lbs., 15 cts.

Beef fat, 14 ozs., 9 cts.

Fish:

Carp, 2 lbs. 13 ozs., 14 cts.

Herring (smoked), 4 ozs., 2 cts.

Eggs, 6 lbs. 6 ozs., 42 cts.

Butter, 2 lbs. 6 ozs., 50 cts.

Cheese:

Cottage, ½ lb., 3 cts.

Schweitzer, 4 ozs., 9 cts.

Milk, 18¾ lbs., 57 cts.

Cream, sour, 1½ lbs., 9 cts.

VEGETABLE FOOD

Cereals:

Barley, ¾ lb., 6 cts.

Wheat flour, 2 lbs., 5 cts.

Oatmeal, 9 ozs., 2 cts.

Rice, ½ lb., 4 cts.

Rye bread, 9 lbs. 11 ozs., 38 cts.

Wheat bread, 14 lbs. 13 ozs., 75 cts.

Sugar, 7 lbs., 31 cts.

Potatoes, 5 lbs. 7 ozs., 6 cts.

Vegetables:

Beets, ½ lb., 2 cts.

Cabbage, 1 lb. 10 ozs., 3 cts.

Lettuce, 10 ozs., 5 cts.

Onions, 3 lbs., 5 cts.

Peas (fresh), 14 ozs., 10 cts.

Radishes, 2 lbs., 10 cts.

Spinach, 1 lb. 3 ozs., 5 cts.

Tomatoes (fresh), 2½ lbs., 10 cts.

Fruits:

Gooseberries,1½ lbs., 10 cts.

Lemons, 1 lb. 12 ozs., 8 cts.

Oranges, 2 lbs., 8 cts.

DIETARY STUDY (NO. 66)

The family consisted of the father, about 36, and the mother, about 35 years old; a girl of 9 years, and three sons aged, respectively, 7 years, 2 years, and 8 months. A woman boarded with the family. They were very poor, and lived in four rooms in a dark, unhealthful basement, for which they paid $7 per month rent. The man worked as a polisher. Besides the food materials enumerated in the table, expenditures were made for what may be called "food accessories," as follows: "Pop," i.e., bottled soda water, 19 cents; tea, 19 cents; horse-radish, 16 cents; vinegar, 5 cents; pepper, 7 cents; baking powder, 15 cents; beer, 5 cents; brandy, 5 cents.

ANIMAL FOOD

Beef:
    Chuck, 18½ lbs., $2.21
    Flauken (plate), 1 lb., 12 cts.
    Beef fat, 1½ lbs., 17 cts.
Fish:
    Carp, 11½ lbs., 58 cts.
    Herring (smoked), 5 ozs., 3 cts.
Eggs, 5 lbs. 12 ozs., 52 cts.
Butter, 4 lbs., $1.12
Cheese (cottage), 6 lbs. 3 ozs., 30 cts.
Milk, 17 lbs., 51 cts.
Cream (sour), 3¼ lbs., 16 cts.

VEGETABLE FOOD

Cereals:
    Rye flour, 13 lbs., 26 cts.
    Rice, 1½ lbs., 9 cts.

Rye bread, 66 lbs., $1.98
Wheat biscuits, 5 lbs., 27 cts.
Sugar, 21½ lbs., $1.05
Potatoes, 32 lbs., 41 cts.
Lima beans (dried), 2½ lbs., 15 cts.
Vegetables:
    Onions, 3½ lbs., 17 cts.
Fruits:
    Apples, 1 lb., 5 cts.
    Lemons, ½ lb., 3 cts.
    Jelly, 1 lb., 3 cts.
    Raisins, ½ lb., 3 cts.

DIETARY STUDY (NO. 114)

The family consisted of a man, 23, and his wife, 20 years of age, and a child about a year old. The income was $7 to $7.50 per week; the rent $7 per month. They are described as "shiftless and filthy." They occupied four back rooms on the second floor.

ANIMAL FOOD

Beef:
    Breast, ½ lb., 4 cts.
    Chuck, 17 lbs. 9 ozs., $1.76
    Beef fat, 1 lb., 6 cts.
Poultry:
    Chicken, 4 lbs., 58 cts.
Fish:
    Carp, 6 lbs. 3 ozs., 43 cts.
    Herring (smoked), ¼ lb., 2 cts.
Eggs, 1 lb. 8 ozs., 20 cts.

Butter, 3½ lbs., 98 cts.

Milk, 13 lbs. 14 ozs., 35 cts.

VEGETABLE FOOD

Cereals:

Wheat flour, 10 ozs., 2 cts.

Barley, 1 lb., 4 cts.

Rye bread, 18 lbs. 8 ozs., 56 cts.

Wheat bread, 4 lbs. 1 oz., 15 cts.

Vegetables:

Onions, 5 lbs., 5 cts.

Turnips, 3 lbs. 6 ozs., 3 cts.

Fruits:

Apples, 22 lbs., 22 cts.

Studies among Bohemian Families

The Bohemian families purchased their food at Bohemian markets, but the character of the food did not vary materially from that of similar articles sold at other markets. A piece of liver and a bone is given at Bohemian markets with each piece of beef purchased. The liver usually weighs about a quarter of a pound and the bone about 6 ounces. No more is given with several pounds of beef than with 1 pound. However, at the better markets the meat is sold cheaper in 3 or 4 pound pieces than in 1-pound pieces. Chopped beef and pork is a common article of diet. The butcher has a platter with chopped beef on one side and chopped pork on the other and mixes them as purchased.

The milkmen carry skim milk and cream separately. Among the Bohemians the term milk is applied exclu-sively to skim milk. They usually buy more or less cream, which is added to the milk. The mixture is called "milk and cream." The amount of cream added depends upon the purse of the purchaser . . .

DIETARY STUDY (NO. 125)

This study was made with a tailor's family, consist-ing of the father, 43, and the mother, 32 years of age; four daughters, aged 13, 9, 8, and 5 years, respectively; and one son 11 years old. The children were born in this country. The family give a good example of what can be done with a small income by thrift and indus-try. The father was connected with a building and loan association and owned a 2-story tenement house with basement, upon which there was still a mortgage. The woman did her own baking, summer and winter, and was very neat. She also found time to do some sew-ing, thus earning a little money. Their combined earn-ings were about $9 a week. Rentals amounting to $26 a month were received, making the actual income at least $15 or $16 per week. The four oldest children went to school. Perishable foods were purchased at the smaller markets. All other foods were purchased in large quan-tities at the large markets. The lard used was from a winter's supply of untried lard, purchased at the rate of 19 pounds for $1. The beef, round and chuck, was made into soup, and eaten with homemade noodles. The beef rib and the veal were roasted. The pork chops and chopped pork and beef were fried. The food acces-sories used during the study and their cost were as fol-lows: Coffee, 56 cents; yeast, 15 cents; nutmegs, 2 cents;

chowchow, 2 cents; pepper, 2 cents; vinegar, 2 cents; poppy seed, 7 cents.

ANIMAL FOOD

Beef:

    Chuck, 12 lbs., 71 cts.

    Rib roast, 2½ lbs., 25 cts.

    Rib ends, 1 lb., 6 cts.

    Round steak, 2½ lbs., 20 cts.

    Rump (no bone), 5 lbs. 5½ ozs., 38 cts.

    Rump, 2 lbs. 14ozs., 17 cts.

    Beef and pork (chopped together), 5½ lbs., 50 cts.

    Veal, rib, and kidney, 13 lbs. 1 oz., $1.10

    Liver, 2¼ lbs., [no cost given]

Pork:

    Chops, 2½ lbs., 20 cts.

    Boiled ham, 1 lb., 20 cts.

    Ham sausage, 1½ lbs., 15 cts.

    Sausage, 1 lb., 1½ ozs., 11 cts.

    Lard, 5 lbs. 7 ozs., 29 cts.

Eggs, 12 lbs. 10 ozs., $1.20

Butter, 1 lb., 24 cts.

Cheese, ½ lb., 8 cts.

Milk, 71 lbs. 10 ozs., $1.72

VEGETABLE FOOD

Cereals:

    Wheat flour, 22 lbs., 46 cts.

    Rye flour, 14 lbs. 10 ozs., 27 cts.

    Barley, 2 lbs., 8 cts.

    Farina, 1 lb. 10 ozs., 7 cts.

    Oatmeal, ½ lb., 2 cts.

    Rice, 1 lb., 8 cts.

    Wheat bread (baker's), 1 lb. 7 ozs., 8 cts.

    Soda crackers, 1 lb., 8 cts.

Sugar, 10½ lbs., 58 cts.

Sirup, ½ lb., 2 cts.

Cocoa, 7 oz., 20 cts.

Potatoes, 32½ lbs., 20 cts.

Vegetables:

    Onions, ½ lb., 1 ct.

    Sauerkraut, 2 lbs., 5 cts.

Fruits:

    Apples, 8 lbs., 15 cts.

    Bananas, 6 lbs., 10 cts.

    Lemons, 11 ozs., 4 cts.

    Prunes (dried), 7 lbs., 56 cts.

Dietary Studies in Eastern Virginia, 1897

In the spring of 1897 a series of dietary studies among the negroes of Franklin County, Va., was made under the auspices of Hampton Institute . . . [6] These studies were carried on for the purpose of obtaining some definite information concerning the actual food consumption of the negroes in this region of Virginia . . .

The families studied were scattered over a large area of country, necessitating a daily round of some 15 miles. The outward trip was taken along the highways and the return trip made by plantation roads. More or less opposition was manifested by some of the white population toward the carrying on of these investigations among the negroes. It is often a difficult matter, and one requiring considerable tact, to explain the purpose of such investigation. There is a suspicion of interference, or some other prejudice is encountered . . .

General Conditions

The dietary studies were carried on in the region bordering the Great Dismal Swamp. The land in the vicinity was low and swampy, and malaria was exceedingly prevalent. The houses were small and constructed in a very crude and simple manner. They were, as a rule, board cabins, rather than log cabins like those found in the "Black Belt" of Alabama, where the dietary studies previously referred to were made. Few of the families studied had lamps or candles. The cabins were not lighted in the evening except by the open fireplace . . .

Nearly all the families studied had very little means. Notwithstanding the fact that food was in many cases none too abundant, most of the families kept a number of dogs and cats.

Character of the Food

As among the negroes of Alabama, "hog and hominy" literally form the larger part of the diet. Side bacon is the principal meat, and, with some fish and a little milk, formed the major portion of the animal food. Large quantities of fish are obtained from the waters of the neighboring Chesapeake Bay and form an important source of food. Frogs, turtles, and even snakes were not infrequently eaten by some of the families at certain seasons of the year. Unbolted corn meal, costing about a cent a pound and containing a very large amount of bran, furnishes a large proportion of the nutriment of the diet. The coarse bran is removed by sifting, but the meal actually used still contains a large proportion. The bread is made simply of meal wet up, without salt or leavening material, and baked, as a rule, in the ashes ("ash cake").

Drinking water is almost invariably obtained from shallow surface wells, which are mere holes dug in the swampy land, with very rarely any side walls other than the clay of the soil. The water is, as a rule, stagnant and brackish, and often muddy.

The families selected for study were believed to be typical of the region, both in their food consumption and in their methods of cooking, etc. Cook stoves were unknown, all the cooking being done in the open fireplace, which was an important feature of all the cabins. Side bacon was almost invariably fried, as was, in fact, a large proportion of all the food. Pork shoulder and ham frequently were boiled . . .

DIETARY STUDY (NO. 211)

The family consisted of the father, 52 years of age, weighing 140 pounds; the mother, 60 years old, weighing 150 pounds; sister of the latter, 52 years of age, weighing 144 pounds; and a son, 28 years of age, weighing 140 pounds. The father was permanently lame and incapable of hard work. He cultivated 5 acres of land on shares, receiving two-thirds of the crop. He obtained about $25 per year in cash for odd jobs. The mother was a midwife, earning about $35 per year. Her sister was very feeble and unable to work. The son did odd jobs at farming, thus earning about $70 per year. He also provided a large part of the food eaten by the family by hunting. The family used little or no beef, mutton, or other lean meats, as they believed that these made them ill. Muskrat, opossum, raccoon, and other game, fish, frogs, turtle, and even snakes in certain seasons, furnished part of the diet. Cash was paid for all food purchased, since the family could obtain no credit. They lived in a two room house with 1 acre of ground surrounding it. There were no improvements, and the location was very unhealthful.

In addition to the food materials used, 48 cents' worth of green coffee and 4 cents' worth of salt were consumed during the study.

ANIMAL FOOD

Beef: Dried, 1¾ lbs. 35 cts.
Pork:
    Bacon, 14½ lbs., $1.21
    Cracklings, 1 lb. 5 oz., 13 cts.
    Ham, ½ lb., 6 cts.
    Salt sides, 11 lbs. 5 oz., $1.21
    Shoulder, 3 lbs. 2 oz., 32 cts.
    Lard, 2¼ lbs., 23 cts.
Fish:
    Eel, 6 oz., 26 cts.
    Catfish, 3 lbs., 15 cts.
    Smoked herring, 6 lbs. 11 oz., 8 cts.
    Mullet, 5 lbs. 13 oz., 2 cts.
    Perch, 5 oz., 1 ct.
    Roach, 2 lbs. 11 oz., 11 cts.
    Snapping turtle, 13 lbs. 3 oz., 16 cts.
Dairy products:
    Sweet milk, 3¼ lbs., 11 cts.
    Sour milk, 8 lbs., 4 cts.

VEGETABLE FOOD

Cereals:
    Corn meal, 7½ lbs., 85 cts.
    Flour, 21 lbs. 14 oz., 74 cts.
    Bread, ¼ lb., 1 ct.
Sugars and starches:
    Brown sugar, 6½ lbs., 33 cts.
    Granulated sugar, 6 lbs. 11 oz., 39 cts.
Potatoes: Sweet, 21 lbs. 7 oz., 23 cts.

Vegetables:

Cabbage, 3½ lbs., 11 cts.

Mustard salad, 8 lbs. 2 oz., 8 cts.

DIETARY STUDY (NO. 214)

This study . . . was made with a family consisting of the grandfather, 81 years of age; the father, 39 years of age, and his brother, 28 years of age; the mother, 24 years of age; an adopted daughter, aged 11 years; and three young children, a boy of 4, a boy of 2, and an infant 10 months old. The weights of the different members of the family were 150, 135, 175, 150, 51, 40, 25, and 14 pounds, respectively. The children in this family were in poor health. The infant died during the study and the two other children were very feeble. The family lived in a house consisting of two rooms and a loft. It was situated in 105 acres of ground, of which the father "owned the holding." They had a few farm implements and some live stock. Provisions were bought by the week in the market at Franklin, and payments were made each month. The grandfather, though feeble, worked on the farm. The father earned about $150 a year teaching school, and in addition did such farm work as was available. His brother carried on the farm. The older children attended school. During the month covered by the study, 11 cents' worth of green coffee, 1 cent's worth of tea, 7 cents' worth of baking powder, 2 cents' worth of vinegar, and 1 cent's worth of salt were used in addition to the food materials.

ANIMAL FOOD

Pork:

Bacon, 42 lbs. 2 oz., $3.84

Ham, 4½ lbs., 56 cts.

Salt sides, 21¼ lbs., $2.13

Shoulders, 3 lbs. 11 oz., 44 cts.

Fish:

Salt herring, 61 lbs., 67 cts.

Roach, 13 oz., 3 cts.

Snapping turtle, 3 lbs. 11 oz., 5 cts.

VEGETABLE FOOD

Cereals:

Corn meal, 218 lbs. 9 oz., $2.25

Flour, 55 lbs. 1 oz., $1.91

Sugars and starches:

Granulated sugar, 4 lbs. 14 oz., 29 cts.

Brown sugar, 2 lbs., 10 cts.

Potatoes: Sweet, 2 lbs., 2 cts.

Vegetables:

Cabbage, 10 lbs. 7 oz., 11 cts.

Mustard salad, 8 lbs. 9 oz., 12 cts.

Fruits: Dried apples, 14 oz., 4 cts.

DIETARY STUDY (NO. 215)

The family consisted of the mother, 34 years of age; four daughters, 18, 14, 12, and 3 years of age, respectively; two sons, 10 and 5 years of age; and a farm laborer, 41 years of age. The weights of the members of the family were 135, 135, 120, 98, 30, 65, 50, and 145 pounds, respectively. The family lived in two cabins, with one room and a loft in each, on 25 acres of ground. They paid one-half their crops for rent. The farm laborer carried on the farm and received one-third of the remainder of the crops in payment. The mother, three daughters, and one son worked on the farm. The water supply was better than ordinarily found. The family owned a few farm implements and some live stock, including 1 steer, 1 mule, 1 cow and calf, and 2 pigs, besides some poultry. The house was made of rough boards put on perpendicularly, without weather strips; the chimney was built of dirt and sticks. The whole building was on piles, and the fowls and dogs occupied the space beneath it. A small log shed adjacent served as a barn. The family were clothed in rags. The oldest daughter was sick during most of the study. With the exception of 3 cents for salt, no money was spent for condiments during the time of the study.

ANIMAL FOOD

Pork:

Bacon, 10 lbs. 10½ oz., $1.07

Jowl, 2½ lbs., 25 cts.

Salt sides, 16 lbs. 6 oz., $1.64

Fish:

Smoked herring, 18 lbs.

VEGETABLE FOOD

Cereals:

Corn meal, 57 lbs. 3 oz., 66 cts.

Corn bread, 1¾ lbs., 1 ct.

Flour, 29 lbs. 13 oz., $1.06

Sugars and starches:

N[ew] O[rleans] molasses, 6¼ lbs., 6 cts.

Granulated sugar, 2 lbs. 1 oz., 12 cts.

Legumes: Green peas, 3 lbs.

Vegetables:

Cabbage, 7 lbs. 5 oz., 7 cts.

Cabbage salad, 7 lbs. 9 oz., 8 cts.

Kale, 3 lbs. 14 oz., 4 cts.

Mustard salad, 4¾ lbs., 5 cts.

DIETARY STUDY (NO. 219)

The family consisted of a man 38 years of age, his wife 40 years of age, and a great aunt said to be 102 years of age. The weights of the individuals were 176, 136, and 120 pounds, respectively. They lived in a very old clapboarded house with brick chimney, containing two rooms and a loft, and situated in a tract of 15 acres of land, which was owned by the family. In addition to the house the premises contained a small barn and smokehouse, chicken house, and work shed, all of logs. The water supply was from an unusually deep well. The live stock consisted of 1 horse, 1 steer, 2 cows, 1 calf, 6 pigs, and a considerable number of chickens. The family also owned quite a number of farm implements. The soil was a dark clay loam. Not far from 1½ acres were planted to cotton and garden truck, the remainder of the land being about equally divided between corn and peanuts.

During the time of the study the family used 11 cents' worth of green coffee, 8 cents' worth of roasted coffee, 1 cent's worth of tea, 2 cents' worth of pepper, 5 cents' worth of lemon extract, 1 cent's worth of vinegar, 8 cents' worth of baking powder, 6 cents' worth of yeast, and 4 cents' worth of salt.

ANIMAL FOOD

Beef:

    Flank, 5¾ lbs., 17 cts.

    Kidney fat, 9 lbs. 5 oz., 28 cts.

    Liver, 4½ lbs., 3 cts.

    Shoulder bone, 2 lbs. 1 oz., 12 cts.

    Scraps, 6 lbs. 14 oz., 22 cts.

Pork:

    "Chittlings," 1 lb. 2 oz., 1 ct.

    Ham, 3 lbs. 15 oz., 40 cts.

    Haslet, 2 lbs., 6 cts.

    Liver, 1½ lbs., 3 cts.

    Salt sides, 9 lbs. 2 oz., 93 cts.

    Cured shoulder, 13 lbs. 10 oz., $1.50

    Lard, 3 lbs. 9 oz., 36 cts.

Fish: Smoked herring, 8 lbs. ½ oz., 8 cts.

Eggs: 5 lbs. 2 oz., 30 cts.

Dairy products:

    Butter, ¼ lb., 6 cts.

    Milk, 116¾ lbs., $4.09

VEGETABLE FOOD

Cereals:

    Corn meal, 67 lbs. 13 oz., 68 cts.

Corn bread, 2 lbs. 9 oz., 3 cts.

Sponge cake, ½ lb., 2 cts.

Flour, 26 lbs. 7 oz., $1.06

Sugars and starches:

    Sugar, 7¼ lbs., 44 cts.

    New Orleans molasses, 3 lbs. 11 oz., 3 cts.

Potatoes: Sweet, 33 lbs. 11 oz., 44 cts.

Vegetables:

    Cabbage, 7 1bs. 6oz., 8 cts.

    Cabbage salad, 2 lbs. 7 oz., 4 cts.

    Onions, 4¾ lbs., 18 cts.

    Artichoke pickles, ½ lb., 4 cts.

    Cucumber pickles, 2 lbs. 6 oz., 23 cts.

    Canned tomatoes, 2 lbs. 2 oz., 11 cts.

    Collards, 1 lb. 5 oz., 2 cts.

Fruits:

    Apples, 10 oz., 1 ct.

    Cherries, 1 lb. 11 oz., 4 cts.

    Preserved citron, 5 lbs. 15 oz., 30 cts.

    Huckleberries, 2 lbs. 2 oz., 11 cts.

    Canned peaches, 2 lbs. 5 oz., 11 cts.

    Dried pears, 8 lbs. 7 oz., 51 cts.

    Canned pears, 1 lb. 3 oz., 5 cts.

    Strawberries, 1 lb. 14 oz., 8 cts.

DIETARY STUDY (NO. 220)

This study . . . was made with a family consisting of a man 30 years old, and his wife, 29 years old, weighing respectively 130 and 92 pounds. They lived in a two-roomed log cabin, situated in a tract of 20 acres of land, which was worked on half shares. The place was surrounded by heavy timber. The water supply was from a very poor shallow well containing nothing but surface water. There were no sanitary arrangements. The live stock included 1 cow, 7 pigs, and considerable poultry. Farm implements of good quality and in sufficient quantity were furnished by the owner of the land. The soil was a heavy clay and fairly productive, being recently cleared land.

About equal areas were planted to corn and peanuts, and 1 acre was planted to garden truck. The condition of this family was considerably above the average in the region. During this study 9 cents' worth of green coffee, 5 cents' worth of baking powder, 1 cent's worth of salt, and 12 cents' worth of yeast were used in addition to the food materials.

ANIMAL FOOD

Pork:

Salt sides, 19 lbs., $1.90

Cured shoulder, 9 lbs. 15 oz., $1.02

Lard, 6 lbs. 6 oz., 64 cts.

VEGETABLE FOOD

Cereals:

Corn meal, 50 lbs. 7 oz., 55 cts.

Flour, 46 lbs. 11 oz., $1.64

Sugars and starches: Sugar, 3 lbs. 13 oz., 23 cts.

Potatoes: Sweet, 1 lb. 2 oz., 1 ct.

Vegetables:

Cabbage, 3 lbs. 5 oz., 4 cts.

Mustard salad, 1 lb. 15 oz., 2 cts.

Onions, 1¾ lbs. 5 cts.

Turnip salad, 1 lb. 1 oz. 1 ct.

Fruits: Strawberries, 5 oz., 2 cts.

Dietary Study in New Mexico, 1897

Dietary Study of a Poor Mexican Family

The dietary work consists of a study of one of the families (No. 163) studied last year and reported elsewhere.[7] It was thought by continuing the investigation with a family whose dietary had already been studied that some idea could be obtained of the difference in the amounts of the various nutrients consumed at different times by the same people.

Conditions of Life

The family, consisting of the father, mother, and 3-year-old son, is one of a colony of some twenty families in the same circumstances attached to one of the large ranches near Las Cruces. The rent of the dwellings and small plats of land, upon which they raise the greater part of their food, is paid in grain. The houses are all built of adobe or sun-dried brick, with an earth floor and a flat roof made of sticks and brush covered with mud, and generally contain but one room about 20 feet square. There are usually a single door and one or two unglazed windows. [T]he houses and the household furnishings are of the simplest and most primitive kind . . .

[There is] an oven in which some of the cooking is done. The greater part of the cooking, however, is done over an open fire in one corner of the house.

In general the diet of such families consists almost entirely of vegetable foods, meats being very rarely purchased. The family studied used no meat during the fourteen days of the experiment previously reported and but 1½ pounds during the present study. "Frijoles," or beans, "chili" (a variety of red pepper), and "tortillas," i.e., cakes made from flour or from the small blue corn, which is pounded in stone mortars by the women, make up the greater part of the food eaten. In the dietary reported, "fideos," a native product resembling macaroni, was also used to some extent. The amount of fat in the vegetable food eaten is comparatively small. The deficiency is made up by the use of lard or lard substitutes used freely in cooking.

The total income of the family derived from the irregular employment of the man for short periods at various kinds of work upon the ranch, did not exceed $100 per year.

Details of the Study

ANIMAL FOOD
Beef:
    Ribs, 595 grams, $0.10
    Lard, 1,730 grams, $0.40

VEGETABLE FOOD
Frijoles, native beans, 2,980 grams, $0.25
Chili, red pepper, 1,105 grams, $0.42
Flour, native, 10,720 grams, $0.82
Corn, native blue, 10,570 grams, $0.30
Fideos, 770 grams, $0.10
Sugar, 1,080 grams, $0.15

Food Accessories:
    Coffee, roasted, 765 grams, $0.21
    Salt, 370 grams, $.01

The food accessories in this dietary consisted of coffee only, for which 21 cents was paid out of a total food expenditure of $2.78 during the period. That the family were accustomed to make the most of what they had is shown by the small amount of waste in this dietary. The waste was estimated to cost but 4 cents. This is an example of careful management that might well be imitated by others in more favored circumstances.

It is interesting to note that the Mexican family obtained for 7 cents more protein, more carbohydrates, and a greater fuel value than the negro family for 8 cents. The negro family, however, had more fat. This difference is due to the use of large amounts of fat pork (an expensive source of protein) by the negro families, while the Mexican family used but little meat and derived the protein in their diet almost entirely from vegetable sources.

It must be understood that the dietary standard here given is not in any way absolute, but represents what is considered at present, as the result of careful investigation, to be the closest estimate possible as to the actual amounts or relation between the amounts of protein, carbohydrates, and fat required to properly nourish a man engaged in moderately hard work. A diet made up on this basis should enable a man to do each day a fair amount of work and at the same time to keep his body in a well-balanced and well-nourished condition.

The great trouble with the dietary of the Mexican family as well as that of the negro is that the amount of protein is too small. Approximately stated, the food of the Mexican family furnished but two-thirds of the amount of protein called for by the standard, and the food of the negro families furnished but one-half the protein that is considered to be necessary, according to the best knowledge at the present, for proper nourishment.

At the same time the Mexican as well as the negro families ate an undue proportion, but not amount, of the fuel ingredients. A proper ratio is generally considered to be established when the quantity of protein is to the quantity of fuel ingredients—starch, sugar, and fat—as 1 to 5.8 or thereabouts. In both the negro and Mexican families the dietaries are deficient in protein and in fuel ingredients.

Gilded Age Banquet Menus, 1880–1899

Gilded Age banquets were not light. Take the dinner held by the Daughters of the American Revolution in honor of George Washington's Birthday in February 1894, at the Ebbitt House Hotel in Washington, DC. Diners started with oysters and horseradish, followed by a choice between Consommé Royale and clear calf's head soup, followed by olives, celery, and pickled peppers—popularly called mangos. This was the merest hint of what was to come. Lobster patties came next, followed by shad caught in the nearby Potomac River, served with a parsley sauce. Then there were Saratoga chips, a kind of fried potatoes, followed by capon—rooster that had been castrated in its youth to make the meat more tender, along with smoked jowl—probably hog's jowl—with spinach. Still, the eaters were only getting warmed up. Next came larded sweetbreads, followed by succotash with French peas, followed by a beef filet, followed by potatoes and mushrooms, followed by fritters flavored with orange. Incredibly, more was still to come: roast turkey, then prime rib and cranberries, then stewed tomatoes. Next there was a brief break, albeit one that involved ingesting more calories in the form of a kirsch punch. Then diners plunged into still more courses: pheasant with grape jelly, bread sauce,

chicken salad, boned turkey, and a green salad. Finally, the desserts began to arrive. First came a plum pudding with cognac sauce, followed by mince and cherry pies, followed by Neapolitan ice cream and assorted cakes, followed by various fruits and Champagne jelly. Then, at long last, the arrival of the post-dessert savory courses signaled that the end was near: cheeses and crackers, nuts and raisins, and finally, black coffee.

A Gilded Age banquet like this one would have taken hours (Mary Henderson noted that some dinners lasted up to five hours), and it would have been exhausting, even for those who most enjoyed it. On the most basic level, how did diners manage to eat it all? In her 1877 *Practical Cooking and Dinner Giving*, Henderson—who would have regularly hosted and attended banquets on this scale herself—offered specific advice. To get through hours of different courses, she wrote, even "the most voracious appetite must be satisfied with a little of each." In other words, to still have room for even a single one of the nuts that would arrive at the end, a diner could have no more than small tastes of everything all night. Of course, that would have entailed great waste, with plate after plate sent back to the kitchen with most of its contents uneaten.[1]

Plum pudding, which Americans today might think of as an English dish, was a popular dessert among Americans in the Gilded Age, in part because of its theatrical presentation: it was often doused with brandy or rum and set alight just before serving. From Mrs. Mary F. Henderson, *Practical Cooking and Dinner Giving* (New York: Harper and Bros., 1877), 269, Special Collections, Michigan State University Libraries.

But waste was part of the point. Perhaps nowhere more nakedly than at a banquet did wealthy Americans in the Gilded Age show off their ability to command resources for their own and their guests' pleasure, to select only the very choicest morsels from a choice dish, and to leave most of the carefully prepared, expensive food for the slop bucket or the servants. There would have been plenty of servants or waiters on hand because they were absolutely necessary to pull off a feast like the ones described here. Paid staff would not only have cooked the food, a herculean task in itself, but multiple people would have been required to bring in every new course, to clear previous courses away, to quietly wash dishes, and to be on hand to attend to the smallest need of any diner. Although most menus here did not men-

tion the attending waitstaff, one did, and it hints at elite attitudes toward the people who served them. The menu of the 1891 Michigan Club dinner in Detroit noted, "A member of the banquet committee will be seated at each table, and guests are requested to promptly report to him any failure of service or inattention on the part of the waiters." Gilded Age feasting involved a superabundance of food, and usually of alcohol, too; it required long stretches of leisure time; and it demonstrated to everyone present the diners' ability to command and to be waited upon. Banquets were a powerful way for diners simultaneously to display and to reinforce their social positions: what the sociologist Thorstein Veblen would famously describe as "conspicuous consumption" in his 1899 book, *The Theory of the Leisure Class*.[2]

And yet Gilded Age banquets were not *only* about position and power. They were also about food. As the historian Paul Freedman writes, the pleasures of lavish dining "were not just symbolic and cumulative but actual and immediate."[3] A banquet was a sensual event on a major scale, one where diners knew they could afford to peck at delectable dishes only because so many other delectable dishes were sure to follow. The mania for French cooking styles ensured a surfeit of butter and cream and eggs, usually served alongside a variety of meats and pastries, and followed by multiple rounds of sweets. Most of the meals described here would have been, above all, absolutely delicious, and, indeed, a main reason these menus survived at all was because it was a fad of the era to give banquet guests souvenir copies of the menu so that they could long remember the delights

A state dinner at the White House under President Grover Cleveland. The accompanying article said that receiving an invitation to one was the "greatest distinction that can be won socially in Washington." The author also claimed that guests preserved their invitations and place-cards, keeping them as heirlooms to be "handed down with glowing accounts of the floral decorations, the gorgeous uniforms, the superb dresses of the ladies, the delightful music." From *Harper's Weekly* 32, no. 1624 (February 4, 1888), engraved plate between pp. 78 and 79, Special Collections, Michigan State University Libraries.

of the night. Banquets represented a predictable, ritualized series of satisfactions.

And predictable they were. Most Gilded Age banquets followed a rigid structure, from the opening oysters to the final black coffee. The coffee was virtually always black at formal meals, even when a menu, such as that for the Daughters of the American Revolution banquet, did not specify as much; it was a truism among elite diners of the era that it was vulgar to put cream in coffee after dinner. The black coffee rule was only one of many strict conventions that gave shape and coherence to Gilded Age fine dining. Peruse the menus here—menus that span two decades and that detail meals held by a variety of groups in cities across the country, including Washington, New York, New Orleans, Detroit, San Fran-

cisco, Saint Paul, Chicago, Cincinnati, Philadelphia, St. Louis, and Boston, and it becomes clear how formalized the shape and order of Gilded Age feasting was, and how consistently certain iconic dishes appeared.

Almost always, oysters came first—often Blue Points, harvested in the northeastern United States and renowned for their briny firmness. Soup followed, often either consommé, turtle soup, or mock turtle soup—which was made from meat from a calf's head, thought to resemble turtle. Although calf's head sounds like an alarmingly exotic ingredient to many eaters today, in the mid-nineteenth century it was common enough to be considered a mundane stand-in for more fashionable—and harder to obtain—turtle meat. Already by the time Lewis Carroll published *Alice's Adventures in Wonderland*

Mock Turtle Soup, made with meat from a calf's head, was so common in the mid-nineteenth century that Lewis Carroll winkingly creating a character in *Alice's Adventures in Wonderland* called the Mock Turtle, which had a turtle's body and a calf's head. Illustration by John Tenniel, Lewis Carroll, *Alice's Adventures in Wonderland* (Chicago: M.A. Donohue, 1904), Special Collections, Michigan State University Libraries.

in 1865, mock turtle soup was so ubiquitous in English and American dining rooms that Carroll made a joke out of it by creating a miserable hybrid creature called the Mock Turtle: a turtle with a calf's head.

After the soup came a course of raw or pickled vegetables, such as radishes and olives. Canvasback duck was an enormous favorite, as were sweet, mild sweetbreads. Celery mayonnaise, Saratoga chips, and green beans all showed up regularly. Striped bass often appeared, or quail, or beef with mushrooms—and sometimes all of them. For dessert, it was as likely as not that Neapoli-

tan ice cream would be served, often flanked by assorted fruits and cakes. Cigars or cigarettes are occasionally listed as part of the menu, and even when the menu did not mention them, male diners often smoked together at the table somewhere toward the end of a meal. Black coffee was the inevitable finale. There were sometimes variations—the 1883 Saint Paul banquet included bear steaks and venison, for example—and occasionally a banquet deviated more aggressively, such as the one held by the Musicians Club of San Francisco in 1897, which followed a familiar order of courses (cold nibbles, soup, fish, meat, poultry, salad, dessert, fruit, and coffee) but which featured exclusively Italian dishes, and included such anomalies as a pasta course. Despite variations, however, the overwhelming impression from surviving Gilded Age banquet menus is one of ritual culinary conformity.

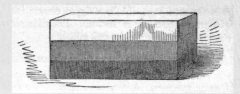

Ice cream and other frozen desserts became much more common in the final decades of the nineteenth century, as mechanical ice-making technology made ice available year-round to those who could afford it. Neapolitan ice cream—blocks of chocolate, strawberry, and vanilla ice creams stacked on top of each other to form decorative stripes—was a particular favorite during the Gilded Age, and it was almost ubiquitous at formal banquets. From Mrs. Mary F. Henderson, *Practical Cooking and Dinner Giving* (New York: Harper and Bros., 1877), 309, Special Collections, Michigan State University Libraries.

Dinner for New Hampshire Club
Young's Hotel, Boston
December 8, 1880

Oysters on Shell

SOUP
Mock Turtle/Clam Chowder

FISH
Cusk à la Crême au Gratin

REMOVES
Roast Turkey/Roast Goose
Boiled Leg of Kentucky Mutton/Roast Red Head Duck

ENTREES
Oyster Patties/Fried Oysters/Croustade of Kidneys
Apple Fritters/Vol au Vent of Venison
Rice Croquettes
Chicken Salad/Lobster Salad

SWEETS
Apple Dumplings/Assorted Pies/Charlotte Russe
Wine Jellies/Ice Cream/Sherbet

DESSERT
Apples/Oranges/Grapes/Nuts/Raisins
Figs/Cheese/Olives/Coffee

Seventh Annual Dinner of the
Harvard Club of San Francisco
Palace Hotel, San Francisco
Thursday, October 21, 1880

HUITRES

POTAGES
A la Rohan
Consommeè à la Rachel

HORS D'OEUVRES
Salad d'anchois/Salad de Crevettes
Olives d'Espagne

POISSON
Truite à la Cambacèrès/Pomme de terre en Surprise

RELEVEES
Filet de Boeuf à la Providence/Haricot Verts

ENTREES
Timbale de Volaille à la Parisienne
Croustades de Grenouille à la Poulette
Petits Pois
Aspic de patè foie gras
Punch au champagne

ROTIS
Selle de moutton puree de marron
Canard, canvas back an [sic] celeri
Chouxfleur au gratin
Artichaut Barigoule
Salad laitues et chicoree

DESSERT
Pudding à la Florentine/Charlotte à l'angelica
Geleè Macedoine/Gateaux Varieè
Nougat Monte à la Modernne/Glacee Napolitenne

FRUIT/CAFÉ

Dinner of the
Crane Re-Union
Martinelli's, New York City
Wednesday, October 5, 1881

Radiches [*sic*]/Blue Points/Olives

POTAGES
Consommé/Royale

POISSON
Bass á l'Hollandaise/Pommes-Duchesse

1ST ENTREE
Filet de Boeuf Piqué Aux Champignons

2D ENTREE
Salmi de Perdreaux aux Riz

3D ENTREE
Rissolé de Ris de Veau Petit Pois

RÔTIS
Philadelphia Chickens Aux Cresson

SALADE
De Saisons

DESSERT
Glaces—Fantasie Napolitaine
Fruits Assorted/Fromage

CAFÈ NOIR

Mixed fruits. From Mrs. Mary F. Henderson, *Practical Cooking and Dinner Giving* (New York: Harper and Bros., 1877), 337, Special Collections, Michigan State University Libraries.

Annual Dinner of the
New England Society in the City of New York
Delmonico's, New York City
December 22, 1882

Huîtres

POTAGES
Consommé Sévigné/Fausse tortue

HORS D'OEUVRES
Olives/Radis
Bouchées à la régence

RELEVES
Bass à la rouennaise/Eperlans frits, rémoulade
Filet de boeuf à la Matignon

ENTREES
Dindonneaux à la viennoise aux champignons
Mignons de chevreuil à la Berthier
Cailles braisées à la macédoine

SORBET
Vénitienne

ROTÍ
Canvas-back
Salade

ENTREMETS
Pommes/Petits Pois/Flageolets

SUCRES
Plum pudding au rhum
Gelée au kirsch/Meringues à la crême
Pièces montées
Petits fours/Gâteaux variés
Soufflé macarons/Napolitaine
Fruits & dessert
Café

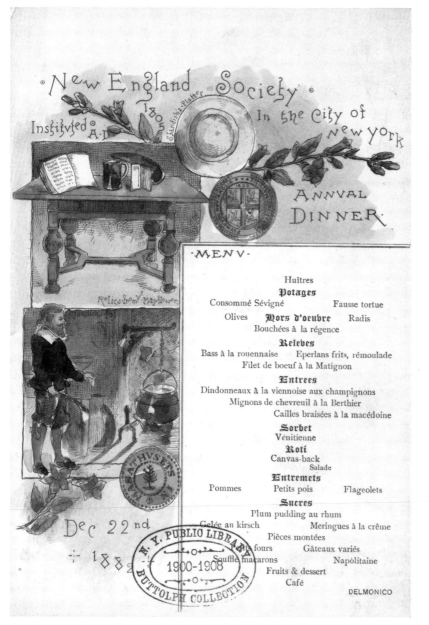

Banquet menus, often lavishly illustrated, were printed for each guest and intended to serve as souvenirs of the occasion. Menu card for banquet of the New England Society in the City of New York, December 22, 1882, New York Public Library Menu Collection.

Banquet Given by the Municipality of Saint Paul on the Completion of the Northern Pacific Railroad
Hotel Lafayette, Saint Paul, Minnesota
September 3, 1883

Blue Points Sur Coquille

POTAGES
Bisque de crevettes/Consommé d'Orsay

HORS D'OEUVRE
Variés/Petites bouchées au salpicon/Variés

POISSONS
Bass rayée à la hollandaise
Filet de sole à la Joinville
Concombres/Pommes croquettes

RELEVES
Selle de chevreuil à la Cumberland
Jambon d'ourson au chasseur
Tomates Farcies

ENTREES
Cotelettes de pigeonneaux, chevalière
Petits pois français
Poitrine de cailles à l'Andalouse
Quenelles de perdreaux à la St Hubert
Flageolets à l'anglaise
Ballottines d'ortolans à la Périgueux
Fonds d'artichauts, lyonnaise

Dinner in Honor of
Lieut. Gen'l Philip Henry Sheridan
on the Occasion of
Leaving Chicago to Assume Command of
the United States Army at Washington
Calumet Club, Chicago, Illinois
Nov. 24th, 1883

"He is a soldier fit to stand
by Caesar,
And give direction."

Blue Points

Consomme with Stuffed Lettuce

Pompano, New Orleans style

Potato Croquettes

Crepenettes of Turkey, a la puree de marrons

Spinach

Sweetbreads en Papillotes

Croquettes of Terrapin a la Bontoux

Asparagus

Roman Punch

Breast of Partridge

Celery Salad

Nesselrode and Bisquit of Pineapple

Roquefort and Brie

Fruit

Coffee

Dinner of the National Board of Trade
Willard's Hotel, Washington, D.C.
January 24, 1884

Blue Points on Shell
(Haut Sauterne)

SOUP
Green Turtle/Consommé, Brunoise
(Vino De Pasto)

FISH
Broiled Whitefish, Maitre d'Hotel
Celery/French Fried Potatoes
(Assmannshanser)

REMOVES
Boiled Capon, With Celery, à la Creme
Roast Young Pig, stuffed, Apple sauce
Roast Sirloin of Beef, Mushroom sauce
Stewed Tomatoes/Potatoes/Green Peas
(St Estephe)

ENTREES
Chicken Croquettes, à la Duchesse
Terrapin, stewed, à la Willards
Banana Fritters, glace, au Rhum
Chicken Salad/Shrimp Salad
(Dry Monopole)

SORBET
Punch, à la Romaine

GAME
Roast Canvas Back Duck/Broiled Quail
Currant Jelly/Dressed Lettuce
(Clos De Vougeot)

PASTRY AND DESSERT
Charlotte Russe/Champagne Jelly
Tutti Frutti/Assorted Cake
Napolitaine Ice Cream
Fruits/Nuts/Raisins/Figs

COFFEE
Cognac et Liqueurs

One Hundred and First Anniversary Dinner
of the Friendly Sons of St. Patrick
Delmonico's, New York City
March 17, 1885

Huîtres

POTAGES
Consommé a la d'Orleans/Bisque aux crevettes
Olives/Radis

HORS D'OEUVRE
Timbales au Cardinal

POISSONS
Bass rayée à la dieppoise/Eperlans Frits
Pommes Persillade

RELEVÉ
Filet de boeuf à la pièmontaise
Tomates au gratin

ENTRÉES
Dinde Braiseé à la Chévreuse
Petits Pois à la française
Ris De Veau Aux Marrons
Haricots Verts

SORBET A LA DALMATIE

ROTIS
Redhead Duck/Selle D' Agneau
Salade

ENTREMETS SUCRÉS
Pudding à la Bagration/Gelée au reine-claude
Cornets Chantilly

PIECES MONTEES
Glace napolitaine/Toronchino
Dessert/Fruits/Café

Dinner of the
Marine Society of New York
New York City
January 11, 1886

Huîtres
Chateau Sauterne
Celeri/Radis/Olives

POTAGES
Printanière Parisienne
Vino De Pasto

POISSON
Bass farcie garnie aux éperlans
Pommes de terre

RELEVE
Filet de boeuf aux champignons
Haricots verts/Tomates
Floirac

SORBET AU KIRSCH

ENTREE
Caille Piquée aux petits pois

ROTI
Grouse à L'anglaise
Gelée de groseilles/Salade de laitue
Pommery Sec

DESSERT
Pudding Nesselrode
Glaces fantaisies/Petits fours
Dessert assorti/Pièce montée
Café

Fourth Annual Dinner
of the Commandery of
The State of Ohio Military Order of the
Royal Legion of the United States
Burnet House, Cincinnati
May 4, 1887

Sherry/Consommé, l'Osentiville

Filets Of Sole, Rochembeau

Cucumbers/Bermuda Potatoes/Tomatoes

Sauterne/Tenderloin Beef, larded, a l'Independance

Asperges en Branche

Claret/ Ris de veau, braisé, a l'Oncle Sam

Petits Pois Francais

Union Punch

Champagne/Broiled Spring Chicken

Dressed Lettuce

Glace a la Vanille/Petits Four Assortis

Strawberries

Cheese/Crackers

Cigars

Coffee

Dinner Given by
Mrs. Cornelius Vanderbilt
1 West 57th Street
New York City
January 23, 1888

CHAUD

Consommé en Tasse

Huîtres à la Poulette

Bouchées à la Reine

Croquettes de Volaille

Térrapène à la Maryland

Canvas Back Duck

FROID

Galantine de Chapon

Filet de Boeuf, Jardinière

Aspic de Foie Gras, Belle Vue

Pâté de Gibier, Chasseur

Chaufroid de Mauviette

Pâté de Strasbourg, Naturel

Jambon à La Gelée

Saumon à La Vatel

Salade de Homard

Salade de Poulet

Sandwiches Variés

Volière de Cailles

ENTREMETS

Charlotte Moderne

Gelée Macédoine aux Fruits

Glaces Assorties

Dessert

Beef à la Jardinière, that is, trimmed with vegetables. From Mrs. Mary F. Henderson, *Practical Cooking and Dinner Giving* (New York: Harper and Bros., 1877), 137, Special Collections, Michigan State University Libraries.

Dinner Given by
William Waldorf Astor
Delmonico's, New York City
October 9, 1889

Huitres en coquille (Ruedesheimer)

Potage tortue verte (Amontillado)

Caviare sur canapé (Medoc)

Homard à la Maryland (Royal Charter)

Ris de veau aux champignons

Selle de mouton/Haricots verts/Pommes parisiennes

Suprême de volaille

Pâté de foie-gras, Belle-vue (Steinberger Cabinet)

Sorbet à la romaine/Cigarettes

Teal duck, celery mayonnaise (Clos De Vougeot)

Fromage (Duque Port Wine)

Glace à la napolitaine (Chateau Lafitte, Old Reserve Madeira)

Dinner of the
Free and Accepted Masons of Pennsylvania
Masonic Temple
Philadelphia, Pennsylvania
January 2, 1889

Blue Point Oysters on Half Shell/Chateau Sauterne

Puree of Crab/A. A. Amintillado

Fish, a la Crème/Smelts/Cucumbers

Potato Croquets/Roedesheimer

Partridges Larded/French Asparagus/Roedesheimer

Sweet Breads and French Peas/Broiled Oysters Bergundy [sic]

Arrack Punch/Roasted Almonds/Salt

Terrapin, a la Wiener/Saratoga Chips

Champagne/Cliquot, Tellen Label/L. Roederer

Canvas-Back Duck/Curled Mayonnaise Celery

Champagne/Cliquot, Tellen Label/L. Roederer

Chicken Salad/Rochfort, Fromarge [sic] de Brie

Crackers/Olives

Champagne/Cliquot, Tellen Label/L. Roederer

Frozen Cherries/Frozen Coffee/Montrose Pudding, Glace

French Meringues/Chocolate Meringues

Croquants/Wafers/Maccaroons/Assorted Fruits

Favors/Menth/Café/Cigars

Dinner Given by Mr. Shiuzo Isukahra
Imperial Department of Japan
in Honor of Delegates of the
International Marine Conference
Chamberlin's, Washington, D.C.
Friday, December 20, 1889

Blue Points/Celery

(Sauterne)

Julienne Soup

(Amontillado Sherry)

Boiled King of The Sea

Saddle of Venison

Potato Croquettes/French String Beans

(G. H. Mumm's Extra Dry)

Lobster Patties

Stewed Terrapin

Saratoga Chips

Orange Romaine

(Cigarettes)

Broiled Quail

Lettuce Salad

(Pontet Canet)

Cheese/Olives/Coffee

(Cognac)

Fruit

(Cigars)

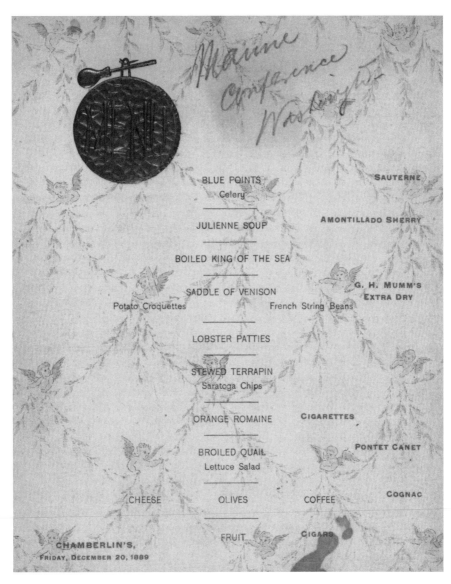

Menu card for banquet given by Mr. Shiuzo Isukahra, Imperial Department of
Japan, in honor of delegates of the International Marine Conference, Washington,
DC, December 20, 1889, New York Public Library Menu Collection.

157th Anniversary
Birthday of Washington
Annual Dinner
Order of United Americans
Friday, February 22, 1889
at Mazzetti's

Oysters on Half Shell

SOUP
Consomme Royale

HORS D'OEUVRES
Olives/Radishes/Celery

FISH
Lobster Chop/Sauce Tartar/Boiled Potatoes

JOINT
Filet of Beef With Mushrooms/String Beans

ENTREE
Chicken Pattie [*sic*] with Green Peas

SORBET
Roman Punch

ROAST
Roast Turkey or Goose/Currant Jelly
Celery Mayonaise

GLACE
Fancy Forms/Biscuit Mazzetti

DESSERT
Fancy Cakes/Bon Bons
Mottoes/Fruits/Coffee
Nougat Pyramid Appropriate

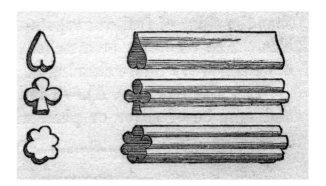

Tin cutters like these were used to make fancy cakes and to cut out bread into decorative shapes. From Mrs. Mary F. Henderson, *Practical Cooking and Dinner Giving* (New York: Harper and Bros., 1877), 55, Special Collections, Michigan State University Libraries.

Banquet in Honor of the Officers of the Cruiser "Baltimore"
Given by the Citizens of Baltimore
Hotel Rennert, Baltimore
May 9, 1890

Olives

Cherry Stone Oysters

Haute Sauterne

Consommé

Amontillado Sherry

Terrapin, à la Rennert

Moet & Chandon (White Seal)

Broiled Spring Chicken

Smithfield Ham

Green Peas/Bermuda Potatoes

The Rennert

Roman Punch

Cigarettes

Soft Shell Crabs

Tomato Salad

La Rose

Plover

Saratoga Chips

Asparagus, Vinaigrette

Ices/Strawberries/Cake

Cafe Noir

Strontia

Cigars

The Michigan Club Sixth Annual Banquet
Detroit Rink
Detroit
February 23, 1891

"His thirst he slakes at some neighboring brook,
Nor seeks for sauce where Appetite stands cook."
—Churchill

Blue Point Oysters
Green Turtle Soup/Fillet of Beef with Mushrooms
Boned Turkey in Aspic/Ham/Tongue/Wine Jelly
Chicken Salad/Shrimp Salad/Celery/Cross &
    Blackwell's Pickles/Olives
Decorated Ham and Tongue
Ornamented Cakes/Neapolitan Ice Cream
California Pears/Florida Oranges/Tangerines/
    Almedia Grapes
Catawba Grapes/Bananas/Apples
Mixed Nuts/Raisins/Pine Apple Cheese
Coffee

Wine jelly filled with whipped cream. From
Mrs. Mary F. Henderson, *Practical Cooking and
Dinner Giving* (New York: Harper and Bros.,
1877), 59, Special Collections, Michigan State
University Libraries.

A member of the banquet committee will be seated
at each table, and guests are requested to promptly report
to him any failure of service or inattention on the part
of the waiters.

Third Annual Banquet
of the Trustees of the Missouri Botanical Garden
at the Mercantile Club, St. Louis
Thursday, May 19, 1892

(Tower Grove Sherry)

Little Neck Clams

Bisque of Crab

Radishes/Olives/Salted Almonds

(Haute Sauterne)

California Salmon, Genoise

Cucumbers/New Potatoes Resolette

Fillet Of Beef, Cheron

Stuffed Tomatoes

(Chateau Lafitte)

Sweet Breads, Velorette

Asparagus Tops

Fresh Mushrooms, Glace

Punch au Kirsch

Snipe, Sur Canape

Lettuce

(Pomery Sec)

Strawberries and Ice Cream

Assorted Cake

Roquefort and Brie Cheese

Coffee

(Henry Shaw's Port)

Cigars/Brandy

Formal meals frequently included a fish course, in addition to an opening course of shellfish. For this St. Louis banquet held for the trustees of the Missouri Botanical Garden in May 1892, there was a course of clams, followed by a lobster bisque, followed by a salmon, before the heavier meat dishes. From Mrs. Mary F. Henderson, *Practical Cooking and Dinner Giving* (New York: Harper and Bros., 1877), 106, Special Collections, Michigan State University Libraries.

Sunset Club
The Grand Pacific Hotel, Chicago
December 7, 1893

Blue Points

Mock Turtle

Celery/Queen Olives

Baked Trout, Fine Herbs

Saratoga Chips

Tenderloin of Beef, Financiere

Potatoes Anglaise

Jamaica Punch

Deviled Crabs, Sauce Tartar

Rice Cakes with Raisins

Dressed Celery

Charlotte Glace/Assorted Cake

Fruit/Coffee

Daughters of the American Revolution
Dinner in Honor of George Washington's Birthday
Ebbitt House, Washington, D.C.
February 22, 1894

Norfolk Oysters/Horseradish

Consommé Royale/Clear Calf's Head

Olives/Mango Peppers/Celery

Patties Of Lobster

Potomac Shad/Broiled Parsley Sauce

Saratoga Chips

Philadelphia Capon/Smoked Jowl with Spinach

Sweetbreads Larded

Succotash/French Peas

Small Filet Beef

White Potatoes/Mushrooms

Queen Fritters—Orange Flavor

Roast Young Turkey

Cranberries/Prime Ribs of Beef

Stewed Tomatoes

Punch au Kirsch

Gold Pheasant/Grape Jelly

Bread Sauce

Chicken Salad/Dressed Lettuce/Boned Turkey

Plum Pudding/Hard and Cognac Sauce

Cherry Pie/Mince Pie

Neapolitan Ice Cream/Assorted Cake

Fruits/Champagne Jelly

Roquefort Cheese/Crackers/Dairy Cheese

Nuts/Raisins

Coffee

Banquet for the
Twenty-Seventh Reunion of the Army of Tennessee
Grand Hotel, Cincinnati
September 17, 1895

Blue Points

Amontillado[4]

Salted Almonds/Radishes/Olives

Green Sea Turtle Soup—au Quennells

Filet Of Flounder—al a [sic] Joinville

Pressed Cucumbers

Sweetbreads In Cases—Delmonico French Peas

Chateau Margaux

Supreme of Chicken—Perigeax Cauliflower au Gratin

Punch Militaire

Roast Pheasant—au Cresson/Julienne Potatoes/
   Fried Hominy

G. H. Mumm's Extra Dry and Piper Heiseick

Lettuce and Tomatoes en Mayonnaise

Fancy Ices/Sweets

Fruits

Neufchatel Cheese/Toasted Wafers

Coffee

Cigars

Grand Banquet
Tendered to New Orleans Base Ball Club
by the Rooters' Club
at Lecourt's Hotel,
West End, Louisiana
Thursday, June 11, 1896

Absinthe and Anisette

SOUPS
Turtle/Crawfish Bisque/Consomme
Queen Olives/Pickles

FISH
Tenderloin Trout, White Wine Sauce
Julienne Potatoes
Sauterne

ENTREE
Filet of Beef Pique, Mushroom Sauce
Stuffed Tomatoes a la Italienne
Roman Punch
Chateau Margaux

ROAST
Roast Spring Chicken/Green Peas

SALADS
Lettuce/Tomatoe [*sic*]
Sweet Peppers

DESSERT
Fruit/Cheese and Jelly
Peaches with Ice Cream/Coffee

The Musicians Club of San Francisco
Martinelli's
San Francisco, California
February 26, 1897

ANTIPASTO
Acciughe/Salame/Tonno Olive
Verdura Assortita

ZUPPA
Gallina

PESCE
Ciuppino all' Italiana

PASTA
Taglarini all' Napolitana

ENTRATA
Vitella Saltata alla Cacciatora

ARROSTO
Gallina
Insalata Fresca Di Stagione

DESSERT
Crema Fritta/Frutta/Formaggio
Caffé

Banquet
The Chamber of Commerce of Nashville
in Honor of Rear Admiral Winfield Scott Schley
and Commander Washburn Maynard
The Maxwell, Nashville, Tennessee
December 6, 1898

Blue Points	Margaux
Celery	Admiral Punch
Consomme, Printanier Royale	Quail, Barde au Cresson
Salted Almonds/Olives	Mumm's
Broiled Pompano, Maitre d'Hotel	Lobster Mayonnaise
Potato Croquettes	Ices/Cake
Amontillado	Crackers/Cheese
Filet of Beef, Pique aux Cepes	Coffee
French Peas	Cigars

Complimentary Dinner
Twenty-fifth Annual Meeting
of the Mississippi Valley Medical Association
at the Chicago Athletic Association
Thursday, October 5, 1899

Blue Points

Hors d'oeuvres varies

Consommè printanier, royal

Striped bass valois

Pommes rosalind

Filet Mignon, Prèviolot

Cauliflower villeroi/Potatoes marquise

Benedictine Sherbet

Breast of chicken, piquè pèrigord

Hearts of lettuce, mayonnaise

Mousse aux macarons

Fromage de brie and Roquefort

Toasted crackers

Café noir

Fannie Merritt Farmer,
The Boston Cooking-School Cook Book, 1896

Fannie Farmer was a vigorous woman who loved to eat, loved to cook, and loved to teach, and her 1896 *The Boston Cooking-School Cook Book* became one of the best-selling and most iconic American cookbooks in history. As a teenager, Farmer had been a bright and energetic student, bent on attending college, when she suffered a sudden attack of paralysis in her legs—possibly polio—that left her unable to finish high school. Although she spent years as a semi-invalid, Farmer had recovered enough by her early thirties to reenter school, this time as a student in the Boston Cooking School, founded a few years earlier. After completing the basic course, she was hired on as a teacher and administrator, eventually rising through the ranks to become school principal at age 36, in 1893. A few years later she would publish *The Boston Cooking-School Cook Book* with Little, Brown, and Company, a heavy revision of the 1884 *Mrs. Lincoln's Boston Cook Book*, written by Mary J. Lincoln, the Boston Cooking School's first principal.[1]

In some ways, Farmer's *The Boston Cooking-School Cook Book* looked like many other nineteenth-century cookbooks in its encyclopedic scope and its inclusion of reci-pes like mock turtle soup, potted pigeons, croquettes, and all sorts of dishes using organ meat. Like other Gilded Age authors, Farmer also included a number of recipes with French names and cooking techniques. On the whole, however, Farmer turned away from the obsessively Frenchified styles that had dominated middle- and upper-class American cooking for the previous two decades. Instead, she concentrated more on classic American recipes like Parker House Rolls, Mint Juleps, Graham Bread, Carrots and Peas, and endless varieties of creamed vegetables, as well as a wide assortment of regional American recipes like Corn à la Southern, Maryland Chicken, Saratoga Chips, Succotash, Gumbo, and Boston Brown Bread.

This book was more than a compendium of established culinary Americana, however; an impressive number of Farmer's recipes strained toward the future, not the past. For example, her recipes for Hamburg Steaks and French Fried Potatoes would become hallmarks of American cuisine in the twentieth century as hamburgers and french fries. Her recipe for Fruit Sandwiches, which called for figs to be cooked down to a jammy paste, spread on bread, and then sprinkled with peanuts, was really an early prototype of a peanut butter and jelly sandwich. In fact, including sandwiches in a cookbook at all was fairly novel, even if most of Farmer's sandwiches would have been sliced tea-sandwich-thin and served on a doily. She also included recipes for macaroni and cheese, brownies, peanut cookies, and many varieties of chocolate cakes and candies, all dishes that had been relatively rare in the nineteenth century but would become enormously popular in the twentieth. Not only did Farmer have a gift for picking up on preexisting impulses that were just coming to life, but *The Boston Cooking-School Cook Book's* wild popularity itself helped to shape what American cuisine would be in the future.

More than anything else, perhaps, Farmer's recipes were delicious. There are Panned Oysters with Lemon Butter, Cheese Canapés, Lobster Bisque, Fried Ham and Eggs, Pineapple Lemonade, Chocolate Cream, and many, many other dishes that would have appealed to readers at the time as rich, flavorful, and exciting. Not all recipes may look exciting to today's readers, however. The turn of the twentieth century was a time of declining tolerance of spices and strong flavors, and Farmer was influenced by this trend, too.[2] Dietary reformers of the era increasingly rejected the spicy, pungent condiments that had enlivened nineteenth-century meals, instead exalting mildness, simplicity, and digestibility as culinary virtues of the highest order. Although many of Farmer's recipes would have been unusually flavorful, others were insipid. For instance, her Turkish Pilaf, compelling as it might sound, consisted of nothing but rice, stewed tomatoes, and a little butter. Most of her pasta dishes called for no accompaniment beyond a white sauce. In fact, Farmer called for cooks to blanket dish after dish with floury white sauces that would have added richness but tamped down flavor. In her recipe for a "chapon," Farmer instructed readers to rub a slice of French bread with garlic, and then to add the bread to a salad so that it would impart only the mildest suggestion of garlic to the vegetables. Even as she praised the "agreeable additional flavor" given by a chapon, never again in the cookbook did she call for garlic, an ingredient that native-born Americans at the time would have associated overwhelmingly with immigrants.

Farmer's recipes also stood out for the artistic flare she brought to them, with an emphasis on decoration and whimsy that was striking even in an age renowned for its attention to food's visual aesthetics. There are fanciful recipes like Apple Porcupine, baked apples bristling with spines of slivered almonds, and Strawberry Baskets, fresh berries nestled into fried pastry cups. There are geometric presentations like Turban of Fish, seasoned fish shaped into a pyramid, and Spinach Salad, tightly molded cooked spinach topped with circles of tongue. There are instructions designed purely to maximize the visual interest of a dish, like Ribbon Cake's alternating light and dark layers, or directions to bore holes into a block of ice with a smoking flat iron in order to create cavities in which to lodge raw oysters.

But imagination stopped at the measuring cup. Mingled with the recipes' whimsical content was an extraordinarily modern emphasis on precise measurement. In most of Farmer's recipes, a comprehensive, quantity-focused ingredient list leads the way, followed by instructions. While this format is commonplace today, it was still relatively unusual when she wrote, a time when many recipes still consisted mainly of vague, prosy instructions that hardly specified quantities at all. Most revolutionary was Farmer's emphasis on absolute precision. Instead of calling for cooks to measure with tumblers or coffee cups or salt spoons or any other changeable vessels, Farmer insisted that cooks use standard measuring implements that were just becoming available across the country. And then she went further, calling for ultraspecific amounts like seven-eighths of a cup or a quarter teaspoon. Above all, Farmer crusaded for level measurements. Before Farmer, recipe authors often intended cooks to round their measurements, heaping as much sugar or other ingredients as they could onto a cup or spoon. Since the narrowness or breadth of individual implements varied greatly, rounded measuring resulted in very different quantities—and thus in very different dishes. Farmer was so inexhaustible in calling for cooks to level off their measuring cups and spoons that she became known as the "Mother of Level Measurements."[3]

Although Farmer was part of growing efforts to apply science to cooking, she was not deeply interested in the hygienic and managerial sides of running a kitchen that were fascinating her colleagues in the budding home economics movement. Instead, she was more interested in producing delicious and imaginative dishes. Partly

Unlike most nineteenth-century cookbook authors, who described ingredient quantities in vague terms or not at all, Fannie Farmer insisted that cooks use standardized measuring implements and that they level off all ingredients to make quantities as accurate as possible. From Fannie Farmer, *The Original 1896 Boston Cooking-School Cook Book* (Mineola, NY: Dover Publications, 1997), 410, Special Collections, Michigan State University Libraries.

because of diverging interests, a few years after publishing *The Boston Cooking-School Cook Book* Farmer left the Boston Cooking School itself and founded her own school, Miss Farmer's School of Cookery, which focused more on home cooking and less on teacher training. Her name was so famous by the early twentieth century that students flocked to her school, abandoning the Boston Cooking School with such speed that it shuttered a mere year after Farmer's departure.[4]

Like many female authors in the nineteenth century, Farmer had emphasized in her original preface that she wrote *The Boston Cooking-School Cook Book* because friends and fellow teachers urged her to do so—not out of, say, personal ambition. The truth was, though, that whatever Farmer's ambitions may or may not have been, it turned out to be a very important book. Printed at her own expense because her publisher, Little, Brown and Company had so little faith in its salability, the book turned out to have mammoth popular appeal. Farmer's direct, technical-minded cooking instructions combined with her abundance of delicious and decidedly American recipes answered a demand in the late nineteenth century that no one else knew existed. Her book was an immediate best-seller, and its print runs sold out again and again. Because Farmer had financed the book's initial printing herself, she recouped an unusually high percentage of its profits and became very wealthy. By the time she died in 1915, not quite twenty years after the book first appeared, 360,000 copies had been sold, and there was no sign of declining appeal.[5] *The Boston Cooking-School Cook Book*, which by the mid-twentieth century would be widely known simply as *The Fannie Farmer Cookbook*, would eventually sell millions of copies, making it one of the best-selling and most influential cookbooks of the twentieth century.[6]

Preface

But for life the universe were nothing;
and all that has life requires nourishment.

With the progress of knowledge the needs of the human body have not been forgotten. During the last decade much time has been given by scientists to the study of foods and their dietetic value, and it is a subject which rightfully should demand much consideration from all. I certainly feel that the time is not far distant when a knowledge of the principles of diet will be an essential part of one's education. Then mankind will eat to live, will be able to do better mental and physical work, and disease will be less frequent.

At the earnest solicitation of educators, pupils, and friends, I have been urged to prepare this book, and I trust it may be a help to many who need its aid. It is my wish that it may not only be looked upon as a compilation of tried and tested recipes, but that it may awaken an interest through its condensed scientific knowledge which will lead to deeper thought and broader study of what to eat.

F. M. F.

How to Measure

Correct measurements are absolutely necessary to insure the best results. Good judgment, with experience, has taught some to measure by sight; but the majority need definite guides.

Tin measuring-cups, divided in quarters or thirds, holding one half-pint, and tea and table spoons of regulation sizes,—which may be bought at any store where kitchen furnishings are sold,—and a case knife, are essentials for correct measurement. Mixing-spoons, which are little larger than tablespoons, should not be confounded with the latter.

Measuring Ingredients. Flour, meal, powdered and confectioners' sugar, and soda should be sifted before measuring. Mustard and baking-powder, from standing in boxes, settle, therefore should be stirred to lighten; salt frequently lumps, and these lumps should be broken. A cupful is measured level. To measure a cupful, put in the ingredient by spoonfuls or from a scoop, round slightly, and level with a case knife, care being taken not to shake the cup. A tablespoonful is measured level. A teaspoonful is measured level.

To measure tea or table spoonfuls, dip the spoon in the ingredient, fill, lift, and level with a knife, the sharp edge of knife being toward tip of spoon. Divide with knife lengthwise of spoon, for a half-spoonful; divide halves crosswise for quarters, and quarters crosswise for eighths. Less than one-eighth of a teaspoonful is considered a few grains.

Measuring Liquids. A cupful of liquid is all the cup will hold.

A tea or table spoonful is all the spoon will hold.

Measuring Butter, Lard, etc. To measure butter, lard, and other solid fats, pack solidly into cup or spoon, and level with a knife.

When dry ingredients, liquids, and fats are called for in the same recipe, measure in the order given, thereby using but one cup.

Chocolate

1½ squares Baker's chocolate.

4 tablespoons sugar.

Few grains salt.

1 cup boiling water.

3 cups milk.

Scald milk. Melt chocolate in small saucepan placed over hot water, add sugar, salt, and gradually boiling water; when smooth, place on range and boil one minute; add to scalded milk, mill, and serve in chocolate cups with whipped cream. One and one-half ounces vanilla chocolate may be substituted for Baker's chocolate; being sweetened, less sugar is required.

Lemonade

1 cup sugar.

⅓ cup lemon juice.

1 pint water.

Make syrup by boiling sugar and water twelve minutes; add fruit juice, cool, and dilute with ice water to suit individual tastes. Lemon syrup may be bottled and kept on hand to use as needed.

Pineapple Lemonade

1 pint water.

1 cup sugar.

1 quart ice water.

1 can grated pineapple.

Juice 3 lemons.

Make syrup by boiling water and sugar ten minutes; add pineapple and lemon juice, cool, strain, and add ice water.

Mint Julep

1 quart water.

2 cups sugar.

1 pint claret wine.

1 cup strawberry juice.

1 cup orange juice.

Juice 8 lemons.

1½ cups boiling water.

12 sprigs fresh mint.

Make syrup by boiling quart of water and sugar twenty minutes. Separate mint in pieces, add to the boiling water, cover, and let stand in warm place five minutes, strain, and add to syrup; add fruit juices, and cool. Pour into punch-bowl, add claret, and chill with a large piece of ice; dilute with water. Garnish with fresh mint leaves and whole strawberries.

Ginger Punch

1 quart cold water.
1 cup sugar.
½ lb. Canton ginger.
½ cup orange juice.
½ cup lemon juice.

Chop ginger, add to water and sugar, boil fifteen minutes; add fruit juice, cool, strain, and dilute with crushed ice.

Unfermented Grape Juice

10 lbs. grapes.
1 cup water.
3 lbs. sugar.

Put grapes and water in granite stew-pan. Heat until stones and pulp separate; then strain through jellybag, add sugar, heat to boiling-point, and bottle. This will make one gallon. When served, it should be diluted one-half with water.

Bread and Bread Making

Water Bread

2 cups of boiling water.
1 tablespoon butter.
1 tablespoon lard.
1 tablespoon sugar.
1½ teaspoons salt.
¼ yeast cake dissolved in
¼ cup lukewarm water.
6 cups sifted flour.

Put butter, lard, sugar, and salt in bread raiser, or large bowl without a lip; pour on boiling water; when lukewarm, add dissolved yeast cake and five cups of flour; then stir until thoroughly mixed, using a knife or mixing-spoon. Add remaining flour, mix, and turn on a floured board, leaving a clean bowl; knead until mixture is smooth, elastic to touch, and bubbles may be seen under the surface. Some practice is required to knead quickly, but the motion once acquired will never be forgotten. Return to bowl, cover with a clean cloth kept for the purpose, and board or tin cover; let rise over night in temperature of 65° F. In morning cut down; this is accomplished by cutting through and turning over dough several times with a case knife, and checks fermentation for a short time; dough may be again raised, and recut down if it is not convenient to shape into loaves or biscuit after first cutting. When properly cared for, bread need never sour. Toss on board slightly floured, knead, shape into loaves or biscuits, place in greased pans, having pans nearly half full. Cover, let rise again to double its bulk, and bake in hot oven . . . This recipe will make a double loaf of bread and pan of biscuit. Cottolene, coto-suet, or beef drippings may be used for shortening, one-third less being required. Bread shortened with butter has a good flavor, but is not as white as when lard is used.

Entire Wheat Bread

2 cups scalded milk.

¼ cup sugar or ⅓ cup molasses.

1 teaspoon salt.

¼ yeast cake dissolved in ¼ cup lukewarm water.

4⅓ cups entire wheat flour.

Add sweetening and salt to milk, cool, and when luke-warm add dissolved yeast cake and flour; beat well, cover, and let rise to double its bulk. Again beat, and turn into greased bread pans, having pans one-half full; let rise, and bake. Entire Wheat Bread should not quite double its bulk during last rising. This mixture may be baked in gem pans.

Graham Bread

2½ cups hot liquid (water, or milk and water).

⅓ cup molasses.

1½ teaspoons salt.

¼ yeast cake dissolved in

⅓ cup lukewarm water.

3 cups flour.

3 cups Graham flour.

Prepare and bake as Entire Wheat Bread. The bran remaining in sieve after sifting Graham flour should be discarded.

Quaker Oats Bread

2 cups boiling water.

½ cup molasses.

½ tablespoon salt.

½ yeast cake dissolved in

½ cup lukewarm water.

1 cup Quaker Rolled Oats.

4¾ cups flour.

Add boiling water to oats and let stand one hour; add molasses, salt, dissolved yeast cake, and flour; let rise, beat thoroughly, turn into buttered bread pans, let rise again, and bake. By using one-half cup less flour, the dough is better suited for biscuits, but, being soft, is difficult to handle. To make shaping of biscuits easy, take up mixture by spoonfuls, drop into plate of flour, and have palms of hands well covered with flour before attempting to shape.

Boston Brown Bread

1 cup rye-meal.

1 cup granulated corn-meal.

1 cup Graham flour.

¾ tablespoons soda.

1 teaspoon salt.

¾ cup molasses.

2 cups sour milk, or 1¾ cups sweet milk or water.

Mix and sift dry ingredients, add molasses and milk, stir until well mixed, turn into a well-buttered mould, and steam three and one-half hours. The cover should be buttered before being placed on mould, and then tied down with string; otherwise the bread in rising might force off cover. Mould should never be filled more than two-thirds full. A melon-mould or one-pound baking powder boxes make the most attractive-shaped loaves, but a five-pound lard pail answers the purpose. For steaming, place mould on a trivet in kettle containing boiling water, allowing water to come half-way up around mould, cover closely, and steam, adding, as needed, more boiling water.

Indian Bread

1½ cups Graham flour.
1 cup Indian meal.
½ tablespoon soda.
1 teaspoon salt.
½ cup molasses.
1⅔ cups milk.

Mix and steam as Boston Brown Bread.

Parker House Rolls

2 cups scalded milk.
3 tablespoons butter.
2 tablespoons sugar.
1 teaspoon salt.
1 yeast cake dissolved in
¼ cup lukewarm water.
Flour.

Add butter, sugar, and salt to milk; when lukewarm, add dissolved yeast cake and three cups of flour. Beat thoroughly, cover, and let rise until light; cut down, and add enough flour to knead (it will take about two and one-half cups). Let rise again, toss on slightly floured board, knead, pat, and roll out to one-third inch thickness. Shape with biscuit-cutter, first dipped in flour. Dip the handle of a case knife in flour, and with it make a crease through the middle of each piece; brush over one-half of each piece with melted butter, fold, and press edges together. Place in greased pan, one inch apart, cover, let rise, and bake in hot oven twelve to fifteen minutes. As rolls rise they will part slightly, and if hastened in rising are apt to lose their shape.

Parker House Rolls may be shaped by cutting or tearing off small pieces of dough, and shaping round like a biscuit; place in rows on floured board, cover, and let rise fifteen minutes. With handle of large wooden spoon, or toy rolling-pin, roll through centre of each biscuit, brush edge of lower halves with melted butter, fold, press lightly, place in buttered pan one inch apart, cover, let rise, and bake.

Coffee Cakes (Brioche)

1 cup scalded milk.
¼ cup yolks of eggs.
½ cup whole eggs.
⅔ cup butter.
½ cup sugar.
2 yeast cakes.

½ teaspoon extract lemon, or

2 pounded cardamom seeds.

4⅔ cups flour.

French Confectioner.

Cool milk; when lukewarm, add yeast cakes, and when they are dissolved add remaining ingredients, and beat thoroughly with hand ten minutes; let rise six hours. Keep in ice-box over night; in morning turn on floured board, roll in long rectangular piece one-fourth inch thick; spread with softened butter, fold from sides toward centre to make three layers. Cut off pieces three-fourths inch wide; cover and let rise. Take each piece separately in hands and twist from ends in opposite directions, coil and bring ends together at top of cake. Let rise in pans and bake twenty minutes in a moderate oven; cool and brush over with confectioners' sugar, moistened with enough boiling water to spread.

Hot Cross Buns

1 cup scalded milk.

¼ cup sugar.

2 tablespoons butter.

½ teaspoon salt.

½ yeast cake dissolved in

¼ cup lukewarm water.

¾ teaspoon cinnamon.

3 cups flour.

1 egg.

¼ cup raisins stoned and quartered, or

¼ cup currants.

Add butter, sugar, and salt to milk; when lukewarm, add dissolved yeast cake, cinnamon, flour, and egg well beaten; when thoroughly mixed, add raisins, cover, and let rise over night. In morning, shape in forms of large biscuits, place in pan one inch apart, let rise, brush over with beaten egg, and bake twenty minutes; cool, and with ornamental frosting make a cross on top of each bun.

Squash Biscuits

½ cup squash (steamed and sifted).

¼ cup sugar.

½ teaspoon salt.

½ cup scalded milk.

¼ yeast cake dissolved in

¼ cup lukewarm water.

¼ cup butter.

2½ cups flour.

Add squash, sugar, salt, and butter to milk; when lukewarm, add dissolved yeast cake and flour; cover, and let rise over night. In morning shape into biscuits, let rise and bake.

Milk Toast

1 pint scalded milk.

2 tablespoons butter.

1½ tablespoons bread flour.

½ teaspoon salt.

1 cup milk.

Cold water.

6 slices dry toast.

Add cold water gradually to flour to make a smooth, thin paste. Add to milk, stirring constantly until thickened, cover, and cook twenty minutes; then add salt and butter in small pieces. Dip slices of toast separately in sauce; when soft, remove to serving dish. Pour remaining sauce over all.

Tomato Cream Toast

1½ cups stewed and strained tomato.

½ cup scalded cream.

¼ teaspoon soda.

3 tablespoons butter.

3 tablespoons flour.

½ teaspoon salt.

6 slices toast.

Put butter in saucepan; when melted and bubbling, add flour, mixed with salt, and stir in gradually tomato, to which soda has been added, then cream and butter. Dip slices of toast in sauce. Serve as soon as made.

Quaker Muffins

⅔ cup rolled oats.

1⅓ cups flour.

3 tablespoons sugar.

3 tablespoons baking powder.

½ teaspoon salt.

1 cup scalded milk.

1 egg.

1 tablespoon melted butter.

Turn scalded milk on rolled oats, let stand five minutes; add sugar, salt, and melted butter; sift in flour and baking powder, mix thoroughly, and add egg well beaten.

Golden Corn Cake

¾ cup corn meal.

1¼ cups flour.

¼ cup sugar.

4 teaspoons baking powder.

½ teaspoon salt.

1 cup milk.

1 egg.

1 tablespoon melted butter.

Mix and sift dry ingredients; add milk, egg well beaten, and butter; bake in shallow buttered pan in hot oven twenty minutes.

Susie's Spider Corn Cake

1½ cups corn meal.

2 cups sour milk.

1 teaspoon soda.

1 teaspoon salt.

2 eggs.

2 tablespoons butter.

Mix soda, salt, and corn meal; gradually add eggs well beaten and milk. Heat frying-pan, grease sides and bottom of pan with butter, turn in the mixture, place on middle grate in hot oven, and cook twenty minutes.

Pop-overs

1 cup flour.

¼ teaspoon salt.

⅞ cup milk.

1 egg.

½ teaspoon melted butter.

Mix salt and flour; add milk gradually, in order to obtain a smooth batter. Add egg, beaten until light, and butter; beat two minutes,—using Dover egg-beater,—turn into hissing hot buttered iron gem pans, and bake thirty to thirty-five minutes in a hot oven. They may be baked in buttered earthen cups, when the bottom will have a glazed appearance. Small round iron gem pans are best for Pop-overs.

Fadges

1 cup entire wheat flour.

1 cup cold water.

Add water gradually to flour, and beat with Dover egg-beater until very light. Bake as Pop-overs.

Sour Milk Griddle-Cakes

2½ cups flour.

½ teaspoon salt.

2 cups sour milk.

½ teaspoon soda.

1 egg.

Mix and sift flour, salt, and soda; add sour milk, and egg well beaten. Drop by spoonfuls on a greased hot griddle; cook on one side. When puffed, full of bubbles, and cooked on edges, turn, and cook other side. Serve with butter and maple syrup.

Corn Griddle-Cakes

2¼ cups flour.

½ cup corn meal.

1¼ tablespoons baking powder.

1½ teaspoons salt.

⅓ cup sugar.

1½ cups boiling water.

1 cup milk.

1 egg.

2 tablespoons melted butter.

Add meal to boiling water, and boil five minutes; turn into bowl, add milk, and remaining dry ingredients mixed and sifted, then the egg well beaten, and butter. Cook as other griddle-cakes.

Buckwheat Cakes

⅓ cup fine bread crumbs.
2 cups scalded milk.
½ teaspoon salt.
¼ yeast cake.
½ cup lukewarm water.
Buckwheat flour.
1 tablespoon molasses.

Pour milk over crumbs, and soak thirty minutes; add salt, yeast cake dissolved in lukewarm water, and buckwheat to make a batter thin enough to pour. Let rise over night; in the morning, stir well, add molasses, and cook as griddle-cakes. Save enough batter to raise another mixing, instead of using yeast cake; it will require one-half cup.

Waffles

2 cups flour.
3 teaspoons baking powder.
½ teaspoon salt.
1 cup milk.
Yolks 2 eggs.
Whites 2 eggs.
1 tablespoon melted butter.

Mix and sift dry ingredients; add milk gradually, yolks of eggs well beaten, butter, and whites of eggs beaten stiff; cook on a greased hot waffle iron. Serve with maple syrup.

A waffle iron should fit closely on range, be well heated on one side, turned, heated on other side, and thoroughly greased before iron is filled. In filling, put a tablespoonful of mixture in each compartment near centre of iron, cover, and mixture will spread to just fill iron. If sufficiently heated, it should be turned almost as soon as filled and covered. In using a new iron, special care must be taken in greasing, or waffles will stick.

Doughnuts

4 cups flour.
1½ teaspoons salt.
1¾ teaspoons soda.
1¾ teaspoons cream tartar.
¼ teaspoon grated nutmeg.
¼ teaspoon cinnamon.
½ tablespoon butter.
1 cup sugar.
1 cup sour milk.
1 egg.

Put flour in shallow pan; add salt, soda, cream tartar, and spices. Work in butter with tips of fingers; add sugar, egg well beaten, and sour milk. Stir thoroughly, and toss on board thickly dredged with flour; knead slightly, using more flour if necessary. Pat and roll out to one-fourth inch thickness; shape, fry, and drain. Sour milk doughnuts may be turned as soon as they come to top of fat, and frequently afterwards.

Strawberry Short Cake

2 cups flour.

4 teaspoons baking powder.

½ teaspoon salt.

2 teaspoons sugar.

¾ cup milk.

¼ cup butter.

Mix dry ingredients, sift twice, work in butter with tips of fingers, and add milk gradually. Toss on floured board, divide in two parts. Pat, roll out, and bake twelve minutes in a hot oven in buttered Washington pie or round layer cake tins. Split and spread with butter. Sweeten strawberries to taste, place on back of range until warmed, crush slightly, and put between and on top of Short Cakes; cover top with Cream Sauce. Allow from one to one and one-half boxes berries to each Short Cake.

Cereals

Oatmeal Mush with Apples

Core apples, leaving large cavities; pare, and cook until soft in syrup made by boiling sugar and water together. Fill cavities with oatmeal mush; serve with sugar and cream. The syrup should be saved and re-used.

Cereal with Fruit

¾ cup Wheat Germ.

¾ cup cold water.

2½ cups boiling water.

1 teaspoon salt.

½ lb. dates, stoned, and cut in pieces.

Mix cereal, salt, and cold water; add to boiling water placed on front of range. Boil five minutes, steam in double boiler thirty minutes; stir in dates, and serve with cream. To serve for breakfast, or as a simple dessert.

Fried Mushes

Mush left over from breakfast may be packed in greased, one pound baking-powder box, and covered, which will prevent crust from forming. The next morning remove from box, slice thinly, dip in flour, and sauté. Serve with maple syrup.

Steamed Rice

1 cup rice.

1 teaspoon salt.

2¾ to 3¼ cups boiling water (according to age of rice).

Put salt and water in top of double boiler, place on range, and add gradually well-washed rice, stirring with a fork to prevent adhering to boiler. Boil five minutes, cover, place over [the] under part [of a] double boiler, and steam forty-five minutes, or until kernels are soft;

uncover, that steam may escape. When rice is steamed for a simple dessert, use one-half quantity of water given in recipe, and steam until rice has absorbed water; then add scalded milk for remaining liquid.

To wash rice. Put rice in strainer, place strainer over bowl nearly full of cold water; rub rice between hands, lift strainer from bowl, and change water. Repeat process three or four times, until water is quite clear.

Rice with Cheese

Steam one cup rice, allowing one tablespoon salt; cover bottom of buttered pudding-dish with rice, dot over with three-fourths tablespoon butter, sprinkle with thin shavings mild cheese and a few grains cayenne; repeat until rice and one-fourth pound cheese are used. Add milk to half the depth of contents of dish, cover with buttered cracker crumbs, and bake until cheese melts.

Turkish Pilaf

Wash and drain one-half cup rice, cook in one tablespoon butter until brown, add one cup boiling water, and steam until water is absorbed. Add one and three-fourths cups hot stewed tomatoes, cook until rice is tender, and season with salt and pepper.

Boiled Macaroni

¾ cup macaroni, broken in inch pieces.
2 quarts boiling water.
1 tablespoon salt.
½ cup cream.

Cook macaroni in boiling salted water twenty minutes or until soft, drain in strainer, pour over it cold water to prevent pieces from adhering; add cream, reheat, and season with salt.

Macaroni with White Sauce

¾ cup macaroni broken in inch pieces.
2 quarts boiling water.
1 tablespoon salt.
1½ cups white sauce.

Cook as for Boiled Macaroni, and reheat in white sauce. White Sauce. Melt two tablespoons butter, add two tablespoons flour with one-half teaspoon salt, and pour on slowly one and one-half cups scalded milk.

Baked Macaroni with Cheese

Put a layer of boiled macaroni in buttered baking dish, sprinkle with grated cheese; repeat, pour over White Sauce, cover with buttered crumbs, and bake until crumbs are brown.

Spaghetti

Spaghetti may be cooked in any way in which macaroni is cooked, but is usually served with tomato sauce.

It is cooked in long strips rather than broken in pieces; to accomplish this, hold quantity to be cooked in the hand, and dip ends in boiling salted water; as spaghetti softens it will bend, and may be coiled under water.

Eggs

Scrambled Eggs with Anchovy Toast

Spread thin slices of buttered toast with Anchovy Paste. Arrange on platter, and cover with scrambled eggs.

Buttered Eggs with Tomatoes

Cut tomatoes in one-third inch slices. Sprinkle with salt and pepper, dredge with flour, and sauté in butter. Serve a buttered egg on each slice of tomato.

Eggs à la Goldenrod

3 hard boiled eggs.
1 tablespoon butter.
1 tablespoon flour.
1 cup milk.
½ teaspoon salt.
⅛ teaspoon pepper.
5 slices toast.
Parsley.

Make a thin white sauce with butter, flour, milk, and seasonings. Separate yolks from whites of eggs. Chop whites finely, and add them to the sauce. Cut four slices of toast in halves lengthwise. Arrange on platter, and pour over the sauce. Force the yolks through a potato ricer or strainer, sprinkling over the top. Garnish with parsley and remaining toast, cut in points.

Curried Eggs

3 hard boiled eggs.
2 tablespoons butter.
2 tablespoons flour.
¼ teaspoon salt.
½ teaspoon curry powder.
⅛ teaspoon pepper.
1 cup hot milk.

Melt butter, add flour and seasonings, and gradually hot milk. Cut eggs in eighths lengthwise, and re-heat in sauce.

Stuffed Eggs in a Nest

Cut hard boiled eggs in halves, lengthwise. Remove yolks, and put whites aside in pairs. Mash yolks, and add half the amount of devilled ham and enough melted butter to make of consistency to shape. Make in balls size of original yolks, and refill whites. Form remainder of mixture into a nest. Arrange eggs in the nest, and pour over one cup White Sauce. Sprinkle with buttered crumbs, and bake until crumbs are brown.

Plain Omelet

4 eggs.
½ teaspoon salt.
Few grains pepper.
4 tablespoons hot water.
1 tablespoon butter.
1½ cups Thin White Sauce.

Separate yolks from whites. Beat yolks until thick and lemon colored; add salt, pepper, and hot water. Beat whites until stiff and dry, cutting and folding them into first mixture until they have taken up mixture. Heat omelet pan, and butter sides and bottom. Turn in mixture, spread evenly, place on range where it will cook slowly, occasionally turning the pan that omelet may brown evenly. When well "puffed" and delicately browned underneath, place pan on centre grate of oven to finish cooking the top. The omelet is cooked if it is firm to the touch when pressed by the finger. If it clings to the finger like the beaten white of egg, it needs longer cooking. Fold and turn on hot platter, and pour around one and one-half cups Thin White Sauce.

Milk is sometimes used in place of hot water, but hot water makes a more tender omelet.

Oyster Omelet

Mix and cook Plain Omelet. Fold in one pint oysters, parboiled, drained from their liquor, and cut in halves. Turn on platter, and pour around Thin White Sauce.

Orange Omelet

3 eggs.
2 tablespoons powdered sugar.
Few grains salt.
1 teaspoon lemon juice.
2 oranges.
½ tablespoon butter.
2½ tablespoons orange juice.

Follow directions for Plain Omelet. Remove skin from oranges and cut in slices, lengthwise. Fold in one-third of the slices of orange, well sprinkled with powdered sugar; put remaining slices around omelet, and sprinkle with sugar.

Jelly Omelet

Mix and cook Plain Omelet, omitting pepper and one-half the salt, and adding one tablespoon sugar. Spread before folding with jam, jelly, or marmalade. Fold, turn, and sprinkle with sugar.

Bread Omelet

4 eggs.
½ cup milk.
½ cup stale bread crumbs.
¾ teaspoon salt.
⅛ teaspoon pepper.
1 tablespoon butter.

Soak bread crumbs fifteen minutes in milk, add beaten yolks and seasonings, fold in whites. Cook and serve as Plain Omelet.

Soups

Brown Soup Stock

6 lbs. shin of beef.

3 quarts cold water.

½ teaspoon peppercorns.

6 cloves.

½ bay leaf.

3 sprigs thyme.

1 sprig marjoram.

2 sprigs parsley.

Carrot, ½ cup, cut in dice.

Turnip, ½ cup, cut in dice.

Onion, ½ cup, cut in dice.

Celery, ½ cup, cut in dice.

1 tablespoon salt.

Wipe beef, and cut the lean meat in inch cubes. Brown one-third of meat in hot frying-pan in marrow from a marrow-bone. Put remaining two-thirds with bone and fat in soup kettle, add water, and let stand for thirty minutes. Place on back of range, add browned meat, and heat gradually to boiling point. As scum rises it should be removed. Cover and cook slowly six hours, keeping below boiling point during cooking. Add vegetables and seasonings, cook one and one-half hours, strain, and cool as quickly as possible.

Bouillon

5 lbs. lean beef from middle of round.

2 lbs. marrow-bone.

3 quarts cold water.

1 teaspoon peppercorns.

1 tablespoon salt.

Carrot, ⅓ cup, cut in dice.

Turnip, ⅓ cup, cut in dice.

Onion, ⅓ cup, cut in dice.

Celery, ⅓ cup, cut in dice.

Wipe, and cut meat in inch cubes. Put two-thirds of meat in soup kettle, and soak in water thirty minutes. Brown remainder in hot frying-pan with marrow from marrow-bone. Put browned meat and bone in kettle. Heat to boiling point; skim thoroughly, and cook at temperature below boiling point five hours. Add seasonings and vegetables, cook one hour, strain and cool. Remove fat and clear. Serve in bouillon cups.

Ox-Tail Soup

1 small oxtail.

6 cups Brown Stock.

Carrot, 1 cup each, cut in fancy shapes.

Turnip, 1 cup each, cut in fancy shapes.

Onion, 1 cup, cut in fancy shapes.

Celery, 1 cup, cut in fancy shapes.

½ teaspoon salt.

Few grains cayenne.

¼ cup Madeira wine.

1 teaspoon Worcestershire Sauce.

1 teaspoon lemon juice.

Cut ox-tail in small pieces, wash, drain, sprinkle with salt and pepper, dredge with flour, and fry in butter ten minutes. Add to Brown Stock, and simmer one hour. Then add vegetables, which have been parboiled twenty minutes; simmer until vegetables are soft, add salt, cayenne, wine, Worcestershire Sauce, and lemon juice.

White Soup Stock

The water in which a fowl or chicken is cooked makes White Stock.

Hygienic Soup

6 cups White Stock.

¼ cup oatmeal.

2 cups scalded milk.

2 tablespoons butter.

2 tablespoons flour.

Salt and pepper.

Heat stock to boiling point, add oatmeal, and boil one hour; rub through sieve, add milk, and thicken with butter and flour cooked together. Season with salt and pepper.

Farina Soup

4 cups White Stock.

¼ cup farina.

2 cups scalded milk.

1 cup cream.

Few gratings of nutmeg.

Salt and pepper.

Heat stock to boiling point, add farina, and boil fifteen minutes; then add milk, cream, and seasonings.

Turkish Soup

5 cups Brown Soup Stock.

¼ cup rice.

1½ cups stewed and strained tomatoes.

Bit of bay leaf.

2 slices onion.

10 peppercorns.

¼ teaspoon celery salt.

2 tablespoons butter.

1½ tablespoons flour.

Cook rice in Brown Stock until soft. Cook bay leaf, onion, peppercorns, and celery salt with tomatoes thirty minutes. Combine mixtures, rub through sieve, and bind with butter and flour cooked together. Season with salt and pepper if needed.

Potage à la Reine

4 cups White Stock.
½ teaspoon peppercorns.
1 stalk celery.
1 slice onion.
½ tablespoon salt.
Yolks 3 hard boiled eggs.
⅓ cup cracker crumbs.
Breast meat from a boiled chicken.
2 cups scalded milk.
½ cup cold milk.
3 tablespoons butter.
3 tablespoons flour.

Cook stock with seasonings twenty minutes. Rub yolks of eggs through sieve. Soak cracker crumbs in cold milk until soft; add to eggs. Chop meat and rub through sieve; add to egg and cracker mixture. Then pour milk on slowly, and add to strained stock; boil three minutes. Bind with butter and flour cooked together.

Imperial Soup

4 cups White Stock.
2 cups stale bread crumbs.
2 stalks celery, broken in pieces.
2 slices carrot, cut in cubes.
1 small onion.
3 tablespoons butter.
Sprig of parsley.
2 cloves.
½ teaspoon peppercorns.
Bit of bay leaf.
Blade of mace.
1 teaspoon salt.
½ breast boiled chicken.
⅓ cup blanched almonds.
1 cup cream.
½ cup milk.
2 tablespoons flour.

Cook celery, carrot, and onion in one tablespoon butter, five minutes; tie in cheese cloth with parsley, cloves, peppercorns, bay leaf, and mace; add to stock with salt and bread crumbs, simmer one hour, remove seasonings, and rub through a sieve. Chop chicken meat and rub through sieve; pound almonds to a paste, add to chicken, then add cream. Combine mixtures, add milk, reheat, and bind with remaining butter and flour cooked together.

Cream of Lima Bean Soup

1 cup dried lima beans.
3 pints cold water.
2 slices onion.
4 slices carrot.
1 cup cream or milk.
4 tablespoons butter.
2 tablespoons flour.
1 teaspoon salt.
½ teaspoon pepper.

Soak beans over night; in the morning drain and add cold water; cook until soft, and rub through a sieve. Cut vegetables in small cubes, and cook five minutes in half the butter; remove vegetables, add flour, salt, and pepper, and stir into boiling soup. Add cream, reheat, strain, and add remaining butter in small pieces.

Cream of Lettuce Soup

2½ cups White Stock.
2 heads lettuce finely cut.
2 tablespoons rice.
½ cup cream.
¼ tablespoon onion, finely chopped.
1 tablespoon butter.
Yolk 1 egg.
Few grains nutmeg.
Salt.
Pepper.

Cook onion five minutes in butter, add lettuce, rice, and stock. Cook until rice is soft, then add cream, yolk of egg slightly beaten, nutmeg, salt, and pepper. Remove outer leaves from lettuce, using only tender part for soup.

Chestnut Purée

4 cups White Stock.
2 cups French chestnuts boiled and mashed.
1 slice onion.
¼ teaspoon celery salt.

2 cups scalded milk.
¼ cup butter.
¼ cup flour.
Salt.
Pepper.

Cook stock, chestnuts, onion, and celery salt ten minutes; rub through sieve, add milk, and bind. Season with salt and pepper.

Mock Turtle Soup

1 calf's head.
6 cloves.
½ teaspoon peppercorns.
6 allspice berries.
2 sprigs thyme.
⅓ cup sliced onion.
⅓ cup carrot, cut in dice.
2 cups brown stock.
¼ cup butter.
½ cup flour.
1 cup stewed and strained tomatoes.
Juice ½ lemon.
Madeira wine.

Clean and wash calf's head; soak one hour in cold water to cover. Cook until tender in three quarts boiling salted water (to which seasoning and vegetables have been added). Remove head; boil stock until reduced to one quart. Strain and cool. Melt and brown butter, add flour, and stir until well browned; then pour on slowly brown stock. Add head-stock, tomato, one cup face meat cut in dice, and lemon juice. Simmer five minutes; add Royal Custard cut in dice, and Egg Balls, or Force-meat Balls. Add Madeira wine, salt, and pepper to taste.

Consommé

3 lbs. beef, poorer part of round.

1 lb. marrow-bone.

3 lbs. knuckle of veal.

1 quart chicken stock.

Carrot, ⅓ cup, cut in dice.

Turnip, ⅓ cup, cut in dice.

Celery, ⅓ cup, cut in dice.

⅓ cup sliced onion.

2 tablespoons butter.

1 tablespoon salt.

1 teaspoon peppercorns.

4 cloves.

3 sprigs thyme.

1 sprig marjoram.

2 sprigs parsley.

½ bay leaf.

Cut beef in one and one-half inch cubes, and brown one-half in some of the marrow from marrow-bone; put remaining half in kettle with cold water, add veal cut in pieces, browned meat, and bones. Let stand one-half hour. Heat slowly to boiling point, and let simmer three hours, removing scum as it forms on top of kettle. Add one quart liquor in which a fowl was cooked,

and simmer two hours. Cook carrot, turnip, onion, and celery in butter five minutes; then add to soup, with remaining seasonings. Cook one and one-half hours, strain, cool quickly, remove fat, and clear.

Consommé à la Royale

Consommé, served with Royal Custard.

Soups with Fish Stock

Oyster Stew

1 quart oysters.

4 cups scalded milk.

¼ cup butter.

½ tablespoon salt.

⅛ teaspoon pepper.

Clean oysters by placing in a colander and pouring over them three-fourths cup cold water. Carefully pick over oysters, reserve liquor, and heat it to boiling point; strain through double cheese cloth, add oysters, and cook until oysters are plump and edges begin to curl. Remove oysters with skimmer, and put in tureen with butter, salt, and pepper. Add oyster liquor, strained a second time, and milk. Serve with oyster crackers.

Oyster Gumbo

1 pint oysters.

4 cups fish stock.

¼ cup butter.

1 tablespoon chopped onion.

½ can okra.

⅓ can tomatoes.

Salt.

Pepper.

Clean, pick over, and parboil oysters, drain, and add oyster liquor to fish stock. Cook onion five minutes in one-half the butter; add to stock. Then add okra, tomatoes heated and drained from some of their liquor, oysters, and remaining butter. Season with salt and pepper.

Lobster Bisque

2 lb. lobster.

2 cups cold water.

4 cups milk.

¼ cup butter.

¼ cup flour.

1½ teaspoons salt.

Few grains of cayenne.

Remove meat from lobster shell. Add cold water to body bones and tough end of claws, cut in pieces; bring slowly to boiling point, and cook twenty minutes. Drain, reserve liquor, and thicken with butter and flour cooked together. Scald milk with tail meat of lobster,

finely chopped; strain, and add to liquor. Season with salt and cayenne; then add tender claw meat, cut in dice, and body meat. When coral is found in lobster, wash, wipe, force through fine strainer, put in a mortar with butter, work until well blended, then add flour, and stir into soup.

If a richer soup is desired, White Stock may be used in place of water.

Soup without Stock

Black Bean Soup

1 pint black beans.

2 quarts cold water.

1 small onion.

2 stalks celery, or

¼ teaspoon celery salt.

½ tablespoon salt.

⅛ teaspoon pepper.

¼ teaspoon mustard.

Few grains cayenne.

3 tablespoons butter.

1½ tablespoons flour.

2 hard boiled eggs.

1 lemon.

Soak beans over night; in the morning drain and add cold water. Slice onion, and cook five minutes with half the butter, adding to beans, with celery stalks broken in pieces. Simmer three or four hours, or until beans are soft; add more water as water boils away. Rub through a sieve, reheat to the boiling point, and add salt, pepper, mustard, and cayenne well mixed. Bind with remaining butter and flour cooked together. Cut eggs in thin slices, and lemon in thin slices, removing seeds. Put in tureen, and strain the soup over them.

Kornlet Soup

1 can kornlet.
1 pint cold water.
1 quart milk, scalded.
4 tablespoons butter.
1 tablespoon chopped onion.
4 tablespoons flour.
1½ teaspoons salt.
Few grains pepper.

Cook kornlet in cold water twenty minutes, rub through a sieve, and add milk. Fry butter and onion three minutes; remove onion, add flour, salt, and pepper, and stir into boiling soup.

Tomato Soup

1 can tomatoes.
1 pint water.
12 peppercorns.
Bit of bay leaf.
4 cloves.
2 teaspoons sugar.

1 teaspoon salt.
⅛ teaspoon soda.
2 tablespoons butter.
3 tablespoons flour.

Cook the first six ingredients twenty minutes; strain, add salt and soda; bind, and strain into tureen.

Chowders

Corn Chowder

1 can corn.
4 cups potatoes, cut in ¼ inch slices.
1½ inch cube fat salt pork.
1 sliced onion.
4 cups scalded milk.
8 common crackers.
3 tablespoons butter.
Salt and pepper.

Cut pork in small pieces and try out; add onion and cook five minutes, stirring often that onion may not burn; strain fat into a stewpan. Parboil potatoes five minutes in boiling water to cover; drain, and add potatoes to fat; then add two cups boiling water; cook until potatoes are soft, add corn and milk, then heat to boiling point. Season with salt and pepper; add butter, and crackers split and soaked in enough cold milk to moisten. Remove crackers, turn chowder into a tureen, and put crackers on top.

Fish Chowder

4 lb. cod or haddock.
6 cups potatoes cut in ¼ inch slices, or
4 cups potatoes cut in ¾ inch cubes.
1 sliced onion.
1½ inch cube fat salt pork.
1 tablespoon salt.
⅓ teaspoon pepper.
3 tablespoons butter.
4 cups scalded milk.
8 common crackers.

Order the fish skinned, but head and tail left on. Cut off head and tail and remove fish from backbone. Cut fish in two-inch pieces and set aside. Put head, tail, and backbone broken in pieces, in stewpan; add two cups cold water and bring slowly to boiling point; cook twenty minutes. Cut salt pork in small pieces and try out, add onion, and fry five minutes; strain fat into stewpan. Parboil potatoes five minutes in boiling water to cover; drain, and add potatoes to fat; then add two cups boiling water and cook five minutes. Add liquor drained from bones and fish; cover, and simmer ten minutes. Add milk, salt, pepper, butter, and crackers split and soaked in enough cold milk to moisten. Pilot bread is sometimes used in place of common crackers.

Connecticut Chowder

4 lb. cod or haddock.
4 cups potatoes cut in ¾ inch cubes.
1½ inch cube fat salt pork.
1 sliced onion.
2½ cups stewed and strained tomatoes.
3 tablespoons butter.
⅔ cup cracker crumbs.
Salt and pepper.

Prepare as Fish Chowder, using liquor drained from bones for cooking potatoes, instead of additional water. Use tomatoes in place of milk and add cracker crumbs just before serving.

Soup Garnishings and Force-Meats

Croûtons (Duchess Crusts)

Cut stale bread in one-third inch slices, remove crusts, and spread thinly with butter. Cut slices in one-third inch cubes, put in pan and bake until delicately browned, or fry in deep fat.

Egg Balls

Yolks 2 hard boiled eggs.
⅛ teaspoon salt.
Few grains cayenne.
½ teaspoon melted butter.

Rub yolks through sieve, add seasonings, and moisten with raw egg yolk to make of consistency to handle. Shape in small balls, roll in flour, and sauté in butter. Serve in Brown Soup Stock, Consommé, or Mock Turtle Soup.

Egg Custard

Yolks 2 eggs.
Few grains salt.
2 tablespoons milk.

Beat eggs slightly, add milk and salt. Pour into small buttered cup, place in pan of hot water and bake until firm; cool, remove from cup, and cut in fancy shapes with French vegetable cutters.

Royal Custard

Yolks 3 eggs.
1 egg.
½ cup Consommé.
⅛ teaspoon salt.
Slight grating nutmeg.
Few grains cayenne.

Beat eggs slightly, add Consommé and seasonings. Pour into a small buttered tin mould, place in pan of hot water and bake until firm; cool, remove from mould, and cut in fancy shapes.

Noodles

1 egg.
½ teaspoon salt.
Flour.

Beat egg slightly, add salt, and flour enough to make very stiff dough; knead, toss on slightly floured board, and roll thinly as possible, which may be as thin as paper. Cover with towel, and set aside for twenty minutes; then cut in fancy shapes, using sharp knife or French vegetable cutter; or the thin sheet may be rolled like jelly-roll, cut in slices as thinly as possible, and pieces unrolled. Dry, and when needed cook twenty minutes in boiling salted water; drain, and add to soup.

Noodles may be served as a vegetable.

Pâte au Chou

2½ tablespoons milk.
½ teaspoon lard.
½ teaspoon butter.
⅛ teaspoon salt.
¼ cup flour.
1 egg.

Heat butter, lard, and milk to boiling point, add flour and salt, and stir vigorously. Remove from fire, add egg unbeaten, and stir until well mixed. Cool, and drop small pieces from tip of teaspoon into deep fat. Fry until brown and crisp, and drain on brown paper.

Fish Force-meat

¼ cup fine stale bread crumbs.
¼ cup milk.
1 egg.
⅔ cup raw fish.
Salt.

Cook bread and milk to a paste, add egg well beaten, and fish pounded and forced through a purée strainer. Season with salt. A meat chopper is of great assistance in making force-meats, as raw fish or meat may be easily forced through it. Bass, halibut, or pickerel are the best fish to use for force-meat. Force-meat is often shaped into small balls.

Chicken Force-meat

½ cup fine stale bread crumbs.
½ cup milk.
2 tablespoons butter.
White 1 egg.
⅔ cup breast raw chicken.
Salt.
Few grains cayenne.
Slight grating nutmeg.

Cook bread and milk to a paste, add butter, white of egg beaten stiff, and seasonings; then add chicken pounded and forced through purée strainer.

Broiled Scrod

A young cod, split down the back, and backbone removed, except a small portion near the tail, is called a scrod. Scrod are always broiled, spread with butter, and sprinkled with salt and pepper.

Haddock is also so dressed.

Baked Halibut with Stuffing

Clean a four-pound haddock, sprinkle with salt inside and out, stuff and sew. Cut five diagonal gashes on each side of backbone and insert narrow strips of fat salt pork, having gashes on one side come between gashes on other side. Shape with skewers in form of letter S,

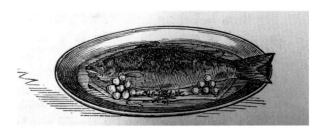

A baked fish garnished with potato balls. From Mrs. Mary F. Henderson, *Practical Cooking and Dinner Giving* (New York: Harper and Bros., 1877), 107, Special Collections, Michigan State University Libraries.

and fasten skewers with small twine. Place on greased fish-sheet in a dripping-pan, sprinkle with salt and pepper, brush over with melted butter, dredge with flour, and place around fish small pieces of fat salt pork. Bake one hour in hot oven, basting as soon as fat is tried out, and continue basting every ten minutes. Serve with Drawn Butter, Egg or Hollandaise Sauce.

Baked Cod with Oyster Stuffing

Clean a four-pound cod, sprinkle with salt and pepper, brush over with lemon juice, stuff, and sew. Gash, skewer, and bake as Baked Halibut with Stuffing. Serve with Oyster Sauce.

Oyster Stuffing

1 cup cracker crumbs.
¼ cup melted butter.
½ teaspoon salt.
⅛ teaspoon pepper.
1½ teaspoons lemon juice.
½ tablespoon finely chopped parsley.
1 cup oysters.

Add seasonings and butter to cracker crumbs. Clean oysters, and remove tough muscles; add soft parts to mixture, with enough oyster liquor to moisten.

Baked Halibut with Lobster Sauce

Clean a piece of halibut weighing three pounds. Cut gashes in top, and insert a narrow strip of fat salt pork in each gash. Place in dripping-pan on fish-sheet, sprinkle with salt and pepper, and dredge with flour. Cover bottom of pan with water, add sprig of parsley, slice of onion, two slices carrot cut in pieces, and bit of bay leaf. Bake one hour, basting with one-fourth cup butter, and the liquor in pan. Serve with Lobster Sauce.

Baked Stuffed Smelts

Clean and wipe as dry as possible twelve selected smelts. Stuff, sprinkle with salt and pepper, and brush over with lemon juice. Place in buttered shallow plate, cover with buttered paper, and bake five minutes in hot oven. Remove from oven, sprinkle with buttered crumbs, and bake until crumbs are brown. Serve with Sauce Béarnaise.

Stuffing. Cook one tablespoon finely chopped onion with one tablespoon butter three minutes. Add one-fourth cup finely chopped mushrooms, one-fourth cup soft part of oysters (parboiled, drained, and chopped), one-half teaspoon chopped parsley, three tablespoons Thick White Sauce, and one-half cup Fish Force-meat.

Fried Cod Steaks

Clean steaks, sprinkle with salt and pepper, and dip in granulated corn meal. Try out slices of fat salt pork in frying-pan, remove scraps, and sauté steaks in fat.

Fried Smelts

Clean smelts, leaving on heads and tails. Sprinkle with salt and pepper, dip in flour, egg, and crumbs, and fry three to four minutes in deep fat. As soon as smelts are put into fat, remove fat to back of range so that they may not become too brown before cooked through. Arrange on hot platter, garnish with parsley, lemon, and fried gelatine. Serve with Sauce Tartare.

Smelts are fried without being skewered, but often are skewered in variety of shapes.

To fry gelatine. Take up a handful and drop in hot, deep fat; it will immediately swell and become white; it should at once be removed with a skimmer, then drained.

Phosphated or granulated gelatine cannot be used for frying.

Fried Eels

Clean eels, and cut in two-inch pieces. Sprinkle with salt and pepper, dip in corn meal, and sauté in pork fat.

Soft-shell Crabs

Clean crabs, sprinkle with salt and pepper, dip in crumbs, egg, and crumbs, fry in deep fat, and drain. Being light they will rise to top of fat, and should be turned while frying. Soft-shell crabs are usually fried.

To Clean a Crab

Lift and fold back the tapering points which are found on each side of the back shell, and remove spongy substance that lies under them. Turn crab on its back, and with a pointed knife remove the small piece at lower part of shell, which terminates in a point; this is called the apron.

Frogs' Hind Legs

Trim and clean. Sprinkle with salt and pepper, dip in crumbs, egg, and crumbs again, then fry three minutes in deep fat, and drain. If used as an entrée, serve with Sauce Tartare.

Terrapin

To prepare terrapin for cooking, plunge into boiling water and boil five minutes. Lift out of water with skimmer, and remove skin from feet and tail by rubbing with a towel. Draw out head with a skewer and rub off skin.

To Cook Terrapin. Put in a kettle, cover with boiling salted water, add two slices each of carrot and onion, and a stalk of celery. Cook until meat is tender, which may be determined by pressing feet-meat between thumb and finger. The time required will be from thirty-five to forty minutes. Remove from water, cool, draw out nails from feet, cut under shell close to upper shell and remove.

Empty upper shell and carefully remove and discard bags, and thick, heavy part of intestines. Any of the gall-bladder would give bitter flavor to the dish. The liver, small intestines, and eggs are used with the meat.

Turban of Fish

2½ cups cold flaked fish (cod, haddock, halibut, or cusk).
1½ cups milk.
1 slice onion.
Blade of mace.
Sprig of parsley.
¼ cup butter.
¼ cup flour.
½ teaspoon salt.
⅛ teaspoon pepper.
Lemon juice.
Yolks 2 eggs.
⅔ cup buttered cracker crumbs.

Scald milk with onion, mace, and parsley; remove seasonings. Melt butter, add flour, salt, pepper, and gradually the milk; then add eggs, slightly beaten. Put a layer of fish on buttered dish, sprinkle with salt and pepper, and add a few drops of lemon juice. Cover with sauce, continuing until fish and sauce are used, shaping in pyramid form. Cover with crumbs, and bake in hot oven until crumbs are brown.

Fish Hash

Take equal parts of cold flaked fish and cold boiled potatoes finely chopped. Season with salt and pepper.

Try out fat salt pork, remove scraps, leaving enough fat in pan to moisten fish and potatoes. Put in fish and potatoes, stir until heated, then cook until well browned underneath; fold and turn like an omelet.

Fish Croquettes

To two cups cold flaked halibut or salmon add one cup Thick White Sauce. Season with salt and pepper, and spread on a plate to cool. Shape, roll in crumbs, egg, and crumbs, and fry in deep fat; drain, arrange on hot dish for serving, and garnish with parsley. If salmon is used, add lemon juice and finely chopped parsley.

Salmon Box

Line a bread pan, slightly buttered, with warm steamed rice. Fill the centre with cold boiled salmon, flaked, and seasoned with salt, pepper, and a slight grating of nutmeg. Cover with rice, and steam one hour. Turn on a hot platter for serving, and pour around Egg Sauce II.

Oysters on the Half Shell

Serve oysters on deep halves of the shells, allowing six to each person. Arrange on plates of crushed ice, with one-fourth of a lemon in the centre of each plate.

Raw Oysters

Raw oysters are served on oyster plates, or in a block of ice. Place block of ice on a folded napkin on platter, and garnish the base with parsley and quarters of lemon, or ferns and lemons.

To Block Ice for Oysters. Use a rectangular piece of clear ice, and with hot flatirons melt a cavity large enough to hold the oysters. Pour water from cavity as rapidly as it forms.

Panned Oysters

Clean one pint large oysters. Place in dripping-pan small oblong pieces of toast, put an oyster on each piece, sprinkle with salt and pepper, and bake until oysters are plump. Serve with Lemon Butter.

Lemon Butter. Cream three tablespoons butter, add one-half teaspoon salt, one tablespoon lemon juice, and a few grains of cayenne.

Oyster Fricassee

1 pint oysters.
Milk or cream.
2 tablespoons butter.
2 tablespoons flour.
¼ teaspoon salt.
Few grains cayenne.
1 teaspoon finely chopped parsley.
1 egg.

Clean oysters, heat oyster liquor to boiling point and strain through double thickness of cheese cloth; add oysters to liquor and cook until plump. Remove oysters with skimmer and add enough cream to liquor to make a cupful. Melt butter, add flour, and pour on gradually hot liquid; add salt, cayenne, parsley, oysters, and egg slightly beaten.

Scalloped Oysters

1 pint oysters.
4 tablespoons oyster liquor.
2 tablespoons milk or cream.
½ cup stale bread crumbs.
1 cup cracker crumbs.
½ cup melted butter.
Salt.
Pepper.

Mix bread and cracker crumbs, and stir in butter. Put a thin layer in bottom of a buttered shallow baking-dish, cover with oysters, and sprinkle with salt and pepper; add one-half each of oyster liquor and cream. Repeat, and cover top with remaining crumbs. Bake thirty minutes in hot oven. Never allow more than two layers of oysters for Scalloped Oysters; if three layers are used, the middle layer will be underdone, while others are properly cooked. A sprinkling of mace or grated nutmeg to each layer is considered by many an improvement. Sherry wine may be used in place of cream.

Fried Scallops

Clean one quart scallops, add one and one-half cups boiling water, and let stand two minutes; drain, and dry between towels. Season with salt and pepper, roll in fine cracker crumbs, dip in egg, again in crumbs, and fry two minutes in deep fat; then drain on brown paper.

Fried Lobster

Remove lobster meat from shell. Use tail meat, divided in fourths, and large pieces of claw meat. Sprinkle with salt, pepper, and lemon juice; dip in crumbs, egg, and again in crumbs; fry in deep fat, drain, and serve with Sauce Tartare.

Buttered Lobster

2 lb. lobster.
3 tablespoons butter.
Salt and pepper.
Lemon juice.

Remove lobster meat from shell and chop slightly. Melt butter, add lobster, and when heated, season and serve garnished with lobster claws.

Beef

Beefsteak with Oyster Blanket

Wipe a sirloin steak, cut one and one-half inches thick, broil five minutes, and then remove to platter. Spread with butter and sprinkle with salt and pepper. Clean one pint oysters, cover steak with same, sprinkle oysters with salt and pepper and dot over with butter. Place on grate in hot oven, and cook until oysters are plump.

Cutlets of Tenderloin with Chestnut Purée

Shape slices of tenderloin, one inch thick, in circular pieces. Broil five minutes. Spread with butter, sprinkle with salt and pepper. Arrange on platter around a mound of Chestnut Purée.

Broiled Meat Cakes

Chop finely lean raw beef, season with salt and pepper, shape in small flat cakes, and broil in a greased broiler or frying-pan. Spread with butter, or serve with Maître d'Hôtel Butter. In forming the cakes, handle as little as possible; for if pressed too compactly, cakes will be found solid.

Hamburg Steaks

Chop finely one pound lean raw beef; season highly with salt, pepper, and a few drops onion juice or one-half shallot finely chopped. Shape, cook, and serve as Meat Cakes. A few gratings of nutmeg and one egg slightly beaten may be added.

Yorkshire Pudding

1 cup milk.
1 cup flour.
2 eggs.
¼ teaspoon salt.
　　　　Miss C. J. Wills.

Mix salt and flour, and add milk gradually to form a smooth paste; then add eggs beaten until very light. Cover bottom of hot pan with some of beef fat tried out from roast, pour mixture in pan one-half inch deep. Bake twenty minutes in hot oven, basting after well risen, with some of the fat from pan in which meat is roasting. Cut in squares for serving. Bake, if preferred, in greased, hissing hot iron gem pans.

Corned Beef

Corned beef has but little nutritive value. It is used to give variety to our diet in summer, when fresh meats prove too stimulating. It is eaten by the workingman to give bulk to his food. The best pieces of corned beef are the rattle rand and fancy brisket . . .

To Boil Corned Beef. Wipe the meat and tie securely in shape, if this has not been already done at market. Put in kettle, cover with cold water, and bring slowly to boil-

Corned beef, from Mrs. Mary F. Henderson, *Practical Cooking and Dinner Giving* (New York: Harper and Bros., 1877), 139, Special Collections, Michigan State University Libraries.

ing point. Boil five minutes, remove scum, and cook at a lower temperature until tender. Cool slightly in water in which it was cooked, remove to a dish, cover, and place on cover a weight, that meat may be well pressed. The lean meat and fat may be separated and put in alternate layers in a bread pan, then covered and pressed.

Boiled Dinner

A boiled dinner consists of warm unpressed corned beef, served with cabbage, beets, turnips, carrots, and potatoes. After removing meat from water, skim off fat and cook vegetables (with exception of beets, which require a long time for cooking) in this water. Carrots require a longer time for cooking than cabbage or turnips. Carrots and turnips, if small, may be cooked whole; if large, cut in pieces. Cabbage and beets are served in separate dishes, other vegetables on same dish with meat.

Boiled Tongue

A boiled corned tongue is cooked the same as Boiled Corned Beef. If very salt, it should be soaked in cold water several hours, or over night, before cooking. Take from water when slightly cooled and remove skin.

Braised Tongue

A fresh tongue is necessary for braising. Put tongue in kettle, cover with boiling water, and cook slowly two hours. Take tongue from water and remove skin and roots. Place in deep pan and surround with one-third

cup each carrot, onion, and celery, cut in dice, and one sprig parsley; then pour over four cups sauce. Cover closely, and bake two hours, turning after the first hour. Serve on platter and strain around the sauce.

Sauce for Tongue. Brown one-fourth cup butter, add one-fourth cup flour and stir together until well browned. Add gradually four cups of water in which tongue was cooked. Season with salt and pepper and add one teaspoon Worcestershire Sauce. One and one-half cups stewed and strained tomatoes may be used in place of some of the water.

Broiled Liver

Cover with boiling water slices of liver cut one-half inch thick, let stand five minutes to draw out the blood; drain, wipe, and remove the thin outside skin and veins. Sprinkle with salt and pepper, place in a greased wire broiler and broil five minutes, turning often. Remove to a hot platter, spread with butter, and sprinkle with salt and pepper.

Liver and Bacon

Prepare as for Broiled Liver, cut in pieces for serving, sprinkle with salt and pepper, dredge with flour, and fry in bacon fat. Serve with bacon.

Broiled Tripe

Fresh honeycomb tripe is best for broiling. Wipe tripe as dry as possible, dip in fine cracker dust and olive oil or melted butter, draining off all fat that is possible, and again dip in cracker dust. Place in a greased broiler and broil five minutes, cooking smooth side of tripe the first three minutes. Place on a hot platter, honeycomb side up, spread with butter and sprinkle with salt and pepper. Broiled tripe is at its best when cooked over a charcoal fire.

Cottage Pie

Cover bottom of a small greased baking-dish with hot mashed potato, add a thick layer of roast beef, chopped or cut in small pieces (seasoned with salt, pepper, and a few drops of onion juice) and moistened with some of the gravy; cover with a thin layer of mashed potato, and bake in a hot oven long enough to heat through.

Corned Beef Hash

Remove skin and gristle from cooked corned beef, then chop the meat. When meat is very fat, discard most of the fat. To chopped meat add an equal quantity of cold boiled chopped potatoes. Season with salt and pepper, put into a hot buttered frying-pan, moisten with milk or cream, stir until well mixed, spread evenly, then place on a part of the range where it may slowly brown underneath. Turn, and fold on a hot platter. Garnish with sprig of parsley in the middle.

Corned Beef Hash with Beets

When preparing Corned Beef Hash, add one-half as much finely chopped cooked beets as potatoes. Cold roast beef or one-half roast beef and one-half corned beef may be used.

Dried Beef with Cream

¼ lb. smoked dried beef, thinly sliced.
1 cup scalded cream.
1½ tablespoons flour.

Remove skin and separate meat in pieces, cover with hot water, let stand ten minutes, and drain. Dilute flour with enough cold water to pour easily, making a smooth paste; add to cream, and cook in double boiler ten minutes. Add beef, and reheat.

Lamb and Mutton

Mutton Curry

Wipe and cut meat from fore-quarter of mutton in one-inch pieces; there should be three cupfuls. Put in kettle, cover with cold water, and bring quickly to boiling point; drain in colander and pour over one quart cold water. Return meat to kettle, cover with one quart boiling water, add three onions cut in slices, one-half teaspoon peppercorns, and a sprig each of thyme and parsley. Simmer until meat is tender, remove meat, strain liquor, and thicken with one-fourth cup each of butter and flour cooked together; to the flour add one-half tablespoon curry powder, one-half teaspoon salt, and one-eighth teaspoon pepper. Add meat to gravy, reheat, and serve with border of steamed rice.

Irish Stew with Dumplings

Wipe and cut in pieces three pounds lamb from the fore-quarter. Put in kettle, cover with boiling water, and cook slowly two hours or until tender. After cooking one hour, add one-half cup each carrot and turnip cut in one-half inch cubes, and one onion cut in slices. Fifteen minutes before serving add four cups potatoes cut in one-fourth inch slices, previously parboiled five minutes in boiling water. Thicken with one-fourth cup flour, diluted with enough cold water to form a thin smooth paste. Season with salt and pepper, serve with Dumplings.

Dumplings

2 cups flour.
4 teaspoons baking powder.
½ teaspoon salt.
2 teaspoons butter.
¾ cup milk.

Mix and sift dry ingredients. Work in butter with tips of fingers, add milk gradually, using a knife for mixing. Toss on a floured board, pat, and roll out to one-half inch in thickness. Shape with biscuit cutter, first dipped in flour. Place closely together in a buttered steamer, put over kettle of boiling water, cover closely, and steam twelve minutes. A perforated tin pie plate may be used in place of steamer. A little more milk may be used in the mixture, when it may be taken up by spoonfuls, dropped and cooked on top of stew. In this case some of the liquid must be removed, that dumplings may rest on meat and potato, and not settle into liquid.

Scotch Broth

Wipe three pounds mutton cut from fore-quarter. Cut lean meat in one-inch cubes, put in kettle, cover with three pints cold water, bring quickly to boiling point, skim, and add one-half cup barley which has been soaked in cold water over night; simmer one and one-half hours, or until meat is tender. Put bones in a second kettle, cover with cold water, heat slowly to boiling point, skim, and boil one and one-half hours. Strain water from bones and add to meat. Fry five minutes in two tablespoons butter, one-fourth cup each of carrot, turnip, onion, and celery, cut in one-half inch dice, add to soup with salt and pepper to taste, and cook until vegetables are soft. Thicken with two tablespoons each of butter and flour cooked together. Add one-half tablespoon finely chopped parsley just before serving.

Rice may be used in place of barley.

Saddle of Mutton

Mutton for a saddle should always be dressed at market. Wipe meat, sprinkle with salt and pepper, place on rack in dripping-pan, and dredge meat and bottom of pan with flour. Bake in hot oven one and one-fourth hours, basting every fifteen minutes. Serve with Currant Jelly Sauce.

To Carve a Saddle of Mutton, cut thin slices parallel with backbone, then slip the knife under and separate slices from ribs.

Lamb's Kidneys

Pare and cut in slices six kidneys, and sprinkle with salt and pepper. Melt two tablespoons butter in hot frying-pan, put in kidneys, and cook five minutes; dredge thoroughly with flour, and add two-thirds cup boiling water or hot Brown Stock. Cook five minutes, add more salt and pepper if needed. Lemon juice, onion juice, or Madeira wine may be used for additional flavor. Kidneys must be cooked a short time, or for several hours; they are tender after a few minutes' cooking, but soon toughen, and need hours of cooking to again make them tender.

Salmi of Lamb

Cut cold roast lamb in thin slices. Cook five minutes two tablespoons butter with one-half tablespoon finely chopped onion. Add lamb, sprinkle with salt and pepper, and cover with one cup Brown Sauce, or one cup cold lamb gravy seasoned with Worcestershire, Harvey, or Elizabeth Sauce. Cook until thoroughly heated. Arrange slices overlapping one another lengthwise of platter, pour around sauce, and garnish with toast points. A few sliced mushrooms or stoned olives improve this sauce.

Minced Lamb on Toast

Remove dry pieces of skin and gristle from remnants of cold roast lamb, then chop meat. Heat in well buttered frying-pan, season with salt, pepper, and celery salt, and moisten with a little hot water or stock; or, after seasoning, dredge well with flour, stir, and add enough stock to make thin gravy. Pour over small slices of buttered toast.

Veal

Veal Birds

Wipe slices of veal from leg, cut as thinly as possible, then remove bone, skin, and fat. Pound until one-fourth inch thick and cut in pieces two and one-half inches long by one and one-half inches wide, each piece making a bird. Chop trimmings of meat, adding for every three birds a piece of fat salt pork cut one inch square and one-fourth inch thick; pork also to be chopped. Add to trimmings and pork one-half their measure of fine cracker crumbs, and season highly with salt, pepper, cayenne, poultry seasoning, lemon juice, and onion juice. Moisten with beaten egg and hot water or stock.

Spread each piece with thin layer of mixture and avoid having mixture come close to edge. Roll, and fasten with skewers. Sprinkle with salt and pepper, dredge with flour, and fry in hot butter until a golden brown. Put in stewpan, add cream to half cover meat, cook slowly twenty minutes or until tender. Serve on small pieces of toast, straining cream remaining in pan over birds and toast, and garnish with parsley.

A Thin White Sauce in place of cream may be served around birds.

Veal Loaf

Separate a knuckle of veal in pieces by sawing through bone. Wipe, put in kettle with one pound lean veal and one onion; cover with boiling water and cook slowly until veal is tender. Drain and chop finely meat, season highly with salt and pepper. Garnish bottom of mould with slices of hard boiled eggs and parsley. Put in layer of meat, layer of thinly sliced hard boiled eggs, sprinkle with finely chopped parsley, and cover with remaining meat. Pour over liquor, which should be reduced to one cupful. Press and chill, turn on a dish, and garnish with parsley.

Broiled Sweetbread

Parboil a sweetbread, split cross-wise, sprinkle with salt and pepper, and broil five minutes. Serve with Lemon Butter.

Pork

Pork Chops with Fried Apples

Arrange Pork Chops on a platter, and surround with slices of apples, cut one-half inch thick, fried in the fat remaining in pan.

Fried Salt Pork with Codfish

Cut fat salt pork in one-fourth inch slices, cut gashes one-third inch apart in slices, nearly to rind. Try out in a hot frying-pan until brown and crisp, occasionally turning off fat from pan. Serve around strips of codfish which have been soaked in pan of lukewarm water and allowed to stand on back of range until soft. Serve with Drawn Butter Sauce, boiled potatoes, and beets.

Fried Pigs' Feet

Wipe, sprinkle with salt and pepper, dip in crumbs, egg, and crumbs, fry in deep fat, and drain.

Fried Ham and Eggs

Wipe ham, remove one-half outside layer of fat, and place in frying-pan. Cover with tepid water and let stand on back of range thirty minutes; drain, and dry on a towel. Heat pan, put in ham, brown quickly on one side, turn and brown other side; or soak ham over night, dry, and cook in hot frying-pan. If cooked too long, ham will become hard and dry. Serve with fried eggs cooked in the tried-out ham fat.

Boston Baked Beans

Pick over one quart pea beans, cover with cold water, and soak over night. In morning, drain, cover with fresh water, heat slowly (keeping water below boiling point), and cook until skins will burst,—which is best determined by taking a few beans on the tip of a spoon and blowing on them, when skins will burst if sufficiently cooked. Beans thus tested must, of course, be thrown away. Drain beans, throwing bean-water out of doors, not in sink.

Scald rind of one-half pound fat salt pork, scrape, remove one-fourth inch slice and put in bottom of bean-pot. Cut through rind of remaining pork every one-half inch, making cuts one inch deep. Put beans in pot and bury pork in beans, leaving rind exposed. Mix one table-spoon salt, one tablespoon molasses, and three table-spoons sugar; add one cup boiling water, and pour over beans; then add enough more boiling water to cover beans. Cover bean-pot, put in oven, and bake slowly six or eight hours, uncovering the last hour of cooking, that rind may become brown and crisp. Add water as needed. Many feel sure that by adding with seasonings one-half tablespoon mustard, the beans are more easily digested. If pork mixed with lean is preferred, use less salt.

The fine reputation which Boston Baked Beans have gained, has been attributed to the earthen bean-pot with small top and bulging sides in which they are sup-posed to be cooked. Equally good beans have often been eaten where a five-pound lard pail was substituted for the broken bean-pot.

Yellow-eyed beans are very good when baked.

Roast Chicken

Dress, clean, stuff, and truss a chicken. Place on its back on rack in a dripping-pan, rub entire surface with salt, and spread breast and legs with three tablespoons butter, rubbed until creamy and mixed with two table-spoons flour. Dredge bottom of pan with flour. Place in a hot oven, and when flour is well browned, reduce the heat, then baste. Continue basting every ten minutes until chicken is cooked. For basting, use one-fourth cup butter, melted in two-thirds cup boiling water, and after this is gone, use fat in pan, and when necessary to pre-vent flour burning, add one cup boiling water. During cooking, turn chicken frequently, that it may brown evenly. If a thick crust is desired, dredge bird with flour two or three times during cooking. If a glazed surface is preferred, spread bird with butter, omitting flour, and do not dredge during baking. When breast meat is tender, bird is sufficiently cooked. A four pound chicken requires about one and one-half hours.

Gravy

Pour off liquid in pan in which chicken has been roasted. From liquid skim off four tablespoons fat; return fat to pan and brown with four tablespoons flour; add two cups stock in which giblets, neck, and tips of wings have been cooked. Cook five minutes, season with salt and pepper, then strain. The remaining fat may be used, in place of butter, for frying potatoes, or for basting when roasting another chicken.

For Giblet Gravy, add to the above, giblets (heart, liver, and gizzard) finely chopped.

Maryland Chicken

Dress, clean, and cut up two chickens. Sprinkle with salt and pepper, dip in flour, egg, and crumbs, place in a well-greased dripping-pan, and bake twenty minutes in a hot oven, basting after first five minutes of cooking with one-third cup melted butter. Arrange on platter and pour over two cups Cream Sauce.

Chicken Gumbo

Dress, clean, and cut up a chicken. Sprinkle with salt and pepper, dredge with flour, and sauté in pork fat. Fry one-half finely chopped onion in fat remaining in frying-pan. Add four cups sliced okra, sprig of parsley, and one-fourth red pepper finely chopped, and cook slowly fifteen minutes. Add to chicken, with one and one-half cups tomato, three cups boiling water and one and one-half teaspoons salt. Cook slowly until chicken is tender, then add one cup boiled rice.

Chicken Stew

Dress, clean, and cut up a fowl. Put in a stewpan, cover with boiling water, and cook slowly until tender, adding one-half tablespoon salt and one-eighth teaspoon pepper when fowl is about half cooked. Thicken stock with one-third cup flour diluted with enough cold water to pour easily. Serve with Dumplings. If desired richer, butter may be added.

Chicken Pie

Dress, clean, and cut up two fowls or chickens. Put in a stewpan with one-half onion, sprig of parsley, and bit of bay leaf; cover with boiling water, and cook slowly until tender. When chicken is half cooked, add one-half tablespoon salt and one-eighth teaspoon pepper. Remove chicken, strain stock, skim off fat, and then cook until reduced to four cups. Thicken stock with one-third cup flour diluted with enough cold water to pour easily. Place a small cup in centre of baking-dish, arrange around it pieces of chicken, removing some of the larger bones; pour over gravy, and cool. Cover with pie crust, in which several incisions have been made that there may be an outlet for escape of steam and gases. Wet edge of crust and put around a rim, having rim come close to edge. Bake in a moderate oven until crust is well risen and browned. Roll remnants of pastry and cut in diamond-shaped pieces, bake, and serve with pie when reheated. If puff paste is used, it is best to bake top separately.

Jellied Chicken

Dress, clean, and cut up a four-pound fowl. Put in a stewpan with two slices onion, cover with boiling water, and cook slowly until meat falls from bones. When half cooked, add one-half tablespoon salt. Remove chicken;

reduce stock to three-fourths cup, strain, and skim off fat. Decorate bottom of a mould with parsley and slices of hard boiled eggs. Pack in meat freed from skin and bone and sprinkled with salt and pepper. Pour on stock and place mould under heavy weight. Keep in a cold place until firm. In summer it is necessary to add one teaspoon dissolved granulated gelatine to stock.

Roast Goose with Potato Stuffing

Singe, remove pinfeathers, wash and scrub a goose in hot soapsuds; then draw (which is removing inside contents). Wash in cold water and wipe. Stuff, truss, sprinkle with salt and pepper, and lay six thin strips fat salt pork over breast. Place on rack in dripping-pan, put in hot oven and bake two hours. Baste every fifteen minutes with fat in pan. Remove pork last half-hour of cooking. Place on platter, cut string, and remove string and skewers. Garnish with watercress and bright red cranberries, and place Potato Apples between pieces of watercress. Serve with Apple Sauce.

Potato Stuffing

2 cups hot mashed potato.
1¼ cups soft stale bread crumbs.
¼ cup finely chopped fat salt pork.
1 finely chopped onion.
⅓ cup butter.
1 egg.
1½ teaspoon salt.
1 teaspoon sage.

Add to potato, bread crumbs, butter, egg, salt, and sage; then add pork and onion.

Roast Wild Duck

Dress and clean a wild duck and truss as goose. Place on rack in dripping-pan, sprinkle with salt and pepper, and cover breast with two very thin slices fat salt pork. Bake twenty to thirty minutes in a very hot oven, basting every five minutes with fat in pan; cut string and remove string and skewers. Serve with Orange or Olive Sauce. Currant jelly should accompany a duck course. Domestic ducks should always be well cooked, requiring little more than twice the time allowed for wild ducks.

Ducks are sometimes stuffed with apples, pared, cored, and cut in quarters, or three small onions may be put in body of duck to improve flavor. Neither apples nor onions are to be served. If a stuffing to be eaten is desired, cover pieces of dry bread with boiling water; as soon as bread has absorbed water, press out the water; season bread with salt, pepper, melted butter, and finely-chopped onion.

Potted Pigeons

Clean, stuff, and truss six pigeons, place upright in a stewpan, and add one quart boiling water in which celery has been cooked. Cover, and cook slowly three hours or until tender; or cook in oven in a covered earthen dish. Remove from water, cool slightly, sprinkle with salt and pepper, dredge with flour, and brown entire surface in pork fat. Make a sauce with one-fourth cup each butter and flour cooked together and stock remaining in pan; there should be two cups. Place each bird on a slice of dry toast, and pour gravy over all. Garnish with parsley.

Chicken and Oysters à la Métropole

¼ cup butter.

¼ cup flour.

½ teaspoon salt.

⅛ teaspoon pepper.

2 cups cream.

2 cups cold cooked chicken cut in dice.

1 pint oysters cleaned and drained.

⅓ cup finely chopped celery.

Make a sauce of first five ingredients, add chicken dice and oysters; cook until oysters are plump. Serve sprinkled with celery.

Fish and Meat Sauces

Thin White Sauce

2 tablespoons butter.

1½ tablespoons flour.

1 cup scalded milk.

¼ teaspoon salt.

Few grains pepper.

Put butter in saucepan, stir until melted and bubbling; add flour mixed with seasonings, and stir until thoroughly blended. Pour on gradually the milk, adding about one-third at a time, stirring until well mixed, then beating until smooth and glossy. If a wire whisk is used, all the milk may be added at once; and although more quickly made if milk is scalded, it is not necessary.

Thick White Sauce (for Cutlets and Croquettes)

2½ tablespoons butter.

¼ cup corn-starch or

½ cup flour.

1 cup milk.

¼ teaspoon salt.

Few grains pepper.

Make same as Thin White Sauce.

White Sauce

2 tablespoons butter.

2 tablespoons flour.

1 cup milk.

¼ teaspoon salt.

Few grains pepper.

Make same as Thin White Sauce.

Cream Sauce

Make same as Thin White Sauce, using cream instead of milk.

Drawn Butter Sauce

⅓ cup butter.

3 tablespoons flour.

1½ cups hot water.

½ teaspoon salt.

⅛ teaspoon pepper.

Melt one-half the butter, add flour with seasonings, and pour on gradually hot water. Boil five minutes, and add remaining butter in small pieces. To be served with boiled or baked fish.

Egg Sauce I

To Drawn Butter Sauce add two hard boiled eggs cut in one-fourth inch slices.

Egg Sauce II

To Drawn Butter Sauce add beaten yolks of two eggs and one teaspoon lemon juice.

Brown Sauce

2 tablespoons butter.

½ slice onion.

2½ tablespoons flour.

1 cup Brown Stock.

¼ teaspoon salt.

⅛ teaspoon pepper.

Cook onion in butter until slightly browned; remove onion and stir butter constantly until well browned; add flour mixed with seasonings, and brown the butter and flour; then add stock gradually.

Sauce Piquante

To one cup Brown Sauce add one tablespoon vinegar, one-half small shallot finely chopped, one tablespoon each chopped capers and pickle, and a few grains of cayenne.

Béchamel Sauce

1½ cups White Stock.

1 slice onion.

1 slice carrot.

Bit of bay leaf.

Sprig of parsley.

6 peppercorns.

¼ cup butter.

¼ cup flour.

1 cup scalded milk.

½ teaspoon salt.

⅛ teaspoon pepper.

Cook stock twenty minutes with onion, carrot, bay leaf, parsley, and peppercorns, then strain; there should be one cupful. Melt the butter, add flour, and gradually hot stock and milk. Season with salt and pepper.

Cucumber Sauce

Grate two cucumbers, drain, and season with salt, pepper, and vinegar. Serve with Broiled Fish.

Maître d'Hôtel Butter

¼ cup butter.
½ teaspoon salt.
⅛ teaspoon pepper.
½ tablespoon finely chopped parsley.
¾ tablespoon lemon juice.

Put butter in a bowl, and with small wooden spoon work until creamy. Add salt, pepper, and parsley, then lemon juice very slowly.

Tartar Sauce

1 tablespoon vinegar.
1 teaspoon lemon juice.
¼ teaspoon salt.
1 tablespoon Worcestershire Sauce.
⅓ cup butter.
    The Boston Cook Book.

Mix vinegar, lemon juice, salt, and Worcestershire Sauce in a small bowl, and heat over hot water. Brown the butter in an omelet pan and strain into first mixture.

Anchovy Butter

¼ cup butter.
Anchovy essence.

Cream the butter, and add Anchovy essence to taste.

Lobster Butter

¼ cup butter.
Lobster coral.

Clean, wipe, and force coral through a fine sieve. Put in a mortar with butter, and pound until well blended. This butter is used in Lobster Soup and Sauces to give color and richness.

Hollandaise Sauce

½ cup butter.
Yolks 2 eggs.
1 tablespoon lemon juice.
¼ teaspoon salt.
Few grains cayenne.
⅓ cup boiling water.

Put butter in a bowl, cover with cold water and wash, using a spoon. Divide in three pieces; put one piece in a saucepan with yolks of eggs and lemon juice, place saucepan in a larger one containing boiling water, and stir constantly with a wire whisk until butter is melted; then add second piece of butter, and, as it thickens, third piece. Add water, cook one minute, remove from fire, then add salt and cayenne.

Lobster Sauce

1¼ lb. lobster.
¼ cup butter.
¼ cup flour.
½ teaspoon salt.
Few grains cayenne.
½ tablespoon lemon juice.
3 cups cold water.

Remove meat from lobster, and cut tender claw meat in one-half inch dice. Chop remaining meat, add to body bones, and cover with water; cook until stock is reduced to two cups, strain, and add gradually to butter and flour cooked together, then add salt, cayenne, lemon juice, and lobster dice.

If the lobster contains coral, prepare Lobster Butter, add flour, and thicken sauce therewith.

Suprème Sauce

¼ cup butter.
¼ cup flour.
1½ cups hot chicken stock.
½ cup hot cream.
1 tablespoon mushroom liquor.
¾ teaspoon lemon juice.
Salt and pepper.

Make same as Thin White Sauce, and add seasonings.

Horseradish Sauce

3 tablespoons grated horseradish root.
1 tablespoon vinegar.
¼ teaspoon salt.
Few grains cayenne.
4 tablespoons heavy cream.

Mix first four ingredients, and add cream beaten stiff.

Olive Sauce

Remove stones from ten olives, leaving meat in one piece. Cover with boiling water and cook five minutes. Drain olives, and add to two cups Brown Sauce.

Orange Sauce

¼ cup butter.
¼ cup flour.
1⅓ cups Brown Stock.
½ teaspoon salt.
Few grains cayenne.
Juice 2 oranges.
2 tablespoons sherry wine.
Rind of 1 orange cut in fancy shapes.

Brown the butter, add flour, with salt and cayenne, and stir until well browned. Add stock gradually, and just before serving, orange juice, sherry, and pieces of rind.

Sauce Tartare

½ teaspoon mustard.

1 teaspoon powdered sugar.

½ teaspoon salt.

Few grains cayenne.

Yolks 2 eggs.

½ cup olive oil.

1½ tablespoons vinegar.

Capers, ½ tablespoon, finely chopped.

Pickles, ½ tablespoon, finely chopped.

Olives, ½ tablespoon, finely chopped.

Parsley, ½ tablespoon, finely chopped.

½ shallot finely chopped.

¼ teaspoon powdered tarragon.

Mix mustard, sugar, salt, and cayenne; add yolks of eggs, and stir until thoroughly mixed, setting bowl in pan of ice water. Add oil, at first drop by drop, stirring with a wooden spoon or wire whisk. As mixture thickens, dilute with vinegar, when oil may be added more rapidly. Keep in cool place until ready to serve, then add remaining ingredients.

Currant Jelly Sauce

To one cup Brown Sauce, from which onion has been omitted, add one-fourth tumbler currant jelly and one tablespoon sherry wine; or, add currant jelly to one cup gravy made to serve with roast lamb. Currant Jelly Sauce is suitable to serve with lamb.

Cranberry Sauce

Pick over and wash three cups cranberries. Put in a stewpan, add one and one-fourth cups sugar and one cup boiling water. Cover, and boil ten minutes. Care must be taken that they do not boil over. Skim and cool.

Vegetables

Boiled Artichokes

Cut off stem close to leaves, remove outside bottom leaves, trim artichoke, cut off one inch from top of leaves, and with a sharp knife remove choke; then tie artichoke with a string to keep its shape. Soak one-half hour in cold water. Drain, and cook thirty to forty-five minutes in boiling, salted, acidulated water. Remove from water, place upside down to drain, then take off string. Serve with Béchamel or Hollandaise Sauce. Boiled Artichokes often constitute a course at dinner. Leaves are drawn out separately with fingers, dipped in sauce, and fleshy ends only eaten, although the bottom is edible.

Fried Artichokes

Sprinkle Boiled Artichokes cut in quarters with salt, pepper, and finely chopped parsley. Dip in Batter I., fry in deep fat, and drain. In preparing artichokes, trim off tops of leaves closer than when served as Boiled Artichokes.

Boiled Asparagus

Cut off lower parts of stalks as far down as they will snap, untie bunches, wash, remove scales, and retie. Cook in boiling salted water fifteen minutes or until soft, leaving tips out of water first ten minutes. Drain, remove string, and spread with soft butter, allowing one and one-half tablespoons butter to each bunch asparagus. Asparagus is often broken in inch pieces for boiling, cooking tips a shorter time than stalks.

Asparagus on Toast

Serve Boiled Asparagus on Buttered or Milk Toast.

Cream of Lima Beans

Soak one cup dried beans over night, drain, and cook in boiling salted water until soft; drain, add three-fourths cup cream, and season with butter and salt. Reheat before serving.

Sugared Beets

4 hot boiled beets.

3 tablespoons butter.

1½ tablespoons sugar.

½ teaspoon salt.

Cut beets in one-fourth inch slices, add butter, sugar, and salt; reheat for serving.

Brussels Sprouts in White Sauce

Pick over, remove wilted leaves, and soak in cold water fifteen minutes. Cook in boiling salted water twenty minutes, or until easily pierced with a skewer. Drain, and to each pint add one cup White Sauce.

German Cabbage

Slice red cabbage and soak in cold water. Put one quart in stewpan with two tablespoons butter, one-half teaspoon salt, one tablespoon finely chopped onion, few gratings of nutmeg, and few grains cayenne; cover, and cook until cabbage is tender. Add two tablespoons vinegar and one-half tablespoon sugar, and cook five minutes.

Cole-Slaw

Select a small, heavy cabbage, take off outside leaves, and cut in quarters; with a sharp knife slice very thinly. Soak in cold water until crisp, drain, dry between towels, and mix with Cream Salad Dressing.

Hot Slaw

Slice cabbage as for Cole-Slaw, using one-half cabbage. Heat in a dressing made of yolks of two eggs slightly beaten, one-fourth cup cold water, one tablespoon butter, one-fourth cup hot vinegar, and one-half teaspoon salt, stirred over hot water until thickened.

Carrots and Peas

Wash, scrape, and cut young carrots in small cubes or fancy shapes; cook until soft in boiling salted water or stock. Drain, add an equal quantity of cooked green peas, and season with butter, salt, and pepper.

Cauliflower au Gratin

Place a whole cooked cauliflower on dish for serving, cover with buttered crumbs, and place on oven grate to brown crumbs; remove from oven and pour one cup Thin White Sauce around cauliflower.

Creamed Cauliflower

Remove leaves, cut off stalk, and soak thirty minutes (head down) in cold water to cover. Cook (head up) twenty minutes or until soft in boiling salted water; drain, separate flowerets, and reheat in one and one-half cups White Sauce.

Celery in White Sauce

Wash, scrape, and cut outer celery stalks in one-inch pieces; cook twenty minutes or until soft in boiling salted water; drain, and to two cups celery add one cup White Sauce.

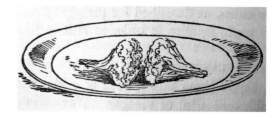

Cauliflower with white sauce, from Mrs. Mary F. Henderson, *Practical Cooking and Dinner Giving* (New York: Harper and Bros., 1877), 198, Special Collections, Michigan State University Libraries.

Succotash

Cut hot boiled corn from cob, add equal quantity of hot boiled shelled beans; season with butter and salt; reheat before serving.

Corn Oysters

Grate raw corn from cobs. To one cup pulp add one well beaten egg, one-fourth cup flour, and season highly with salt and pepper. Drop by spoonfuls and fry in deep fat, or cook on a hot, well greased griddle. They should be made about the size of large oyster.

Corn à la Southern

To one can chopped corn add two eggs slightly beaten, one teaspoon salt, one-eighth teaspoon pepper, one and one-half tablespoons melted butter, and one pint scalded milk; turn into a buttered pudding-dish and bake in slow oven until firm.

Chestnut Purée

Remove shells from chestnuts, cook until soft in boiling salted water; drain, mash, moisten with scalded milk, season with salt and pepper, and beat until light. Chestnuts are often boiled, riced, and piled lightly in centre of dish, then surrounded by meat.

Boiled Cucumbers

Old cucumbers may be pared, cut in pieces, cooked until soft in boiling salted water, drained, mashed, and seasoned with butter, salt, and pepper.

Fried Cucumbers

Pare cucumbers and cut lengthwise in one-third inch slices. Dry between towels, sprinkle with salt and pepper, dip in crumbs, egg, and crumbs again, fry in deep fat, and drain.

Stuffed Egg-plant

Cook egg-plant fifteen minutes in boiling salted water to cover. Cut a slice from top, and with a spoon remove pulp, taking care not to work too closely to skin. Chop pulp, and add one cup soft stale bread crumbs. Melt two tablespoons butter, add one-half tablespoon finely chopped onion, and cook five minutes; or try out three slices of bacon, using bacon fat in place of butter. Add to chopped pulp and bread, season with salt and pepper, and if necessary moisten with a little stock or water; cook five minutes, cool slightly, and add one beaten egg. Refill egg-plant, cover with buttered bread crumbs, and bake twenty-five minutes in a hot oven.

Boiled Beet Greens

Wash thoroughly and scrape roots, cutting off ends. Drain, and cook one hour or until tender in a small quantity boiling salted water. Season with butter, salt, and pepper. Serve with vinegar.

Dandelions

Wash thoroughly, remove roots, drain, and cook one hour or until tender in boiling salted water. Allow two quarts water to one peck dandelions. Season with butter, salt, and pepper. Serve with vinegar.

Boiled Onions

Put onions in cold water and remove skins while under water. Drain, put in a saucepan, and cover with boiling salted water; boil five minutes, drain, and again cover with boiling salted water. Cook one hour or until soft, but not broken. Drain, add a small quantity of milk, cook five minutes, and season with butter, salt, and pepper.

Onions in Cream

Prepare and cook as Boiled Onions, changing the water twice during boiling; drain, and cover with Cream or Thin White Sauce.

Creamed Oyster Plant (Salsify)

Wash, scrape, and put at once into cold acidulated water to prevent discoloration. Cut in inch slices, cook in boiling salted water until soft, drain, and add to White Sauce. Oyster plant is in season from October to March.

Salsify Fritters

Cook oyster plant as for Creamed Oyster Plant. Mash, season with butter, salt, and pepper. Shape in small flat cakes, roll in flour, and sauté in butter.

Parsnips

Parsnips are not so commonly served as other vegetables; however, they often accompany a boiled dinner. They are raised mostly for feeding cattle. Unless young, they contain a large amount of woody fibre, which extends through centre of roots and makes them undesirable as food.

Parsnips with Drawn Butter Sauce

Wash and scrape parsnips, and cut in pieces two inches long and one-half inch wide and thick. Cook five minutes in boiling salted water, or until soft. Drain, and to two cups add one cup Drawn Butter Sauce.

Parsnip Fritters

Wash parsnips and cook forty-five minutes in boiling salted water. Drain, plunge into cold water, when skins will be found to slip off easily. Mash, season with butter, salt, and pepper, shape in small flat round cakes, roll in flour, and sauté in butter.

Boiled Peas

Remove peas from pods, cover with cold water, and let stand one-half hour. Skim off undeveloped peas which rise to top of water, and drain remaining peas. Cook until soft in a small quantity of boiling water, adding salt the last fifteen minutes of cooking. There should be but little, if any, water to drain from peas when they are cooked. Season with butter, salt, and pepper. If peas have lost much of their natural sweetness, they are improved by the addition of a small amount of sugar.

Boiled Spinach

Remove roots, carefully pick over (discarding wilted leaves), and wash in several waters to be sure that it is free from all sand. When young and tender put in a stew-pan, allow to heat gradually, and cook twenty-five minutes, or until tender, in its own juices. Old spinach is better cooked in boiling salted water, allowing two quarts water to one peck spinach. Drain thoroughly, chop finely, reheat, and season with butter, salt, and pepper. Garnish with slices of hard boiled eggs. The green color of spinach is better retained by cooking in a large quantity of water in an uncovered vessel.

Baked Winter Squash I

Cut in pieces two inches square, remove seeds and stringy portion, place in a dripping-pan, sprinkle with salt and pepper, and allow for each square one-half teaspoon molasses and one-half teaspoon melted butter. Bake fifty minutes, or until soft, in a moderate oven, keeping covered the first half-hour of cooking. Serve in the shell.

Baked Winter Squash II

Cut squash in halves, remove seeds and stringy portion, place in a dripping-pan, cover, and bake two hours, or until soft, in a slow oven. Remove from shell, mash, and season with butter, salt, and pepper.

Broiled Tomatoes

Wipe and cut in halves crosswise, cut off a thin slice from rounding part of each half. Sprinkle with salt and pepper, dip in crumbs, egg, and crumbs again, place in a well-buttered broiler, and broil six to eight minutes.

Devilled Tomatoes

3 tomatoes.
Salt and pepper.
Flour.
Butter for sautéing.
4 tablespoons butter.
2 teaspoons powdered sugar.
1 teaspoon mustard.
¼ teaspoon salt.
Few grains cayenne.
Yolk 1 hard boiled egg.
1 egg.
2 tablespoons vinegar.

Wipe, peel, and cut tomatoes in slices. Sprinkle with salt and pepper, dredge with flour, and sauté in butter. Place on a hot platter and pour over the dressing made by creaming the butter, adding dry ingredients, yolk of egg rubbed to a paste, egg beaten slightly, and vinegar, then cooking over hot water, stirring constantly until it thickens.

Mashed Turnip

Wash and pare turnips, cut in slices or quarters, and cook in boiling salted water until soft. Drain, mash, and season with butter, salt, and pepper.

Turnip Croquettes

Wash, pare, and cut in quarters new French turnips. Steam until tender, mash, pressing out all water that is possible. This is best accomplished by wringing in cheese cloth. Season one and one-fourth cups with salt and pepper, then add yolks of two eggs slightly beaten. Cool, shape in small croquettes, dip in crumbs, egg, and crumbs again, fry in deep fat, and drain.

Mushrooms à la Sabine

Wash one-half pound mushrooms, remove stems, and peel caps. Sprinkle with salt and pepper, and cook three minutes in a hot frying-pan, with two tablespoons butter. Add one and one-third cups Brown Sauce, and cook slowly five minutes. Sprinkle with three tablespoons grated cheese. As soon as cheese is melted, arrange mushrooms on pieces of toast, and pour over sauce.

Mushrooms à la Algonquin

Wash large selected mushrooms. Remove stems, peel caps, and sauté caps in butter. Place in a small buttered shallow pan, cap side being up; place on each a large oyster, sprinkle with salt and pepper, and place on each a bit of butter. Cook in a hot oven until oysters are plump. Serve with Brown or Béchamel Sauce.

Boiled Potatoes

Select potatoes of uniform size. Wash, pare, and drop at once in cold water to prevent discoloration; soak one half-hour in the fall, and one to two hours in winter and spring. Cook in boiling salted water until soft, which is easily determined by piercing with a skewer. For seven potatoes allow one tablespoon salt, and boiling water to cover. Drain from water, and keep uncovered in warm place until serving time. Avoid sending to table in a covered vegetable dish. In boiling large potatoes, it often happens that outside is soft, while centre is underdone. To finish cooking without potatoes breaking apart, add one pint cold water, which drives heat to centre, thus accomplishing the cooking.

Riced Potatoes

Force hot boiled potatoes through a potato ricer or coarse strainer. Serve lightly piled in a hot vegetable dish.

Mashed Potatoes

To five riced potatoes add three tablespoons butter, one teaspoon salt, few grains pepper, and one-third cup hot milk; beat with fork until creamy, reheat, and pile lightly in hot dish.

Potato Omelet

Prepare Mashed Potatoes, turn in hot omelet pan greased with one tablespoon butter, spread evenly, cook slowly until browned underneath, and fold as an omelet.

Duchess Potatoes

To two cups hot riced potatoes add two tablespoons butter, one-half teaspoon salt, and yolks of three eggs slightly beaten. Shape, using pastry bag and tube, in form of baskets, pyramids, crowns, leaves, roses, etc. Brush over with beaten egg diluted with one teaspoon water, and brown in a hot oven.

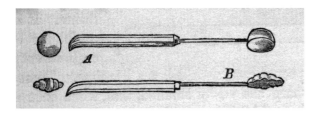

Specialized tin scoops could cut hard vegetables like potatoes into decorative balls. From Mrs. Mary F. Henderson, *Practical Cooking and Dinner Giving* (New York: Harper and Bros., 1877), 55, Special Collections, Michigan State University Libraries.

Potato Balls

Select large potatoes, wash, pare, and soak. Shape in balls with a French vegetable cutter. Cook in boiling salted water until soft; drain, and to one pint potatoes add one cup Thin White Sauce. Turn into hot dish, and sprinkle with finely chopped parsley.

Brabant Potatoes

Prepare as for Boiled Potatoes, using small potatoes, and trim egg-shaped; parboil ten minutes, drain, and place in baking-pan and bake until soft, basting three times with melted butter.

Shadow Potatoes (Saratoga Chips)

Wash and pare potatoes. Slice thinly (using vegetable slicer) into a bowl of cold water. Let stand two hours, changing water twice. Drain, plunge in a kettle of boiling water and boil one minute. Drain again, and cover with cold water. Take from water and dry between towels. Fry in deep fat until light brown, keeping in motion with a skimmer. Drain on brown paper and sprinkle with salt.

Shredded Potatoes

Wash, pare, and cut potatoes in one-eighth inch slices. Cut slices in one-eighth inch strips. Soak one hour in cold water. Take from water, dry between towels, and fry in deep fat. Drain on brown paper and sprinkle with salt. Serve around fried or baked fish.

French Fried Potatoes

Wash and pare small potatoes, cut in eighths lengthwise, and soak one hour in cold water. Take from water, dry between towels, and fry in deep fat. Drain on brown paper and sprinkle with salt.

Care must be taken that fat is not too hot, as potatoes must be cooked as well as browned.

Potato Marbles

Wash and pare potatoes. Shape in balls, using a French vegetable cutter. Soak fifteen minutes in cold water, take from water and dry between towels. Fry in deep fat, drain, and sprinkle with salt.

Potato Curls

Wash and pare large long potatoes. Shape with a potato curler, soak one hour in cold water, drain, dry between towels, fry in deep fat, drain, and sprinkle with salt.

Potato Croquettes

2 cups hot riced potatoes.
2 tablespoons butter.
½ teaspoon salt.
⅛ teaspoon pepper.
¼ teaspoon celery salt.
Few drops onion juice.
Yolk 1 egg.
1 teaspoon finely chopped parsley.

Mix ingredients in order given, and beat thoroughly. Shape, dip in crumbs, egg, and crumbs again, fry one minute in deep fat, and drain on brown paper. Croquettes are shaped in a variety of forms. The most common way is to first form a smooth ball by rolling one rounding tablespoon mixture between hands. Then roll on a board until of desired length, and flatten ends.

Potato Apples

2 cups hot riced potatoes.
2 tablespoons butter.
⅓ cup grated cheese.
½ teaspoon salt.
Few grains cayenne.
Slight grating nutmeg.
2 tablespoons thick cream.
Yolks 2 eggs.

Mix ingredients in order given, and beat thoroughly. Shape in form of small apples, roll in flour, egg, and crumbs, fry in deep fat, and drain on brown paper. Insert a clove at both stem and blossom end of each apple.

Sweet Potato Balls

To two cups hot riced sweet potatoes add three tablespoons butter, one-half teaspoon salt, few grains pepper, and one beaten egg. Shape in small balls, roll in flour, fry in deep fat, and drain. If potatoes are very dry, it will be necessary to add hot milk to moisten.

Hashed Brown Potatoes

Try out fat salt pork cut in small cubes, remove scraps; there should be about one-third cup of fat. Add two cups cold boiled potatoes finely chopped, one-eighth teaspoon pepper, and salt if needed. Mix potatoes thoroughly with fat; cook three minutes, stirring constantly; let stand to brown underneath. Fold as an omelet and turn on hot platter.

Salads and Salad Dressings

A Chapon

Remove a small piece from end of French loaf and rub over with a clove of garlic, first dipped in salt. Place in bottom of salad bowl before arranging salad. A chapon is often used in vegetable salads, and gives an agreeable additional flavor.

French Dressing

½ teaspoon salt.
¼ teaspoon pepper.
2 tablespoons vinegar.
4 tablespoons olive oil.

Mix ingredients and stir until well blended. French Dressing is more easily prepared and largely used than any other dressing.

Cream Dressing

½ tablespoon salt.
½ tablespoon mustard.
1¼ tablespoons sugar.
1 egg slightly beaten.
2½ tablespoons melted butter.
¾ cup cream.
¼ cup vinegar.

Mix ingredients in order given, adding vinegar very slowly. Cook over boiling water, stirring constantly until mixture thickens, strain and cool.

Boiled Dressing

½ tablespoon salt.
1 teaspoon mustard.
1½ tablespoons sugar.
Few grains cayenne.
½ tablespoon flour.
Yolks 2 eggs.
1½ tablespoons melted butter.
¾ cup milk.
¼ cup vinegar.

Mix dry ingredients, add yolks of eggs slightly beaten, butter, milk, and vinegar very slowly. Cook over boiling water until mixture thickens; strain, and cool.

German Dressing

½ cup thick cream.

3 tablespoons vinegar.

¼ teaspoon salt.

Few grains pepper.

Beat cream until stiff, using Dover Egg-beater. Add salt, pepper, and vinegar very slowly, continuing the beating.

Mayonnaise Dressing

1 teaspoon mustard.

1 teaspoon salt.

1 teaspoon powdered sugar.

Few grains cayenne.

Yolks 2 eggs.

2 tablespoons lemon juice.

2 tablespoons vinegar.

1½ cups olive oil.

Mix dry ingredients, add egg yolks, and when well mixed, add one-half teaspoon vinegar. Add oil gradually, at first drop by drop, and stir constantly. As mixture thickens, thin with vinegar or lemon juice. Add oil, and vinegar or lemon juice alternately, until all is used, stirring or beating constantly. If oil is added too rapidly, dressing will have a curdled appearance. A smooth consistency may be restored by taking yolk of another egg and adding curdled mixture slowly to it. It is desirable to have bowl containing mixture placed in a larger bowl of crushed ice, to which a small quantity of water has been added. Olive oil for making Mayonnaise should always be thoroughly chilled. A silver fork, wire whisk, small wooden spoon, or Dover Egg-beater may be used as preferred. If one has a Keystone Egg-beater, dressing may be made very quickly by its use. Mayonnaise should be stiff enough to hold its shape. It soon liquefies when added to meat or vegetables; therefore it should be added just before serving time.

Lettuce and Cucumber Salad

Place a chapon in bottom of salad bowl. Wash, drain, and dry one head lettuce, arrange in bowl, and place between leaves one cucumber cut in thin slices. Serve with French Dressing.

Watercress and Cucumber Salad

Prepare watercress and add one cucumber, pared, chilled, and cut in one-half inch dice. Serve with French Dressing.

Dressed Celery

Wash, scrape, and cut stalks of celery in thin slices. Mix with Cream Dressing.

Celery and Cabbage Salad

Remove outside leaves from a small solid white cabbage, and cut off stalk close to leaves. Cut out centre and with a sharp knife shred finely. Let stand one hour in cold or ice water. Drain, wring in double cheese cloth, to make as dry as possible. Mix with equal parts celery cut in small pieces. Moisten with Cream Dressing and refill cabbage. Arrange on a folded napkin and garnish with celery tips and parsley between folds of napkin and around top of cabbage.

Potato Salad

Cut cold boiled potatoes in one-half inch cubes. Sprinkle four cupfuls with one-half tablespoon salt and one-fourth teaspoon pepper. Add four tablespoons oil and mix thoroughly; then add two tablespoons vinegar. A few drops of onion juice may be added, or one-half tablespoon chives finely cut. Arrange in a mound and garnish with whites and yolks of two hard boiled eggs, cold boiled red beets, and parsley. Chop whites and arrange on one-fourth of the mound; chop beets finely, mix with one tablespoon vinegar, and let stand fifteen minutes; then arrange on fourths of mound next to whites. Arrange on remaining fourth of mound, yolks chopped or forced through a potato ricer. Put small sprigs of parsley in lines dividing beets from eggs; also garnish with parsley at base.

Macédoine Salad

Marinate separately cold cooked cauliflower, peas, and carrots, cut in small cubes, and outer stalks of celery finely cut. Arrange peas and carrots in alternate piles in centre of a salad dish. Pile cauliflower on top. Arrange celery in four piles at equal distances. At top of each pile place a small gherkin cut lengthwise in very thin slices, beginning at blossom end and cutting nearly to stem end. Open slices to represent a fan. Place between piles of celery a slice of tomato.

Almost any cold cooked vegetables on hand may be used for a Macédoine Salad, and if care is taken in arrangement, they make a very attractive dish.

Tomato Jelly Salad

To one can stewed and strained tomatoes add one teaspoon each of salt and powdered sugar, and one box gelatine which has soaked fifteen minutes in one-half cup cold water. Pour into small cups and chill. Run a knife around inside of moulds, so that when taken out shapes may have a rough surface suggesting a fresh tomato. Place on lettuce leaves and garnish top of each with Mayonnaise Dressing.

Spinach Salad

Pick over, wash, and cook one-half peck spinach. Drain, and chop finely. Season with salt, pepper, and lemon juice, and add one tablespoon melted butter. Butter slightly small tin moulds and pack solidly with mixture.

Chill, remove from moulds, and arrange on thin slices of cold boiled tongue cut in circular pieces. Garnish base of each with a wreath of parsley, and serve on top of each Sauce Tartare.

Lenten Salad

Separate yolks and whites of four hard boiled eggs. Chop whites finely, marinate with French Dressing, and arrange on lettuce leaves. Force yolks through a potato ricer and pile on the centre of whites. Serve with French Dressing.

Cheese Salad

Arrange one head of lettuce on a salad dish, sprinkle with one-fourth pound Edam cheese broken in very small pieces, and pour over it French Dressing.

Nut and Celery Salad

Mix equal parts of English walnut or pecan nut meat cut in pieces, and celery cut in small pieces. Marinate with French Dressing. Serve with a border of shredded lettuce.

Banana Salad

Remove one section of skin from each of four bananas. Take out fruit, scrape, and cut fruit from one banana in thin slices, fruit from other three bananas in one-half inch cubes. Marinate cubes with French Dressing. Refill skins and garnish each with slices of banana. Stack around a mound of lettuce leaves.

Chicken and Oyster Salad

Clean, parboil, and drain one pint oysters. Remove tough muscles, and mix soft parts with an equal quantity of cold boiled fowl cut in one-half inch dice. Moisten with any salad dressing, and serve on a bed of lettuce leaves.

Sweetbread and Cucumber Salad

Parboil a pair of sweetbreads twenty minutes; drain, cool, and cut in one-half inch cubes. Mix with an equal quantity of cucumber cut in one-half inch dice. Season with salt and pepper, and moisten with German Dressing. Arrange in nests of lettuce leaves or in cucumber cups, and garnish with watercress. To prepare cucumber cups, pare cucumbers, remove thick slices from each end, and cut in halves crosswise. Take out centres, put cups in cold water, and let stand until crisp; drain, and dry for refilling. Small cucumbers may be pared, cut in halves lengthwise, centres removed, and cut pointed at ends to represent a boat.

Batter I

1 cup bread flour.
½ teaspoon salt.
Few grains pepper.
⅔ cup milk.
2 Eggs.

Mix flour, salt, and pepper. Add milk gradually, and eggs well beaten.

Batter II

1 cup bread flour.
1 tablespoon sugar.
¼ teaspoon salt.
⅔ cup water.
½ tablespoon olive oil.
White 1 egg.

Mix flour, sugar, and salt. Add water gradually, then olive oil and white of egg beaten until stiff.

Apple Fritters

Sour apples.
Powdered sugar.
Lemon juice.
Batter II.

Core, pare, and cut apples in one-third inch slices. Sprinkle with powdered sugar and few drops lemon juice; cover, and let stand one-half hour. Drain, dip pieces in batter, fry in deep fat, and drain. Arrange on a folded napkin in form of a circle, and serve with . . . Hard Sauce.

Cold Cooked Cauliflower

Batter I.
Salt and pepper.

Sprinkle pieces of cauliflower with salt and pepper and dip in Batter I. Fry in deep fat, and drain on brown paper.

Farina Cakes with Jelly

2 cups scalded milk.
½ cup farina (scant).
¼ cup sugar.
½ teaspoon salt.
1 egg.

Add farina, sugar, and salt to milk, and cook in double boiler twenty minutes, stirring constantly until mixture has thickened. Add egg slightly beaten, pour into a buttered shallow pan, and brush over with one egg slightly beaten and diluted with one tablespoon milk. Brown in oven. Cut in squares, and serve with a cube of jelly on each square.

Gnocchi à la Romaine

¼ cup butter.
¼ cup flour.
¼ cup corn-starch.
½ teaspoon salt.
2 cups scalded milk.
Yolks 2 eggs.
¾ cup grated cheese.

Melt butter, and when bubbling, add flour, corn-starch, salt, and milk, gradually. Cook three minutes, stirring constantly. Add yolks of eggs slightly beaten, and one-half cup cheese. Pour into a buttered shallow pan, and cool. Turn on a board, cut in squares, diamonds, or strips. Place on a platter, sprinkle with remaining cheese, and brown in oven.

Chestnut Croquettes

1 cup mashed French chestnuts.
2 tablespoons thick cream.
Yolks 2 eggs.
1 teaspoon sugar.
¼ teaspoon vanilla.

Mix ingredients in order given. Shape in balls, dip in crumbs, egg, and crumbs again, fry in deep fat, and drain.

Oyster and Macaroni Croquettes

⅓ cup macaroni broken in ½ inch pieces.
1 pint oysters.
1 cup Thick White Sauce.
Few grains cayenne.
Few grains mace.
½ teaspoon lemon juice.
¼ cup grated cheese.

Cook macaroni in boiling salted water until soft, drain in a colander, and pour over macaroni two cups cold water. Clean and parboil oysters, remove tough muscles, and cut soft parts in pieces. Reserve one-half cup oyster liquor and use in making Thick White Sauce in place of all milk. Mix macaroni and oysters, add Thick White Sauce and seasonings. Spread on a plate to cool. Shape, dip in crumbs, egg, and crumbs again, fry in deep fat, and drain.

Lobster Cutlets

2 cups chopped lobster meat.

½ teaspoon salt.

Few grains cayenne.

Few gratings nutmeg.

1 teaspoon lemon juice.

Yolk 1 egg.

1 teaspoon finely chopped parsley.

1 cup Thick White Sauce.

Mix ingredients in order given, and cool. Shape in form of cutlets, crumb, and fry same as croquettes. Make a cut at small end of each cutlet, and insert in each the tip end of a small claw. Stack around a mound of parsley. Serve with Sauce Tartare.

A photograph of Lobster Cutlets, from Fannie Farmer, *The Original 1896 Boston Cooking-School Cook Book* (Mineola, NY: Dover Publications, 1997), 311, Special Collections, Michigan State University Libraries.

Chicken Croquettes

1¾ cups chopped cold cooked fowl.

½ teaspoon salt.

¼ teaspoon celery salt.

Few grains cayenne.

1 teaspoon lemon juice.

Few drops onion juice.

1 teaspoon finely chopped parsley.

1 cup Thick White Sauce.

Mix ingredients in order given. Cool, shape, crumb, and fry same as other croquettes.

White meat of fowl absorbs more sauce than dark meat. This must be remembered if dark meat alone is used. Croquette mixtures should always be as soft as can be conveniently handled, when croquettes will be soft and creamy inside.

Rice Croquettes with Jelly

½ cup rice.

½ cup boiling water.

1 cup scalded milk.

½ teaspoon salt.

Yolks 2 eggs.

1 tablespoon butter.

Wash rice, add to water with salt, cover, and steam until rice has absorbed water. Then add milk, stir lightly with a fork, cover, and steam until rice is soft. Remove from fire, add egg yolks and butter; spread on a shallow plate to cool. Shape in balls, roll in crumbs, then shape in form of nests. Dip in egg, again in crumbs, fry in deep fat, and drain. Put a cube of jelly in each croquette. Arrange on a folded napkin and garnish with parsley, or serve around game.

Swedish Timbales

¾ cup flour.
½ teaspoon salt.
1 teaspoon sugar.
½ cup milk.
1 egg.
1 tablespoon olive oil.

Mix dry ingredients, add milk gradually, and beaten egg; then add olive oil. Shape, using a hot timbale iron, fry in deep fat until crisp and brown; take from iron and invert on brown paper to drain.

To Heat Timbale Iron. Heat fat until nearly hot enough to fry uncooked mixtures. Put iron into hot fat, having fat deep enough to more than cover it, and let stand until heated. The only way of knowing when iron is of right temperature is to take it from fat, shake what fat may drip from it, lower in batter to three-fourths its depth, raise from batter, then immerse in hot fat. If batter does not cling to iron, or drops from iron as soon as immersed in fat, it is either too hot or not sufficiently heated.

To Form Timbales. Turn timbale batter into a cup. Lower hot iron into cup, taking care that batter covers iron to only three-fourths its depth. When immersed in fat, mixture will rise to top of iron, and when crisp and brown may be easily slipped off. If too much batter is used, in cooking it will rise over top of iron, and in order to remove timbale it must be cut around with a sharp knife close to top of iron. If the cases are soft rather than crisp, batter is too thick and must be diluted with milk. Fill cases with Creamed Oysters, Chicken, Sweetbreads, or Chicken and Sweetbreads in combination with Mushrooms.

Strawberry Baskets

Fry Swedish Timbales, making cases one inch deep. Fill with selected strawberries, sprinkled with powdered sugar. Serve as a first course at a ladies' luncheon.

Macaroni Timbales

Line slightly buttered Dario moulds with boiled macaroni. Cut strips the length of height of mould, and lace closely together around inside of mould. Fill with chicken, or Salmon Force-meat. Put in a pan, half surround with hot water, cover with buttered paper, and bake thirty minutes in a moderate oven. Serve with Lobster, Béchamel, or Hollandaise Sauce.

Spaghetti Timbales

Line bottom and sides of slightly buttered Dario moulds with long strips of boiled spaghetti coiled around the inside. Fill and bake as Macaroni Timbales.

Lobster Timbales

Sprinkle slightly buttered Dario or timbale moulds with lobster coral rubbed through a strainer. Line moulds with Fish Force-meat, fill centres with Creamed Lobster, and cover with force-meat. Put in a pan, half surround with hot water, place over moulds buttered paper, and bake twenty minutes in a moderate oven. Serve with Lobster or Béchamel Sauce.

Suprème of Chicken

Breast and second joints of uncooked chicken
   weighing 4 lbs.
4 eggs.
⅔ cup thick cream.
Salt and pepper.

Force chicken through a meat chopper, or chop very finely. Beat eggs separately, add one at a time, stirring until mixture is smooth. Add cream, and season with salt and pepper. Turn into slightly buttered Dario moulds, and bake as Lobster Timbales, allowing thirty minutes for baking. Serve with Suprème or Béchamel Sauce.

Lobster Cream

2 lb. lobster.
½ cup soft stale bread crumbs.
½ cup milk.
¼ cup cream.
2 teaspoons Anchovy essence.
½ teaspoon salt.
Few grains cayenne.
Whites 3 eggs.

Remove lobster meat from shell and chop finely. Cook bread and milk ten minutes. Add cream, seasonings, and whites of eggs beaten until stiff. Turn into one slightly buttered timbale mould and two slightly buttered Dario moulds. Bake as Lobster Timbales. Remove to serving-dish, having larger mould in centre, smaller moulds one at either end. Pour around Lobster Sauce, sprinkle with coral rubbed through a sieve, and garnish with pieces of lobster shell from tail, and parsley.

Devilled Crabs

1 cup chopped crab meat.
¼ cup mushrooms finely chopped.
2 tablespoons butter.
2 tablespoons flour.
⅔ cups White Stock.
Yolks 2 eggs.
2 tablespoons sherry wine.
1 teaspoon finely chopped parsley.
Salt and pepper.

Make a sauce of butter, flour, and stock; add yolks of eggs, seasonings (except parsley), crab meat, and mushrooms. Cook three minutes, add parsley, and cool mixture. Wash and trim crab shells, fill rounding with mixture, sprinkle with stale bread crumbs mixed with a small quantity of melted butter. Crease on top with a case knife, having three lines parallel with each other across shell and three short lines branching from outside parallel lines.

Cheese Soufflé

2 tablespoons butter.
3 tablespoons flour.
½ cup scalded milk.
½ teaspoon salt.
Few grains cayenne.
¼ cup grated Old English or Young America cheese.
Yolks 3 eggs.
Whites 3 eggs.

Melt butter, add flour, and when well mixed add gradually scalded milk. Then add salt, cayenne, and cheese. Remove from fire, add yolks of eggs beaten until lemon-colored. Cool mixture, and cut and fold in whites of eggs beaten until stiff and dry. Pour into a buttered baking-dish, and bake twenty minutes in a slow oven. Serve at once.

Hot Puddings

Indian Pudding

5 cups scalded milk.
⅓ cup Indian meal.
½ cup molasses.
1 teaspoon salt.
1 teaspoon ginger.

Pour milk slowly on meal, cook in double boiler twenty minutes, add molasses, salt, and ginger; pour into buttered pudding-dish and bake two hours in slow oven; serve with cream. If baked too rapidly it will not whey. Ginger may be omitted.

Tapioca Custard Pudding

4 cups scalded milk.
⅔ cup pearl tapioca.
3 eggs.
½ cup sugar.
1 teaspoon salt.
1 tablespoon butter.

Soak tapioca one hour in cold water to cover, drain, add to milk, and cook in double boiler thirty minutes; beat eggs slightly, add sugar and salt, pour on gradually hot mixture, turn into buttered pudding-dish, add butter, bake thirty minutes in slow oven.

Bread Pudding

2 cups stale bread crumbs.

1 quart scalded milk.

⅓ cup sugar.

¼ cup melted butter.

2 eggs.

½ teaspoon salt.

1 teaspoon vanilla or

¼ teaspoon spice.

Soak bread crumbs in milk, set aside until cool; add sugar, butter, eggs slightly beaten, salt, and flavoring; bake one hour in buttered budding-dish in slow oven; serve with Vanilla Sauce. In preparing bread crumbs for puddings avoid using outside crusts. With a coarse grater there need be but little waste.

Chocolate Bread Pudding

2 cups stale bread crumbs.

4 cups scalded milk.

2 squares Baker's chocolate.

⅔ cup sugar.

2 eggs.

¼ teaspoon salt.

1 teaspoon vanilla.

Soak bread in milk thirty minutes; melt chocolate in saucepan placed over hot water, add one-half sugar and enough milk taken from bread and milk to make of consistency to pour; add to mixture with remaining

sugar, salt, vanilla, and eggs slightly beaten; turn into buttered pudding-dish and bake one hour in a moderate oven. Serve with Hard or Cream Sauce.

Lemon Soufflé

Yolks 4 eggs.

Grated rind and juice 1 lemon.

1 cup sugar.

Whites 4 eggs.

Beat yolks until thick and lemon colored, add sugar gradually and continue beating, then add lemon rind and juice. Cut and fold in whites of eggs beaten until dry; turn into buttered pudding-dish, set in pan of hot water, and bake thirty-five to forty minutes. Serve with or without sauce.

Steamed Cranberry Pudding

½ cup butter.

1 cup sugar.

3 eggs.

3½ cups flour.

1¼ tablespoons baking powder.

½ cup milk.

1½ cups cranberries.

Cream the butter, add sugar gradually, and eggs well beaten. Mix and sift flour and baking powder and add alternately with milk to first mixture, stir in berries previously washed, turn into buttered mould, cover, and steam three hours. Serve with thin cream, sweetened and flavored with nutmeg.

Suet Pudding

1 cup finely chopped suet.
1 cup molasses.
1 cup milk.
3 cups flour.
1 teaspoon soda.
1½ teaspoons salt.
Ginger, ½ teaspoon.
Clove, ½ teaspoon.
Nutmeg, ½ teaspoon.
1 teaspoon cinnamon.

Mix and sift dry ingredients. Add molasses and milk to suet; combine mixtures. Turn into buttered mould, cover, and steam three hours; serve with Egg Sauce. Raisins and currants may be added.

English Plum Pudding

½ lb. stale bread crumbs.
1 cup scalded milk.
¼ lb. sugar.
4 eggs.
½ lb. raisins, seeded, cut in pieces, and floured.
¼ lb. currants.
¼ lb. finely chopped figs.
2 oz. finely cut citron.
½ lb. suet.

¼ cup wine and brandy mixed.
½ grated nutmeg.
¾ teaspoon cinnamon.
⅓ teaspoon clove.
½ teaspoon mace.

Soak bread crumbs in milk, let stand until cool, add sugar, beaten yolks of eggs, raisins, currants, figs, and citron; chop suet, and cream by using the hand; combine mixtures, then add wine, brandy, nutmeg, cinnamon, clove, mace, and whites of eggs beaten stiff. Turn into buttered mould, cover, and steam six hours.

Apple Porcupine

Make a syrup by boiling eight minutes one and one-half cups sugar and one and one-half cups water. Wipe, core, and pare eight apples. Put apples in syrup as soon as pared, that they may not discolor. Cook until soft, occasionally skimming syrup during cooking. Apples cook better covered with the syrup; therefore it is better to use a deep saucepan and have two cookings. Drain apples from syrup, cool, fill cavities with jelly, marmalade, or preserved fruit, and stick apples with almonds blanched and split in halves lengthwise. Serve with Cream Sauce.

Lemon Sauce

½ cup sugar.

1 cup boiling water.

2 tablespoons corn-starch.

2 tablespoons butter.

1½ tablespoons lemon juice.

Few gratings nutmeg.

Mix sugar and corn-starch, add water gradually, stirring constantly; boil five minutes, remove from fire, add butter, lemon juice, and nutmeg.

Vanilla Sauce

Make as Lemon Sauce, using one teaspoon vanilla in place of lemon juice and nutmeg.

Hard Sauce

⅓ cup butter.

1 cup powdered sugar.

⅓ teaspoon lemon extract.

⅔ teaspoon vanilla.

Cream the butter, add sugar gradually, and flavoring.

Cream Sauce

¾ cup thick cream.

¼ cup milk.

⅓ cup powdered sugar.

½ teaspoon vanilla.

Mix cream and milk, beat until stiff, using egg beater; add sugar and vanilla.

Cold Desserts

Chocolate Cream

2 cups scalded milk.

5 tablespoons corn-starch.

½ cup sugar.

¼ teaspoon salt.

⅓ cup cold milk.

1½ squares Baker's chocolate.

3 tablespoons hot water.

Whites 3 eggs.

1 teaspoon vanilla.

Mix corn-starch, sugar, and salt, dilute with cold milk, add to scalded milk, and cook over hot water ten minutes, stirring constantly until thickened; melt chocolate, add hot water, stir until smooth, and add to cooked mixture; add whites of eggs beaten stiff, and vanilla. Mould, chill, and serve with cream.

Caramel Custard

4 cups scalded milk.

5 eggs.

½ teaspoon salt.

1 teaspoon vanilla.

½ cup sugar.

Put sugar in omelet pan, stir constantly over hot part of range until melted to a syrup of light brown color. Add gradually to milk, being careful that milk does not bubble up and go over, as is liable on account of high temperature of sugar. As soon as sugar is melted in milk, add mixture gradually to eggs slightly beaten; add salt and flavoring, then strain in buttered mould. Bake as custard. Chill, and serve with Caramel Sauce.

Caramel Sauce

½ cup sugar.
½ cup boiling water.
> *Miss Parloa.*

Melt sugar as for Caramel Custard, add water, simmer ten minutes; cool before serving.

Wine Cream

Arrange lady fingers or slices of sponge cake in a dish, pour over cream made as follows: Mix one-third cup sugar, grated rind and juice one-half lemon, one-fourth cup sherry wine, and yolks of two eggs; place over fire and stir vigorously with wire whisk until it thickens and is frothy, then pour over beaten whites of two eggs and continue beating[.]

Lemon Jelly

½ box gelatine or 2½ tablespoons granulated gelatine.
½ cup cold water.
2½ cups boiling water.
1 cup sugar.
½ cup lemon juice.

Soak gelatine twenty minutes in cold water, dissolve in boiling water, strain, and add to sugar and lemon juice. Turn into mould, and chill.

Coffee Jelly

½ box gelatine or 2½ tablespoons granulated gelatine.
½ cup cold water.
1 cup boiling water.
⅓ cup sugar.
2 cups boiled coffee.

Make same as Lemon Jelly. Serve with sugar and cream.

Apricot and Wine Jelly

½ box gelatine or 2½ tablespoons granulated gelatine.
½ cup cold water.
1 cup boiling water.
1 cup apricot juice.
1 cup wine.
1 cup sugar.
1 tablespoon lemon juice.

Garnish individual moulds with halves of apricots, fill with mixture made same as for other jellies, and chill. Serve with Cream Sauce.

Wine Jelly

½ box gelatine or 2½ tablespoons granulated gelatine.

½ cup cold water.

1⅔ cups boiling water.

1 cup sugar.

1 cup sherry or Madeira wine.

⅓ cup orange juice.

3 tablespoons lemon juice.

Soak gelatine twenty minutes in cold water, dissolve in boiling water; add sugar, wine, orange juice, and lemon juice; strain, mould, and chill. If a stronger jelly is desired, use additional wine in place of orange juice.

Spanish Cream

¼ box gelatine or 1¼ tablespoons granulated gelatine.

3 cups milk.

Whites 3 eggs.

Yolks 3 eggs.

½ cup sugar (scant).

¼ teaspoon salt.

1 teaspoon vanilla or

3 tablespoons wine.

Scald milk with gelatine, add sugar, pour slowly on yolks of eggs slightly beaten. Return to double boiler and cook until thickened, stirring constantly; remove from range, add salt, flavoring, and whites of eggs beaten stiff. Turn into individual moulds, first dipped in cold water, and chill; serve with cream. More gelatine will be required if large moulds are used.

Charlotte Russe

¼ box gelatine or 1¼ tablespoons granulated gelatine.

¼ cup cold water.

⅓ cup scalded cream.

⅓ cup powdered sugar.

Whip from 3½ cups thin cream.

1½ teaspoons vanilla.

6 lady fingers.

Soak gelatine in cold water, dissolve in scalded cream, strain into a bowl, and add sugar and vanilla. Set bowl in pan of ice water and stir constantly until it begins to thicken, then fold in whip from cream, adding one-third at a time. Should gelatine mixture become too thick, melt over hot water, and again cool before adding whip. Trim ends and sides of lady fingers, place around inside of a mould, crust side out, one-half inch apart. Turn in mixture, spread evenly, and chill. Serve on glass dish

A photograph of Charlotte Russe, a kind of molded trifle, garnished with cubes of wine jelly. From Fannie Farmer, *The Original 1896 Boston Cooking-School Cook Book* (Mineola, NY: Dover Publications, 1997), 360, Special Collections, Michigan State University Libraries.

and garnish with cubes of Wine Jelly. Charlotte Russe is sometimes made in individual moulds; these are often garnished on top with some of mixture forced through a pastry bag and tube. Individual moulds are frequently lined with thin slices of sponge cake cut to fit moulds.

Canton Sherbet

4 cups water.
1 cup sugar.
¼ lb. Canton ginger.
½ cup orange juice.
⅓ cup lemon juice.

Cut ginger in small pieces, add water and sugar, boil fifteen minutes; add fruit juice, cool, strain, and freeze. To be used in place of punch at a course dinner. This quantity is enough to serve twelve persons.

Milk Sherbet

4 cups milk.
1½ cups sugar.
Juice 3 lemons.

Mix juice and sugar, stirring constantly while slowly adding milk; if added too rapidly mixture will have a curdled appearance, which is unsightly, but will not affect the quality of sherbet; freeze and serve.

Nesselrode Pudding

3 cups milk.
1½ cups sugar.
Yolks 5 eggs.
½ teaspoon salt.
1 pint thin cream.
¼ cup pineapple syrup.
1½ cups prepared French chestnuts.

Make custard of first four ingredients, strain, cool; add cream, pineapple syrup, and chestnuts; then freeze. To prepare chestnuts, shell, cook in boiling water until soft, and force through a strainer. Line a two-quart melon mould with part of mixture; to remainder add one-half cup candied fruit cut in small pieces, one-quarter cup sultana raisins, and eight chestnuts broken in pieces, first soaked several hours in Maraschino syrup. Fill mould, cover, pack in salt and ice, and let stand two hours. Serve with whipped cream, sweetened and flavored with Maraschino syrup.

Soft Molasses Gingerbread

1 cup molasses.

⅓ cup butter.

1¾ teaspoons soda.

½ cup sour milk.

1 egg.

2 cups flour.

2 teaspoons ginger.

½ teaspoon salt.

Put butter and molasses in saucepan and cook until boiling point is reached. Remove from fire, add soda, and beat vigorously. Then add milk, egg well beaten, and remaining ingredients mixed and sifted. Bake fifteen minutes in buttered small tin pans, having pans two-thirds filled with mixture.

Peanut Cookies

2 tablespoons butter.

¼ cup sugar.

1 egg.

1 teaspoon baking powder.

¼ teaspoon salt.

½ cup flour.

2 tablespoons milk.

½ cup finely chopped peanuts.

½ teaspoon lemon juice.

Cream the butter, add sugar, and egg well beaten. Mix and sift baking powder, salt, and flour; add to first mixture; then add milk, peanuts, and lemon juice. Drop from a teaspoon on an unbuttered sheet one-inch apart, and place one-half peanut on top of each. Bake twelve to fifteen minutes in a slow oven. This recipe will make twenty-four cookies.

Chocolate Cookies

½ cup butter.

1 cup sugar.

1 egg.

¼ teaspoon salt.

2 oz. Baker's chocolate.

2½ cups flour (scant).

2 teaspoons baking powder.

¼ cup milk.

Cream the butter, add sugar gradually, egg well beaten, salt, and chocolate melted. Beat well, and add flour mixed and sifted with baking powder alternately with milk. Chill, roll very thin, then shape with a small cutter, first dipped in flour, and bake in a hot oven.

Rolled Wafers

¼ cup butter.

½ cup powdered sugar.

¼ cup milk.

⅞ cup bread flour.

½ teaspoon vanilla.

Always an advocate of fanciful presentations, Fannie Farmer recommended dying rolled wafers with food coloring and tying them together in groups of three with a ribbon. From Fannie Farmer, *The Original 1896 Boston Cooking-School Cook Book* (Mineola, NY: Dover Publications, 1997), 410, Special Collections, Michigan State University Libraries.

flavor with one-fourth teaspoon almond and three-fourths teaspoon vanilla. If colored pink, flavor with rose. Colored wafers must be baked in a very slow oven to prevent browning.

Cakes and Pastry Desserts

Cheap Sponge Cake

Yolks 3 eggs.
1 cup sugar.
1 tablespoon hot water.
1 cup flour.
1½ teaspoons baking powder.
¼ teaspoon salt.
Whites 3 eggs.
2 teaspoons vinegar.

Beat yolks of eggs until thick and lemon-colored, add sugar gradually, and continue beating; then add water, flour mixed and sifted with baking powder and salt, whites of eggs beaten until stiff, and vinegar. Bake thirty-five minutes in a moderate oven, in a buttered and floured cake pan.

Cream the butter, add sugar gradually, and milk drop by drop; then add flour and flavoring. Spread very thinly with a broad, long-bladed knife on a buttered inverted dripping pan. Crease in three-inch squares, and bake in a slow oven until delicately browned. Place pan on back of range, cut squares apart with a sharp knife, and roll while warm in tubular or cornucopia shape. If squares become too brittle to roll, place in oven to soften. If rolled tubular shape, tie in bunches with narrow ribbon. These are very attractive, and may be served with sherbet, ice cream, or chocolate. If rolled cornucopia shape, they may be filled with whipped cream just before sending to table. Colored wafers may be made from this mixture by adding leaf green or fruit red. If colored green,

Jelly Roll

3 eggs.
1 cup sugar.
½ tablespoon milk.
1½ teaspoons baking powder.
¼ teaspoon salt.
1 cup flour.
1 tablespoon melted butter.

Beat egg until light, add sugar gradually, milk, flour mixed and sifted with baking powder and salt, then butter. Line the bottom of a dripping-pan with paper; butter paper and sides of pan. Cover bottom of pan with mixture, and spread evenly. Cover bottom of pan with mixture and spread evenly. Bake twelve minutes in a moderate oven. Take from oven and turn on a paper sprinkled with powdered sugar. Quickly remove paper, and cut off a thin strip from sides and ends of cake. Spread with jelly or jam which has been beaten to consistency to spread easily, and roll. After cake has been rolled, roll paper around cake that it may better keep in shape. The work must be done quickly, or cake will crack in rolling.

One Egg Cake

¼ cup of butter.
½ cup sugar.
1 egg.
½ cup of milk.
1½ cups flour.
2½ teaspoons baking powder.

Cream the butter, add sugar gradually, and egg well beaten. Mix and sift flour and baking powder, add alternately with milk to first mixture. Bake thirty minutes in a shallow pan. Spread with Chocolate Frosting.

Chocolate Frosting

1½ squares chocolate.
⅓ cup scalded cream.
Few grains salt.
Yolk 1 egg.
½ teaspoon melted butter.
Confectioners' sugar.
½ teaspoon vanilla.

Melt chocolate over hot water, add cream gradually, salt, yolk of egg, and butter. Stir in confectioners' sugar until of right consistency to spread; then add flavoring.

Chocolate Cake

3 tablespoons butter.
½ cup sugar.
1 egg.
½ cup milk.
1⅓ cups flour.
2 teaspoons baking powder.
1 square chocolate melted.
½ teaspoon vanilla.

Cream the butter, add one-half sugar, egg well beaten, and remaining sugar. Mix and sift flour and baking powder, add alternately with milk to first mixture. Then add chocolate and vanilla. Bake thirty minutes in a shallow pan.

Ribbon Cake

½ cup butter.
2 cups sugar.
Yolks 4 eggs.
1 cup milk.
3½ cups flour.
5 teaspoons baking powder.
Whites 4 eggs.
½ teaspoon cinnamon.
¼ teaspoon mace.
¼ teaspoon nutmeg.
⅓ cup raisins seeded and cut in pieces.
⅓ cup figs finely chopped.
1 tablespoon molasses.

Mix first seven ingredients in order given. Bake two-thirds of the mixture in two layer cake pans. To the remainder add spices, fruit, and molasses, and bake in a layer cake pan. Put layers together with jelly (apple usually being preferred as it has less flavor), having the dark layer in the centre.

Brownies

⅓ cup butter.
⅓ cup powdered sugar.
⅓ cup Porto Rico molasses.
1 egg well beaten.
⅞ cup bread flour.
1 cup pecan meat cut in pieces.

Mix ingredients in order given. Bake in small, shallow fancy cake tins, garnishing top of each cake with one-half pecan.

Pound Cake

1 lb. butter.
1 lb. sugar.
Yolks 10 eggs.
Whites 10 eggs.
1 lb. flour.
½ teaspoon mace.
2 tablespoons brandy.

Cream the butter, add sugar gradually, and continue beating; then add yolks of eggs beaten until thick and lemon colored, whites of eggs beaten until stiff and dry, flour, mace, and brandy. Beat vigorously five minutes. Bake in a deep pan one and one fourth hours in a slow oven; or if to be used for fancy ornamented cakes, bake thirty to thirty-five minutes in a dripping-pan.

Polish Tartlets

Roll puff or plain paste one-eighth inch thick, and cut in two and one-half inch squares; wet the corners, fold toward the centre, and press lightly; bake on a sheet; when cool, press down the centres and fill, using two-thirds quince marmalade and one-third currant jelly.

Confections

Salted Almonds

Blanch one-fourth pound Jordan almonds and dry on a towel. Put one-third cup olive oil in a very small sauce-pan. When hot, put in one-fourth of the almonds and fry until delicately browned, stirring to keep almonds constantly in motion. Remove with a spoon or small skimmer, taking up as little oil as possible. Drain on brown paper and sprinkle with salt; repeat until all are fried. It may be necessary to remove some of the salt by wiping nuts with a napkin.

Parisian Sweets

1 lb. figs.
1 lb. dates.
1 lb. English walnut meat.
Confectioners' sugar.

Pick over and remove stems from figs and stones from dates. Mix fruit with walnut meat, and force through a meat-chopper. Work, using the hands, on a board dredged with confectioners' sugar, until well blended. Roll to one-fourth inch thickness, using confectioners' sugar for dredging board and pin. Shape with a small round cutter, first dipped in sugar, or cut with a sharp knife in three-fourth inch squares. Roll each piece in confectioners' sugar, and shake to remove superfluous sugar. Pack in layers in a tin box, putting paper between each layer. These confections may be used at dinner in place of bonbons or ginger chips.

A combination of nut meat (walnut, almond, and filbert) may be used in equal proportions.

Molasses Candy

2 cups Porto Rico molasses.
⅔ cup sugar.
3 tablespoons butter.
1 tablespoon vinegar.

An iron kettle with a rounding bottom (Scotch kettle), or copper kettle is best for candy making. If one has no copper kettle, a granite kettle is best for sugar candies. Put butter in kettle, place over fire, and when melted, add molasses and sugar. Stir until sugar is dissolved. During the first of the boiling, stirring is unnecessary; but when nearly cooked, it should be constantly stirred. Boil until, when tried in cold water, mixture will become brittle. Add vinegar just before taking from fire. Pour into a well buttered pan. When cool enough to handle, pull until porous and light colored, allowing candy to come in contact with tips of fingers and thumbs, not to be squeezed in the hand. Cut in small pieces, using large shears or a sharp knife, and then arrange on slightly buttered plates to cool.

Vinegar Candy

2 cups sugar.
½ cup vinegar.
2 tablespoons butter.

Put butter into kettle; when melted, add sugar and vinegar. Stir until sugar is dissolved, afterwards occasionally. Boil until, when tried in cold water, mixture will become brittle. Turn on a buttered platter to cool. Pull and cut same as Molasses Candy.

Ice Cream Candy

3 cups sugar.
¼ teaspoon cream of tartar.
½ cup boiling water.
½ tablespoon vinegar.

Boil ingredients together without stirring, until, when tried in cold water, mixture will become brittle. Turn on a well buttered platter to cool. As edges cool, fold towards centre. As soon as it can be handled, pull until white and glossy. While pulling, flavor as desired, using vanilla, orange extract, coffee extract, oil of sassafras, or melted chocolate. Cut in sticks or small pieces.

Butter Scotch

1 cup sugar.
¼ cup molasses.
2 tablespoons vinegar.
2 tablespoons boiling water.
½ cup butter.

Boil ingredients together until, when tried in cold water, mixture will become brittle. Turn into a well buttered pan; when slightly cool, mark with a sharp-pointed knife in squares. This candy is much improved by cooking a small piece of vanilla bean with other ingredients.

Butter Taffy

2 cups light brown sugar.
¼ cup molasses.
2 tablespoons vinegar.
2 tablespoons water.
⅞ teaspoon salt.
¼ cup butter.
2 teaspoons vanilla.

Boil first five ingredients until, when tried in cold water, mixture will become brittle. When nearly done, add butter, and just before turning into pan, vanilla. Cool and mark in squares.

Horehound Candy

¾ square inch pressed horehound.
2 cups boiling water.
3 cups sugar.
½ teaspoon cream of tartar.

Pour boiling water over horehound which has been separated in pieces; let stand one minute, then strain through double cheese cloth. Put into a granite kettle with remaining ingredients, and boil until, when tried in cold water, mixture will become brittle. Turn into a buttered pan, cool slightly, then mark in small squares. Small square packages of horehound may be bought for five cents.

Peanut Nougat

1 lb. sugar.
1 quart peanuts.

Shell, remove skins, and finely chop peanuts. Sprinkle with one-fourth teaspoon salt. Put sugar in a perfectly smooth granite saucepan, place on range, and stir constantly until melted to a syrup, taking care to keep sugar from sides of pan. Add nut meat, pour at once into a warm buttered tin, and mark in small squares. If sugar is not removed from range as soon as melted, it will quickly caramelize.

Chocolate Cream Candy

2 cups sugar.
⅔ cup milk.
1 tablespoon butter.
2 squares chocolate.
1 teaspoon vanilla.

Put butter into granite saucepan; when melted, add sugar and milk. Heat to boiling point; then add chocolate, and stir constantly until chocolate is melted. Boil thirteen minutes, remove from fire, add vanilla, and beat until creamy and mixture begins to sugar slightly around edge of saucepan. Pour at once into a buttered pan, cool slightly, and mark in squares. Omit vanilla, and add, while cooking, one-fourth teaspoon cinnamon.

Maple Sugar Candy

1 lb. soft maple sugar.
¾ cup thin cream.
¼ cup boiling water.
⅔ cup English walnut or pecan meat cut in pieces.

Break sugar in pieces; put into a saucepan with cream and water. Bring to boiling point, and boil until a soft ball is formed when tried in cold water. Remove from fire, beat until creamy, add nut meat, and pour into a buttered tin. Cool slightly, and mark in squares.

Sultana Caramels

2 cups sugar.
½ cup milk.
¼ cup molasses.
¼ cup butter.
2 squares chocolate.
1 teaspoon vanilla.
½ cup English walnut or hickory nut meat cut in pieces.
2 tablespoons Sultana raisins.

Put butter into a saucepan; when melted, add sugar, milk, and molasses. Heat to boiling point, and boil seven minutes. Add chocolate, and stir until chocolate is melted; then boil seven minutes longer. Remove from fire, beat until creamy, add nuts, raisins, and vanilla, and pour at once into a buttered tin. Cool slightly, and mark in squares.

Pralines

1⅞ cups powdered sugar.
1 cup maple syrup.
½ cup cream.
2 cups hickory nut or pecan meat cut in pieces.

Boil first three ingredients until, when tried in cold water, a soft ball may be formed. Remove from fire, and beat until of a creamy consistency; add nuts, and drop from tip of spoon in small piles on buttered paper.

Peppermints

1½ cups sugar.
½ cup boiling water.
6 drops oil of peppermint.

Put sugar and water into a granite saucepan and stir until sugar is dissolved. Boil ten minutes; remove from fire, add peppermint, and beat until of right consistency. Drop from tip of spoon on slightly buttered paper.

Sandwiches and Canapés

In preparing bread for sandwiches, cut slices as thinly as possible, and remove crusts. If butter is used, cream the butter, and spread bread before cutting from loaf. Spread half the slices with mixture to be used for filling, cover with remaining pieces, and cut in squares, oblongs, or triangles. If sandwiches are shaped with round or fancy cutters, bread should be shaped before spreading, that there may be no waste of butter. Sandwiches which are prepared several hours before serving-time may be kept fresh and moist by wrapping in a napkin wrung as dry as possible out of hot water, and keeping in a cool place. Paraffine paper is often used for the same purpose. Bread for sandwiches cuts better when a day old. Serve sandwiches piled on a plate covered with a doily.

Rolled Bread

Cut fresh bread, while still warm, in as thin slices as possible, using a very sharp knife. Spread evenly with butter which has been creamed. Roll slices separately, and tie each with baby ribbon.

Bread and Butter Folds

Remove end slice from bread. Spread end of loaf sparingly and evenly with butter which has been creamed. Cut off as thin a slice as possible. Repeat until the number of slices required are prepared. Remove crusts, put together in pairs, and cut in squares, oblongs, or triangles. Use white, entire wheat, Graham, or brown bread.

Lettuce Sandwiches

Put fresh, crisp lettuce leaves, washed and thoroughly dried, between thin slices of buttered bread prepared as for Bread and Butter Folds, having a teaspoon of Mayonnaise on each leaf.

Sliced Ham Sandwiches

Slice cold boiled ham as thinly as possible. Put between thin slices of buttered bread prepared as for Bread and Butter Folds.

Anchovy Sandwiches

Rub the yolks of hard boiled eggs to a paste. Moisten with soft butter and season with Anchovy essence. Spread mixture between thin slices of buttered bread prepared as for Bread and Butter Folds.

Chicken Sandwiches

Chop cold boiled chicken, and moisten with Mayonnaise or Cream Salad Dressing; or season with salt and pepper, and moisten with rich chicken stock. Prepare as other sandwiches.

Lobster Sandwiches

Remove lobster meat from shell, and chop. Season with salt, cayenne, made mustard, and lemon juice; or moisten with any salad dressing. Spread mixture on a crisp lettuce leaf, and prepare as other sandwiches.

Oyster Sandwiches

Arrange fried oysters on crisp lettuce leaves, allowing two oysters for each leaf, and one leaf for each sandwich. Prepare as other sandwiches.

Nut and Cheese Sandwiches

Mix equal parts of grated Gruyère cheese and chopped English walnut meat; then season with salt and cayenne. Prepare as other sandwiches.

Ginger Sandwiches

Cut preserved Canton ginger in very thin slices. Prepare as other sandwiches.

Fruit Sandwiches

Remove stems and finely chop figs; add a small quantity of water, cook in double boiler until a paste is formed, then add a few drops of lemon juice. Cool mixture and spread on thin slices of buttered bread; sprinkle with finely chopped peanuts and cover with pieces of buttered bread.

Canapés are made by cutting bread in slices one-fourth inch thick, and cutting slices in strips four inches long by one and one-half inches wide, or in circular pieces. Then bread is toasted, fried in deep fat, or buttered and browned in the oven, and covered with a seasoned mixture of eggs, cheese, fish, or meat, separately or in combination. Canapés are served hot or cold, and used in place of oysters at a dinner or luncheon. At a gentlemen's dinner they are served with a glass of sherry before entering the dining-room.

Cheese Canapés

Toast circular pieces of bread, sprinkle with a thick layer of grated cheese, seasoned with salt and cayenne. Place on a tin sheet and bake until cheese is melted. Serve at once.

Sardine Canapés

Spread circular pieces of toasted bread with sardines (from which bones have been removed) rubbed to a paste, with a small quantity of creamed butter and seasoned with Worcestershire Sauce and a few grains cayenne. Place in the centre of each a stuffed olive, made by removing stone and filling cavity with sardine mixture. Around each arrange a border of the finely chopped whites of hard boiled eggs.

Canapés Lorenzo

Toast slices of bread cut in shape of horseshoes, cream two tablespoons butter, and add one teaspoon white of egg. Spread rounding with Crab Mixture, cover with creamed butter, sprinkle with cheese, and brown in the oven. Serve on a napkin, ends toward centre of dish, and garnish with parsley.

Recipes Especially Prepared for the Sick

Statistics prove that two-thirds of all disease is brought about by error in diet. The correct proportions of food-principles have not been maintained, or the food has been improperly cooked. Physicians agree, with but few exceptions, that the proper preparation of food for the sick is of as great importance in the restoration to health as administration of drugs. Time and manner of serving are of equal importance.

Take especial care in setting an invalid's tray. Cover with a spotless tray-cloth or dinner napkin, folding the same, if it is larger than tray, that it may just come over edge. Avoid a fringed cloth, as the fringe is apt to prove annoying.

Select the daintiest china, finest glass, and choicest silver, making changes as often as possible. Cheer the patient with a bright blossom laid on tray, or a small vase of flowers placed in left hand corner. Place plate at front of tray, near the edge; knife at right of plate, with sharp edge toward plate; fork at left of plate, tines up; spoon at head of plate, or, if more convenient for the patient, at right of knife, bowl up; cup and saucer at right of plate, with handle arranged so that cup may be easily lifted; tumbler above knife, and filled two-thirds full of freshly drawn water just before taking into the sick-room. The individual butter, or bread and butter plate, should be placed at left hand corner over fork. The napkin may be placed at right of cup. Salt should appear, but pepper never. Avoid having too many things on the tray at one time. If soup, meat, and a light dessert are to be served to a convalescent, have one course removed before another appears. Foods which are intended to be served hot should be placed in heated dishes and kept covered during transit from kitchen, that patient may receive them hot. Equal care should be taken to have cold foods served cold; never lukewarm. A glass of milk, cup of gruel, or cup of beef-tea should be on a plate covered with a doily.

Never consult the patient as to his menu. If there is anything he especially desires, you will be informed. Anticipation often creates appetite. Serve in small quantities; the sight of too much food often destroys the appetite. If liquid diet must be adhered to, give as great variety as is allowable. If patient is restricted to milk diet, and milk is somewhat objectionable, it may be tolerated by serving in different ways,—such as Koumiss, Albumenized Milk, or by addition of Apollinaris, Seltzer water, or rennet.

After the completion of a meal, the tray should be removed at once from the sick-room. If any solid food remains, it should be burned, and liquids disposed of at once.

Rice Water

2 tablespoons rice.
2 cups cold water.
Milk or cream.
Salt.

Pick over rice, add to water, and boil until rice is tender; strain, and add to rice water, milk or cream as desired.

Season with salt and reheat. A half-inch piece of stick cinnamon may be cooked with rice, and will assist in reducing a laxative condition.

Oatmeal Water

1 cup fine oatmeal.
2 quarts water (which has been boiled and cooled).

Add oatmeal to water, and keep in a warm place (at temperature of 80° F.) one and one-half hours. Strain and cool.

Toast Water

Equal measures of stale bread toasted and boiling water.
Salt.

Cut bread in quarter-inch slices, put in a pan, and dry thoroughly in a slow oven until crisp and brown. Break in pieces, add water, and let stand one hour. Strain through cheese cloth, and season. Serve hot or cold.

Apple Water

1 large sour apple.
2 teaspoons sugar.
1 cup boiling water.

Wipe, core, and pare apple. Put sugar in the cavity. Bake until tender; mash, pour over water, let stand one-half hour, and strain.

Tamarind Water

2 tablespoons preserved tamarinds.
1 cup boiling water.
Sugar.

Pour water over tamarinds; stir until well mixed. Let stand twenty minutes and strain. Sweeten to taste.

Currant Water

2 tablespoons currant juice or
2 teaspoons currant jelly.
⅔ cup cold water.
Sugar.

Mix juice and water, then sweeten; or beat jelly with a fork, dissolve in water, and if not sweet enough add sugar.

Grape Juice

1½ cups Concord grapes.
1 cup cold water.
½ cup sugar.

Wash, pick over, and remove stems from grapes; add water, and cook one and one-half hours in a double boiler. Add sugar, and cook twenty minutes. Strain and cool.

Fannie Farmer provided a recipe for homemade grape juice made from Concord grapes, sugar, and water. While most Americans still squeezed juice themselves if they drank it at all, however, commercially produced fruit juices were starting to become available in the late nineteenth century under brand names like Welch's. Welch's promotional pamphlet, 1896, The Alan and Shirley Brocker Sliker Collection, MSS 314, Special Collections, Michigan State University Libraries.

Flaxseed Lemonade

1 tablespoon whole flaxseed.
1 pint boiling water.
Lemon juice.
Sugar.

Pick over and wash flaxseed, add water, and cook two hours, keeping just below boiling point. Strain, add lemon juice, and sugar to taste.

Egg-nog

1 egg.
⅔ cup milk.
1 tablespoon sugar.
2 tablespoons wine or
1 tablespoon brandy.
Few grains salt.

Beat egg slightly, add salt, sugar, and wine; mix thoroughly, add milk, and strain. Wine may be omitted, and a slight grating nutmeg used.

Wine Whey

1 cup milk.
1 cup sherry or port wine.

Scald milk, add wine, and let stand five minutes. By this time the curd should have separated from whey. Strain and serve, or heat before serving.

Milk Punch

½ cup milk.

1 tablespoon whiskey, rum, or brandy.

Sugar.

Few gratings nutmeg.

Mix ingredients, cover, and shake well.

Cocoa Cordial

1 teaspoon cocoa.

1 teaspoon sugar.

½ cup boiling water.

1½ tablespoons port wine.

Mix cocoa and sugar, add enough of the water to form a paste. Stir in remainder of water and boil one minute, then add wine. Useful in cases of chill or exhaustion.

Broiled Beef Essence

½ lb. steak from top of round (cut ¾ inch thick).

Wipe steak, remove all fat, and place in a heated broiler. Broil three minutes over a clear fire, turning every ten seconds to prevent escape of juices. Put on a hot plate, and cut in one and one-half inch pieces; gash each piece two or three times on each side. Express the juice with a lemon squeezer and turn into a cup, set in a dish of hot water, care being taken that heat is not sufficient to coagulate juices. Season with salt.

Broiled Beef Tea

Dilute Broiled Beef Essence with water.

Frozen Beef Tea.

Freeze Beef Tea to the consistency of a mush.

Indian Gruel

2 tablespoons Indian meal.

1 tablespoon flour.

½ teaspoon salt.

Cold water.

3 cups boiling water.

Milk or cream.

Mix meal, flour, and salt; add cold water to make a thin paste. Add to boiling water, and boil gently one hour. Dilute with milk or cream.

A richer gruel may be made by using milk instead of water, and cooking three hours in double boiler.

Oatmeal Gruel

½ cup coarse oatmeal.

3 cups boiling water.

1 teaspoon salt.

Milk.

Add oatmeal and salt to boiling water and cook three hours in double boiler. Force through a strainer, dilute with milk or cream, reheat, and strain a second time.

Barley Gruel

1 cup boiling water.
3 teaspoons barley flour.
Cold water.
½ cup milk.
¼ teaspoon salt.

Mix barley flour with cold water to form a thin paste. Add to boiling water, and boil fifteen minutes; then add milk, season, reheat, and strain.

Cracker Gruel

½ Boston cracker.
¼ teaspoon salt.
1 cup milk.

Scald milk, and add cracker rolled and sifted. Cook five minutes in double boiler. Season.

Clam Water

Wash and scrub one and one-half dozen clams. Cook in covered kettle with three tablespoons water until shells open. Remove clams, strain liquor through double cheese cloth. Serve hot or as a frappé.

Indian Meal Mush

½ cup Indian meal.
¾ cup milk.
1 cup boiling water.
½ teaspoon salt.

Mix meal and salt, add milk, and stir into boiling water. Cook three hours in double boiler. Serve with sugar and cream.

Raw Beef Sandwiches

Prepare bread as for Bread and Butter Sandwiches. Spread one-half the pieces with scraped beef, generously seasoned with salt; if pepper is desired, use sparingly. Cover with remaining pieces.

Egg Sandwiches

Cut thin slices of stale bread in triangles, then toast. Put together in pairs, having between the pieces thoroughly cooked egg yolk, rubbed to a paste, seasoned with salt, and moistened with soft butter.

Suitable Combinations for Serving

breakfast menus

Sliced Oranges.
Wheat Germ with Sugar and Cream.
Warmed over Lamb.
French Fried Potatoes.
Raised Biscuits.
Buckwheat Cakes with Maple Syrup.
Coffee.

Raspberries.
Shredded Wheat Biscuit.
Dried Smoked Beef in Cream.
Hashed Brown Potatoes.
Baking-Powder Biscuit.
Coffee.

Blackberries.
H-O with Sugar and Cream.
Dropped Eggs on Toast.
Waffles with Maple Syrup.
Coffee.

Wheatena with Sugar and Cream.
Fish Hash.
Buttered Graham Toast.
Strawberry Short Cake.
Coffee.

luncheon menus

Scalloped Oysters.
Rolls.
Dressed Celery.
Polish Tartlets.
Tea.

Salmi of Lamb.
Olives.
Bread and Butter.
Cake.
Chocolate.

Cold Sliced Tongue.
Macaroni and Cheese.
Lettuce Salad.
Crackers.
Wafers.
Coffee.

Cold Sliced Corned Beef.
Corn à la Southern.
Entire Wheat Bread and Butter.
Grapes and Pears.

dinner menus

Kornlet Soup.
Maryland Chicken.
Baked Sweet Potatoes.
Creamed Cauliflower.
Cranberry Sauce.
Dressed Lettuce.
Polish Tartlets.
Café Noir.

Turkish Soup.
Lamb Chops.
French Fried Potatoes.
Apple Fritters.
Beet Greens.
Caramel Custard.
Café Noir.

Cream of Lima Bean Soup.
Roast Duck.
Mashed Sweet Potatoes.
Cauliflower au Gratin.
Rice Croquettes with Currant Jelly.
Grapes.
Pears.
Crackers.
Cheese.
Café Noir.

A Full Course Dinner

FIRST COURSE

Little Neck Clams or Bluepoints, with brown-bread sandwiches. Sometimes canapés are used in place of either. For a gentlemen's dinner, canapés accompanied with sherry wine are frequently served before guests enter the dining-room.

SECOND COURSE

Clear soup, with bread sticks, small rolls, or crisp crackers. Where two soups are served, one may be a cream soup. Cream soups are served with croûtons. Radishes, celery, or olives are passed after the soup. Salted almonds may be passed between any of the courses.

THIRD COURSE

Bouchées or rissoles. The filling to be of light meat.

FOURTH COURSE

Fish, baked, boiled, or fried. Cole slaw, dressed cucumbers, or tomatoes accompany this course; with fried fish potatoes are often served.

FIFTH COURSE

Roast saddle of venison or mutton, spring lamb, or fillet of beef; potatoes and one other vegetable.

SIXTH COURSE

Entrée, made of light meat or fish.

SEVENTH COURSE

A vegetable. Such vegetables as mushrooms, cauliflower, asparagus, artichokes, are served, but not in white sauce.

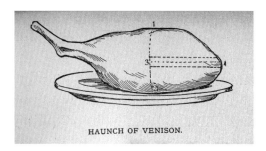

HAUNCH OF VENISON.

Haunch of venison from Fanny Gillette, *The White House Cook Book: A Selection of Choice Recipes Original and Selected* (Chicago: R. S. Peale and Co., 1887), 15, Special Collections, Michigan State University Libraries.

Where wines and liquors are served, the first course is not usually accompanied by either; but if desired, Sauterne or other white wine may be used.

With soup, serve sherry; with fish, white wine; with game, claret; with roast and other courses, champagne.

EIGHTH COURSE

Punch or cheese course. Punch, when served, always precedes the game course.

NINTH COURSE

Game, with vegetable salad, usually lettuce or celery; or cheese sticks may be served with the salad, and game omitted.

TENTH COURSE

Dessert, usually cold.

ELEVENTH COURSE

Frozen dessert and fancy cakes. Bonbons are passed after this course.

TWELFTH COURSE

Crackers, cheese, and café noir. Café noir is frequently served in the drawing and smoking rooms after the dinner.

Champagne was a powerful symbol of fine dining in the Gilded Age. "Dejeuner [held by] Cie Cie Transatlantique Paqueboat: La Champagne (SS)," 1900, Rare Book Division, New York Public Library Menu Collection.

After serving café noir in drawing-room, pass pony of brandy for men, sweet liqueur (Chartreuse, Benedictine, or Parfait d'Amour) for women; then Crème de Menthe to all.

After a short time Apollinaris should be passed. White wines and claret should be served cool; sherry should be thoroughly chilled by keeping in ice box. Champagne should be served very cold by allowing it to remain in salt and ice at least one-half hour before dinner time. Claret, as it contains so small an amount of alcohol, is not good the day after opening.

For a simpler dinner, the third, seventh, eighth, and tenth courses, and the game in the ninth course may be omitted.

For a home dinner, it is always desirable to serve for first course a soup; second course, meat or fish, with potatoes and two other vegetables; third course, a vegetable salad, with French dressing; fourth course, dessert; fifth course, crackers, cheese, and café noir.

At a ladies' luncheon the courses are as many as at a small dinner. In winter, grape fruit is sometimes served in place of oysters; in summer, selected strawberries in small Swedish Timbale cases.

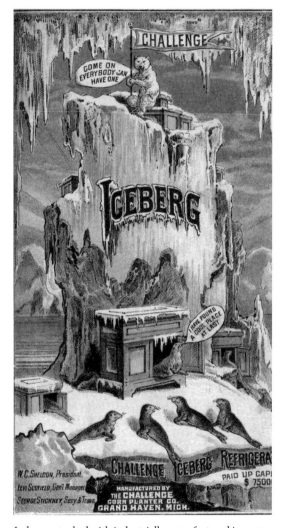

Iceboxes stocked with industrially manufactured ice were becoming more common in middle-class homes throughout the late nineteenth century. Advertisement for Challenge Iceberg Refrigerators, Challenge Corn Planter Company, The Alan and Shirley Brocker Sliker Collection, MSS 314, Special Collections, Michigan State University Libraries.

Menu for Full Course Dinner

Blue Points.

Consommé à la Royal.

Olives.

Celery.

Salted Almonds.

Swedish Timbales with Chicken and Mushrooms.

Fried Smelts.

Sauce Tartare.

Dressed Cucumbers.

Saddle of Mutton.

Currant Jelly Sauce.

Potatoes Brabant.

Brussels Sprouts.

Suprème of Chicken.

Mushrooms à la Sabine.

Canton Sherbet.

Canvasback Duck.

Olive Sauce.

Farina Cakes with Jelly.

Celery Salad.

Apricot and Wine Jelly.

Nesselrode Pudding.

Rolled Wafers.

Parisian Sweets.

Crackers.

Cheese.

Café Noir.

NOTES

A Matter of Class: Food in the United States, 1870–1900

1. Portions of this essay appeared previously in *How the Other Half Ate: A History of Working-Class Meals at the Turn of the Century*, by Katherine Leonard Turner © 2014 by the Regents of the University of California. Published by the University of California Press.

2. "Mrs. William Astor's Ball," *New York Times*, January 18, 1898. Translations and dish identifications by Beckett Graham and Susan Vollenweider, "The Mrs. Astor," *The History Chicks* (http://thehistorychicks.com/show-notes/the-mrs-astor/), May 12, 2011.

3. W. O. Atwater and Chas. D. Woods, *Dietary Studies in New York City in 1895 and 1896* (Washington, DC: Government Printing Office, 1898), 25–28.

4. The following sources have informed my discussion, in addition to those specifically cited: Harvey Levenstein, *Revolution at the Table: The Transformation of the American Diet* (Berkeley: University of California Press, 1988); Susan Williams, *Food in the United States, 1820s–1890* (Westport, CT: Greenwood Press, 2006); Marcie Cohen Ferris, *The Edible South: The Power of Food and the Making of an American Region* (Chapel Hill: University of North Carolina Press, 2014); Hasia R. Diner, *Hungering for America: Italian, Irish, and Jewish Foodways in the Age of Migration* (Cambridge, MA: Harvard University Press, 2001).

5. Sophonisba Breckinridge, *New Homes for Old* (reprint: Montclair, NJ: Patterson Smith, 1971), 171; Moses Rischin, *The Promised City: New York's Jews, 1870–1914* (Cambridge, MA: Harvard University Press, 1962); I. A. Newby, *Plain Folk in the New South: Social Change and Cultural Persistence, 1880–1915* (Baton Rouge: Louisiana State University Press, 1989); Madelon Powers, *Faces along the Bar: Lore and Order in the Workingman's Saloon, 1870–1920* (Chicago: University of Chicago Press, 1998).

6. Dennis F. Brestensky, Evelyn A. Hovanec, and Albert N. Skomra, eds., *Patch/Work Voices: The Culture and Lore of a Mining People* (University of Pittsburgh, 1978); Karen Bescherer Metheny, *From the Miner's Doublehouse: Archaeology and Landscape in a Pennsylvania Coal Company Town* (Knoxville: University of Tennessee Press, 2007).

7. Louise Bolard More, *Wage Earners' Budgets* (New York: Henry Holt and Company, 1907; reprint New York: Arno Press and New York Times, 1971).

8. Williams, *Food in the United States*, 163.

9. Fanny Lemira Gilette, *White House Cook Book: A Selection of Choice Recipes Original and Selected, during a Period of Forty Years' Practical Housekeeping* (Chicago: R.S. Peale & Co, 1887), 503.

10. Condensed milk on bread: More, *Wage Earners' Budgets*, 209.

11. Elizabeth S. D. Engelhardt, *A Mess of Greens: Southern Gender and Southern Food* (Athens and London: University of Georgia Press, 2011).

12. Jen Miller, "Frybread," *Smithsonian Magazine*, July 2008.

13. Diner, *Hungering for America*.

14. Mary Hinman Abel, *Practical Sanitary and Economic Cooking Adapted to Persons of Moderate and Small Means* (New York: American Public Health Association, 1890).

15. Williams, *Food in the United States*, 33.

16. Ferris, *The Edible South*, 128–130.

17. Williams, *Food in the United States*, 28–29.

18. Diner, *Hungering for America*; oral history respondent number I-3-A, pages 11–13 of transcript, in "Women, Ethnicity, and Mental Health: A Comparative Oral History Project, 1975–1977," Archives of Industrial Society, Hillman Library, University of Pittsburgh; Andrew H. Fisher, "'They Mean to Be Indians Always': The Origin of Columbia River Indian Identity, 1860–1885," in Roger L. Nichols, ed., *The American Indian: Past and Present* (Norman: University of Oklahoma Press, 2008).

19. By contrast, a cookbook published in 1730, *The Frugal Housewife*, advocated cooking vegetables only until crisp-tender: cauliflower must be taken out of the pot "before it loses its crispness, for colliflower is good for nothing that boils till it becomes quite soft." The taste for very soft vegetables was peculiar to the nineteenth century. The Women's Centennial Committee, *National Cookery Book* (Philadelphia, 1876), 150–151; Fannie Merritt Farmer, *The Boston Cooking-School Cook Book* (Boston: Little, Brown & Company, 1896), 34; Jean McKibin, ed., *The Frugal Colonial Housewife* (reprint Garden City, NY: Dolphin Books, Doubleday & Company, 1976), 34.

20. Williams, *Food in the United States*, 78–79.

21. Harvey Levenstein, *Fear of Food: A History of Why We Worry about What We Eat* (Chicago: University of Chicago Press, 2012).

22. Williams, *Food in the United States*, 104–112.

23. Williams, *Food in the United States*, 112–121, 135–137.

24. Karen J. Friedmann, "Urban Food Marketing in Los Angeles, 1850–1885," *Agricultural History* 54, no. 3 (1980): 433–444; Robert F. G. Spier, "Food Habits of Nineteenth-Century California Chinese," *California Historical Society Quarterly* 37, no. 1 (1958): 79–84 and 37, no. 2 (1958): 129–136.

25. Gary Paul Nabhan, "Diabetes, Diet, and Native American Foraging Traditions," and Christine E. Miewald, "The Nutritional Impact of European Contact on the Omaha: A Continuing Legacy," in Carole M. Counihan, ed., *Food in the USA: A Reader* (New York: Routledge, 2002).

26. Williams, *Food in the United States*, 122–131.

27. Kristin L. Hoganson, *Consumer's Imperium: The Global Production of American Domesticity, 1865–1920* (Chapel Hill: University of North Carolina Press, 2007), 114.

28. Levenstein, *Revolution at the Table*, 30–32; R. Douglas Hurt, *American Agriculture: A Brief History* (Iowa State University Press, 1994), 184–185; Richard J. Hooker, *Food and Drink in America: A History* (Indianapolis: Bobbs-Merrill, 1981), 229–232.

29. Many of the farmers who moved to the Great Plains had incorrectly believed that there was sufficient rainfall, or that "rain would follow the plow." This did not prove to be the case; farmers were forced to adapt to the dry Plains environment with different farming technologies. New crops were the key: drought-resistant strains of wheat and sorghum, rather than thirstier corn. Gary D. Libecap and Zeynep Kocabiyik Hansen, "'Rain Follows the Plow' and Dryfarming Doctrine: The Climate Information Problem and Homestead Failure in the Upper Great Plains, 1890–1925," *Journal of Economic History* 62, no. 1 (2002): 86–120; Hurt, *American Agriculture*, 179.

30. Leonard A. Carlson, "The Dawes Act and the Decline of Indian Farming," *Journal of Economic History* 38, no. 1 (1978): 274–276.

31. Hurt, *American Agriculture*, 195–200.

32. Ibid., 179.

33. Roger Horowitz, *Putting Meat on the American Table: Taste, Technology, Transformation* (Baltimore: Johns Hopkins University Press, 2006), 30.

34. William Cronon, *Nature's Metropolis: Chicago and the Great West* (New York: W.W. Norton, 1991), 243.

35. Hooker, *Food and Drink in America*, 224–226.

36. Susanne Freidberg, *Fresh: A Perishable History* (Cambridge, MA: Belknap Press of Harvard University Press, 2009), 203–218; Levenstein, *Fear of Food*, chapter 2.

37. Hooker, *Food and Drink in America*, 229.

38. Ibid., 237.

39. Maria Parloa, *Miss Parloa's New Cook Book and Marketing Guide* (Boston: Estes & Lauriat, 1880), 48.

40. Freidberg, *Fresh*, 94–96.

41. "Food Preservation in New York," *Harper's Weekly*, July 4, 1891, 508. The facility stored fabrics and tobacco as well as food: "Woolens and fine dress goods keep best at about 50° Fahr., furs and pelts at about 45°, tobacco of the better grades at 42°, eggs at just above the freezing-point, and fish just below that standard. Poultry, game, and meats are best when kept frozen; fine Philadelphia chickens and capons, Boston ducks, New York turkeys, and venison are best when kept at a temperature of between 15° and 20° above zero. Each room is devoted to one class of goods, and is kept at one temperature."

42. I borrow the phrase "democracy of goods" from Roland Marchand's *Advertising the American Dream: Making Way for Modernity, 1920–1940* (Berkeley: University of California Press, 1985), in which he used it to describe the way advertisers in the 1920–1940s promised social equality through consumption.

43. Lee A. Craig, Barry Goodwin, and Thomas Grennes, "The Effect of Mechanical Refrigeration on Nutrition in the United States," *Social Science History* 28, no. 2 (2004): 325–336.

44. Hoganson, *Consumer's Imperium*, 109–110.

45. Ibid., 115, 122–123.

46. James H. Collins, *The Story of Canned Foods* (New York: E.P. Dutton, 1924), 38; *Historical Statistics of the United States: Colonial Times to 1970* (Washington, DC: U.S. Dept. of Commerce, Bureau of the Census, 1975), 164.

47. Hooker, *Food and Drink in America*, 215; Joseph R. Conlin, *Bacon, Beans, and Galantines* (Reno: University of Nevada Press, 1986), 118–126.

48. In the first half of the nineteenth century, food was "canned" in glass jars or tin cans by a tedious hand process. The tin cans themselves were made by skilled tinsmiths and sealed by hand with solder. Tinsmiths, who had been highly paid, skilled, organized workers, were driven out of the industry with the development of machinery to make and seal the cans in the late nineteenth century. Filling and closing the cans also became mechanized, with the development of the "sanitary can" in 1897, which required no solder but was crimped closed. Collins, *Story of Canned Foods*, 36. Well into the twentieth century, low-paid women and girls still worked the tedious jobs of preparing food for canning: shucking corn or oysters, shelling peas or peeling tomatoes, and feeding the prepared food into the small fill holes in the tin cans. The canning industry succeeded in the late nineteenth century in developing machinery to perform these tasks, culminating in such triumphs as the mechanical peapodder and the "Iron Chink" salmon gutter, which replaced Chinese immigrants in the salmon packing industry. Levenstein, *Revolution at the Table*, 32.

49. In Fannie Farmer's 1905 cookbook, aimed at the urban middle class, a recipe for "Green Peas" began, "Open one can

of peas." Fannie Merritt Farmer, *What to Have for Dinner* (New York: Dodge Publishing Co., 1905).

50. Robert Coit Chapin, *The Standard of Living among Workingmen's Families in New York City* (New York: Charities Publication Committee, 1909), 156.

51. "Italian Housewives' Dishes," *New York Times*, June 7, 1903, 28; Diner, *Hungering for America*, 62.

52. Levenstein, *Revolution at the Table*, 34–37.

53. Levenstein, *Fear of Food*, 44, 62.

54. Caroline L. Hunt, *The Life of Ellen H. Richards* (Boston: Whitcomb & Barrows, 1912), 105–110, 146.

55. Lizabeth A. Cohen, "Embellishing a Life of Labor: An Interpretation of the Material Culture of American Working-Class Homes, 1885–1915," *Journal of American Culture* 3, no. 4 (1980): 752–775.

56. Susan Strasser, *Never Done: A History of American Housework* (New York: Pantheon Books, 1982), 100, 96–103.

57. At least one domestic advisor and cookbook author, Mary Hinman Abel, acknowledged the difficulty of learning this sort of sense-based traditional technique: "One housekeeper says 'hot enough so that you can hold your hand in until you count twelve,' another 'until you can count to thirty,' and the puzzled novice can only inquire 'how fast do you count?'" Abel, *Practical Sanitary and Economic Cooking*, 95.

58. Priscilla J. Brewer, *From Fireplace to Cookstove: Technology and the Domestic Ideal in America* (Syracuse: Syracuse University Press, 2000), 170.

59. Brewer, *From Fireplace to Cookstove*, 229.

60. *Sears, Roebuck Catalogue*, 1897 (reprint Philadelphia: Chelsea House, 1968), 115.

61. Ellen M. Plante, *The American Kitchen, 1700 to the Present* (New York: Facts on File, 1995), 104.

62. *Sears, Roebuck Catalogue, 1897*, 130–132.

63. Williams, *Food in the United States*, 70–72.

64. That is, one dozen forks, one dozen silver spoons, one dozen large knives, one dozen glass tumblers, two dozen wine glasses, one dozen soup plates, and four dozen plates. Susan Williams, *Savory Suppers and Fashionable Feasts: Dining in Victorian America* (New York: Pantheon Books, 1985), 81. The list is from Catharine Beecher, *Miss Beecher's Domestic Receipt Book Designed as a Supplement to Her Treatise on Domestic Economy* (New York : Harper & Brothers, 1852), 237.

65. Williams, *Savory Suppers*, 81–87.

66. "Family of Dometrio Capilluto," December 1911, Call Number: LOT 7481, no. 2689, Reproduction Number: LC-DIG-nclc-04089, National Child Labor Committee Collection, Library of Congress, Prints and Photographs Collection, Library of Congress.

67. In *Building a Housewife's Paradise: Gender, Politics, and American Grocery Stores in the Twentieth Century* (Chapel Hill: University of North Carolina Press, 2010), Tracey Deutsch makes a detailed argument for why food shopping was so physically and emotionally difficult: shoppers faced long treks and long lines to get good prices, made more difficult by the need to bargain shrewdly, the suspicion that one was being cheated, and social conflict between buyers and sellers of different ethnic groups. See particularly chapter 1.

68. Helen Tangires, *Public Markets and Civic Culture in Nineteenth-Century America* (Baltimore: Johns Hopkins University Press, 2003), especially chapter 8; Peter R. Shergold, *Working-Class Life: The "American Standard" in Comparative Perspective, 1899–1913* (Pittsburgh: University of Pittsburgh Press, 1982), 125ff.

69. James D. McCabe, *New York by Sunlight and Gaslight: A Work Descriptive of the Great American Metropolis* (Philadelphia: Douglass Brothers, 1882), 665.

70. Daniel Bluestone, "The Pushcart Evil," in David Ward and Olivier Zunz, eds., *The Landscape of Modernity: Essays on*

New York City, 1900–1940 (New York: Russell Sage Foundation, 1992).

71. Rischin, *The Promised City*, 55–56.

72. Susan Strasser, *Satisfaction Guaranteed: The Making of the American Mass Market* (Washington, DC: Smithsonian Institution Press, 1989), chapter 3.

73. Strasser, *Satisfaction Guaranteed*, 70–71; Chicago Municipal Markets Commission, "Preliminary Report to the Mayor and Aldermen of the City of Chicago" (Chicago, April 27, 1914), 23–24. Most retailers seem not to have put any limits on delivery: they would deliver any amount of goods, of any value, to customers as many times a day as they were requested.

74. Alvan Francis Sanborn, *Moody's Lodging House and Other Tenement Sketches* (Boston: Copeland and Day, 1895), 111. From the *Immigrant in America* microfilm collection, HSP, Reel 69, no. 160.

75. Marcus T. Reynolds, *The Housing of the Poor in American Cities* (1893; reprint College Park, MD: McGrath 1969), 117.

76. On the origins of pepper pot soup, see Evan Jones, *American Food: The Gastronomic Story* (New York: E.P. Dutton, 1975), 70–71.

77. Mark Kurlansky, *The Big Oyster: History on the Half Shell* (New York: Ballantine Books, 2006), 157–162, 214.

78. Levenstein, *Revolution at the Table*, 16; Williams, *Food in the United States*, 165–166.

79. On restaurants and the middle class, see Andrew P. Haley, *Turning the Tables: Restaurants and the Rise of the Middle Class, 1880–1920* (Chapel Hill: University of North Carolina Press, 2011).

80. Hooker, *Food and Drink in America*, 278–279.

81. Diner, *Hungering for America*, 196; recording of oral history with Louis Arenson, National Council of Jewish Women, Oral History Project, Archives of Industrial Society, University of Pittsburgh Library, call number AIS OH 92:2; "Jewish Women," *Daily Jewish Courier*, July 8, 1912, no author, translated for the Chicago Foreign Language Press Survey, filed in Jewish, IK, box 30, University of Chicago Special Collections; Marni Davis, *Jews and Booze: Becoming American in the Age of Prohibition* (New York: New York University Press, 2012); "Unsanitary Factories," *L'Italia*, June 23, 1906, translated by John Grotto, January 19, 1937, for the Chicago Foreign Language Press Survey, filed in Italian, I M: Attitudes/ Health and Sanitation, box 26, University of Chicago Special Collections; also "Italian Housewives' Dishes," *New York Times*, June 7, 1903.

82. Hooker, *Food and Drink in America*, 294.

83. Diner, *Hungering for America*, 201.

84. William D. Panschar, *Baking in America: Economic Development*, vol. 1 (Evanston, IL: Northwestern University Press, 1956), 68.

85. Sanborn, *Moody's Lodging House*, 111.

86. Abraham Cahan, "A Woman of Valor," June 29, 1902, in Rischin, *The Promised City*, 402.

87. Roy Rosenzweig, *Eight Hours for What We Will: Workers and Leisure in an Industrial City, 1870–1920* (New York: Cambridge University Press, 1983), 95; Chicago business directory, 1901, listings for 'Saloons,' 2521–2536, Microfilm at the New York Public Library; Chicago population figure from Campbell Gibson, "Population of the 100 Largest Cities and Other Urban Places in the United States: 1790 to 1990," U.S. Census Bureau, http://www.census.gov/population/www/documentation /twps0027.html; viewed January 15, 2008.

88. Davis, *Jews and Booze*, 86.

89. Powers, *Faces along the Bar*.

90. Upton Sinclair, *The Jungle* (1906; reprint New York: Barnes & Noble, 1995), 87.

91. "The Free Lunch Microbe," *New York Times*, July 31, 1904.

92. Raymond Calkins, *Substitutes for the Saloon*, 2nd ed. (New York: Houghton Mifflin, 1919), 15. The "nickel beer" was a well-established standard, and saloonkeepers increased profits by selling a smaller glass or a lower-quality beer for the nickel price. This caused difficulties when the wholesale price of beer rose, and saloonkeepers were forced to acquire new stocks of smaller glasses in order to maintain profits. Perry R. Duis, *The Saloon: Public Drinking in Chicago and Boston, 1880–1920* (Urbana: University of Illinois Press, 1983), 48.

93. Kathy Peiss reports that respectable working-class women would cross the street to avoid passing a saloon full of harassing loiterers. *Cheap Amusements: Leisure in Turn-of-the-Century New York* (Philadelphia: Temple University Press, 1986), 27.

94. "Family Solidarity," in the Leonard Covello Papers, box 68, folder 1, "Social Backgrounds—reference—Documents and notes," Historical Society of Pennsylvania.

95. Haley, *Turning the Tables*, 150–151.

Seeing the Gilded Age through Its Recipes

1. Paul Andrew Hutton, "Phil Sheridan's Frontier," *Montana: The Magazine of Western History* 38, no. 1 (1988): 16–31.

2. Wolfgang Mieder, "'The Only Good Indian Is a Dead Indian': History and Meaning of a Proverbial Stereotype," *Journal of American Folklore* 106 (1993): 38–60.

3. Mark Twain and Charles Dudley Warner, *The Gilded Age: A Tale of Today* (1873).

4. Andrew P. Haley, *Turning the Tables: Restaurants and the Rise of the Middle Class, 1880–1920* (Chapel Hill: University of North Carolina Press, 2011), 21.

5. Pellagra, caused by protein and niacin deficiencies, resulted in weeping skin lesions, while rickets, caused by vitamin D deficiencies, caused bowed and bent bones, especially obvious in the legs.

6. Andrew Haley writes, "The paucity of French-language education in the United States increased the symbolic value of French to the elite." *Turning the Tables*, 32.

7. Haley notes that "Many restaurants gallicized their menus even when French names did not always indicate genuine French cuisine." *Turning the Tables*, 27.

8. See Haley, *Turning the Tables*, 23–42.

9. Dahlgren was justifying her belief that the wives of senators and generals should be called "Mrs. Senator" or "Mrs. General." Madeline Vinton Dahlgren, *The Social-Official Etiquette of the United States*, 6th ed. (Baltimore: John Murphy & Company, 1894), 62.

10. Susanne Freidberg, *Fresh: A Perishable History* (Cambridge, MA: Belknap Press of Harvard University Press, 2009).

11. Donna Gabaccia, *We Are What We Eat: Ethnic Food and the Making of Americans* (Cambridge, MA: Harvard University Press, 1998), 55–58; Gabriella M. Petrick, "Feeding the Masses: H.J. Heinz and the Creation of Industrial Food," *Endeavour* 33, no. 1 (2009): 29.

12. The Kornlet Company would later hire Farmer to write a promotional recipe booklet. Fannie Farmer, *The Heart of the Kernal: Kornlet Recipes* (Haserot Canneries Company, 1910), Special Collections, University of Iowa Libraries.

13. "'Cook's French' refers to "a long tradition of using specialized French terms for dishes and to the hackneyed, amateurish efforts of American-born chefs to use these specialized terms." Haley, *Turning the Tables*, xiii.

Mrs. Mary F. Henderson, Practical Cooking and Dinner Giving, 1877

1. John B. Henderson, 1900 U.S. Federal Census, Washington, District of Columbia, district 0012, ancestry.com.

2. Anne Marie Rachman, "Biography of Mary Foote Henderson," *Feeding America*, digital.lib.msu.edu/projects/cookbooks/.

3. Mary F. Henderson, 1880 U.S. Federal Census, St. Louis, Missouri, district 351, ancestry.com; Mary F. Henderson, 1900 U.S. Federal Census, Washington, District of Columbia, district 0012, ancestry.com.

Selected Advice on Table Manners, 1872–1903

1. Haley, *Turning the Tables*, 50–51.

2. For more, See Haley, *Turning the Tables*. In his research on manners and gentility in nineteenth-century America, John Kasson found only two books written specifically for black readers and found no books at all written specifically for recent immigrants. John F. Kasson, *Rudeness and Civility: Manners in Nineteenth-Century Urban America* (New York: Hill & Wang, 1990), 54. There was also a dearth of instruction aimed at the solidly working or lower classes, besides the occasional tract on how to be better servants. Linda Young, *Middle-Class Culture in the Nineteenth Century: America, Australia and Britain* (New York: Palgrave Macmillan, 2003), 134.

3. While John Kasson found no book aimed explicitly at immigrants, the ranks of the middle class swelled in the nineteenth century with immigrants or, more often, with their children, and with people who moved to urban areas from farms and villages. Kasson, *Rudeness and Civility*, 54. In *Everybody's Book of Correct Conduct* (1893), Lady Colin and M. French-Sheldon expanded upon the egalitarianism implicit in their title by explaining that the book "will be found most useful either to the inexperienced hostess or to the visitor unaccustomed to society." Lady M. Colin and M. French-Sheldon, *Everybody's Book of Correct Conduct* (New York and London: Harper & Brothers Publishers, 1893), iii–iv.

4. During the nineteenth century, indeed, "refined," "polite," and "fashionable" all became indicative of (if not synonymous with) things metropolitan. Kasson, *Rudeness and Civility*, 55, 112, 114–115.

5. Julia M. Dewey, *Lessons on Manners: Arranged for Grammar Schools, High Schools, and Academies* (New York: Hinds & Noble, 1899), 41.

6. Margaret Livingston, "Table Etiquette," in *Correct Social Usage: A Course of Instruction in Good Form Style and Deportment by Eighteen Distinguished Authors*, vol. 1 (New York: New York Society of Self-Culture, 1903), 64–65.

7. This was risky advice. The pressure necessary to peel an orange with a knife while holding its base only with a spoon, for example, could cause the fruit to ricochet and careen disastrously down the table or onto the floor. Mrs. Florence Marion Hall, *The Correct Thing in Good Society* (Boston: Estes and Lauriat, 1888), 100.

8. Russell Lynes, *The Domesticated Americans* (New York: Harper & Row, 1957), 181.

9. One of the many examples is in *The Complete Bachelor: Manners for Men* (New York: D. Appleton and Company, 1896), 64.

Massachusetts Recipe Manuscript, 1870s and 1880s

1. Paul Freedman notes that Delmonico's "is generally considered to be the country's first fine restaurant." Freedman, "American Restaurants and Cuisine in the Mid-Nineteenth Century," *New England Quarterly* 84, no. 1 (2011): 6.

*Mrs. Peter A. White, The Kentucky Housewife:
A Collection of Recipes for Cooking, 1885*

1. Mrs. Lettice Bryan, *The Kentucky Housewife: Containing Nearly Thirteen Hundred Full Receipts* (Cincinnati: Shepard & Stearns, 1839).

2. The author originally wrote "desertspoonful."

3. The author had originally capitalized "When" in this sentence.

4. The author originally wrote "Peal."

Christine Terhune Herrick, *What to Eat, How to Serve It,* 1891

1. Laura Shapiro, *Perfection Salad: Women and Cooking at the Turn of the Century* (New York: Farrar, Straus and Giroux, 1986), 107.

2. "Left-over, n.," *Oxford English Dictionary.*

Dietary Studies from Alabama, New York, Chicago, Virginia, and New Mexico, 1895–1897

1. For more, see Helen Zoe Veit, *Modern Food, Moral Food: Self-Control, Science, and the Rise of Modern American Eating in the Early Twentieth Century* (Chapel Hill: University of North Carolina Press, 2013).

2. See Charlotte Biltekoff, *Eating Right in America: The Cultural Politics of Food and Health* (Durham, NC: Duke University Press, 2013).

3. W. O. Atwater and Charles D. Woods, *Dietary Studies with Reference to the Food of the Negro in Alabama in 1895 and 1896,* no. 38, U.S. Department of Agriculture, Office of Experiment Stations (Washington, DC: Government Printing Office, 1897).

4. W. O. Atwater and Chas. D. Woods, *Dietary Studies in New York City in 1895 and 1896,* Bulletin No. 46, U.S. Department of Agriculture, Office of Experiment Stations.

5. W. O. Atwater and Arthur Bryant, *Dietary Studies in Chicago in 1895 and 1896,* conducted with the cooperation of Jane Addams and Caroline L. Hunt, of Hull House, USDA No. 55 (Washington, DC: Government Printing Office, 1898).

6. H. B. Frissell and Isabel Bevier, *Dietary Studies of Negroes in Eastern Virginia: Dietary Studies among the Negroes in 1897* (U.S. Office of Experiment Stations, 1899).

7. Arthur Goss, "Nutrition Investigations in New Mexico in 1897," U.S. Department of Agriculture, Office of Experiment Stations (Washington, DC: Government Printing Office, 1898).

Gilded Age Banquet Menus, 1880–1899

1. Paul Freedman points out that "although the Gilded Age is generally set apart for its extravagantly huge meals, frenzy for French chefs, and fancy for elaborate and overstuffed display, the opulence that culminated in the 1890s was evident by midcentury, when American restaurants everywhere served what amounted to an aspirational national cuisine." Freedman, "American Restaurants and Cuisine in the Mid-Nineteenth Century," *New England Quarterly* 84, no. 1 (March 2011): 7.

2. Andrew Haley calls this kind of conspicuous consumption "an honorific investment in social reputation." *Turning the Tables,* 22.

3. Freedman, "American Restaurants and Cuisine," 8.

4. The author originally wrote "Amontilado."

Fannie Merritt Farmer, *The Boston Cooking-School Cook Book,* 1896

1. Shapiro, *Perfection Salad,* 108–112.

2. See Veit, *Modern Food, Moral Food.*

3. Shapiro, *Perfection Salad,* 115–116.

4. Ibid., 106, 118.

5. Ibid., 112.

6. Ibid., 113.

GLOSSARY OF NINETEENTH-CENTURY COOKING TERMS

alum	A chemical compound used as a preservative, a leavening agent, and sometimes as an ingredient in homemade medicinal remedies.
chafing-dish	A dish used to gently heat food or to keep it warm away from the stove, using a small, portable heat source.
Cottolene, or coto-suet	Cooking fats made from a mix of cottonseed oil and beef fat.
dessertspoon	As a unit of measure, the equivalent of two teaspoons.
filee powder	More commonly spelled *filé*, a pungent powder made from dried sassafras leaves, used to thicken and add distinctive taste to gumbo.
haslet	A mixture of chopped pig's offal, usually cooked in loaf form.
horehound	An herb used to flavor drinks, candies, and medicinal lozenges.
leaf fat	The soft, mild fat found around the kidneys or loins of a pig.
loppered milk	More commonly known as clabber, or milk that has been allowed to sour and clot to form firm, edible curds with a tangy, yogurt-like taste.
made mustard	Prepared fluid mustard, as opposed to dry or powdered mustard.
panada	A paste made from bread crumbs mixed with water or another liquid.
pineapple cheese	A popular cheese made in pineapple-shaped mold.
quenelle	A delicate poached dumpling, often made from creamed meat, egg, and bread crumbs.
roach	A kind of fish.
salamander	A metal plate with a long handle. The plate was heated in a fire and then held over the top of a dish to brown it.
saleratus	A form of bicarbonate of potash, roughly equivalent to modern baking soda.
saltpetre	Potassium nitrate, used in curing meat.
saltspoon	As a unit of measure, the rough equivalent of a quarter of a teaspoon.

spider	A long-handled frying pan with legs.
smelt	A variety of small fish.
sweet milk	Milk that has not yet begun to sour.
tea cup	As a unit of measure, the rough equivalent of five ounces, or just over a modern half-cup.
try out	To render lard by melting it slowly. The melted fat could be used immediately or it could be strained and stored.

INDEX

and oysters à la Métropole, 265; pie, 113, 263; purée, 101; roasted, 112, 262; salad, 155; sandwiches, 302; simple, soup, 100; soup for the sick, 101; suprème of, 286

children, 2, 4, 8, 14, 20, 28, 32, 33, 56, 64, 69, 71, 72, 148, 164–194 passim, 321 (n. 3)

chili sauce, 142

chocolate: bread pudding, 288; for cake, 85; cake, 296–297; caramels, 138; carousels, 86; cookies, 294; cream, 290; cream candy, 300; custard, 132; frosting, 296; fruit cake, 134–135; [hot], 229; pudding, 129

cholera mixture, 85

chow-chow, 141

chowder: Connecticut, 248; corn, 247; fish, 248

cinnamon jumbles, 133

citron preserves, 135

Civil War, 30, 87

clam water, 308

Cleveland, President Grover, 197

cob cake, 80

cocoa cordial, 307

coconut, 129

cod: baked with oyster stuffing, 251; fried, steaks, 252

coffee: cakes, 232–233; jelly, 291

cold water cake, 81

Colin, Lady M., 73

Connecticut chowder, 248

consommé, 245; à la royale, 245

conspicuous consumption, 196–198, 322 (n. 2)

cookies, 81, 132; chocolate, 294; peanut, 294. See also ginger: snaps; jumbles

cooking times, nineteenth-century, 8, 316 (n. 19)

cordial(s): blackberry, 137; peach, 137

corn, 58; boiled, bread, 156; golden, cake, 234; chowder, 247; green, 122; green, fritters, 151; grits, 91; muffins, 150; oysters, 271; pudding, 122; à la southern, 271

corn starch pie, 84

corned beef, 106, 256–257; hash, 258

cottage pie, 258

crabs: devilled, 103, 286–287; directions for cleaning, 252; directions for selecting, 104; gumbo soup, 100; soft-shelled, fried, 104, 252

cracker gruel, 308

crackers, toasted, 154

cranberry(ies), 269; steamed, pudding, 288

cream: chocolate, 290; corn soup, 159; dressing, 278; rice pudding, 162; sauce, 265, 290; Spanish, 292; for Washington pie, 126; wine, 291

crème diplomate, 132

croquettes, 110; chestnut, 283; chicken, 284; hominy, 158; oyster and macaroni, 283; potato, 277; rice, with jelly, 284–285; turnip, 275

croutons, 248

crullers, 133

cucumbers: boiled, 272; catsup, 142; fried, 161, 272; pickles, 85, 139; sauce of, 267

currant(s): cake, 82; jelly sauce, 269; spiced, 85; water, 305; wine, 138

curried eggs, 150–151, 239

curried oysters, 157

curry, 113

custard(s): caramel, 290–291; chocolate, 132; egg, 249; royal, 249

D

dandelions, 272

Daughters of the American Revolution, 195, 218

Delaney, Dr. (Isabelle), 176, 179

Delmonico's, 24, 25, 78, 87, 202, 207, 211, 321 (n. 1); pudding, 83. See also restaurants

Dewey, Julia, 63, 74–75

dietary reformers, 2, 39

dietary studies, 37, 40, 164–194. See also nutrition

digestion, 40, 75, 148–149, 151, 155, 170, 225, 262

dinner, 4–5, 146–147; boiled, 257; parties, 1–2, 4, 5, 21, 42–44, 45–62, 66–77, 309–313

domestic science, 17

doughnuts, 82, 132, 236–237

drawn butter sauce, 266

dressing(s): boiled, 278; cold slaw, 119; cream, 278; French, 278; German, 279; mayonnaise, 279; salad, 118

dried beef with cream, 258

duchess potatoes, 276

duck: canvas back, 114; roast, 114; wild, roast, 114, 264

dumplings, 259

E

eels, fried, 252

eggplant(s): pudding, 123; stuffed, 161–162, 272

egg(s): balls, 105, 248–249; bread, 90; buttered, with tomatoes, 239; with cheese, 92; custard, 249; curried, 150–151, 239; à la goldenrod, 239; nog, 137, 306; salad, 156; sandwiches, 308; sauce, 266; scrambled, with anchovy toast, 239; stuffed, in a nest, 239. *See also* omelet(s)

entire wheat bread, 231

etiquette, 31–32, 34, 35, 39–40, 42, 44, 45–62, 63–77, 321 (n. 2)

F

fadges, 235

faith cake, 83

Fannie Farmer Cookbook, The. See *Boston Cooking-School Cook Book, The*

farina: cakes with jelly, 282; soup, 242

Farmer, Fannie Merritt, 8, 37, 39, 41, 224–227, 320 (n. 12)

farmers and rural life, 168–172, 187–192; and access to fresh produce, 13; and bread baking, 5; and gardening, 8; and kitchens, 17, 20; and meals, 3–4; and meats, 37. *See also* sharecropping

feet: boiled, 96; pig's, fried, 261; stewed, 96

fingers, eating with, 66, 68–69, 71, 72, 73, 77

fish: chowder, 248; croquettes, 254; force-meat, 250; hash, 253; leftover, 157; turban of, 253

flaxseed lemonade, 306

food buying, 21–24, 318 (n. 67)

food for the sick. *See* invalid cookery

food prices, 11–12, 164–194

food safety, 9, 12, 28. *See also* hygiene

force-meat(s): balls, 99; chicken, 250; fish, 250

foreign foods, 2, 10. *See also* immigrants

Freedman, Paul, 196

French dishes: dressing, 278; fried potatoes, 277; mustard, 142

French language, 2, 8, 25, 32–35, 44, 49, 50, 53, 320 (n. 6–7), 320 (n. 13)

French-Sheldon, M., 73

fricassee: chicken, 112; general comments on, 113; lobster, 103; oyster, 254

fritters: apple, 282; apricot, 159; bread, 126; green corn, 151; hominy, 124; parsnip, 124

frogs: fried, 104; hind legs of, 253

frosting, chocolate, 296

frozen beef tea, 307

fruit sandwiches, 303

G

gems, rye, 151

German dressing, 279

ginger: cakes, 82, 133; punch, 230; sandwiches, 303; snaps, 154

gingerbread, 156; hard sugar, 84; soft molasses, 294

gnocchi à la Romaine, 283

golden corn cake, 234

goose, roast, with potato stuffing, 264

grape juice, 230, 305

green tomato pickle, 140–141

greengages, brandied, 136

griddle cakes: corn, 235–236: sour milk, 235

grits: corn, 91; oatmeal, 91

graham bread, 231

gravy, 262–263

grocers. *See* food buying

gruel: barley, 308; cracker, 308; Indian, 307; oatmeal, 307

gumbo, 99–100; chicken, 263; crab, 100; oyster, 100–101, 246

H

halibut: baked with lobster sauce, 251; baked with stuffing, 250–251

Hall, Mrs. Florence Marion, 71–73

ham: baked, 108; boiled, 107–108; cured, Kentucky style, 107; devilled, 93; fried, and eggs, 261; omelet, 91; sandwiches, 302

Hamburg steaks, 256

Hampton Institute, 167, 187–192

hard sauce, 290

hard sugar gingerbread, 84

Harland, Marion, 148

Hartley, Cecil B., 66–67

Hartley, Florence, 66

hash: cold mutton, 94; corned beef, 258; corned beef, with beets, 258; dry beef, 93; fish, 253; turkey, 94–95; veal, 94

hashed brown potatoes, 278

Hat's cup cake, 80

Hattie Howe's cup cake, 80

height and growth, childhood nutrition and, 13, 31

Henderson, Mary, 39, 40, 42–44, 195

Herrick, Christine, 37, 40, 148–149

hollandaise sauce, 117, 267

home economics, 17

hominy: baked, 158; boiled, 124; fritters, 124; meal muffins, 89

horehound candy, 300

horse manders, 133

horseradish, 143; sauce, 268

hot cross buns, 233

Hull House, 180–186

hunger, 30, 32–33, 164, 167

hunting, 5, 6, 10, 12, 36, 37, 168, 188

hygiene, 39, 40, 75, 149, 226

hygienic soup, 242

I

ice boxes. *See* refrigeration

ice cream, 130, 198; candy, 299; macaroon, 130–131

immigrants, 29, 31, 34, 164–194 passim; and garlic, 225; and etiquette manuals, 321 (n. 2–3); and meals, 3–5; and meat, 5; and preservation, 8–9; and regional cuisine, 9–10; and restaurants, 24, 26–28; and urbanization, 11

imperial soup, 243

income inequality, 1–2, 31–33, 165

Indian dishes: bread, 232; gruel, 307; meal mush, 308; pudding, 128, 287

industrial meat processing, 12

industrialization, 2, 4, 10, 34, 37, 39, 317 (n. 48)

invalid cookery, 85, 304; chicken soup for the sick, 101

Irish dishes: potato pudding, 127; stew with dumplings, 259

Isukahra, Shiuzo, 212–213

J

jam, red raspberry, 135. *See also* jelly(ies); marmalade(s); preserves

jambalaya of chicken and rice, 112–113

James, William, 30

jelly(ies), 131; apricot and wine, 291; aspec, 111; coffee, 291; lemon, 291; orange, 131; omelet, 240; roll, 296; wine, 292. *See also* jam, red raspberry; marmalade(s); preserves

Jenny Lind cake, 80

Jewish people, 5, 6, 23, 26–27, 180, 183. *See also* immigrants

Jim Crow, 166–167

Johnston, Mrs. S. O., 69–71

juice, unfermented grape, 230

jumbles, 82; cinnamon, 133; *See also* cookies

K

Kellogg's Corn Flakes, 15

Kentucky cured ham, 107

ketchup. *See* catsup(s)

cream rice, 162; Delmonico's, 83; eggplant, 123; hard sauce for, 130; Indian, 128, 287; Irish potato, 127; Nesselrode, 293; plum, 196, 289; pumpkin, 129; raspberry, 160; rice-and-pear, 161; sauce for, 129–130; suet, 128, 289; tapioca custard, 287; Yankee cake, 128–129; Yorkshire, 256

pumpkin(s): baked, 124; pudding, 129

punch(es): ginger, 230; milk, 307; whisky, 137

Pure Food and Drug Act of 1906, 15

purée of chicken, 101

pushcarts, 21–23, 28

Q

quails and truffles, 115

Quaker muffins, 234

Quaker Oats bread, 231

Queen Victoria, 51, 56

quenelles, 110–111; sauce for, 116

R

raspberry(ies): red, jam, 135; pudding, 160

recipes, changing format of, 35, 37, 40, 78–79, 318 (n. 57)

Reconstruction, 31

reed birds, roasted, 115

refrigeration, 9, 10–13, 23–24, 37, 148, 149, 312

regional cuisines, 5, 9, 12, 224

restaurants, 24–29, 165, 322 (n. 1)

Reynolds, Marcus T., 24

ribbon cake, 297

rice, 5, 123; cakes, 157; with cheese, 238; croquettes with jelly, 284–285; steamed, 237–238; water, 304–305

rice-and-pear pudding, 161

Richards, Ellen, 15

rolled bread sandwiches, 302

rolled wafers, 294–295

rolls, Parker House, 232

Rorer, Mrs. (Sarah Tyson), 75–76

rough and ready pickle, 140

royal custard, 249

Ruth, John, 35, 68–69

rye: gems, 151; muffins, 153

S

salad(s): banana, 281; cabbage and celery, 119, 280; cheese, 281; chicken, 155; chicken and oyster, 281; dressing, 118; egg, 156; lettuce and cucumber, 279; Lenten, 281; Macédoine, 280; nut and celery, 281; potato, 156, 280; shrimp, 118; spinach, 280–281; sweetbread, 118; sweetbread and cucumber, 281; tomato jelly, 280; watercress and cucumber, 279

Sally-Lunn, 152

salmi of lamb, 260

salmon: box, 254; soup, 161

salsify(ies): creamed, 273; fritters, 273

salt pork, fried, with codfish, 261

Sandison, G. H., 73

sandwiches: anchovy, 302; bread and butter folds, 302; chicken, 302; egg, 308; fruit, 303; general notes on, 301; ginger, 303; ham, 302; lettuce, 302; lobster, 302; nut and cheese, 302; oyster, 302; raw beef, 308; rolled bread, 302. *See also* canapés

Saratoga potatoes, 120, 276

sardine canapés, 303

sauce(s): asparagus, 121; béchamel, 266; for Boudins à la Richelieu, 111; brown, 116, 266; caramel, 291; champignon, 117; chili, 142; cranberry, 269; cream, 265, 290; cucumber, 267; currant jelly, 269; drawn butter, 266; egg, 266; hard, 290; hollandaise, 117, 267; horseradish, 143, 268; lemon, 290; lobster, 268; mint, 116; olive, 268; orange, 268; piquante, 266; for quenelles, 116; supreme, 268; tartar, 117, 267, 269; thick white, 265; thin white, 265; truffle, 116–117; vanilla, 290; white, 265. *See also* dressing(s)

sausage(s), 95; meat, 95; rolls, 153